AF574883

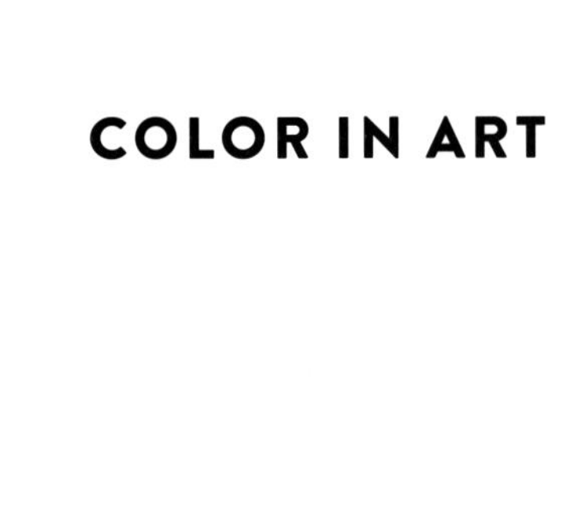

COLOR IN ART

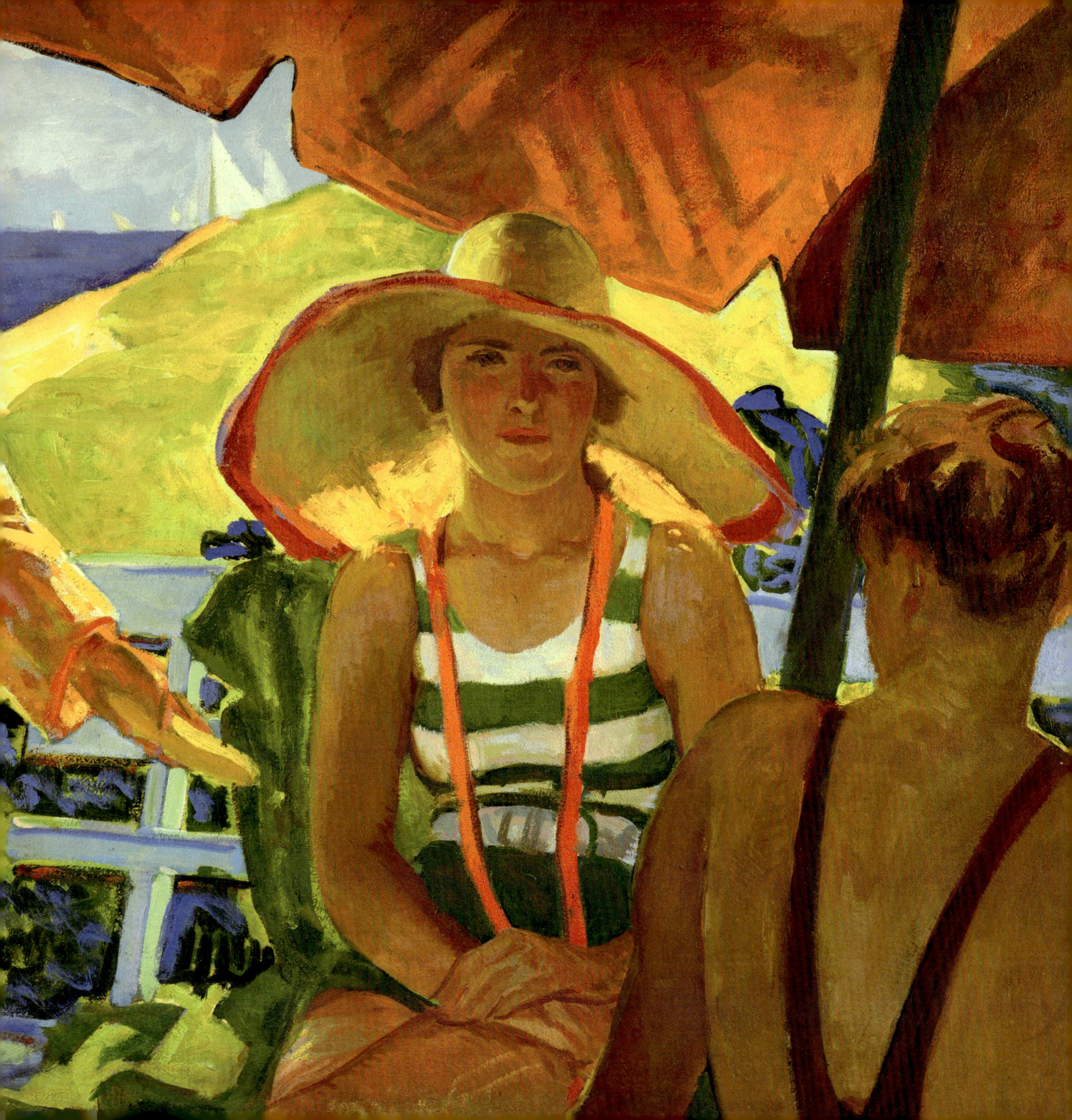

STEFANO ZUFFI

COLOR IN ART

ABRAMS, NEW YORK

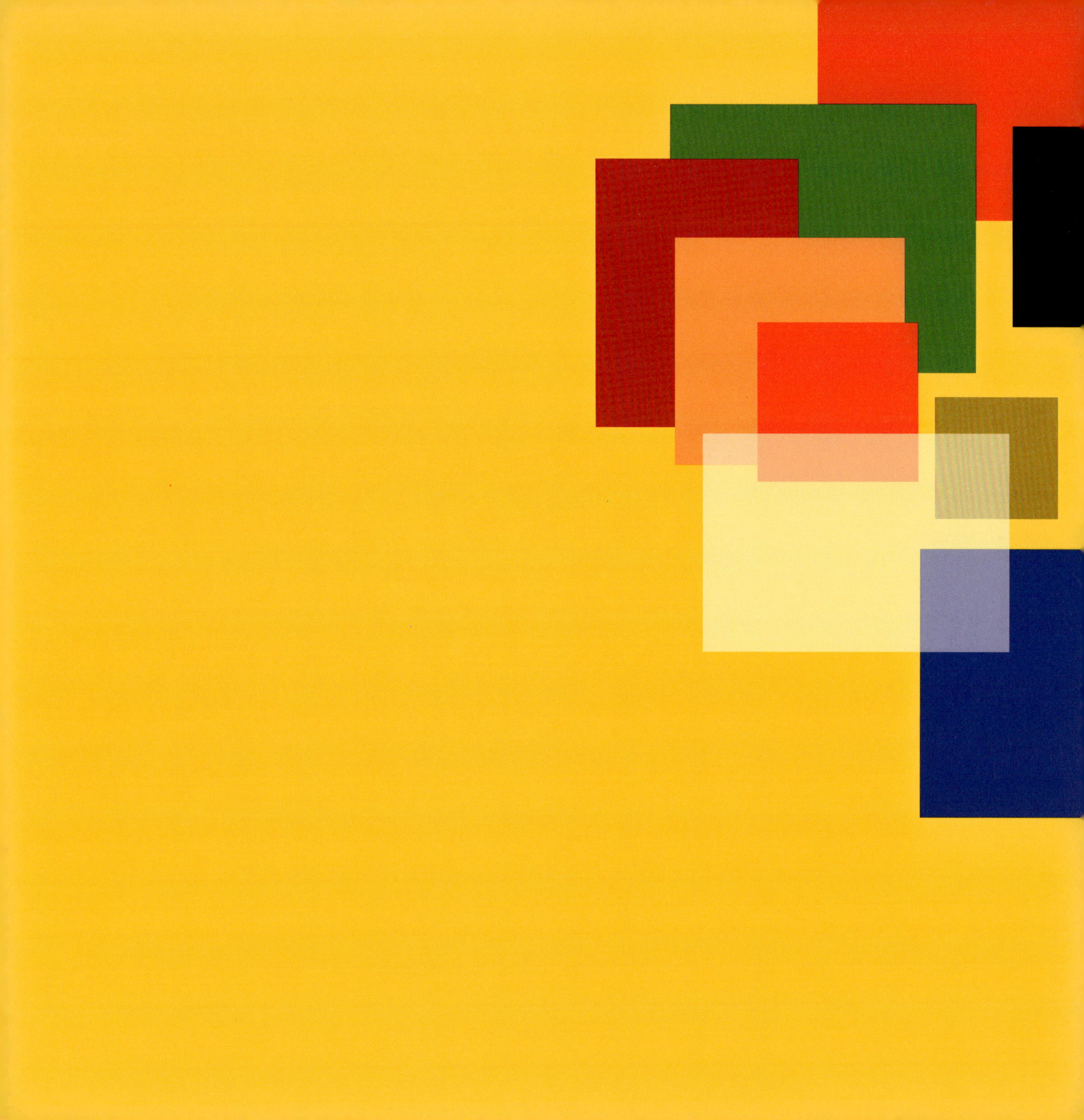

6 **INTRODUCTION**

8 Pigments, binders, varnishes

11 Treatises and theories:
from symbolic interpretation to a scientific approach

13 The apotheosis of colour: impressionism, post-impressionism and neo-impressionism

19 The 'colours' of music and poetry

21 Colour theory in the 20th century: Itten and Albers

25 **RED**

69 **YELLOW**

111 **BLUE**

145 **GREEN**

181 **GOLD**

221 **WHITE**

267 **BLACK**

312 **BIBLIOGRAPHY**

314 **INDEX OF PROPER NAMES**

318 **PHOTOGRAPHIC CREDITS**

INTRODUCTION

Les couleurs ce sont des sensations physiques,

mais ce sont aussi des symboles.

[Colours are physical sensations,

but they are also symbols.]

René-Lucien Rousseau,

Les Couleurs, 1959

The ancient Romans were a very concrete people. They were not given to the poetical refinement and subtle philosophical speculation of the Greeks. For the Romans, it was of primary importance to establish standards, rules and precepts, for every aspect of life had a corresponding law as its solid basis. But even for the Romans there remained three categories that lay outside any normative legalistic scheme: *De gustibus, coloribus et pulchritudine mulierum non est disputandum* –Taste in food, colours and the beauty of women cannot be debated.

In other words, colours are like feminine beauty and flavours: despite scientific theory, each of us perceives them in an individual manner and has our own favourites. In the course of writing this book, three things struck me more clearly each day:

→ first, the dearth of vocabulary for designating colours, regardless of language, ancient or modern. There are about a dozen words, which are modified by adjectives and other specifiers

→ second, the clash that for 350 years has been pitting those who seek to study colours as a physical phenomenon (since Newton) against those who interpret colours as connected solely with individual emotions and subjectivity (since Goethe)

→ and third, the ambiguity and variation in a

colour's symbolic meanings, which can often be completely contradictory.

Instinctively, many of us would give white a 'positive' meaning and black a 'negative' one, following the duality of the Taoist combination of yin and yang. But are we sure that this is so?

In Jungian psychology, the colours are first of all symbols, archetypes of universal value. The historian Michel Pastoreau, who has specialized in the symbolic and expressive value of colour, states in his *Couleurs, Images, Symboles* (1986): 'For a long time, if not always, in Western civilization, white has had two opposites: red and black. Until the height of the Middle Ages, these three colours were three poles around which all symbolic systems were organized.'

Examples of the symbolic values and visual associations of colours may be drawn from such widely diverse fields as liturgy, heraldry and alchemy. The wish to 'describe' colours often leads to definitions that make no reference to the sense of sight. Yellow, red and orange are 'warm' not because if we touch them they actually have a different temperature from blue or green, but because we associate them with the sun and fire. In the same way, we speak of colours as 'dull' or 'bright', and without being poets like Rimbaud or Georg Trakl, we commonly use aural metaphors in trying to convey the idea of a colour's 'tone'. Alongside this universally recognized symbolic value, colour has a profoundly subjective dimension. In 1947, Max Lüscher devised a personality test based on the famous Rorschach inkblot test that introduces the variable of colour as a basic element of subjective interpretation. The Italian psychotherapist Luca Coladarci explains that a 'fundamental characteristic of colours (just as for any other symbol) is the rule of opposites, according to which a single shade may have the opposite value, positive or negative, light or dark, according to the setting and the psychic situation in which it is inserted. This is why black, for example – a colour of death and darkness – can also evoke the original chaos from which new light and life emerge. Or aggressive, violent red can likewise be the shade of love and passion.'

We may also call upon Winston Churchill, a not untalented amateur painter, as a witness beyond suspicion. The great statesman was not insensitive to the inner language of colours: 'I cannot pretend to be impartial about the colours. I rejoice with the brilliant ones, and am genuinely sorry for the poor browns.'

We often ascribe to colours an emotional value of happiness or sadness that, once again, is related not to the colour itself but to symbolic associations with situations in which it is usually found. Franz Marc, an impassioned exponent of the German avant-garde group Der Blaue Reiter who died in the trenches of Verdun in 1916, even attributed a sexual value to colours, giving priority to his beloved yellow: 'Blue is the male principle, stern and spiritual. Yellow the female principle, gentle, cheerful and sensual. Red is matter, brutal and heavy and always the colour which must be fought and vanquished by the other two.'

Through examples of artists' use of seven different colours – white, black, blue, yellow, red, green and gold – this book hopes to show how, as time has unfurled and cultures have waxed and waned, symbolic meanings have been intertwined with other disciplines such as chemistry, poetry and music.

PIGMENTS, BINDERS, VARNISHES

The basis of a colour in painting is the pigment. Pigments are mainly amorphous and crystalline substances (especially earth, minerals and composites) that are prepared in the form of fine coloured powders. They are usually classified in two categories: organic pigments and inorganic (or mineral) pigments. They are essentially not much different from those used by Palaeolithic painters twenty thousand years ago when they painted the walls of the caves of Lascaux: earth, calcite, iron oxide, clay, red ochre, manganese oxide. In medieval and Renaissance workshops, grinding earth and minerals and crushing plants with a mortar and pestle were tasks typically assigned to young apprentices. Some of the great painters produced special pigments of their own, using basic materials in combinations that were jealously guarded secrets. One well-known case is 'Veronese green', a shade between emerald, jade and malachite, which was invented by Paolo Veronese in the second half of the 16th century. It is still used in the figurative arts, although it is poorly regarded because of its instability. In interior decoration, a particular shade of green is called Veronese green or viridian.

Prior to the introduction of industrially produced tubes of colour in the second half of the 19th century, pigments were available in the form of powder or paste. In order to use them in painting (be it on canvas, wooden panel or wall), they were mixed to a fluid consistency with water (for tempera paint) or oil.

The introduction of oil in place of water as a binder for colours was one of the greatest technical revolutions in the history of painting. For almost the entire 15th century, Flemish painters dominated the European art market and influenced stylistic trends in various countries with the lustrous brilliancy of their paintings, filled with minute descriptive details drawn from everyday life. The 'secret' of these paintings, tenaciously sought by competing artists in other countries, was the technique of diluting the colours with oil from flaxseed, walnut or poppyseed. Tempera paint, diluted with water, has a less enamel-like texture and enables less finesse, producing an effect not unlike fresco.

The Gothic practice of using a gold background (a thin layer of pure gold over a bolus ground) and metal insertions had subsided. The Flemish masters applied oil paint in a succession of thin, translucent coats to obtain effects of transparency, exceptionally brilliant light and natural atmosphere. They achieved an optically 'true' result by imitating the play of light on every surface. The first great Flemish masters may also have experimented with optical tools like mirrors and lenses as an aid to thoroughly analysing reality and variations of light. Rare and expensive colours like gold, green from malachite, blue from lapis lazuli and red from the cochineal were appreciated all the more for their material value. Avidly adopted by other European schools, oil became the predominant painting medium. Its status was confirmed when canvas subsequently replaced wood as a support.

Siccative oils are used in painting. Olive oil is unsuitable because it never dries. The most frequently used is the oil extracted from flaxseeds. Not highly soluble, it cracks less readily, limiting the appearance of craquelure (the network of fine cracks that forms on the surface of a painting). Its only defect is that it yellows slightly over time, therefore altering the colours. Various remedies were tested to avert this drawback, such as cooking the linseed oil or combining it with walnut or poppyseed oil. Thanks to the properties of oil paint, an artist such as Hans Memling could graduate the effect of light on the landscape, passing from a dark foreground to a very light horizon, while at the same time creating a celestial vision of the Empyrean circumscribed by a rainbow. Not infrequent in 15th-century Flemish painting, this type of light and colour effect was essentially beyond the reach of painters prior to the advent of oil painting.

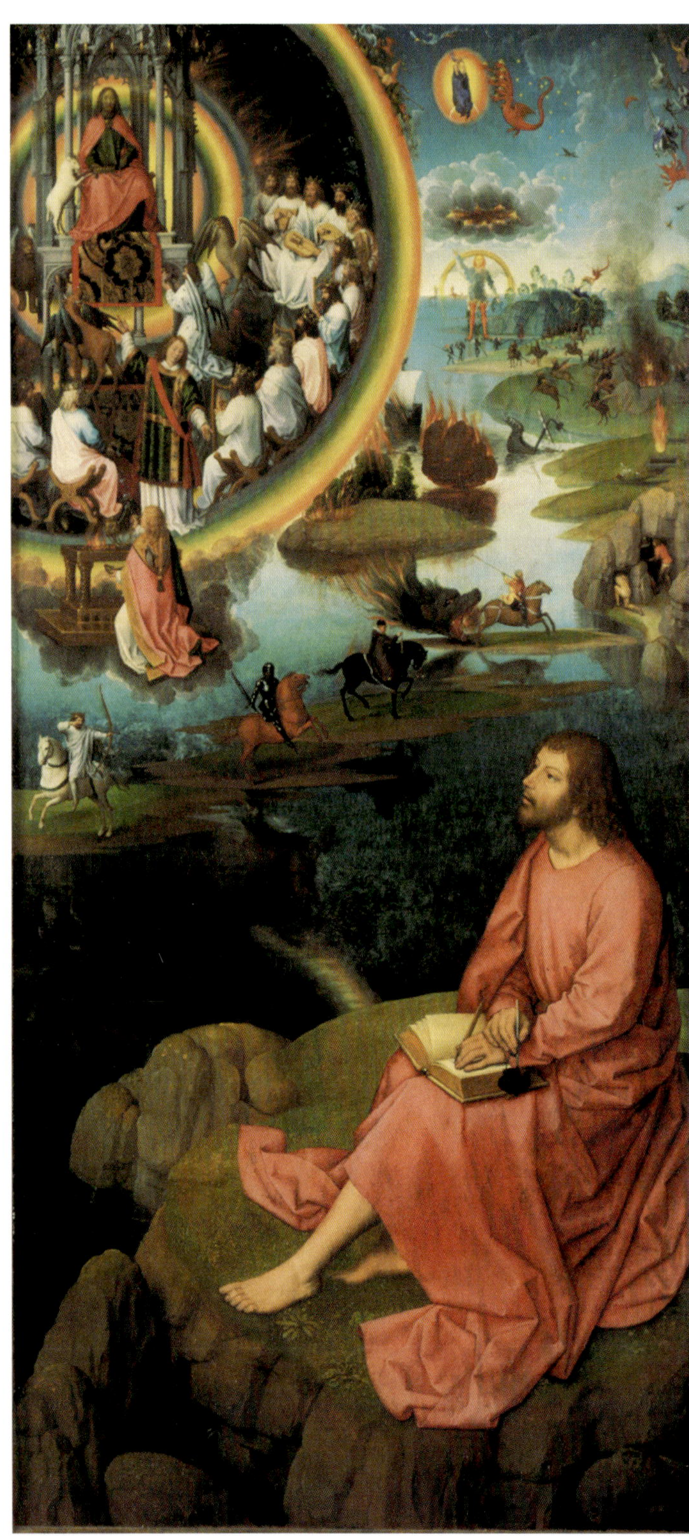

Hans Memling
The Vision of St John on Patmos
side panel of the
Triptych of the Mystic Marriage of St Catherine
1479
oil on panel, 172 x 79 cm
Memlingmuseum, Bruges

Nor was the problem of yellowing and the consequent darkening of lighter colours solved by the introduction of turpentine and essential oils, and yellowing remains the first consideration in restoring all old oil paintings. However, it is often possible to clean the surface of a painting without touching the colours, by confining the operation to the removal of the natural and synthetic varnishes that are applied as a final step to protect paintings from light, dust, smoke and pollution.

TREATISES AND THEORIES: FROM SYMBOLIC INTERPRETATION TO A SCIENTIFIC APPROACH

At the height of the Renaissance, Italy produced many treatises and guides on the meaning and properties of colours that suggest how to express oneself through colours, particularly in relation to human relationships such as love. Outstanding among these manuals of 'colour etiquette' are those by Mario Equicola (*Libro de natura de amore*, 1525), Fulvio Pellegrino Morato (*Del significato de Colori*, 1535, so popular that it was reprinted eight times) and Ludovico Dolce (*Dialogo dei colori*, 1565). This type of book came under the broader 16th-century literary category of guides to behaviour and proper manners, the most famous of which are *The Book of the Courtier* by Baldassare Castiglione and the *Galateo* (The Book of Manners) by Giovanni Della Casa. When dealing with colour, these etiquette manuals pay particular attention to dress, which is considered to reflect a person's nature and intentions, based on a curious correspondence between the planets, the temperaments and colours.

In the 17th century, the eclectic knowledge of the late Renaissance gave way to methodical scientific research, the subdivision of knowledge and experimental verification by means of constantly improved instruments. The year 1666 was one of capital importance for the scientist Isaac Newton, who called it his *annus mirabilis* (year of wonders). His revolutionary discoveries in the field of physics came at the rate of one per season, culminating in the famous episode of the apple falling from the tree. In January, Newton demonstrated that light passing through a prism breaks down into various colours, including the three primary colours: red, blue and yellow. Newton represented humans' perception of colour as a circle, with the seven 'spectral colours' – that is, the colours of the visible spectrum (in the order given by Newton they are red, yellow, green, blue, violet, orange and indigo), which combine through mixture and superimposition into 'an indefinite variety of intermediate graduations'. Newton discussed his theory with his students, while the first publication, in the form of a memoir to the Royal Society, dates from 1672 (*A Letter of Mr. Isaac Newton Containing His New Theory about Light and Colours*); it was later written up in the form of a treatise (*Opticks*, 1704).

Various subsequent studies referred to Newton's theories in an attempt to understand and describe the mechanisms by which the human eye perceives colour. In 1810, Wolfgang Goethe (who was himself a passable amateur painter and draughtsman) published *Zur Farbenlehre* (Theory of Colours) in Tübingen. It is not easy reading, and from the start it was better received by men of letters than by scientists. It mixes science, optical research and personal considerations, passionately maintaining – with the authority of an internationally recognized intellectual – a new point of view, in line with the spread of Romanticism. Colour is above all an individual experience, and the subjective element is no less important than optics and physics.

Also in 1810, the painter Philipp Otto Runge published the treatise *Farben-Kugel* (Colour Sphere). Illustrated with watercolours, it was one of the earliest attempts on the part of a painter to coordinate chromatic tones and values in a coherent whole. Abandoning the traditional 'wheel' and planar projections, Runge conceived and drew up a three-dimensional colour sphere. At the poles were white and black, at the equator the primary colours and saturated mixtures, and over the sphere's surface, the intermediate values. In *Farben-Kugel*, Runge did not address the question of colours' moral connotations but, like Goethe (with whose ideas he was in close contact), he was convinced of the almost mystical value of colour. Runge had planned to adapt the model of the primary colours to the times of day in an allegorical cycle, but of the four projected paintings only *Morning* was completed.

Between 1813 and 1814, the young philosopher Arthur Schopenhauer, recently graduated from university, was Goethe's guest in Weimar. The two intellectuals engaged in intense conversations on the physics and physiology of sight. These reflections resulted in the treatise *Über das Sehn und die Farben* (On Vision and Colours), published by Schopenhauer in 1816 and soon translated into various languages.

The writings of Goethe and Schopenhauer had a particular influence on art, especially through J. M. W. Turner. Spurred on by the two Germans' assertions on the subjectivity of perception, the great English painter freed himself from realistic representation of the landscape to embark upon the evocation of a fantastic vision that went beyond phenomenal facts, projecting them into a spiritual dimension. Following Goethe, Turner interpreted light as the ordering principle of the world, because it reveals the nature of things through colour. Colour thus becomes the 'supreme manifestation of the world and hence its very soul', an assertion borrowed directly from Schopenhauer's essay. In Turner's late works, colour dominates the space without adhering to boundaries imposed by drawing. In accordance with his Romantic concept of nature, Turner depicted many sunsets and dawns, with an important role given to the sun's rays, which create infinite shades of abstract colour.

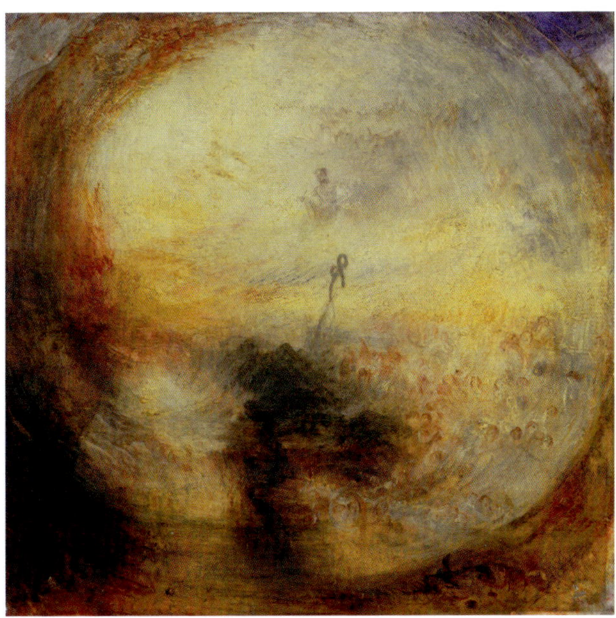

Joseph Mallord William Turner
The Morning after the Deluge
1843
oil on canvas, 78.7 x 78.7 cm
Tate, London

THE APOTHEOSIS OF COLOUR: IMPRESSIONISM, POST-IMPRESSIONISM AND NEO-IMPRESSIONISM

In the 19th century, research on perception and light made extraordinary advances with the invention and rapid improvement of photography. The main characteristic of the Impressionist painters' approach resides in their use of colour and light. These two elements became the image's principal components, replacing the previously dominant approach in Western painting that centred on the definition of forms in space. It was a revolution. The critic Émile Cardon's annoyed and harsh reaction to the first Impressionist exhibition, which took place at the studio of the photographer Nadar, was symptomatic. In *La Presse* of 29 April 1874, Cardon alludes to the title of Monet's painting *Impression: Sunrise,* writing that 'the aim is not to render its form, its relief, its expression – it is enough to give an *impression* with no definite line, no colour, light or shadow; in the implemen-tation of so extravagant a theory, artists fall into hopeless, grotesque confusion, happily without precedent in art, for it is quite simply the negation of the most elementary rules of drawing and painting.'

At the same time, anatomical and optical research provided new clues about the process of colour and light perception. 'Additive synthesis' was discovered. The receptors in the human eye are especially sensitive to red, green and blue. The simultaneous stimulation of all three receptors by three pure lights (red, green and blue) gives rise to white, and the colour we perceive from an object is the light reflected by the object itself. It reflects only some from all the wavelengths that make up the spectrum of visible light, and these define its colour. The artist performs the same function with a white canvas. In effect, colours are filters that prevent the reflection of other colours. Superimposing colours produces a progressive darkening that tends towards black. To avoid this loss of luminosity, the Impressionists used only pure, undiluted colours. They placed complementary colours side by side and never used black (except Manet, who diverged from his colleagues' practice and emphasized black). The Impressionist painters even coloured shadows.

Twenty years after the advent of Impressionism, the use of colour in painting took a new turn with the birth of Pointillism, which combined artistic and scientific enquiry based on the study of optical perception and the decomposition of light into the three primary colours: blue, yellow and red. Through contrast, the juxtaposition of tiny dots of pure colour increases the luminosity of individual colours in the eye of the observer positioned at the proper distance. The exponents of Pointillism first displayed their work to the public at the eighth and final Impressionist exhibition, in 1886, in which they took part at the invitation of Camille Pissarro: it was a symbolic changing of the guard. Painters like Seurat and Signac developed their style by putting into practice the Impressionists' research on colour and light, but went beyond it in terms of technical innovation and expression. They subdivided the surface of the painting into small areas thickly covered in regular uniform touches of colour. Seen close up, it looks like the random distribution of little coloured dots, but from a distance the overall effect is surprising: the composition takes body and volume, and the work acquires movement and depth. At the 1886 exhibition, the public and many critics were astounded and perplexed by the strict geometric execution, considered excessively intellectual and cold, but in a few years, Pointillism spread throughout Europe, spawning various avant-garde movements in the early decades of the 20th century.

Georges Seurat was the main author and theoretician of Pointillism, which he applied with

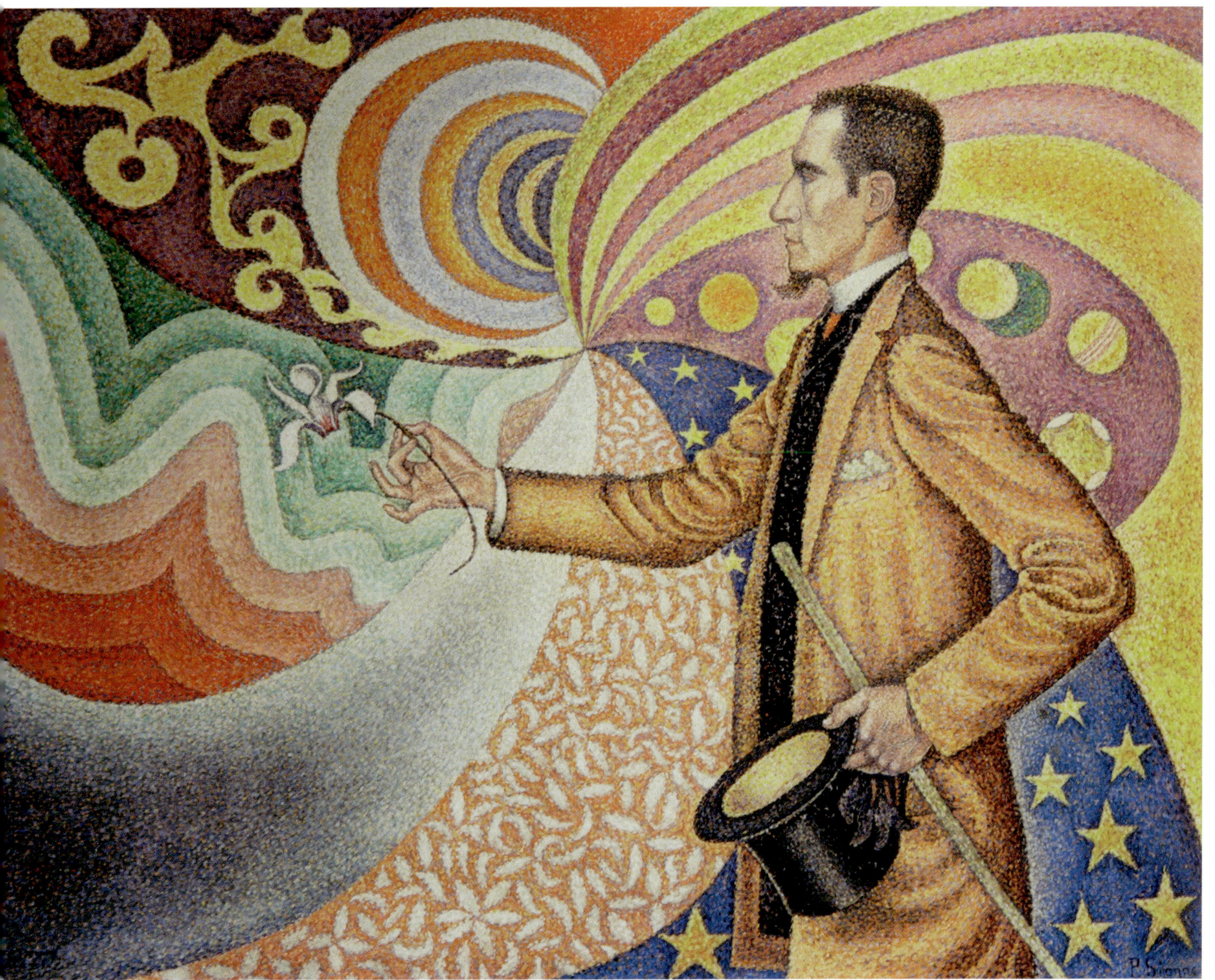

Paul Signac
Portrait of Félix Fénéon
1890
oil on canvas, 73.5 x 92.5 cm
The Museum of Modern Art, New York

almost maniacal scientific rigour. He painted few works in his short life (he died at the age of thirty-one). His meticulousness and technical perfectionism necessitated long execution times, further lengthened by constant rethinking and corrections. In some cases, Seurat also painted the frame to augment the effect of the light and colours. In his last compositions, like *The Circus* (1890-1891), he experimented with increasingly refined drawing (which anticipated the innovations of Art Nouveau and Art Déco) and with a new distribution of colours by which to make perceptible the figures' movement and energy.

Pointillism's other leading figure was Paul Signac, less poetical than Seurat but perhaps even more important for his colour research. Between 1887 and 1889, he collaborated closely with the critic Félix Fénéon and Seurat, attentively reading studies on optics and developing a technique he called 'chromo-luminism'. After the death of Seurat in 1891, Signac's palette was enriched with warmer, more intense tones. Pursuing his experiments in painting, he softened his rigorous style and left more room for emotional values. Through the Belgian painter Théo van Rysselberghe, Pointillism was combined with the English Arts and Crafts movement and found application in the decorative arts on the threshold of Art Nouveau. Furthermore, the investigation of colour had a strong impact on Henri Matisse and the Fauve painters.

Italian Divisionism is an interesting offshoot of Pointillism. In his *Principi scientifici del divisionismo* (Scientific Principles of Divisionism, 1906), the painter Gaetano Previati summarized its essence: 'Painting may be defined as a reduction of reality to lines and coloured dots.' The technique adopted by the Divisionists (who, aside from Previati, included Giovanni Segantini and Giuseppe Pellizza da Volpedo, who focused on social themes and earned international recognition) is similar to Pointillism but is applied in a less strictly scientific manner. Instead of tiny dots of almost all the same size, the Divisionists used irregular brushstrokes, at times threadlike, at times jagged, and not set side by side as in the paintings by their French counterparts but often superimposed or intertwined.

Among the many other late 19th-century artistic groups characterized by the investigation of colour are the Nabis, contemporary with but in a sense the opposite of the Pointillists. Their experience began in 1888 when Paul Sérusier showed some fellow students at the Académie Julian a landscape he had painted on the lid of a cigar box in Pont-

Aven, a resort town in Brittany where Paul Gauguin spent time. Today displayed in the Musée d'Orsay in Paris, this painting is entitled *The Talisman* and is considered the model for these young students, born between 1860 and 1870, who had met at the Lycée Condorcet and the École des Beaux-Arts in Paris. As the painter Maurice Denis wrote, 'It should be remembered that a painting, before being a warhorse, a nude woman or some anecdote is essentially a flat surface covered with colours assembled in a certain order.' The art of the Nabis abandoned perspective and depth in favour of precise lines and strong contrasts of hues, laid out on ample flat backgrounds.

Young and passionate, the Nabis carried some of Gauguin's intuitions to the extreme, such as the anti-naturalistic use of colour and the presence of symbolic elements. For them, art's function was not to reproduce reality; rather, it was a magic tool for investigating the mystery of life. This new concept went beyond the naturalism of the Impressionists and paved the way for the avant-garde experiments of the 20th century.

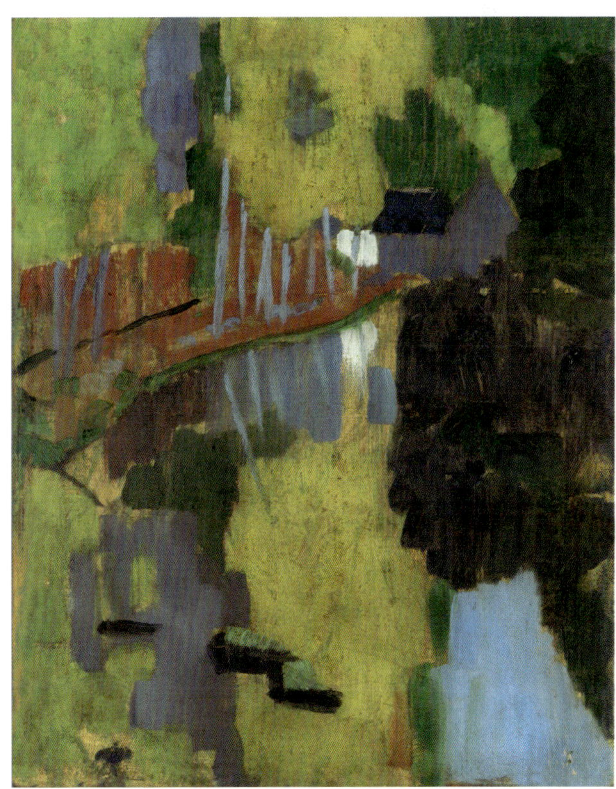

Paul Sérusier
The Talisman (Landscape in the Bois d'Amour)
1888
oil on wooden panel, 27 x 22 cm
Musée d'Orsay, Paris

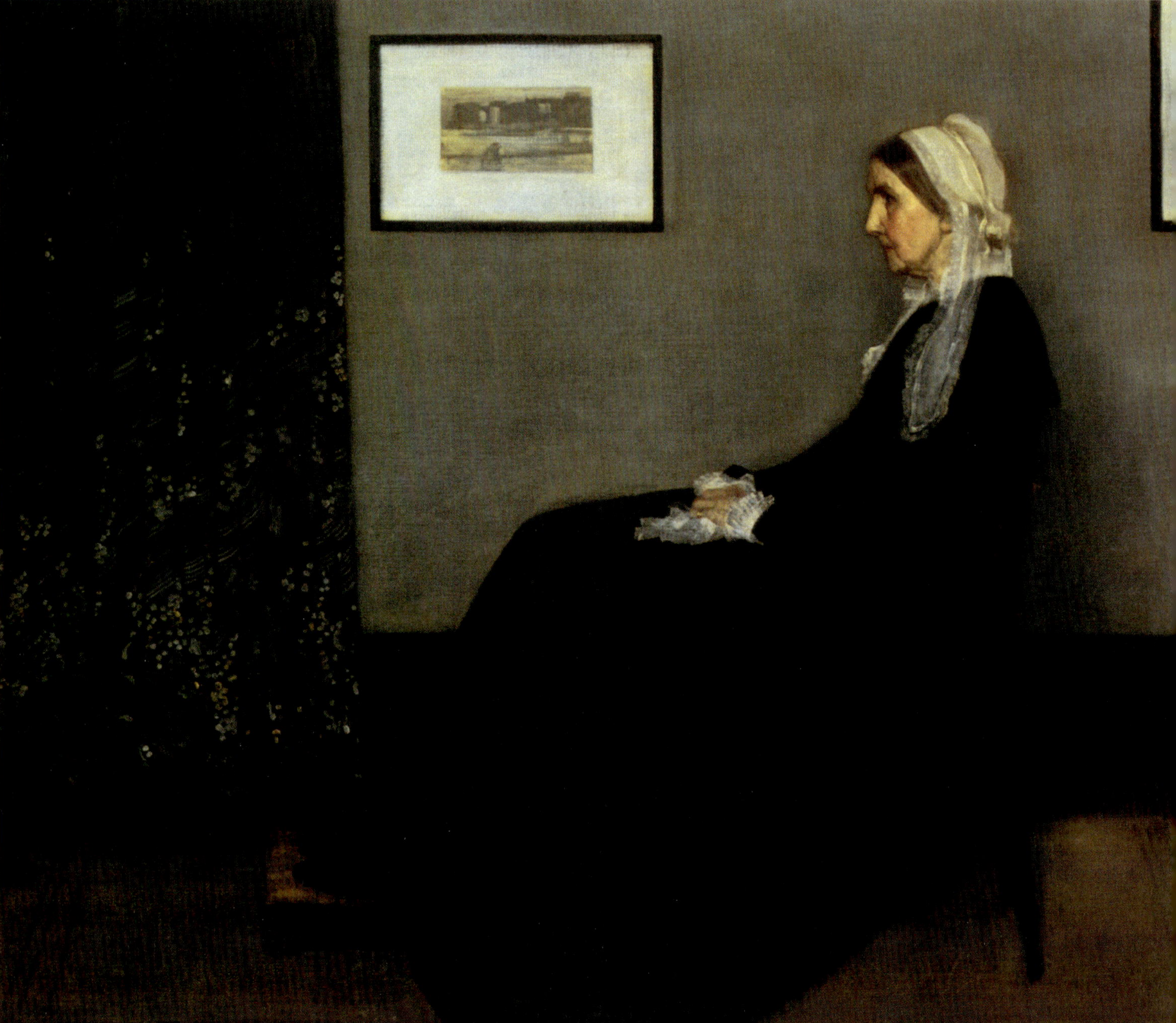

THE 'COLOURS' OF MUSIC AND POETRY

The life of Van Gogh has often been romanticized, but few recall his intense passion for music, stimulated by Wagner's theories of the 'total work of art'. In 1885, when Van Gogh lived in Nuenen, he studied piano and the rudiments of theory with Van der Sanden, an old teacher who was also an organist in Eindhoven. Moreover, as Anton Kerssemakers tells us, music and painting constantly overlapped for the young Vincent: 'During the lessons Van Gogh kept comparing the notes of the piano with Prussian blue and dark green or dark ochre and so on all the way to bright cadmium yellow, and so the poor man thought he must be dealing with a madman and became so afraid of him that he discontinued the lessons.'

Van Gogh's case is far from isolated. From Symbolism on, the interrelationship of painting, music and poetry was very close, and parallels were often drawn between the seven colours of the rainbow and the seven notes of the musical scale. In the 1850s, Whistler had begun entitling his paintings 'Symphonies' and 'Harmonies'; this went on until after the First World War, with the relationship between Kandinsky and Schoenberg.

One of the fundamental passages concerning the correlation between sounds and colours is the sonnet 'Vowels' by Arthur Rimbaud (1871), a masterpiece of Symbolist poetry.

James Abbott McNeill Whistler
Arrangement in Grey and Black (Portrait of the Painter's Mother)
1871
oil on canvas, 144.5 x 162.5 cm
Musée d'Orsay, Paris

Black A, White E, Red I, Green U, Blue, O: vowels.
Someday I'll explain your burgeoning births:
A, a corset; black and hairy, buzzing with flies
Bumbling like bees around a merciless stench,

And shadowy gulfs; E, white vapours and tents, proud
Glacial peaks, white kings, shivering Queen Anne's lace;
I, purples, bloody spittle, lips' lovely laughter
In anger or drunken contrition;

U, cycles, divine vibrations of viridian seas;
Peace of pastures sown with beasts, wrinkles
Stamped on studious brows as if by alchemy;

O, that last Trumpet, overflowing with strange discord,
Silences bridged by Worlds and Angels:
——O the Omega, the violet beam from His Eyes!

Arthur Rimbaud, 'Vowels', 1871

Avant-garde painting may have envied music's freedom of abstraction, unfettered by 'description', yet the composer Mussorgsky sought to depict the 'pictures at an exhibition' in music. A famous juxtaposition of music and visual art came about at the fourteenth exhibition of the Vienna Secession, from 15 April to 27 June 1902, conceived as an homage to Beethoven. The Secession building, designed by Joseph Maria Olbrich a few years earlier, was transformed into a secular temple. In the centre stood a sculpture dedicated to the great composer, a monumental work executed in polychrome marble, alabaster, bronze and ivory by Max Klinger. On the walls of one of the side galleries, Klimt painted one of his masterpieces, the *Beethoven Frieze*: three scenes made up of seven panels more than two metres tall, and twenty-four metres long overall. A Symbolist interpretation of the last movement of the Ninth Symphony, it takes up the themes of the eternal struggle between good and evil and the quest for happiness. Many artists in the early 20th century made liberal use of musical and literary metaphors and parallels: Francis Picabia painted a work significantly entitled *Music Is like Painting*, Sonia Delaunay illustrated long texts in a refined range of colours (and Apollinaire, an advocate of the fusion of painting, literature and music, coined the term 'Orphism'). As often happens, the question of the sound of colours tended to become overly intellectual and rhetorical. Picasso closed the case with one of his irrefutable aphorisms: 'Why do two colours set one beside the other sing? Can one explain this? No. Just as one can never learn to paint.'

COLOUR THEORY IN THE 20TH CENTURY: ITTEN AND ALBERS

Picasso believed that colours, just like forms, must follow the dynamics of the emotions. However, this sentiment was not shared by Johannes Itten and Josef Albers, two mid-20th-century masters who devoted considerable attention to the study of colour while combining painting practice with teaching and writing scientific treatises. Itten and Albers had a number of things in common. Exact contemporaries (both were born in 1888), they had contact with Walter Gropius, taught at the Bauhaus, and had to leave Nazi Germany in the early 1930s. While they were significant artists of geometric abstraction, both were particularly important for their interest in teaching and colour theory.

Josef Albers entered the Weimar Bauhaus in 1920 and continued teaching after the institution's subsequent move to Dessau. From the outset, he focused on regular geometric models and the primary colours. And like Itten, he did not confine himself to painting, but designed furniture and collages of coloured glass.

With the closure of the Bauhaus in 1933 and growing Nazi repression, Albers left Europe and became a US citizen. He taught first at the Black Mountain College in North Carolina (where his students included Cy Twombly and Robert Rauschenberg) and then in New Haven, where he taught at Yale University. Through lectures, lessons and writings (the most famous being *Interaction of Color*), Albers analysed the intrinsic logic governing colours. His pupils included such major figures of North American abstract art as Robert Motherwell and Kenneth Noland. Albers's expressive research concentrated on the effects of perception and, anticipating Op Art, systematically repeated geometric forms. In 1949, he initiated the 'Homage to the Square' series, whose canvases are composed of superimposed squares – planar forms of various colours that suggest an effect of depth. Albers's activity at Yale was carried on by Faber Birren, who assembled the most comprehensive library on colour in existence.

Born in the German-speaking part of Switzerland, Johannes Itten devoted almost all his life to teaching painting, but from a somewhat paradoxical position, for he was convinced it is impossible to 'learn' to paint. For him, the most one could hope to master would be objective technical and material concepts, beginning with line and colour.

Through contact with Alma Mahler and Walter Gropius, in 1920, Itten was made director of the Vorkurs (preliminary course) at the Bauhaus. At the conclusion of this trial semester, a commission evaluated whether or not to admit candidates to the school. Itten stressed the language of forms (curved lines communicate a sense of movement and speed; straight lines convey stable regularity) and the use of contrasts of form, material, light and above all colour, essential for an art in constant development. Above all, however, Itten's lessons aimed to stimulate the creative energies of the students, freeing them from all physical restraint and psychological inhibition. His teaching method was unusual. As Klee wrote in a letter to his wife in 1921, before starting lessons, Itten had his students perform physical exercises to loosen their legs and arms, and taught them how to concentrate, breathe and relax. He accompanied his students outside the classroom to immerse them in nature, and when he proposed the study of Old Masters (Grünewald's Isenheim Altarpiece in Colmar, for example), he concluded that the most useful response is to sit in front of a painting and weep.

Having moved from Weimar to Berlin in 1926, in 1934 Itten left Germany. He went first to Amsterdam and then to Zurich, where he directed the school of applied arts. Only in 1961 did Itten finally publish his own colour theory, an exhaustive study that analyses every aspect of the use of colour. It is still referred to not only by artists but also in the field of visual communications: design, advertising, cinema and fashion. Itten offers a full, well-constructed approach that seeks a balance between science and psychology, the dichotomy that has divided colour studies for over three centuries. Each individual sees and judges colours in an entirely individual way; yet chromatic perception and receptivity have an objective basis in the colours' behaviour within the spectrum of light. Similarly, according to Itten, there exists an exact psychological parallel with the optical, electromagnetic and chemical processes that occur in the eye and the brain when we see colours. Despite the systematic approach of this conclusive book, Itten never lost the impassioned spirit of his early days. In the introduction to his treatise, he writes, 'Colours are children of light, and light is their mother. Light, that first phenomenon of the world, reveals to us the spirit and the living soul of the world through colours.'

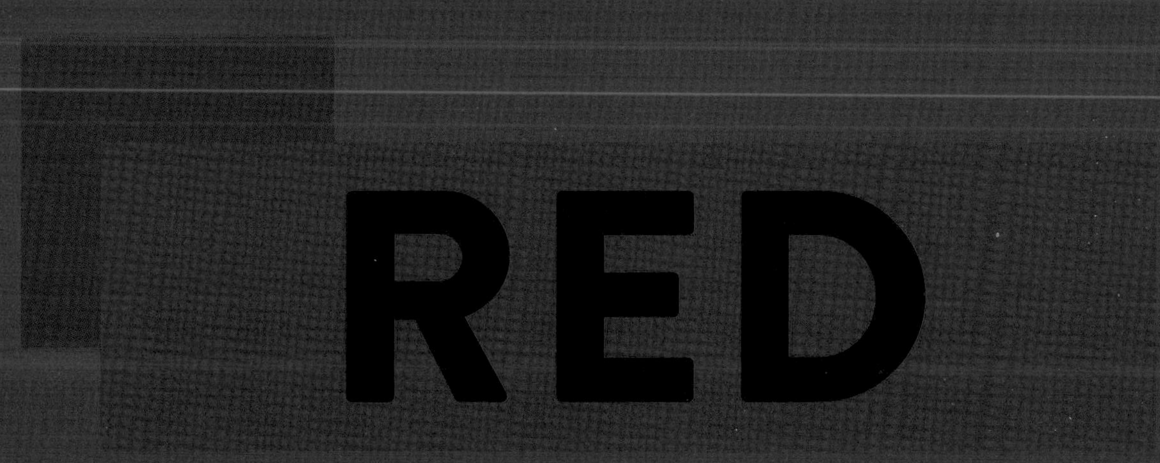
RED

INTRODUCTION

Strong, warm and bright, red is one of the three primary colours, along with blue and yellow. On the edge of the spectrum of colours visible to the human eye (lower frequencies fall into the infrared range), it is the colour of blood and fire, the sun at dawn and sunset, field berries and wild berries. With black, red is an ancient colour, the first to be used by humankind in the remote origins of art. Egyptian scribes and medieval monks filled their quills with it to offset black, while it is one of the two basic colours in a deck of playing cards and on a roulette wheel. Indeed, red is *the* colour, for in Latin (and some languages derived from it), *coloratus* also means 'red'. In Russian, the adjective 'red' also means 'beautiful'.

Red is a fundamental colour in human history, loaded with symbolic meaning. It is easily obtained in nature, in many variants of increasing cost, from simple ochre and madder root to iron oxides to the lavishly expensive Tyrian purple obtained from shellfish of the Murex family and from kermes, the shell of the cochineal. Among the main variants of red, each of which has its own special value, are vermilion, carmine, scarlet, crimson. The term 'miniature', used in the Romance languages to refer to manuscript illustrations (*miniatus* literally means 'painted vermilion'), derives from the name of a reddish dye, *minium* (red lead). Furthermore, the first letter of a chapter in medieval manuscripts was often written in red (Latin *rubeus*) to make it stand out. From this custom came the term 'rubric', originally denoting the text so distinguished and, by extension, 'an authoritative rule'. This practice is also behind the origin of the expression 'red letter day'.

Until colours were produced industrially beginning in the 18th century, one of the most common bases for red was mercury, from which cinnabar and brilliant vermilion are obtained. While cinnabar is easily found in nature (there are abundant deposits in Tuscany on Mount Amiata, in Istria and in some regions of the Iberia Peninsula), vermilion requires an elaborate chemical process of synthesis discovered in the Middle Ages and described in contemporary treatises. In the *Schedula diversarum artium* (c. 1122), the writer Theophilus speaks of a 'dry process' that involves the two materials from which vermilion is obtained – mercury and sulphur – and that produces a black material called *Aethiops mineralis* ('Ethiopian mineral') because of its colour. It is heated before grinding, then recrystallized into an extraordinarily brilliant red-orange colour that assumed an important place in European arts.

The introduction of vermilion had significant consequences for the history of painting. Medieval artists took a decisive step towards the conquest of new chromatic horizons, and from the 12th century onwards began seeking out other bright colours. The contrast between vermilion and the gold background typical of the 14th-century and late Gothic painting is particularly effective.

In general, red expresses extreme feelings and symbols: war, power, wrath, passion, charity, lust, aggression, speed, seduction, sacrifice. The expression 'to see red' means to lose one's calm completely, to be infuriated or in a jealous rage. And tradition holds that redheads are apt to have a fiery temperament.

Owing to its immediacy and universality, red has raised its profile over the past two centuries. Since the international agreement on maritime distress signals, it has become synonymous with danger in traffic lights and street signs. A red carpet receives processions of film stars at the biggest festivals and international award ceremonies.

In many sports, red is a favourite colour for clubs' and national teams' jerseys: Spain's world soccer champions are known as the Red Fury, while the players of Manchester United Football Club are known as the Red Devils. In motor sports, Ferrari cars and Ducati motorcycles are almost always red. In the realm of the automobile, red is a sign of speed – it is rare to see a red family sedan, while some American insurance companies charge higher premiums to red-car owners, whose driving, considered more aggressive, exposes them to greater risks than people who choose a calmer colour for their vehicle.

THE OLDEST COLOUR

Red ochre tools, used for colouring the body, have been found in caves at Blombos, South Africa. This discovery confirms that red is the oldest colour in prehistoric art. Analyses conducted on these primitive 'marker pens' place their fabrication between 70,000 and 75,000 years ago.

Cave paintings of the Upper Palaeolithic era, between 13,000 and 10,000 BC, have given us extraordinary images of animals and hunting scenes, especially in caves in the south-west of Europe (at Lascaux and Chauvet in France, and at Altamira in Spain). The high humidity in the caves favoured the colours' adherence to the rock surface through a chemical process similar to that which occurs in medieval and Renaissance frescoes.

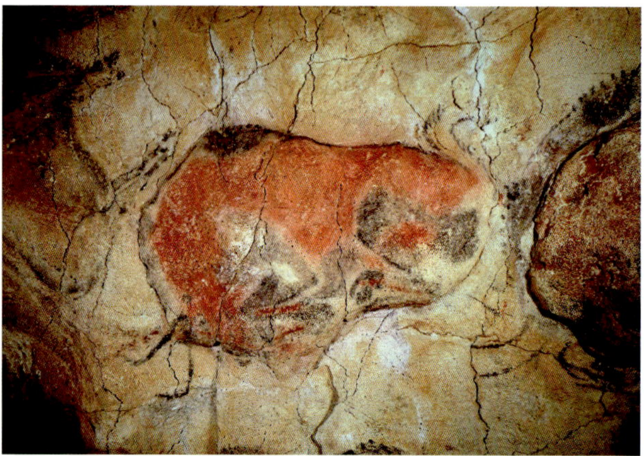

The pictures in the cave at Altamira, on Spain's Cantabrian Coast, are exceptional for both their chromatic variety and their skilled use of colour. Along with black, yellows and earth tones, red is one of the dominant colours that occur most frequently on the cave ceilings. There are many shades of red obtained from mineral pigments such as natural iron oxides and red ochre (the latter a pigment derived from haematite or ferric oxide). Applied with a pad, the fingers or simply blown onto the surface, various shades of red were employed to give the figures volume, as were the natural contours of the rock. The colour was spread only inside the figures, which were outlined in black with charcoal.

Because of their lifelike naturalism and expressive force, the Altamira paintings have been called the 'Sistine Chapel of cave art'. In fact, the same description has been applied to the French caves at Lascaux as well. Without going so far as to liken Stone Age bisons to Michelangelo's Vatican cycle, it is interesting that both use red ochre.

Bison
c. 12,000 BC
cave painting from Altamira, Spain

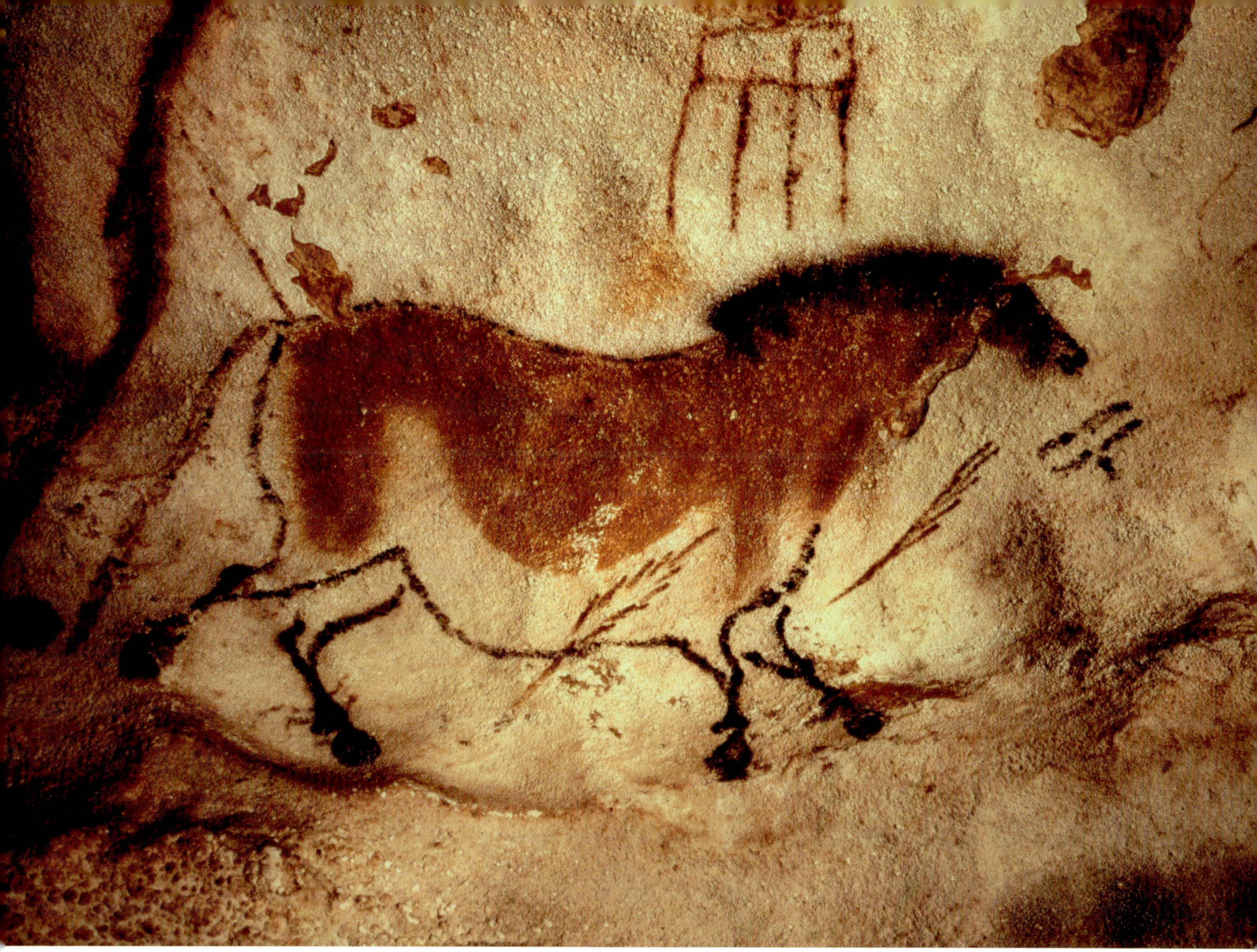

Horse
c. 17,000 BC
cave painting from Lascaux, France

RED-FIGURE POTTERY

Leningrad Painter
Hydria depicting pottery painters at work
480-470 BC
Attic red-figure ware
Collezione d'arte Banca Intesa

Greek pottery can be divided into two main currents according to technique. The 'black figure' technique is characterized by a line incised in the clay body before firing, highlighting the details of the black silhouette executed on a vase's reddish ground. This technique reached its apogee during the middle three decades of the 6th century BC in works by artists of vastly different temperaments. Perhaps the awareness of having reached an expressive peak spawned the sweeping change that began in Attica, the region of Athens. Using a new firing technique, the colours were reversed, so that the preferred style was now 'red' figures on a dense, polished black ground instead.

The new method of 'red figure' vase painting was invented in Athens around 530 BC, at a time when the sculpture being produced was in the so-called Severe Style. In the 'red figure' method, the ground was painted black and the figures, standing out against the red clay ground, could be defined with precise painted – not incised – black lines. Particular attention was paid to the female nude and male musculature, while the early efforts at rendering eyes, shown in profile for the first time, no doubt echo contemporary activity in large-format painting, where there was growing interest in life-like, naturalistic representations of the human figure in realistic, measurable space.

A visual document of exceptional interest, this hydria (water pitcher) was decorated by an anonymous Athenian master in the early 5th century BC. Archaeologists have named its creator the Leningrad Painter. The upper part depicts pottery painters using tools to decorate vessels of various shapes with colours. Some of them are receiving the laurel wreath.

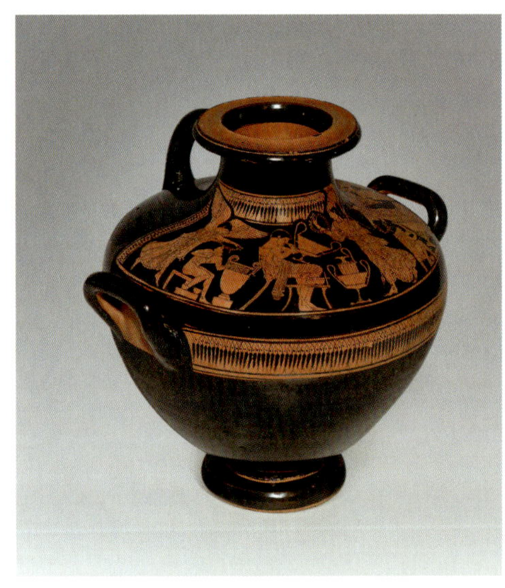

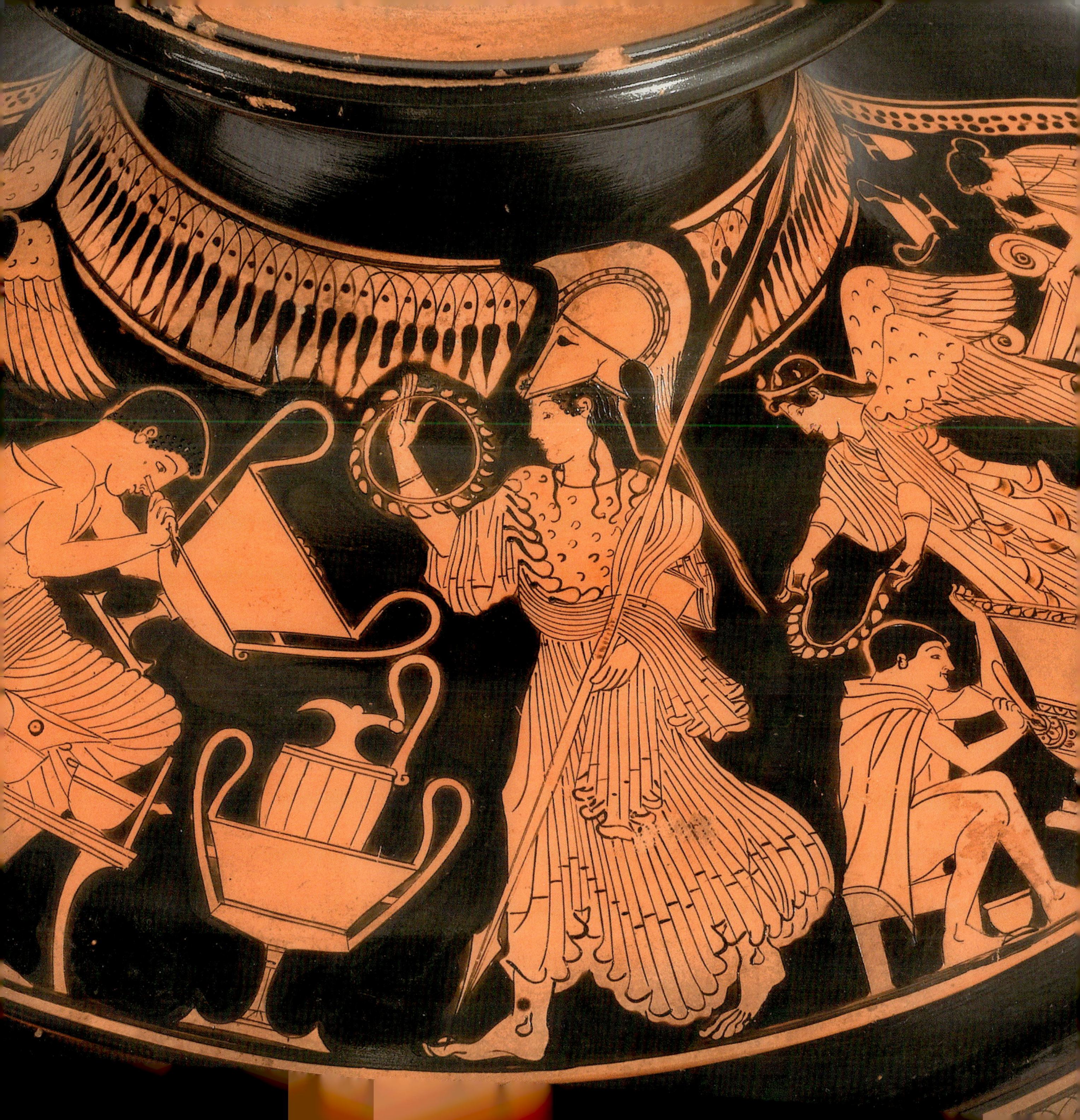

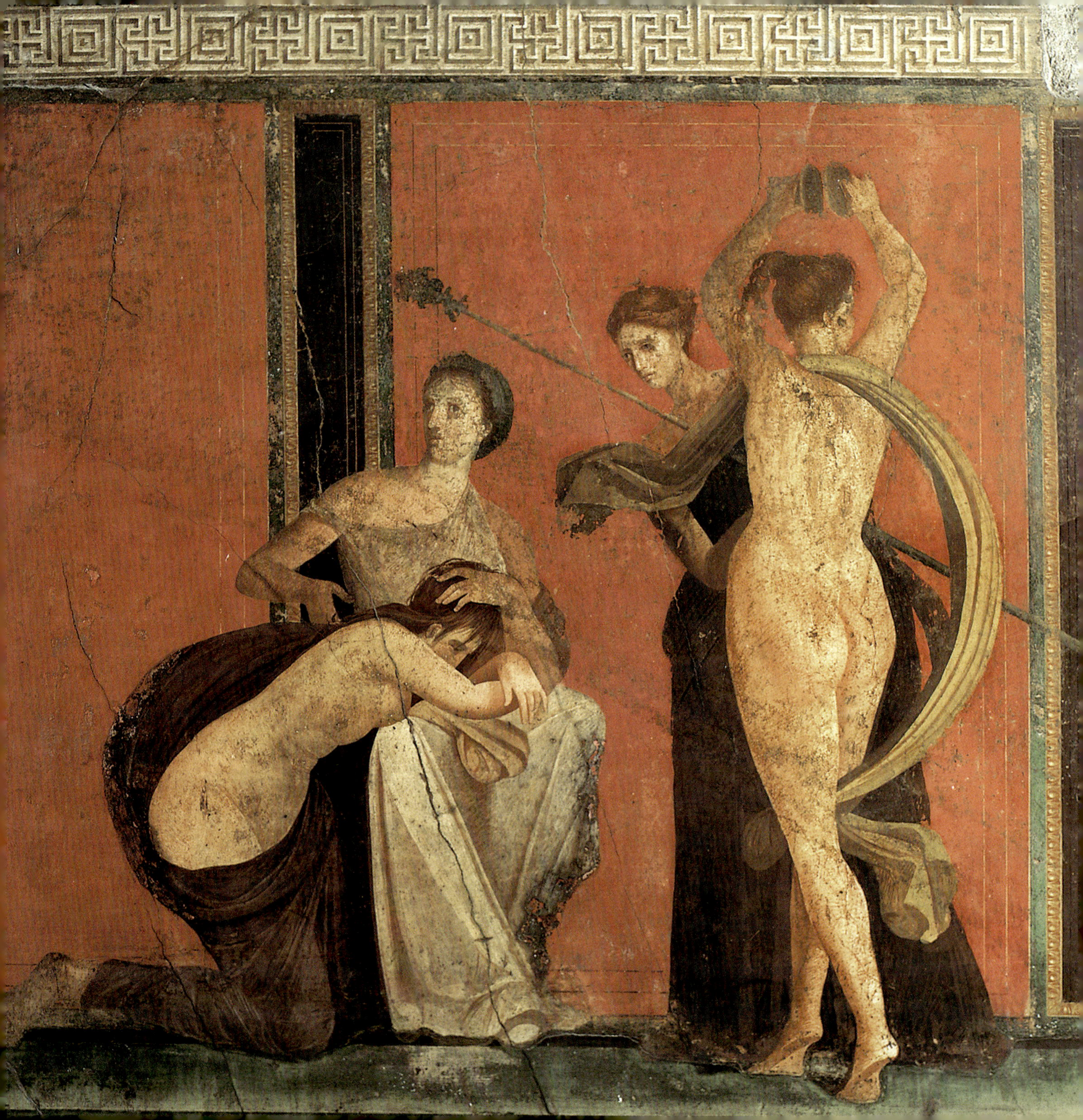

POMPEIAN RED

A common feature of Roman painting, and especially mural painting discovered in the cities buried by the eruption of Vesuvius in AD 79, is the use of a particular shade of red for wall decoration. This surprisingly saturated and bright shade first came to light during the excavations at Pompeii promoted by the Bourbons in the mid-18th century and was immediately dubbed 'Pompeian red'. The rediscovery of highly coloured walls and paintings of large dimensions – a kind of classical art that was believed irretrievably lost – occurred just when the Neoclassical aesthetic was being formulated. For a stylistic theory that proposed white marble statues as the superlative model, the vivid colours of the wall frescoes at Pompeii must have been hard to take!

At first made from very costly cinnabar, Pompeian red (also known as Tuscan red, Herculaneum red, Pozzuoli earth, English red and Verona red earth) was obtained from an inorganic ochre, haematite, whose prefix is Greek for 'blood'. Because of its lesser cost, it was also suitable for use on large wall surfaces, like the distinctive backgrounds of the painting cycle at the Villa of the Mysteries. This cycle is the most important fresco in Pompeii, and one of the greatest examples of classical painting. The red walls depict an almost life-size series of mystic rites associated with Dionysus.

Bacchic rite (detail)
Mid-1st century AD
fresco, Villa of the Mysteries, Pompeii

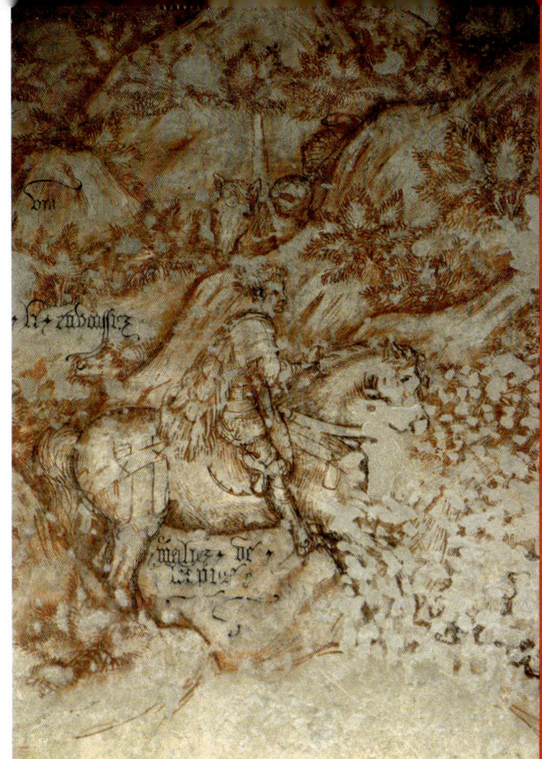

In Ancient Rome, the basic pigment in Pompeian red, consisting of iron oxide, was called *sinopis*, from Sinope, the name of the town in modern-day Turkey where, according to Pliny the Elder, it was first discovered. For centuries, haematite (*lapis haematitis*) was used to make preliminary under-drawings for frescoes in churches, chapels and *palazzi*. Because of their characteristic reddish colour, these drawings are sometimes called 'sinopias'. *Matita*, the Italian word for 'pencil', derives from the Latin *haematites*.

Pisanello
Landscape with Scenes of Chivalry: the Knight Errant Malies de l'Espine (detail)
1440
sinopia
Palazzo Ducale, Mantua

THE PASSION OF CHRIST

Duccio di Buoninsegna
Road to Calvary, detail from the reverse of the *Maestà*
1308-1311
tempera and gold on panel, 51 x 53.3 cm
Museo dell'Opera della Metropolitana, Siena

In Christian art, red has assumed a wide range of at times antithetical symbolic meanings. It is one of the main liturgical colours, and besides being worn by priests at specific periods of the church year, red is worn by cardinals, used for the borders and hats of bishops, and even appears in some of the Pope's accessories. And yet, the Devil and Hell are also represented in red. Charity, one of the three Theological Virtues, is clothed in red, but red is also the colour of Lust, one of the Seven Deadly Sins. Above all, however, red is the colour of the blood shed in sacrifice and martyrdom. In medieval art in particular, it appears frequently in scenes of the Passion of Christ.

On the back of the large panel of the *Maestà*, Duccio di Buoninsegna painted a series of episodes from the Life and Passion of Jesus. In the culminating scenes of the sacred drama, Christ wears red, immediately perceptible as a symbol of his imminent crucifixion: the blood shed on the cross will redeem humankind. Duccio carefully distributed the red shades in the group of figures in the *Road to Calvary*, creating a balanced interplay of references between Christ, in the centre, and those around him, from Mary Magdalene at the far left to Simon of Cyrene, who is supporting the cross at the right.

The blood of Christ is offered in the form of wine at every celebration of Mass, and many Christian images show this blood being collected in a chalice by angels as it flows from Jesus's Five Wounds (the hands, feet and side). With visionary Baroque fantasy, Gian Lorenzo Bernini interpreted this theme from a symbolic perspective: the cross to which Christ was nailed floats above a limitless sea of blood copiously shed for humankind's salvation.

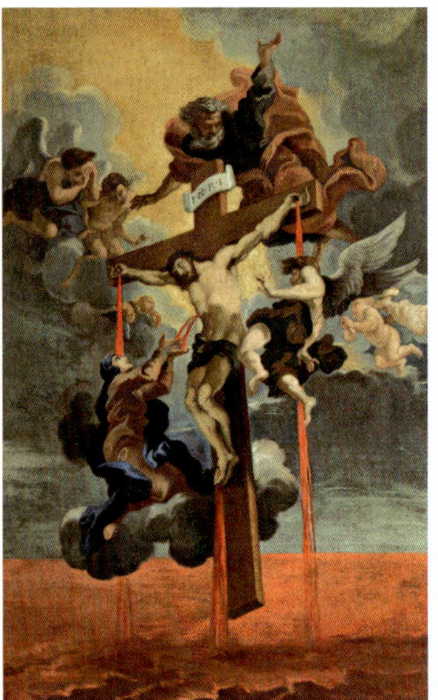

Gian Lorenzo Bernini
The Blood of Christ
1669-1670
oil on canvas, 98 x 64.5 cm
Palazzo Chigi, Ariccia

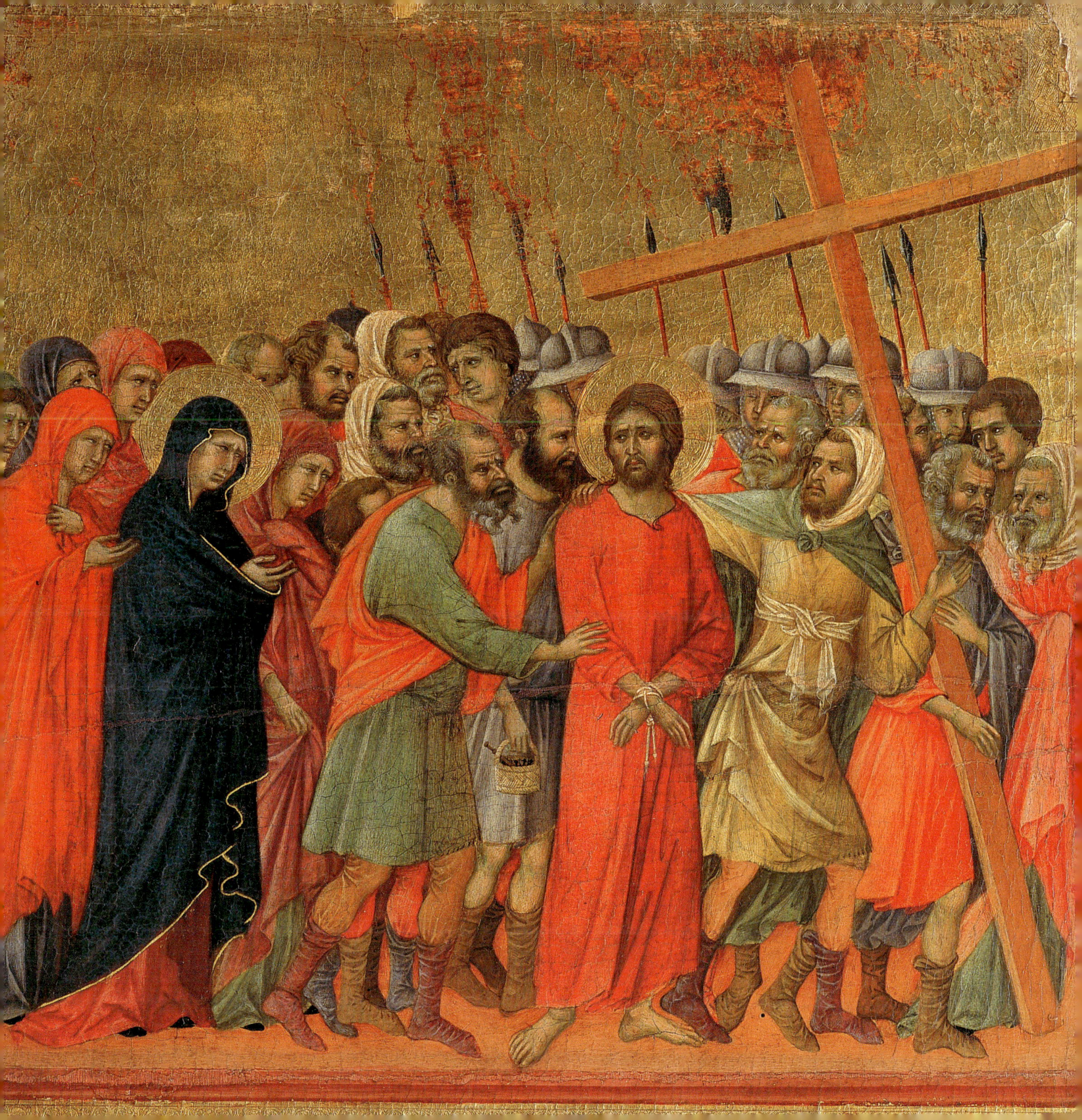

A TOUCH OF ELEGANCE

What is the true colour of elegance, class and style? For centuries, both sexes have been caught in a dilemma between red and black. At least until the 15th century, brightly coloured accessories were widespread among men, though largely confined to the elite social classes who could afford such expensive dress. As is clearly demonstrated in 15th-century art, the quest for sophisticated, colourful accessories attained extraordinary heights of glamour. Headgear in particular was so elaborate that it would make heads turn even today at Ascot racecourse. In fact, the painters most drawn to exploring perspective devoted great attention to hats.

Showing considerable chromatic intuition, Van Eyck begins this marvellous portrait of a man with dark, dull tones, covering the background with a uniform black from which the exotic, somewhat whimsical red turban vividly bursts out. A virtuoso display of folds and knots, this turban confers a note of pleasing elegance on the austerity of a face that is no longer young. Because of the intensity of the gaze turned towards the viewer, some art historians have thought this painting to be a self-portrait, but given the lack of any certain image of the great painter's face, this must remain conjecture. In any case, the painting dates from the late phase of Van Eyck's career, and the age of the man portrayed could correspond to that of the artist.

It is interesting to compare Van Eyck's portrait with Piero della Francesca's profile portrait of Duke Federico da Montefeltro wearing an elegant red jacket and a matching hat. Its simplified forms, reduced to a linear geometric structure so that the hat almost becomes a simple red volume, is diametrically opposed to the free expressiveness of Van Eyck's turban.

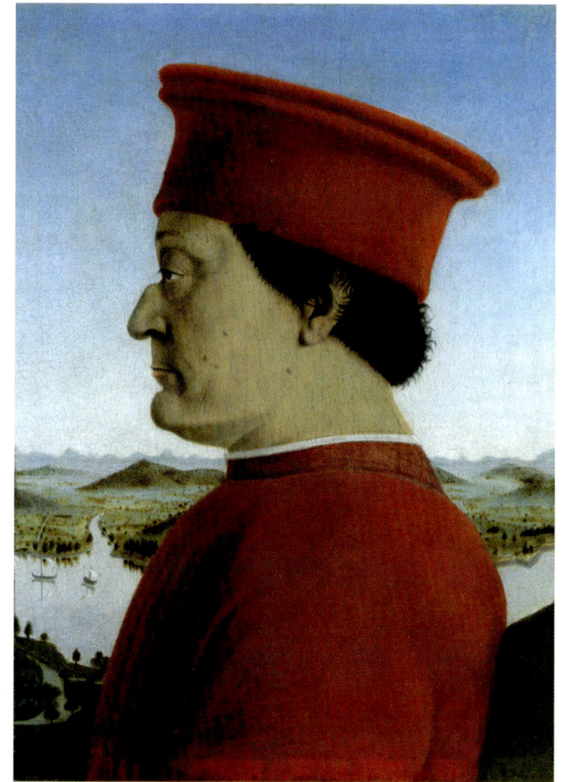

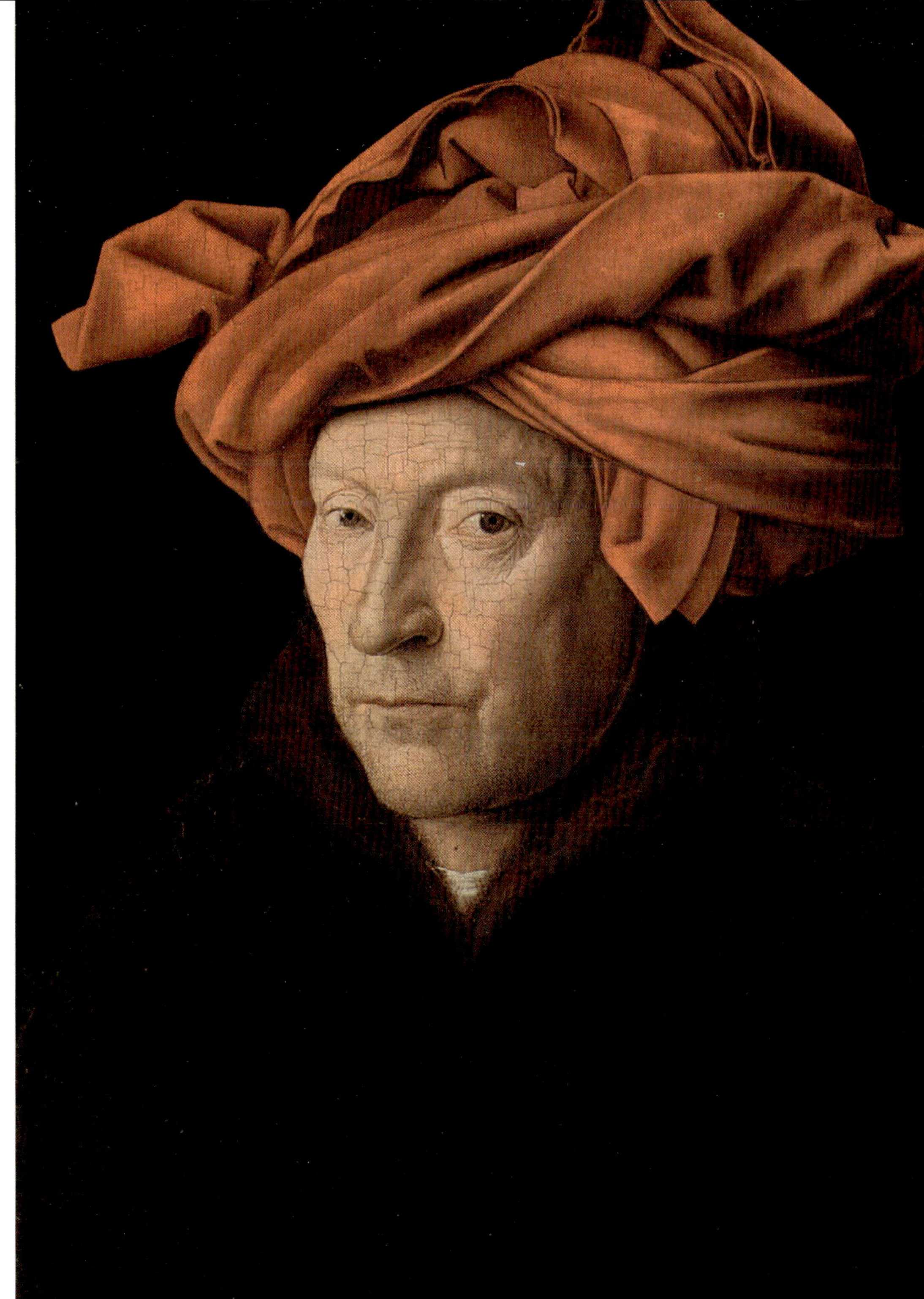

▸

Jan van Eyck
Man in a Red Turban
(Self-portrait?)
1433
oil on panel, 26 x 19 cm
National Gallery, London

◂

Piero della Francesca
Portrait of Federico
da Montefeltro
1465-1472
tempera on panel, 47 x 33 cm
Galleria degli Uffizi, Florence

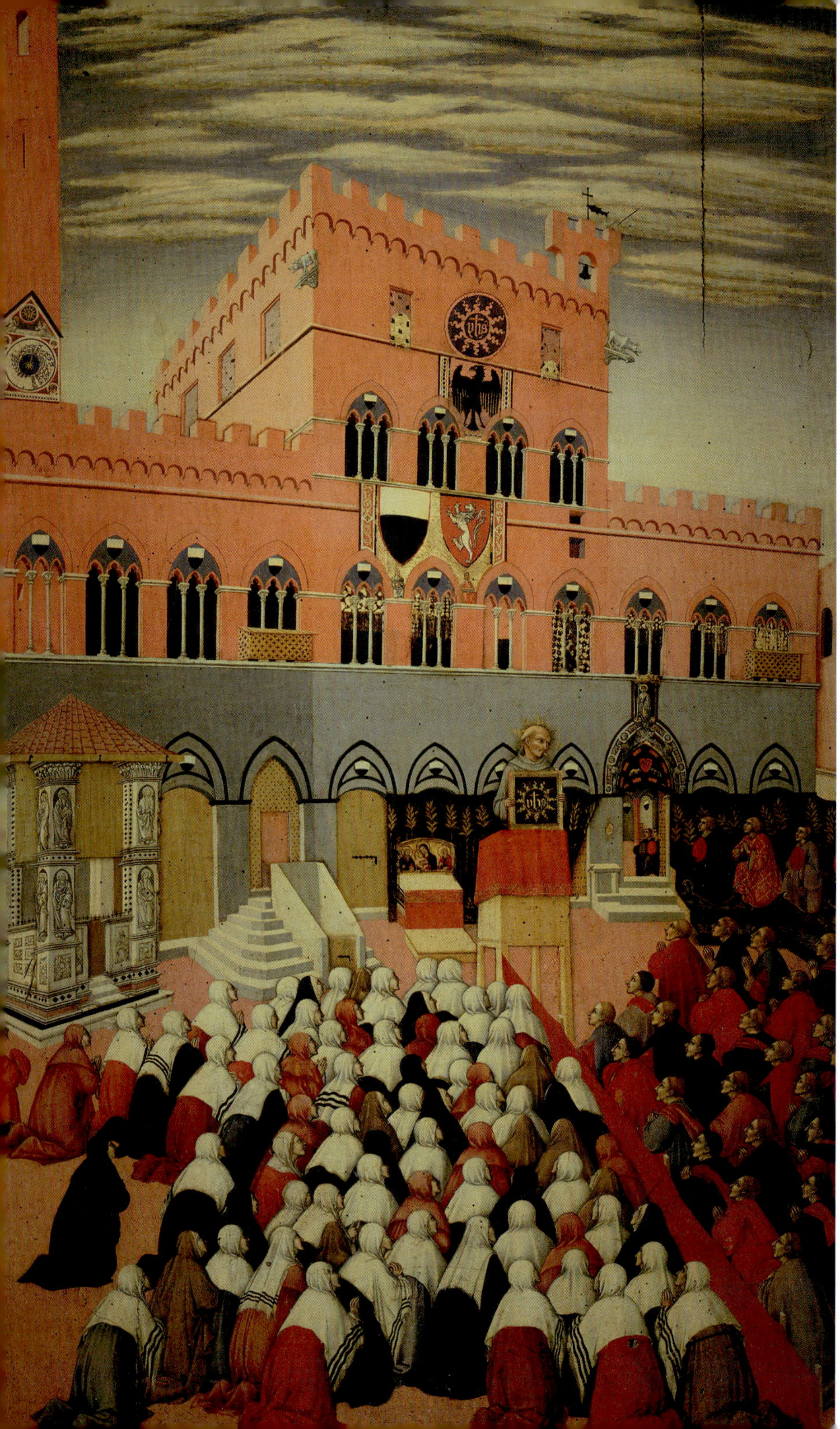

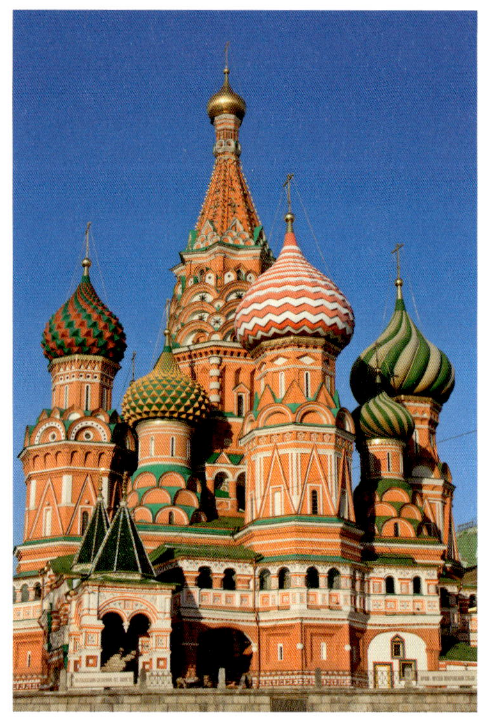

The Cathedral of St Basil
1555-1560
Moscow

Sano di Pietro
St Bernard Preaching in the Piazza del Campo
1445
tempera on panel, 162 x 102 cm
Museo dell'Opera Metropolitana, Siena

BRICK

Brick has often been used for constructions of lesser importance. While nobler construction materials were set aside for a few buildings of high symbolic value, such as the huge Romanesque and Gothic cathedrals of stone and marble, the houses that surrounded them were made of wood, straw and brick. Nevertheless, in some parts of Europe and at particular times in history, brick was used for important buildings. A good example can be found in the almost intact Gothic city of Siena. While marble in the city's emblematic colours black and white is reserved for the cathedral, the grand Palazzo Pubblico is largely brick, and its appearance proudly defines views of the city.

In the Baltic, brick distinguished the solid cities of the Hanseatic League, and between the 14th and 15th centuries spawned its own style of architecture: Backsteingotik, or Brick Gothic. Since the use of a material considered to be modest risked making a town look poor, the merchants of Lübeck adopted an expensive method of enamelling the surface of some bricks to be placed in friezes, along mouldings, around entrances or to enhance other special features of a building.

Red Square in Moscow deserves its name because of the colour of the brick walls of the Kremlin, the museum of history and the Cathedral of St Basil, as well as the granite of Lenin's mausoleum and, of course, of the banners and stars on the pinnacles. But since the Russian word красный (krasnyï) means both 'red' and 'beautiful', it would be more correct to call it Beautiful Square.

RUBY

Ruby and coral are both attributed particular powers, no doubt linked with their bright red colour. Jewellery and ornaments made of these precious materials were not simply adornments but were believed to provide magical protection.

However, the power of stones, jewels and colours is not always sufficient. Domenico Ghirlandaio, usually in his element with narrative scenes full of action and figures, in this case focuses on a particularly inspired moment, a 'freeze frame' full of splendour.

At eighteen, Giovanna degli Albizi married Lorenzo Tornabuoni. They were a celebrated couple on Florence's highest social plane, but Giovanna died in childbirth just two years later, in 1488. Ghirlandaio's painting presents an absorbed, almost abstract image of a beautiful young woman who died tragically.

It is as if the painter had wanted to work a kind of alchemy, making the figure of the woman metallic, enamelled, incorruptible. The Latin inscription is tinged with impotent melancholy: 'Art, would that you could represent character and mind! There would be no more beautiful painting on earth.'

The coral beads suspended in the niche (rather than hung from the neck of a newborn or its mother) probably allude to Giovanna's ill-fated delivery. The young woman is wearing a piece of jewellery set with a ruby, a stone held to be an antidote to sadness and to have the power to overcome every demon and illness (according to Hildegard von Bingen). But another similar jewel, now useless, lies abandoned at the back of the niche.

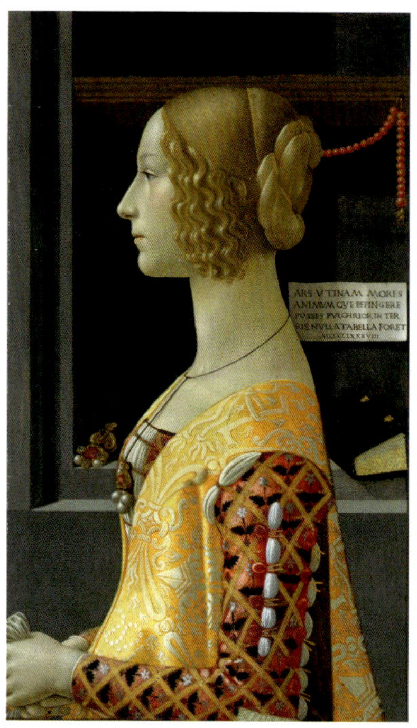

Domenico Ghirlandaio
Portrait of Giovanna Tornabuoni
1488
tempera on panel, 76 x 50 cm
Museo Thyssen-Bornemisza, Madrid

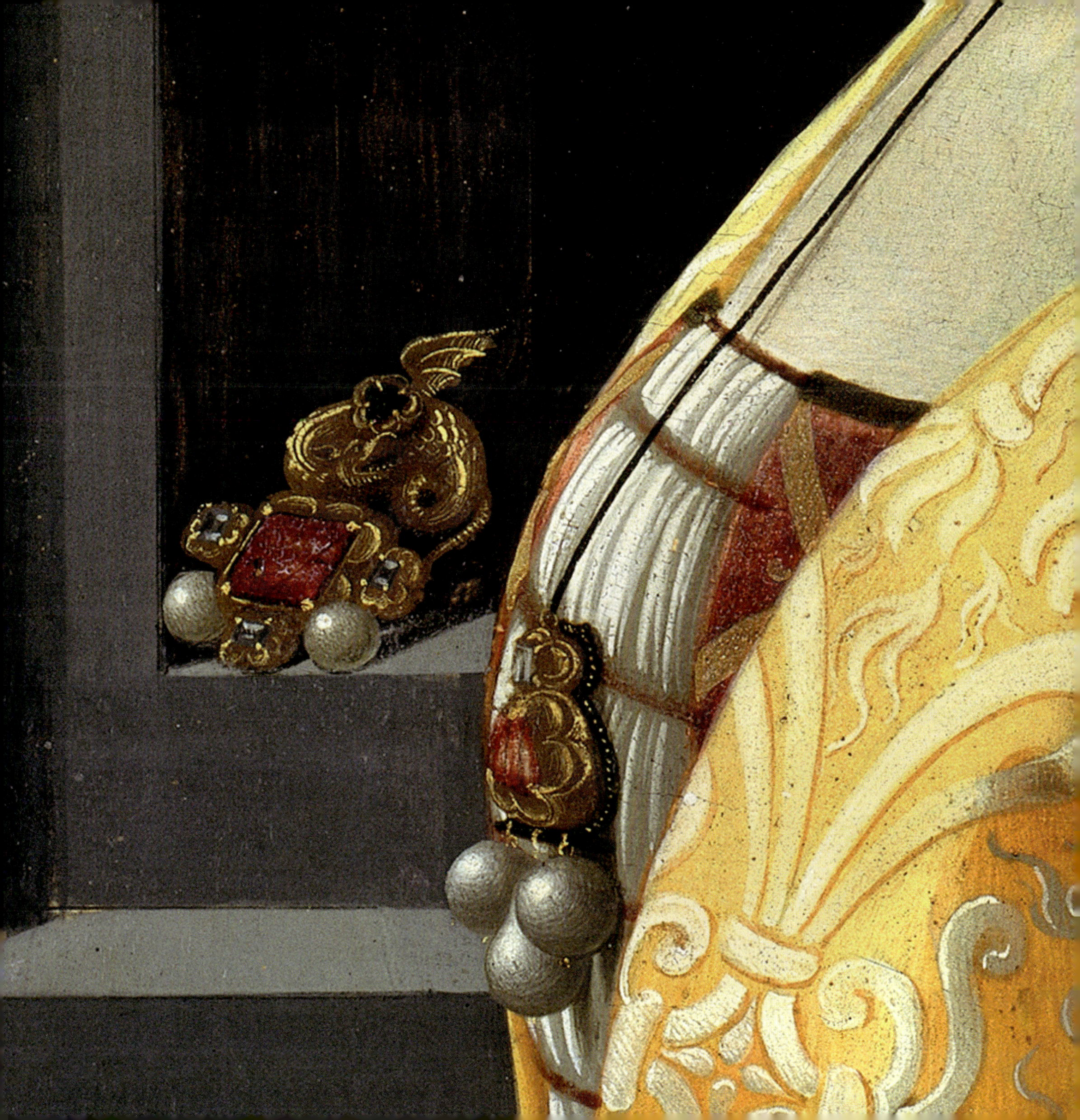

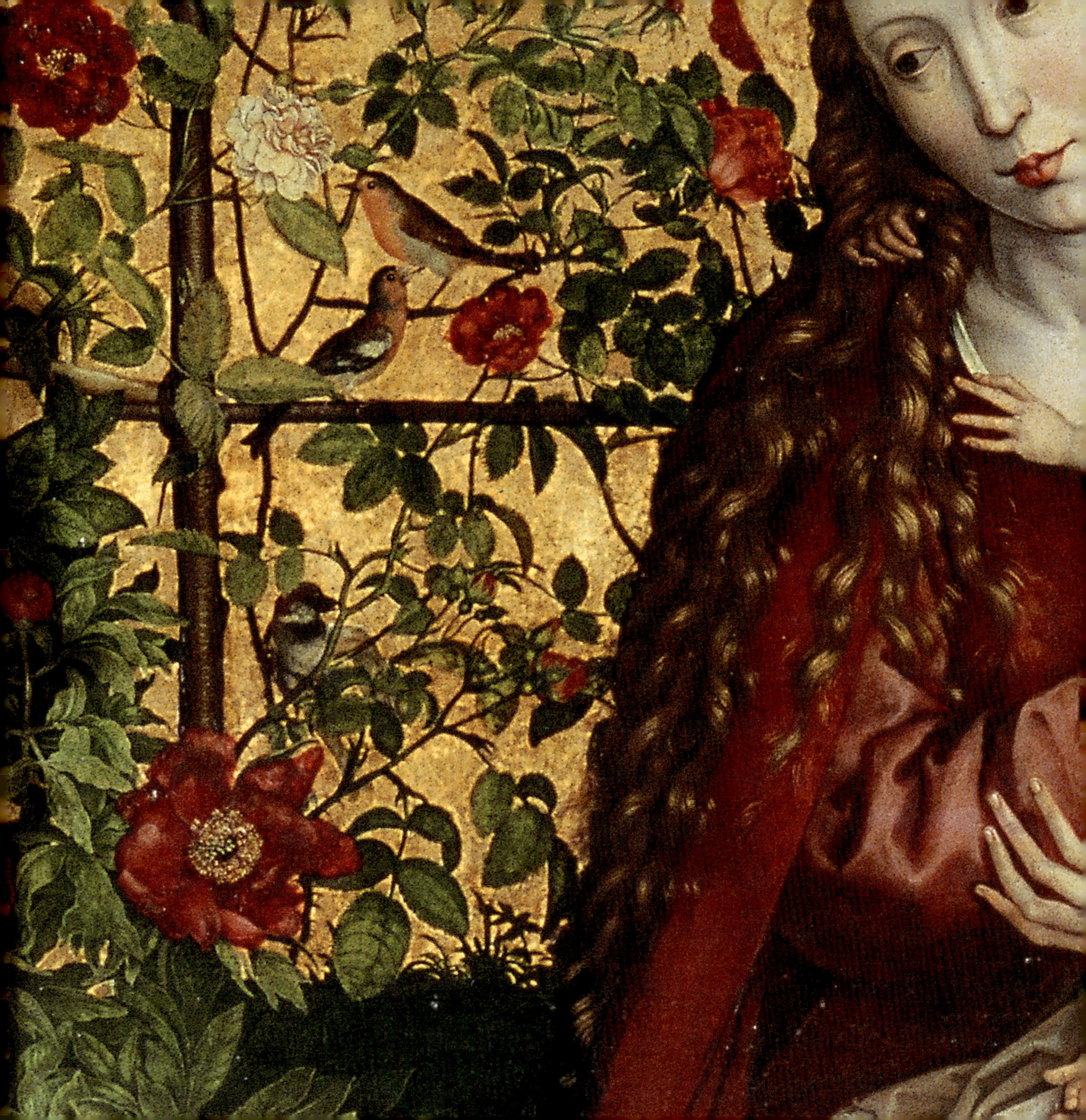

ROSE GARDEN

In late medieval art, Mary is often represented in a garden with hedges or espaliers of red roses, an iconography referring back to old sacred texts, as well as referring to courtly love and the symbolism of the rose as an emblem of love and beauty. 'Mystic Rose' and 'Rose among Roses' are two of the titles reserved for prayers to Mary – invocations that seem to be inspired by passages from the Song of Solomon in which the beloved is likened to 'the rose of Sharon and the lily of the valleys' (Song of Songs, 2:1). The red rose takes on a further meaning in reference to the Passion of Christ, evoking the colour of the blood shed for Man's salvation. The rose's prickly thorns, meanwhile, echo that Crown of Thorns that Christ wore.

In this masterpiece by Martin Schongauer, the flame-red robes match the flowers in the background, transforming Mary into a rose in the heavenly garden, the 'Mystic Rose', the 'Queen of Heaven'. Another interesting detail is the little strawberry bushes in the meadow. The strawberry is often presented allegorically in herbals and sacred artworks. According to medieval symbolism, it represents the three colours of the Theological Virtues: the red (fruit) for Charity; the green (leaves) for Hope; and the white (blossom) for Faith.

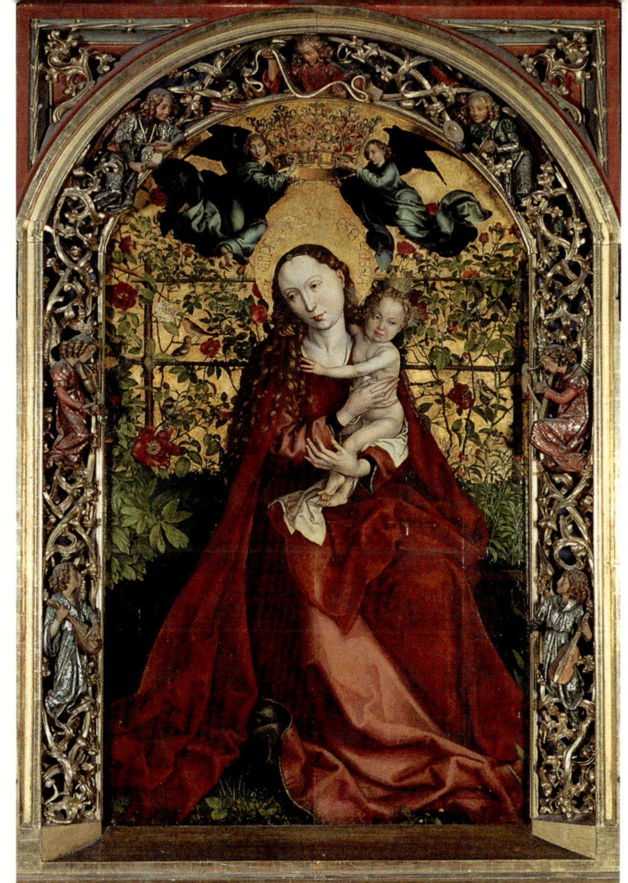

Mary's regal nature, conspicuously confirmed by the crown borne by two angels, justifies the use of a showy tone of red once reserved exclusively for persons of high rank (due to the considerable cost of the brilliant dyes required). Robert Campin's *Madonna of the Flowered Wall* (1425) and Jan van Eyck's *Madonna of Chancellor Rolin* (c. 1437) are two outstanding examples predating the painting by Schongauer.

Martin Schongauer
Madonna of the Rose Bush
1473
oil on panel, 200 x 114.5 cm
St Martin's Church, Colmar

CORAL

Andrea Mantegna
Madonna of Victory
1495-1496
oil on canvas, 280 x 166 cm
Musée du Louvre, Paris

Animal, vegetable or mineral? The ambiguity of coral, its unusual coloration (which lends its name to a shade of red) and the fascinating shapes its 'branches' can assume justify its fame and the role of good-luck charm it has had for thousands of years. Its startling hue recalls blood, and its shape recalls blood vessels – an association that has made coral a symbol of life and regeneration.

In Greek mythology, the first coral sprang from the blood of Medusa, who was beheaded by the Athenian hero Perseus. Coming in contact with the foam of the sea, the blood gushing from the monster's severed neck fell upon some seaweed, tinting it red and turning it to stone.

Since antiquity, red coral has been widely used in precious objects and artworks. The Romans put their trust in coral branches to combat the evil eye, while in the Middle Ages the custom spread of hanging a little coral pendant around a newborn's neck to keep illness away. The apotropaic properties of coral are also associated with its characteristic of hardening on contact with air. This increases the aura of mystery and wonder that has always surrounded it, as abundantly exemplified in art. In representations of the infant Jesus, red coral often foreshadows the blood of the Passion, a reference to Christ's double human and divine nature.

In Andrea Mantegna's *Madonna of Victory*, a branch of coral hangs from the centre of the arch. This not only makes the setting more opulent, in keeping with the widespread custom of adorning churches with coral objects, but also complements the iconographic significance of the painting, which commemorates the victory of Francesco Gonzaga against the French at the battle of Fornovo in 1495. However, the quirks and ironies of history have resulted in the painting today residing in Paris.

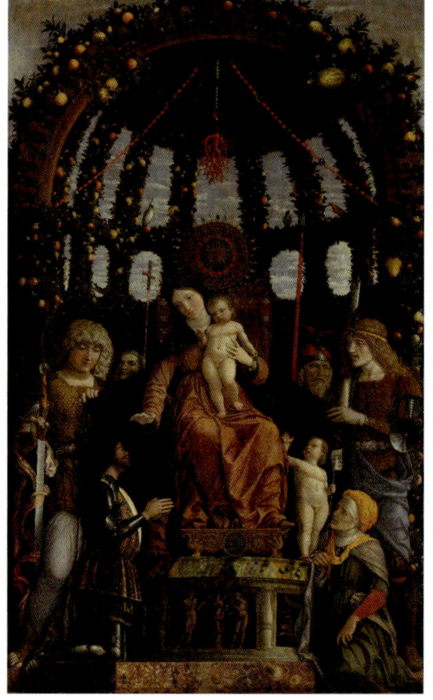

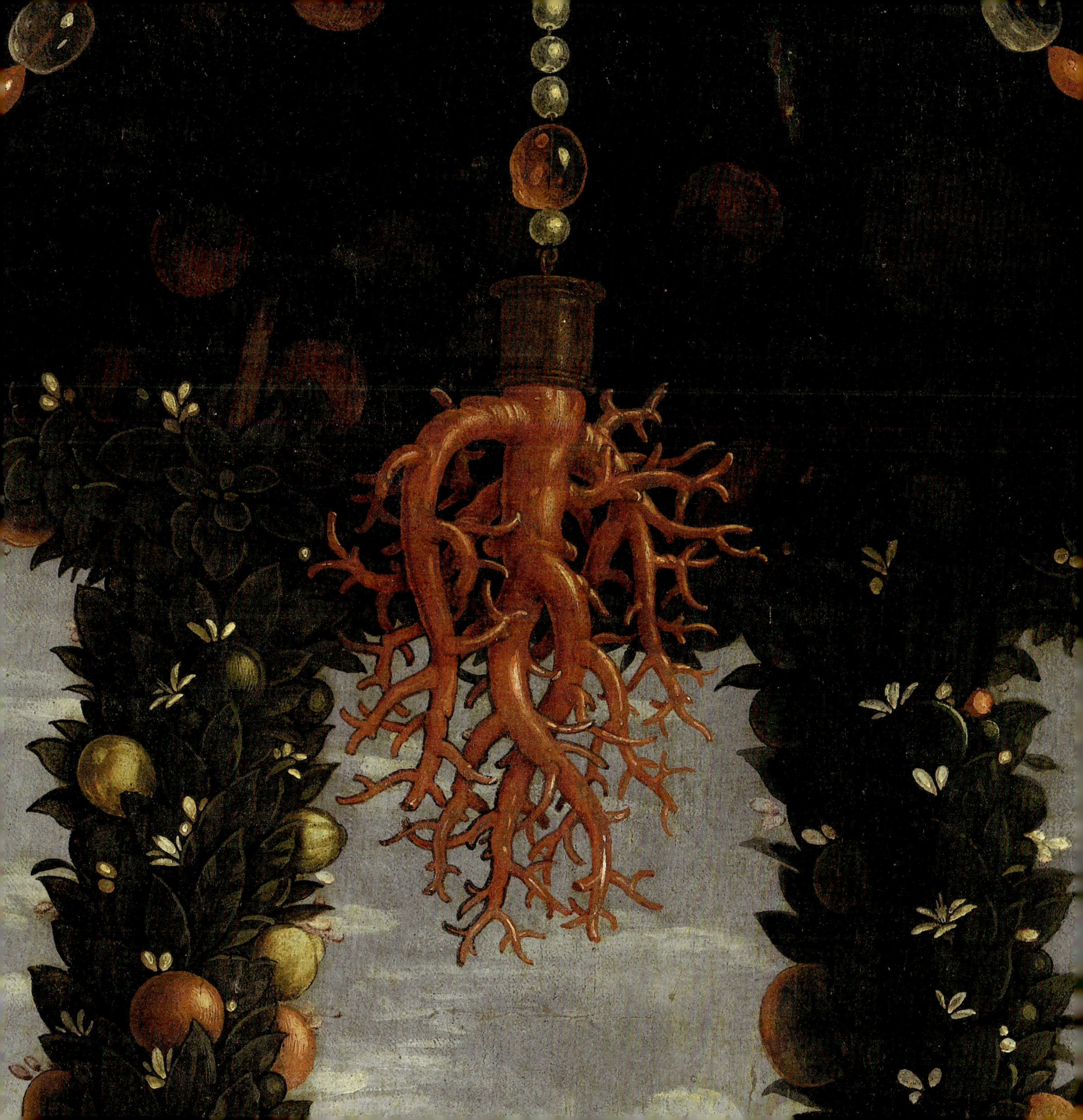

De Predis Brothers
Mars, from the *De Sphaera codex*
c. 1460
parchment
Biblioteca Estense, Modena

WRATH

Red is also the colour of Mars, both the mythological god of war and the planet, and red has been quite prevalent in military uniforms. The English army long wore gaudy red uniforms (and the same colour conventionally designated the nations of the British Empire on world maps). But on the eve of the First World War, when firearms' accuracy and range made it inadvisable to wear uniforms so easily seen and recognized in battle, red was henceforth confined to parades. The 'Thousand' Garibaldi led in conquering Sicily were known as the 'Redshirts', and Canada's Mounted Police are still sometimes referred to as 'red jackets'.

Choleric and irascible people tend to wear all varieties of red, a colour associated with Mars, god of war, and hence with death, violence and uncontrolled passions. For thousands of years, male and female flesh tones have been depicted in different shades. In ancient Egyptian art, men – active mainly outside the home, in the sun – have a denser, reddish complexion. In contrast, women, whose activities took place within the enclosure of the home, had a light complexion. This convention persisted into the late 19th century, when it was considered shameful for a woman's skin to be darkened by the sun's rays.

In Renaissance painting, the cruellest, most despicable characters often wear flame-red clothes, a sign of their brutal nature. An example is Tarquin in this mid-16th-century painting attributable to the circle of Jan Massys.

The chromatic contrast between the innocent purity of the victim and the heinous perversion of her tormentor is not limited to the clothing but encompasses the two figures' flesh tones as well, as if to underscore the equation between colour and temperament.

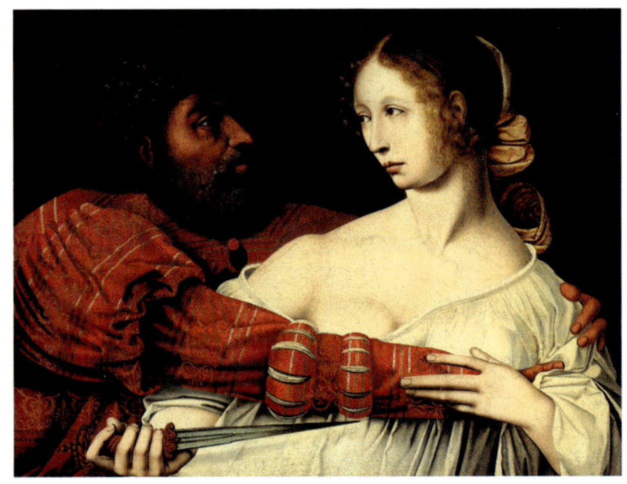

Circle of Jan Massys
Tarquin and Lucretia
c. 1550
oil on panel, 72.8 x 89.5 cm
Palais des Beaux-Arts, Lille

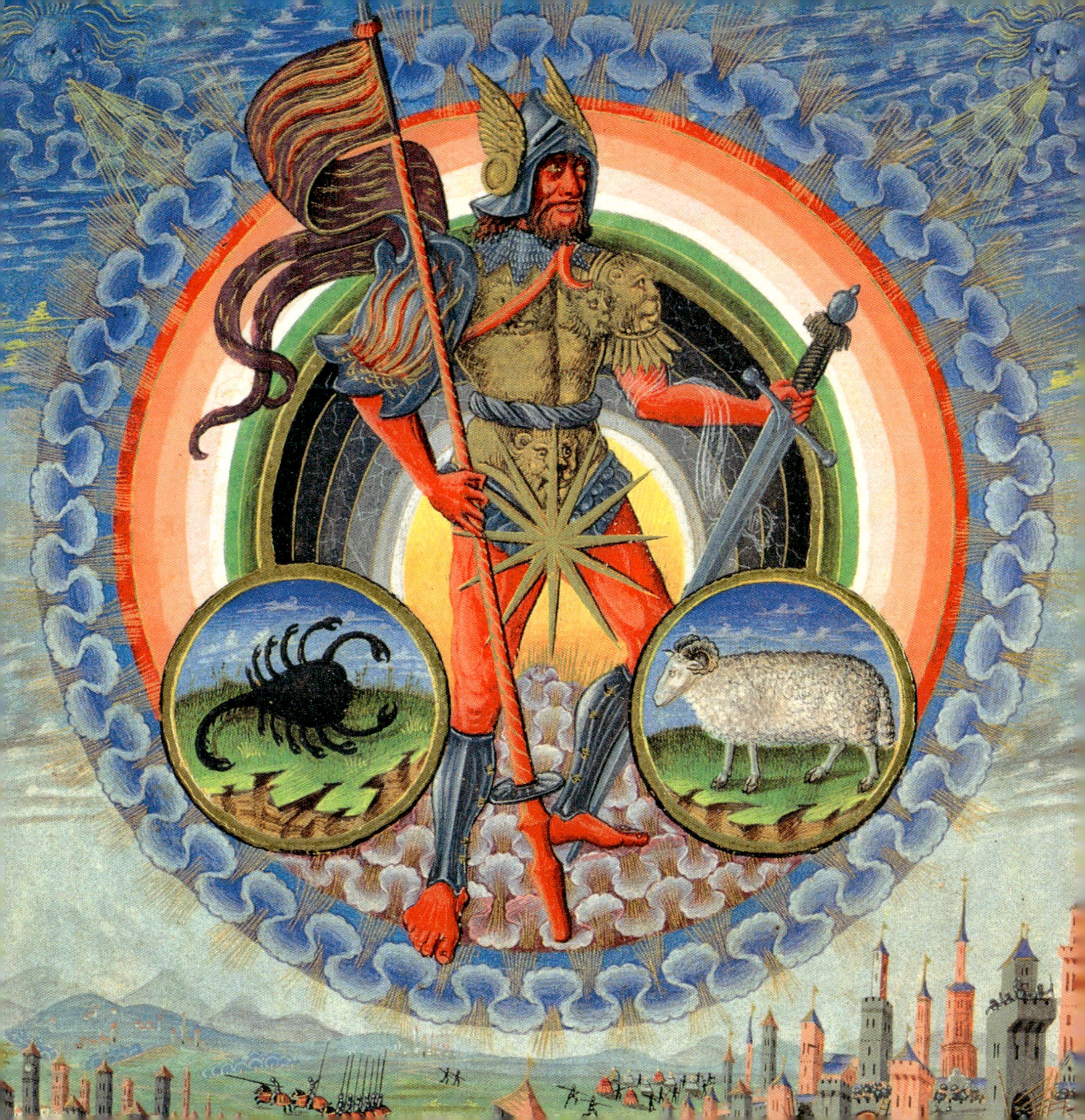

RED BERRIES OF LUST

Hieronymus Bosch
The Garden of Earthly Delights (centre panel)
1500-1505
oil on panel, 220 x 195 cm
Museo Nacional del Prado, Madrid

Red is the colour of extreme passion and therefore also of lust. So it is not surprising that a 'red light' district is a centre of sex for hire, catering to the pleasures of the flesh. The Bible does not specify what fruit Adam and Eve picked from the Tree of Knowledge, but iconographic tradition most often depicts a red apple. The red fruit of temptation also made its way into fairytales: it is a poisoned red apple that makes Snow White fall into a deep stupor.

The theme of red fruit (round berries, huge strawberries, mysterious pods) is abundantly developed in the imposing *Garden of Earthly Delights*, the masterpiece by Hieronymus Bosch and without doubt one of the most fascinating and puzzling paintings in all the European Renaissance.

In the Book of Revelation, red has a negative value, as opposed to the pure white of the Mystic Lamb and the Blessed. One of the four horsemen who bring the world's destruction is red, and the Great Whore of Babylon, dressed in purple and scarlet, sits astride a seven-headed red devil (symbolizing the Seven Deadly Sins). These references tempt us to try and imagine how the most celebrated cycle of Apocalyptic scenes – the extraordinary large woodcuts by Dürer – might have been coloured.

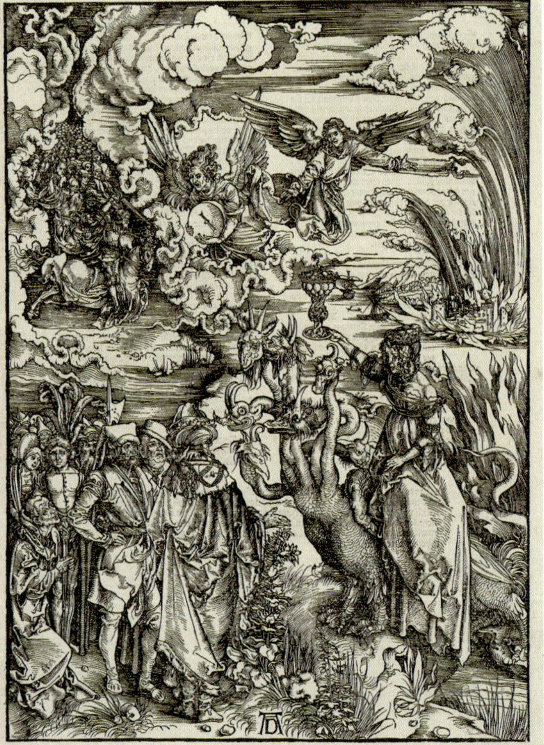

Albrecht Dürer
The Great Whore of Babylon
engraving from the cycle
Apocalypsis cum figuris
1496

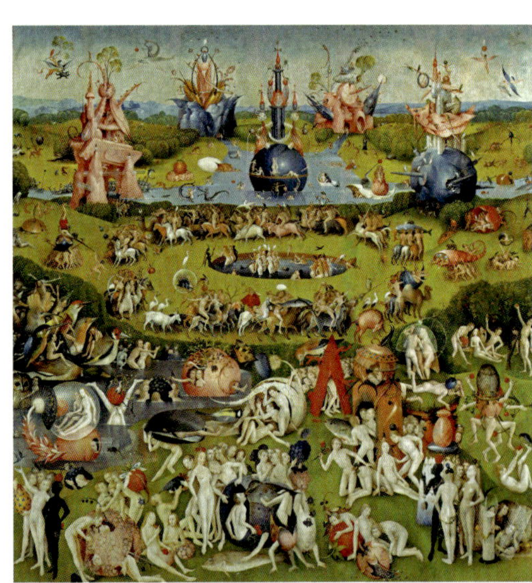

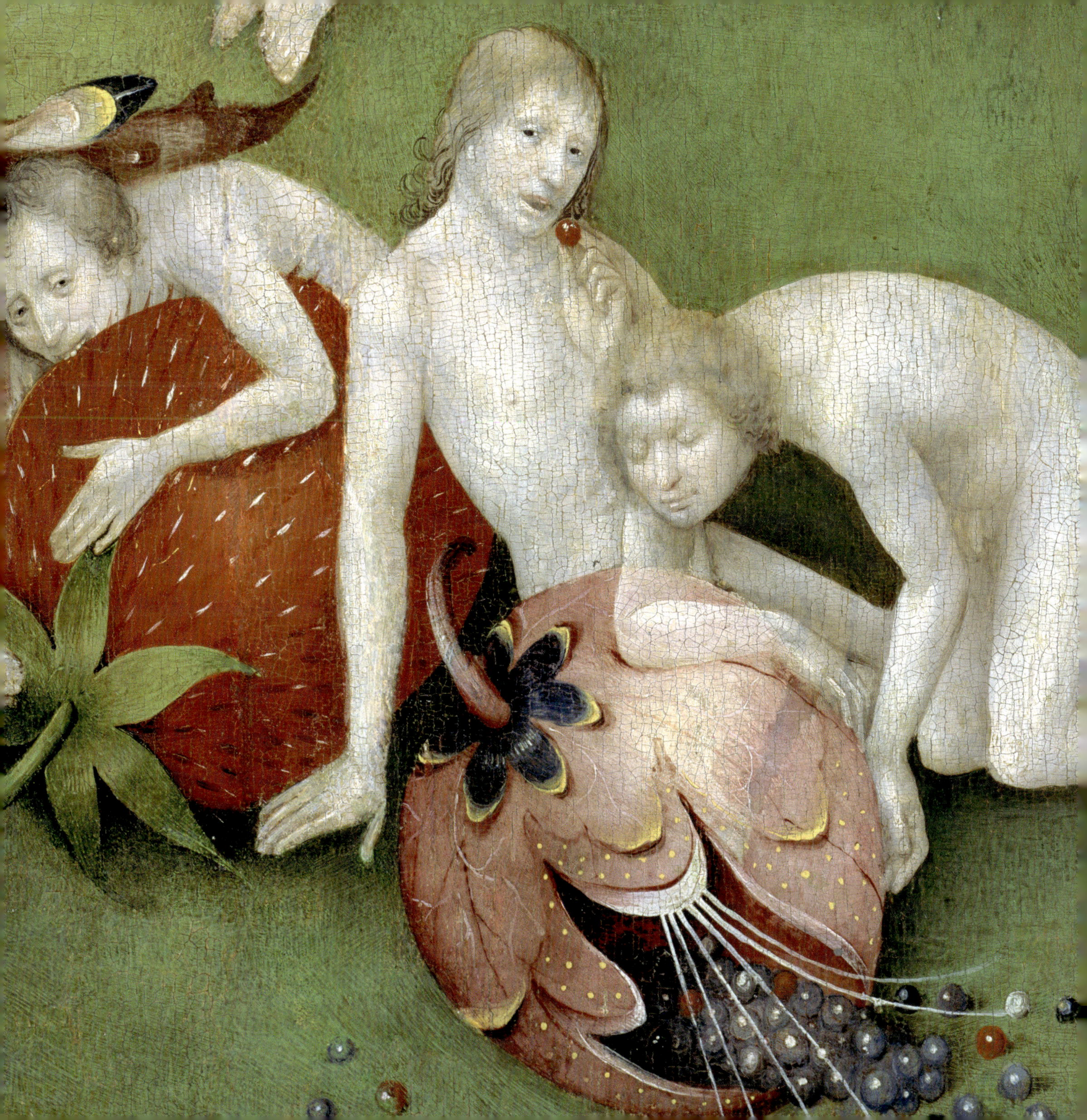

POWER AND INTRIGUE

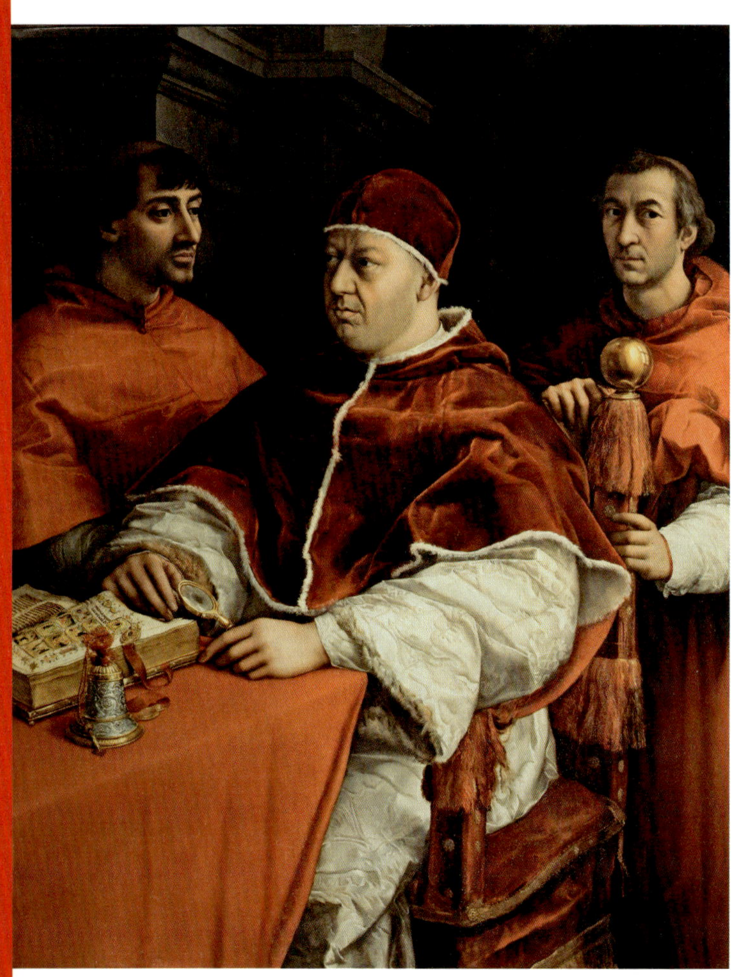

Titian was by far one of the greatest specialists in the use of red. Of course, he was aided by the availability of colours on the market in Venice, where he could acquire brilliant pigments from the eastern Mediterranean. Nevertheless, throughout his long career, his sensitivity in using red remained unsurpassed. Titian even stated that the best way to recognize good painters is to observe whether they know and can manage three colours: white, black and red. And that's all.

During his only visit to Rome, which was memorable, the by now mature Titian had the opportunity to give a spectacular demonstration of this concept in the large group portrait executed for Pope Paul III at the request of the powerful Cardinal Alessandro Farnese, who intended to propose himself as the pope's successor.

Red dominates the painting, but it is not a shrill, vibrant colour. The technique used by Titian is quick, sketchy, unfinished in some details, so it conveys the impression of a suffocating atmosphere of intrigue. The old pope sits hunched over, bony, and casts an intensely pointed look at Ottavio, who is bowing in a parody of Myron's *Discobolus*. Titian uses the symbolic hues of the ecclesiastical hierarchy (the purple-red regalia of the young and ambitious Cardinal Alessandro is a different shade from the pope's hat and mozzetta) and adds the blood-red note of the drapery in the background and the cloth covering the table at the left. This all increases the dramatic narrative effect of a painting that has rightly been described as Shakespearian, on account of its implicit scheming, sentiments and ambitions.

Titian admittedly based his portrait of Pope Paul III with his nephews Alessandro and Ottavio Farnese on a famous portrait of Leo X flanked by two cardinals painted by Raphael about thirty years earlier. Leo X was the son of Lorenzo the Magnificent, and Raphael portrayed him leafing through a priceless illuminated Bible with the hand of a connoisseur. Raphael lingers over the different tones of red seen in the pontifical vestments and the deep purple-red worn by the cardinals.

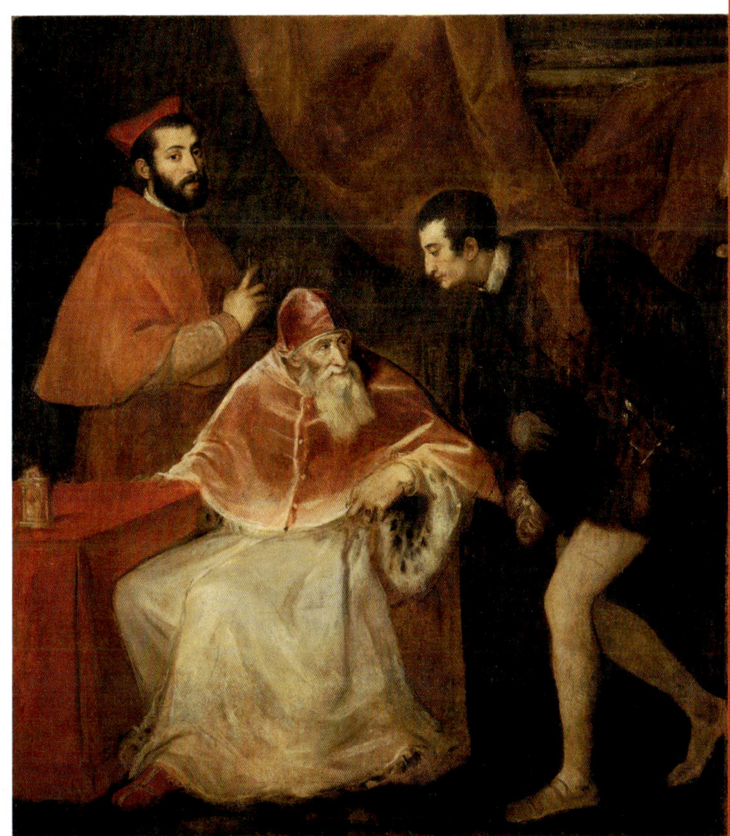

▸
Titian
Portrait of Paul III with His Nephews
1545-1546
oil on canvas, 210 x 174 cm
Museo Nazionale di Capodimonte, Naples

◂
Raphael
Portrait of Leo X with Two Cardinals
1518
oil on panel, 154 x 119 cm
Galleria degli Uffizi, Florence

SCARLET

El Greco
Portrait of Don Fernando Cardinal Niño de Guevara
c. 1600
oil on canvas, 170.8 x 108 cm
The Metropolitan Museum of Art, New York

A cardinal's attire is a distinctive shade of deep purple-red, distinct from the violet of a bishop. It is a colour so characteristic that in Italian, the term *porporato* – literally 'clothed in purple' – also means 'cardinal'. In ancient Rome, purple tunics were worn by patricians and subsequently reserved for the emperor alone, a tradition that was to be maintained in the Byzantine Empire until the mid-15th century. The cardinal's purple-red clothing identifies whoever is wearing it as a person of high rank, and indeed cardinals are the 'princes of the Church'.

Deep red evokes the idea of martyrdom, and a cardinal's vestments symbolize his commitment to Christ and the Church even at the price of martyrdom. Red is furthermore the colour of charity. Popes did not abandon the tradition of deep red in favour of white until 1566. This happened upon the arrival of the Piedmontese pope Pius V Ghislieri, a Dominican monk who, after being elected St Peter's successor, chose to continue wearing the white habit of his order. Since then, red has been reserved for the College of Cardinals, although some papal accessories – for example the cape and shoes – are still red.

In the painting by El Greco, Cardinal de Guevara, a well-known and much-feared Inquisitor, sits in apparent calm in a padded chair. The flash of his gaze behind the unusual eyeglasses, the energy apparent in the left hand that grasps the arm of the chair, and especially the spectacular deep red costume, transmit a formidable sense of power.

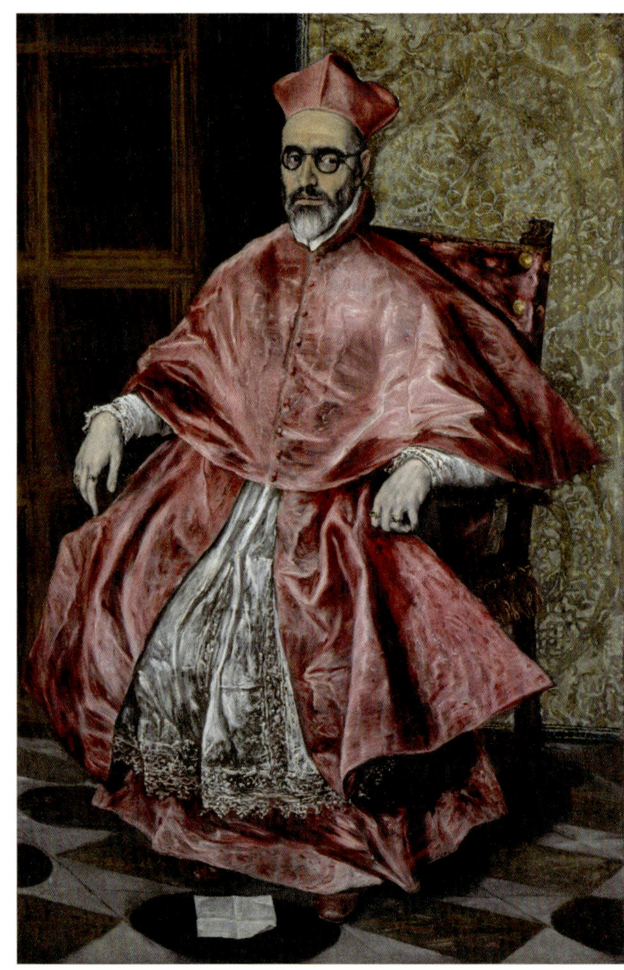

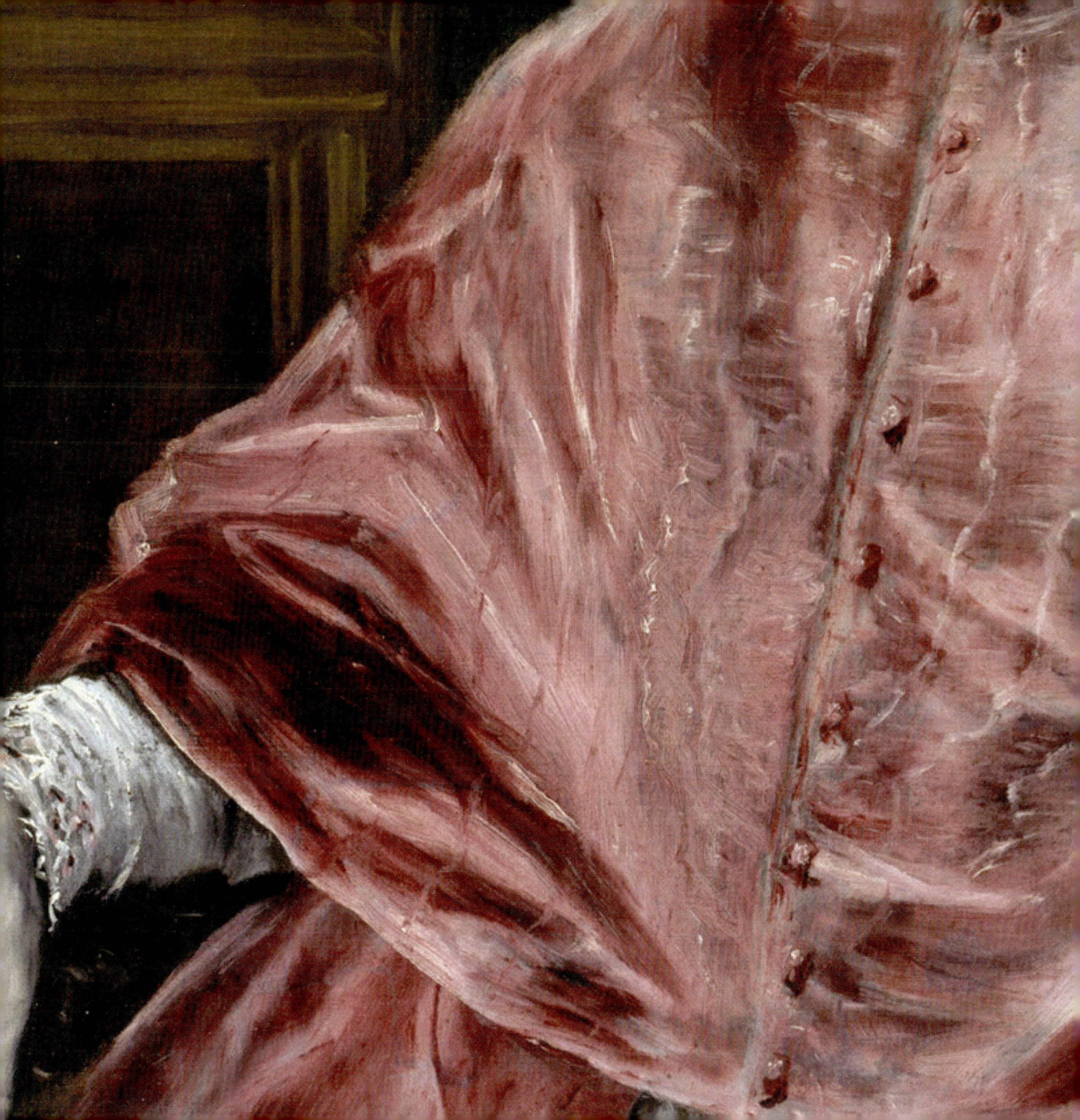

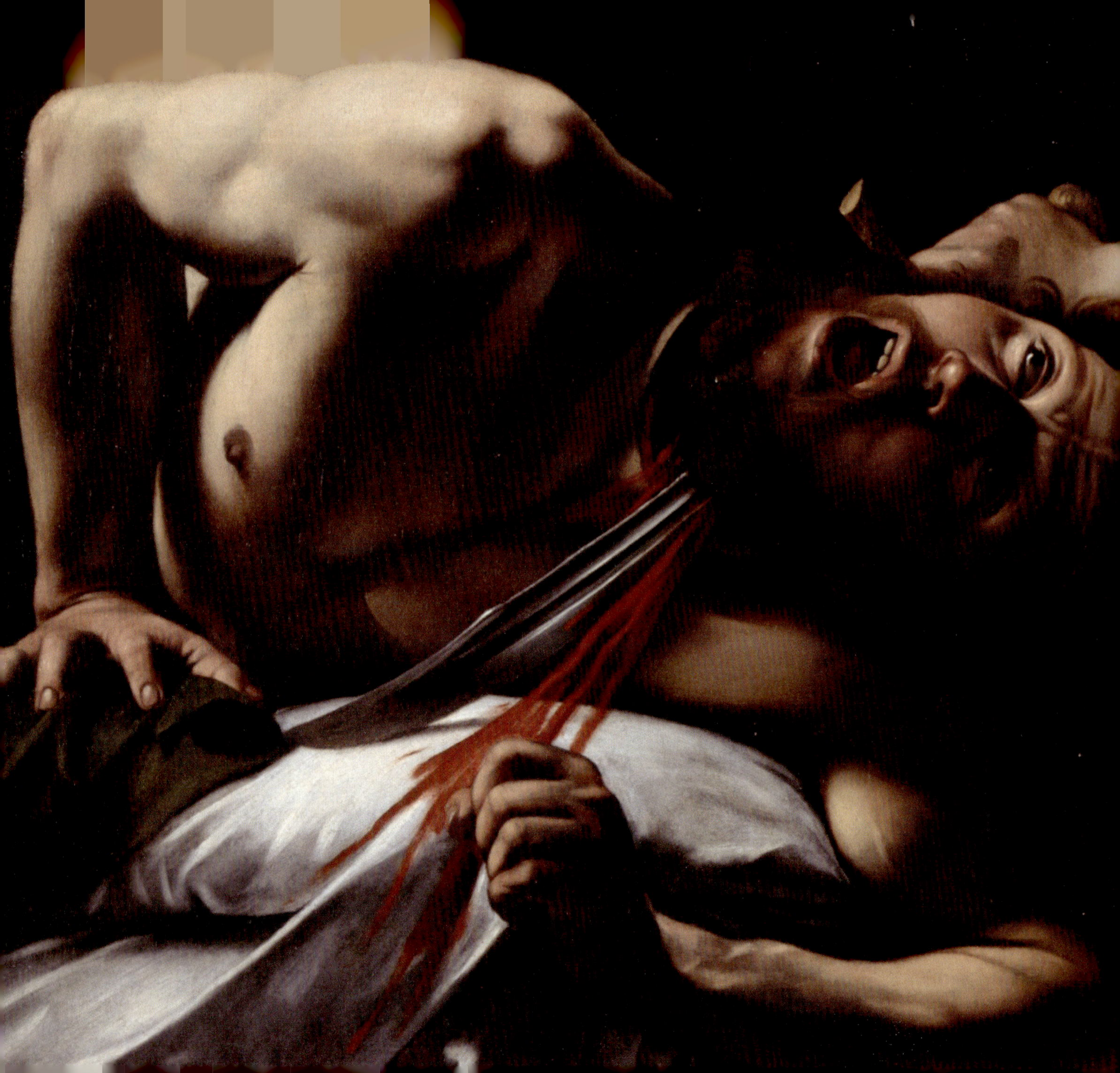

BLOOD

Caravaggio
Judith Beheading Holofernes
1597-1600
oil on canvas, 145 x 195 cm
Galleria Nazionale d'Arte Antica, Rome

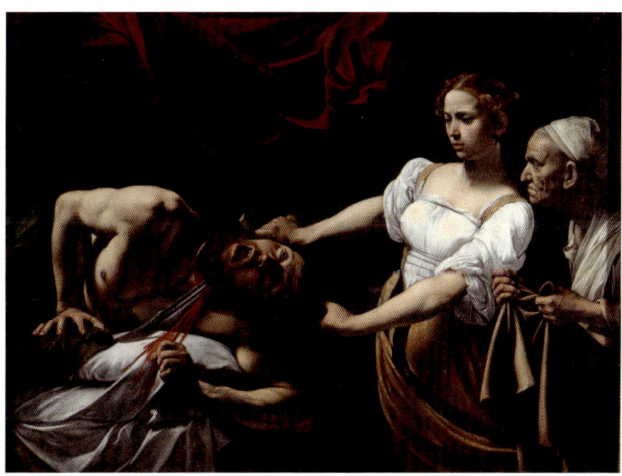

The colour red makes us think first and foremost of blood. Obviously, this instinctual symbolism is present in all cultures at all times. As the great contemporary artist Anish Kapoor has said, 'Red, of course, is the colour of the interior of our bodies. In a way it's inside-out, red.' Kapoor's giant sculpture *Marsyas* filled Tate Modern's Turbine Hall in 2002 with its astonishing red form that paid tribute to the flayed Greek musician.

The red of blood is an integral part of the human being, but whenever it appears it is a sign of trauma: a wound, birth, an intense event. Between the 16th and 17th centuries, artists were urged to witness torture and capital punishment to see with their own eyes the effect of spurting blood and the facial expression of someone who was executed.

Caravaggio is one of the most 'bloodthirsty' artists. Living in a time and context that were far from untroubled, Caravaggio did not shrink from depicting scenes of great violence. In this case, there is an extraordinary contrast between the beautiful and determined Judith (Caravaggio's favourite model Fillide Melandroni posed for this figure) and the bearded general Holofernes, who struggles as the scimitar severs his neck and the blood spurts violently – bright red blood from the carotid arteries. Caravaggio's realistic attention could be related to developments in scientific research on the circulatory system. During the same period, the Englishman William Harvey – the future author of the first treatise on the double circulation of blood – was studying medicine at the University of Padua.

This painting is from Caravaggio's early Roman period, but the theme of beheading was almost an obsession with the artist, who frequently depicted decapitations (Holofernes, Medusa, St John the Baptist, the giant Goliath). This particularly bloody scene took a dramatic autobiographical turn in 1606. After committing murder, Caravaggio was condemned to death; the sentence would have resulted in decapitation. Hurriedly fleeing Rome, he managed to escape execution but died four years later in circumstances that remain unclear.

CHARITY

In Christian tradition, red is the symbolic colour of the theological virtue of Charity. To St Paul, this virtue was the pinnacle of Christian life. Ardent as a flame, quick to sacrifice, Charity is often depicted symbolically as a smiling woman nursing a baby at each breast. The Greco-Roman tradition, too, celebrates examples of charity and dedication to those in need.

A cultivated and refined artist like Peter Paul Rubens lost no opportunity to reaffirm the syncretism – that is, the shared elements – of classical antiquity and Christianity. This painting depicts an episode from ancient history, cited as an exemplar of the virtues of the Roman Republic. Cimon, an old man, had been condemned to languish in prison and die of hunger. His daughter Pero, who had recently become a mother, took advantage of her prison visits to offer her father her breast, swelled with milk. The story, known as 'Roman Charity', overlaps the typical theme of Christian charity, and Rubens underscores the analogy by giving Pero a bright red dress.

Red has retained its meaning of charity and generous aid in the contemporary world. A large red cross on a white field (or a crescent in Islamic countries) is the emblem of the supranational assistance to the wounded inspired by the Swiss businessman Henry Dunant, who was horrified by the aftermath of the Battle of Solferino in 1859. However, the choice of symbol may be related to the Swiss flag, which has the colours reversed.

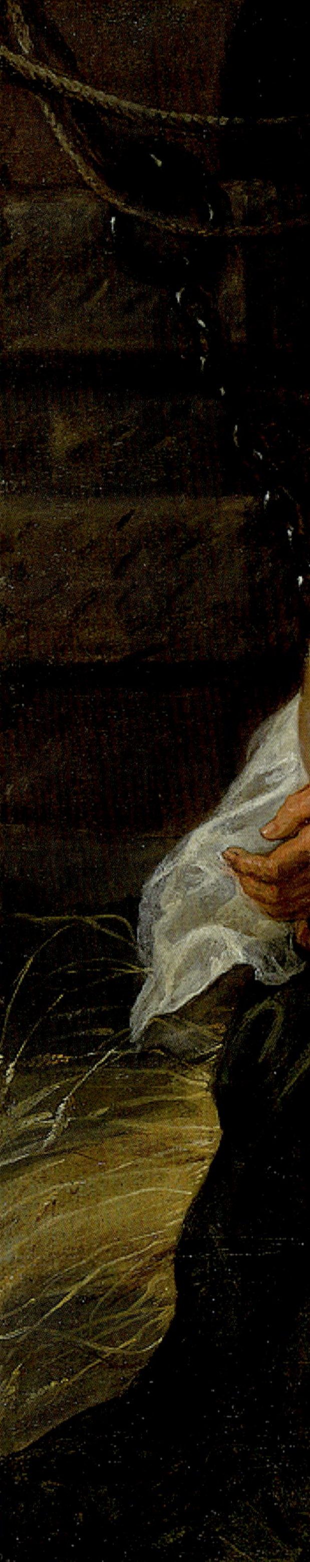

Peter Paul Rubens
Cimon and Pero (Roman Charity)
c. 1630
oil on canvas, 155 x 190 cm
Rijksmuseum, Amsterdam

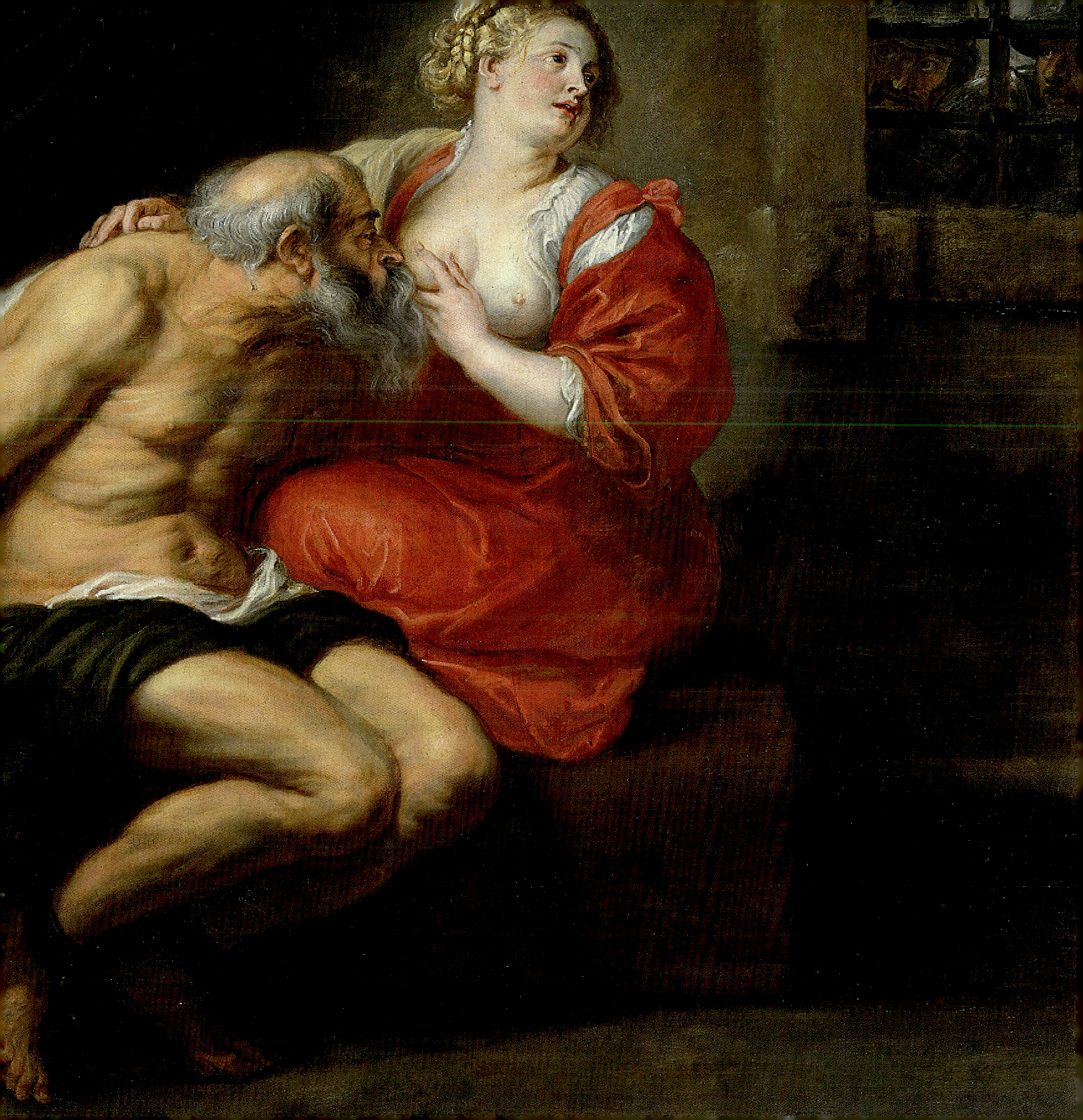

IMPERIAL POWER

Jean-Auguste-Dominique Ingres
Portrait of Napoleon on the Imperial Throne
1806
oil on canvas, 260 x 163 cm
Musée de l'Armée, Paris

For thousands of years purple-red or deep red identified the peak of the social pyramid. And speaking of pyramids, the pharaohs of ancient Egypt wore a double crown – white and red – that symbolized their rule over Upper and Lower Egypt respectively.

Cloth dyed with colours obtained from the murex shellfish was the most expensive, which justified its exclusive use by the elite. During historical periods when symbols and complicated rituals were prevalent – in the Byzantine Empire, for example – the exclusive use of purple-red was not just limited to dress but also extended to materials from which images of emperors were created. Rare and hard to work, red porphyry was the prerogative of the monarch, and the children of some emperors received the honorific title 'porphyrogenitus' (born to the purple), to emphasize their destiny as autocrats while still in the cradle.

In this extraordinary painting, an icon of the imperial Napoleonic myth, the still-young Ingres demonstrated not only his gifts as an academic painter, but also a deep visual and symbolic understanding. This early 19th-century image of peremptory power sums up a series of symbolic values that go back in time through the history of the kingdom of France to the very idea of universal empire.

Exhibited at the Salon the year it was painted, this canvas drew much negative criticism, particularly for the face's pale inexpressiveness, which nevertheless corresponds to the canons of imperturbable majesty derived from Byzantine art. In his right hand, the emperor holds the sceptre of Charles V; in his left, the Hand of Justice and the presumed sword of Charlemagne. The medallions in the border stripe of the carpet (with an imperial eagle prominently displayed in the centre) depict signs of the zodiac. For Virgo, the artist painted a schematic version of the *Madonna of the Chair*, a tribute to his admired Raphael.

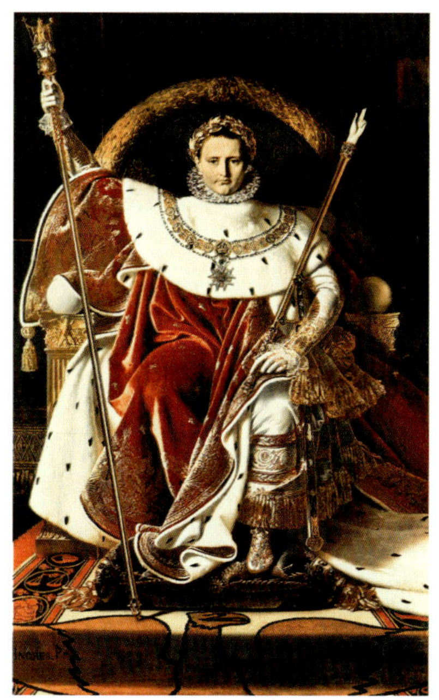

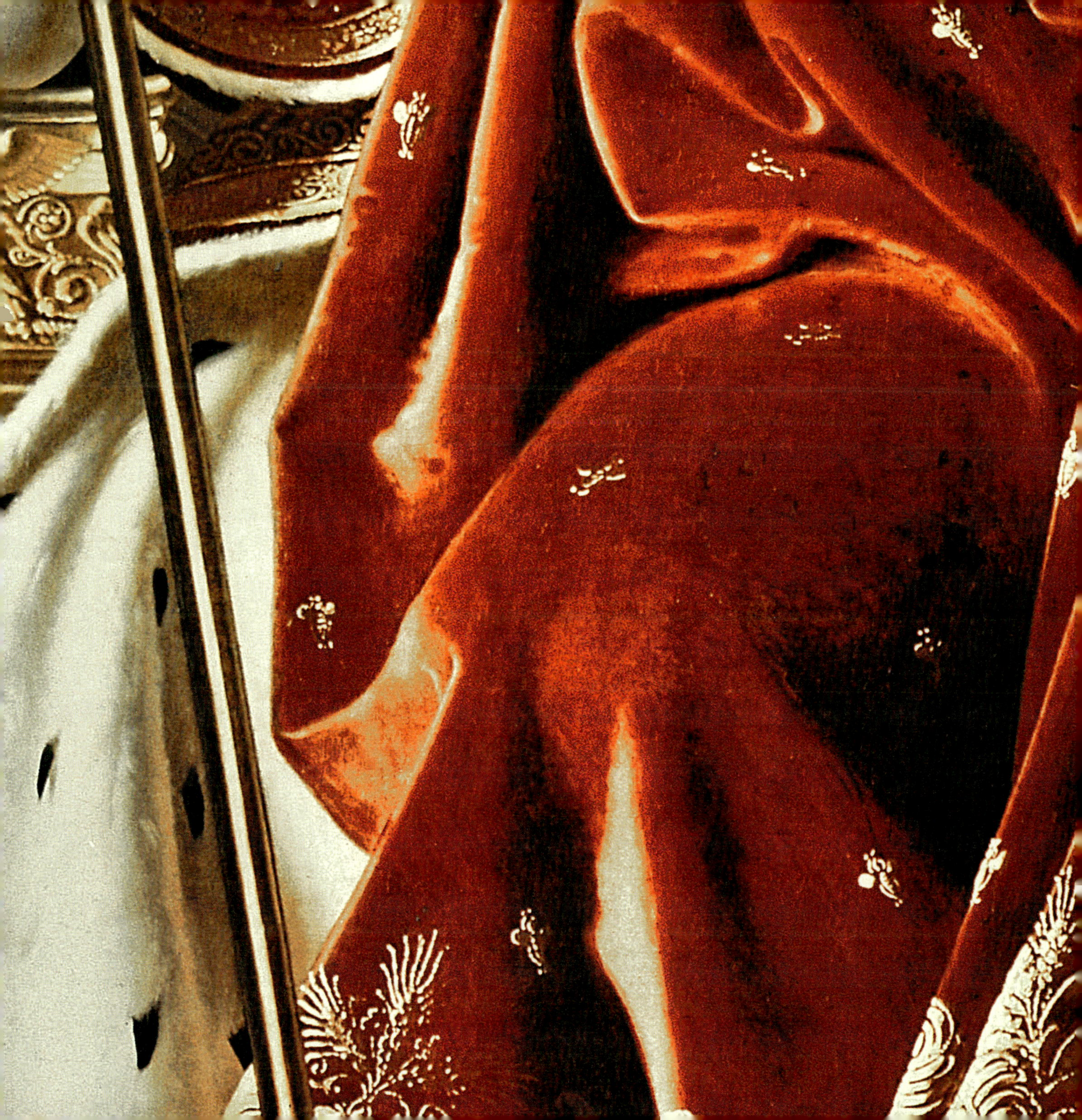

SUNRISE

In the extraordinary tradition of Japanese printmaking, a red disc represents the Rising Sun.

This view of Mount Fuji by Hokusai shows the unmistakable conical shape of the most famous mountain in Japan tinged with the colour of the sun at dawn – an intense red that contrasts fundamentally and most effectively with the blue and white sky, the hazy green of the misty slopes, and the streaks of snow on the mountain's summit. The great master of the *ukiyo-e* explicitly entitled this masterpiece *Red Fuji*.

There can be no doubt that this print depicts the dawn. But in some paintings, it is impossible to determine whether the sun's red-orange shade represents dawn or sunset. A famous case concerns a small painting by Claude Monet that, according to a well-known anecdote, gave the Impressionist movement its name. Just before the exhibition organized in the photographer Nadar's Paris studio on boulevard des Capucines in April 1874, Monet's brother was unsure what title to give the painting. Annoyed, Monet brusquely replied, 'Call it *Impression*.' The painting went down in history as a sunrise, but some have suggested that it might instead represent a sunset at the port of Le Havre.

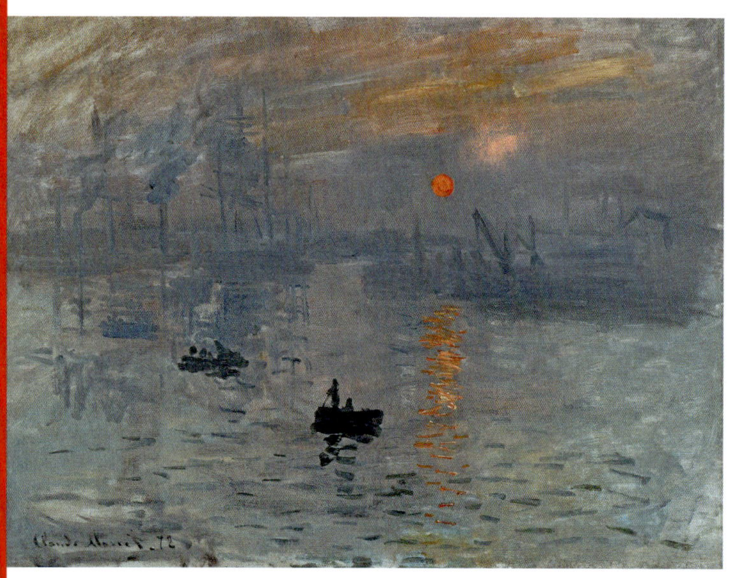

◂
Claude Monet
Impression: Sunrise
1872-1873
oil on canvas, 46 x 63 cm
Musée Marmottan Monet, Paris

▸
Katsushika Hokusai
Red Fuji (Clear Sky, South Wind)
woodcut from the series *Thirty-six Scenes of Mount Fuji*
1829-1833
26.1 x 37.6 cm

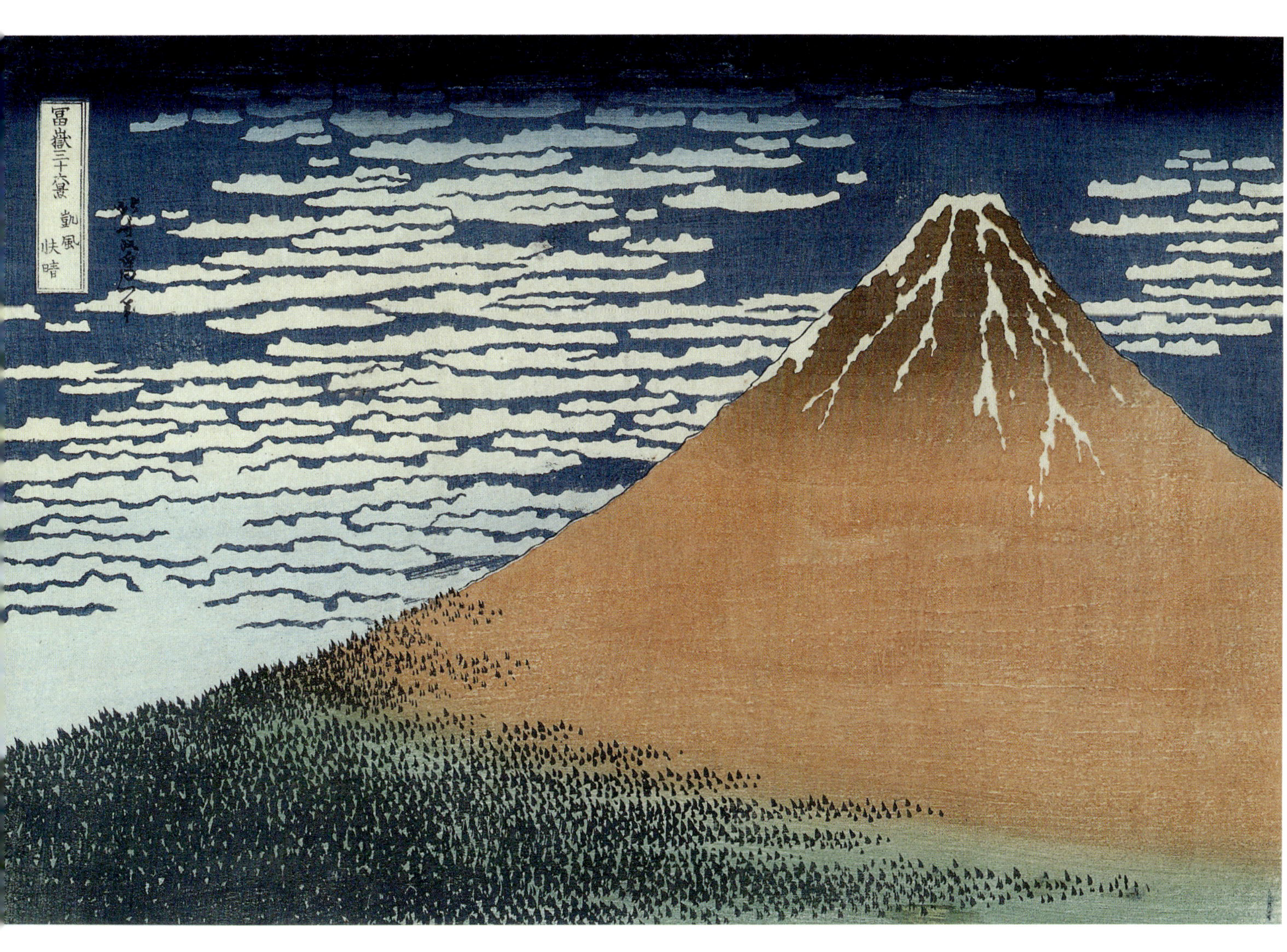
冨嶽三十六景
凱風快晴

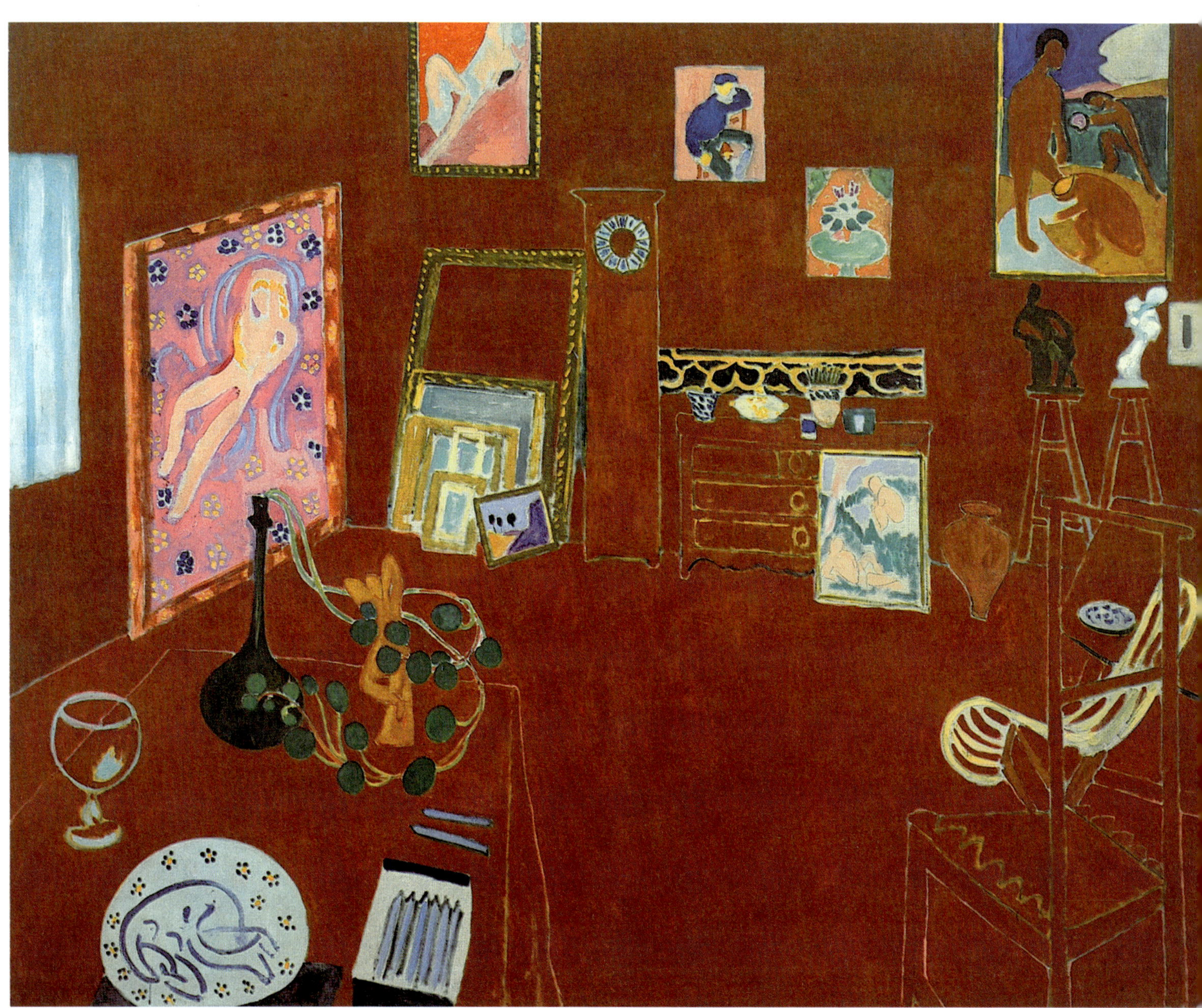

COLOUR, PERCEPTION AND MEMORY

'Where I got the colour red — to be sure, I just don't know. I find that all these things ... only become what they are to me when I see them together with the colour red.'

Henri Matisse

It is not known what led Matisse to abandon his initial intention of using the bluish grey that is still partly visible in some areas of this canvas. It is one of many times when the painter drastically altered a painting's original concept, even going so far as to alter its entire colouring.

As is the case in this canvas, which still shows a Fauvist approach, many of Matisse's works give red a leading role in constructing the pictorial space. Although architectural depth is absent from this depiction of his studio, it is suggested by chromatic interplay wherever the red is interrupted. The paintings, sculptures and ceramics executed by the artist in previous years introduce a sense of movement, coloured objects that stand out against a red background and together form an original and highly personal retrospective.

There is considerable evidence of the extraordinary role played by perceptual experience in Matisse's painting. On more than one occasion, the garden around the artist's studio at Issy-les-Moulineaux prompted him to experiment with surprising new tonalities. One possible explanation for the process that led Matisse to use such strong colours is that the artist saw the walls of the room change from white to intense red after staring through the window at the bright greens in the garden.

A striking example of strong tonality in Matisse's work is *The Red Room* (also known as *Dessert: Harmony in Red*, in the Hermitage Museum, St Petersburg), one of the most astonishing masterpieces among the many works by Matisse acquired by Russian collectors before the October Revolution. In a lively decorative spirit, he had at first painted the walls in this canvas, too, a different colour, but then chose red to highlight the contrast with the other tones in the room and the landscape seen through the window.

Henri Matisse
The Red Studio
1911
oil on canvas, 181 x 219.1 cm
The Museum of Modern Art, New York

SEDUCTION

According to myth, droplets of blood from Venus' heel – pricked by a thorn as the goddess ran in vain to save the life of her beloved Adonis – are what made roses, which symbolize ardent love, turn red. Red has always been the colour of the passions, and touches of red are indispensable to seduction.

In 1935, captivated by Mae West, one of the most provocative American film divas, Dalí designed a living-room suite in the form of a portrait of the actress, who was then at the peak of her fame. Fleshy, painted lips are represented by a soft, inviting sofa, while the nose is a fireplace and the eyes are two picture frames (Dalí had at first considered small home-movie screens).

Executed in his house-studio in Figueres, in Catalonia, the Mae West living room was subsequently replicated at the Art Institute of Chicago, and, as he often did, Dalí also re-created individual components and partial reproductions.

It seems that Mae West was not overly impressed by this tribute from her Catalan admirer. In one of her famous stinging remarks, she is reported to have said that if she had to be turned into a room, she would rather be a bathroom.

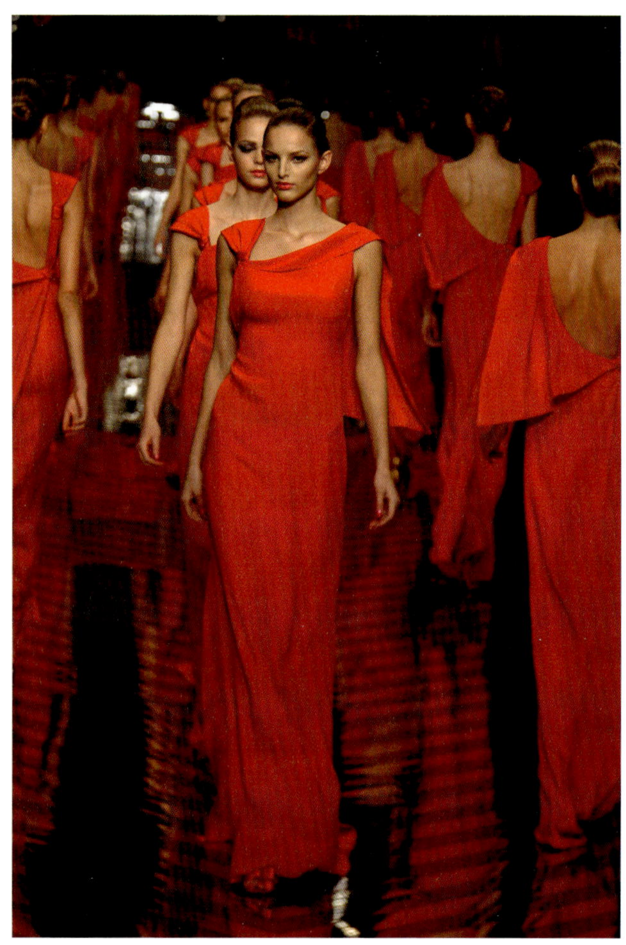

In high fashion, red is associated with the name of Valentino. Since the opening of his first shop in Rome in 1959, his extraordinary flame-red suits have made his international reputation. 'Valentino red' is made using a mix of carmine, purple and cadmium red in various proportions.

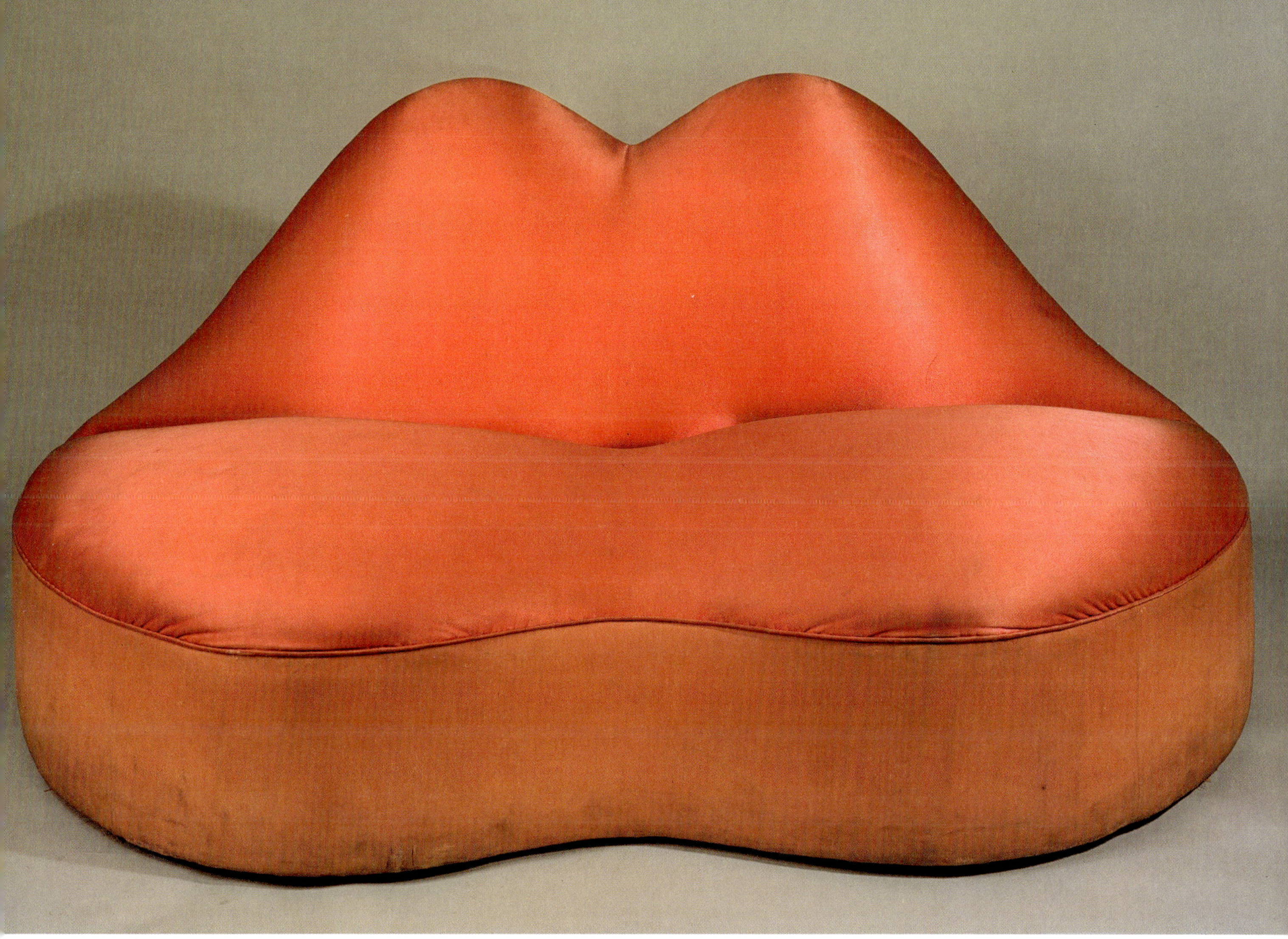

◂

Paris Fashion Week
Valentino Haute Couture
Spring Collection 2008

▴

Salvador Dalí
'Mae West Lips' Sofa
1936-1937
wooden frame, 92 x 213 x 80 cm
The Royal Pavilion Art Gallery and Museum, Borough of Brighton (Sussex)

COMMUNISM

Red has had significant distribution as a political colour, no doubt because it is associated with strength and finality. Beginning with the flag of the French Revolution and again during the Paris Commune, red was adopted as the colour of revolutionaries bent on subverting – violently if necessary – the established order (which itself was usually identified with white). The banners and uniforms of the Bourbon army – fought by the Paris insurgents and then by Garibaldi – were pure white, and the pro-Czarist faction following the October Revolution in Russia were called the 'Whites'.

The red flag raised by Lenin and the Bolsheviks during the October Revolution in Russia became the universal symbol of communism. After communism was established in Russia, the red star became the trademark of the Soviet army, and even today, after the political turnaround of 1989, it remains in the names of important sports teams in various former Warsaw Pact countries and the Balkans (for example, Red Star Belgrade).

In 1949, drawing inspiration from the Russian Revolution, Mao Tse-tung chose to identify the Chinese path to communism with red. Besides flag and insignias, the slender volume of the Great Helmsman's poetic-political pronouncements became known as the 'Little Red Book' and was widely circulated.

In the large painting commemorating the leader of the Italian Communist Party, Renato Guttuso raises Socialist Realism to a supreme level. It eloquently exploits the strong contrast between the flag's bold red and the many black-and-white portraits intermingling ordinary people with notable political figures, including Lenin, who appears in the crowd no fewer than four times.

Renato Guttuso
The Funeral of Palmiro Togliatti
1972
acrylic and collage on paper on four panels, 340 x 440 cm
Galleria d'Arte Moderna, Bologna

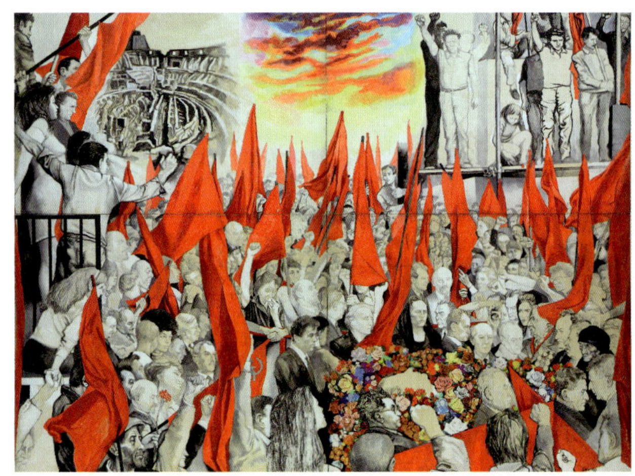

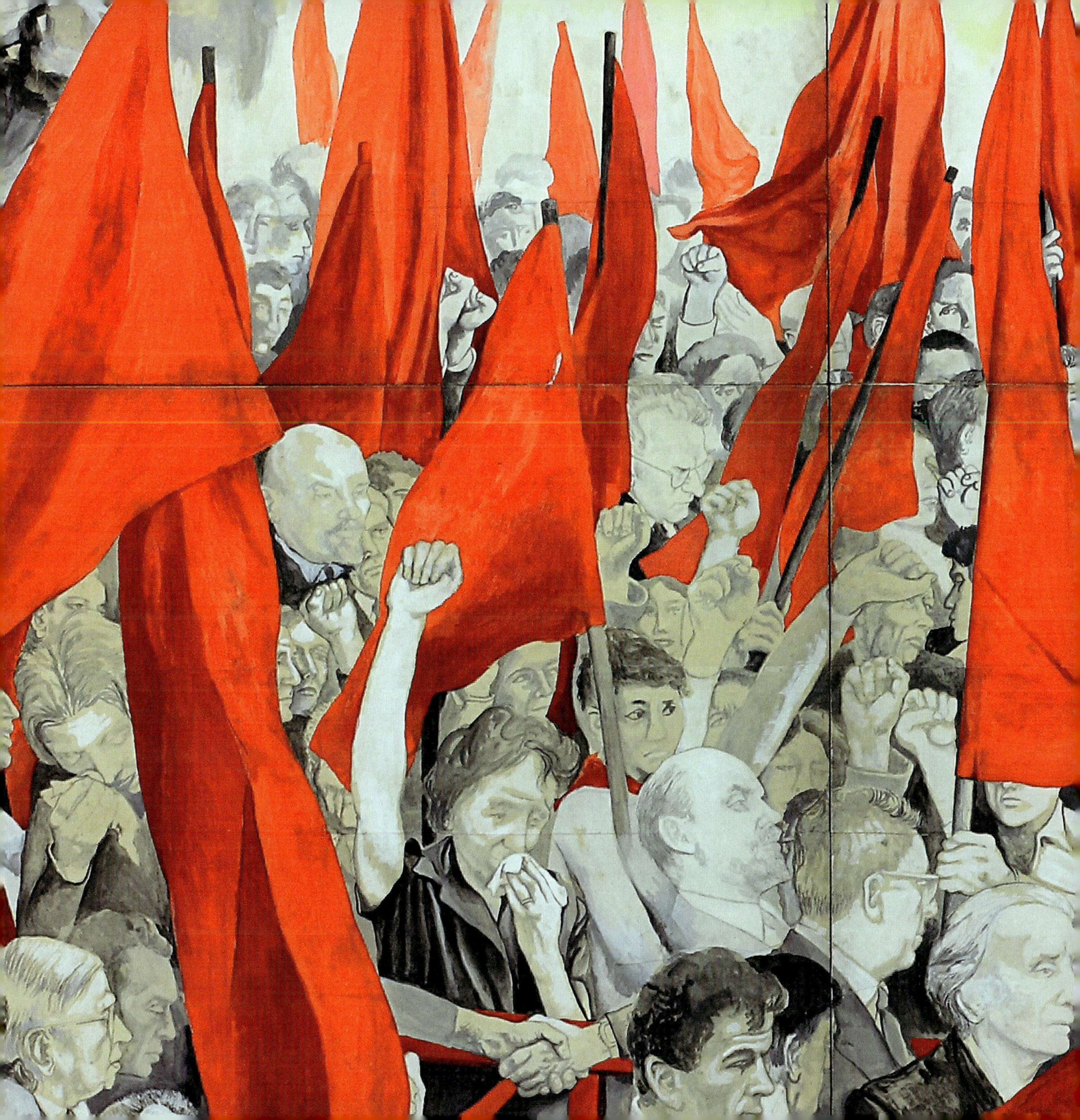

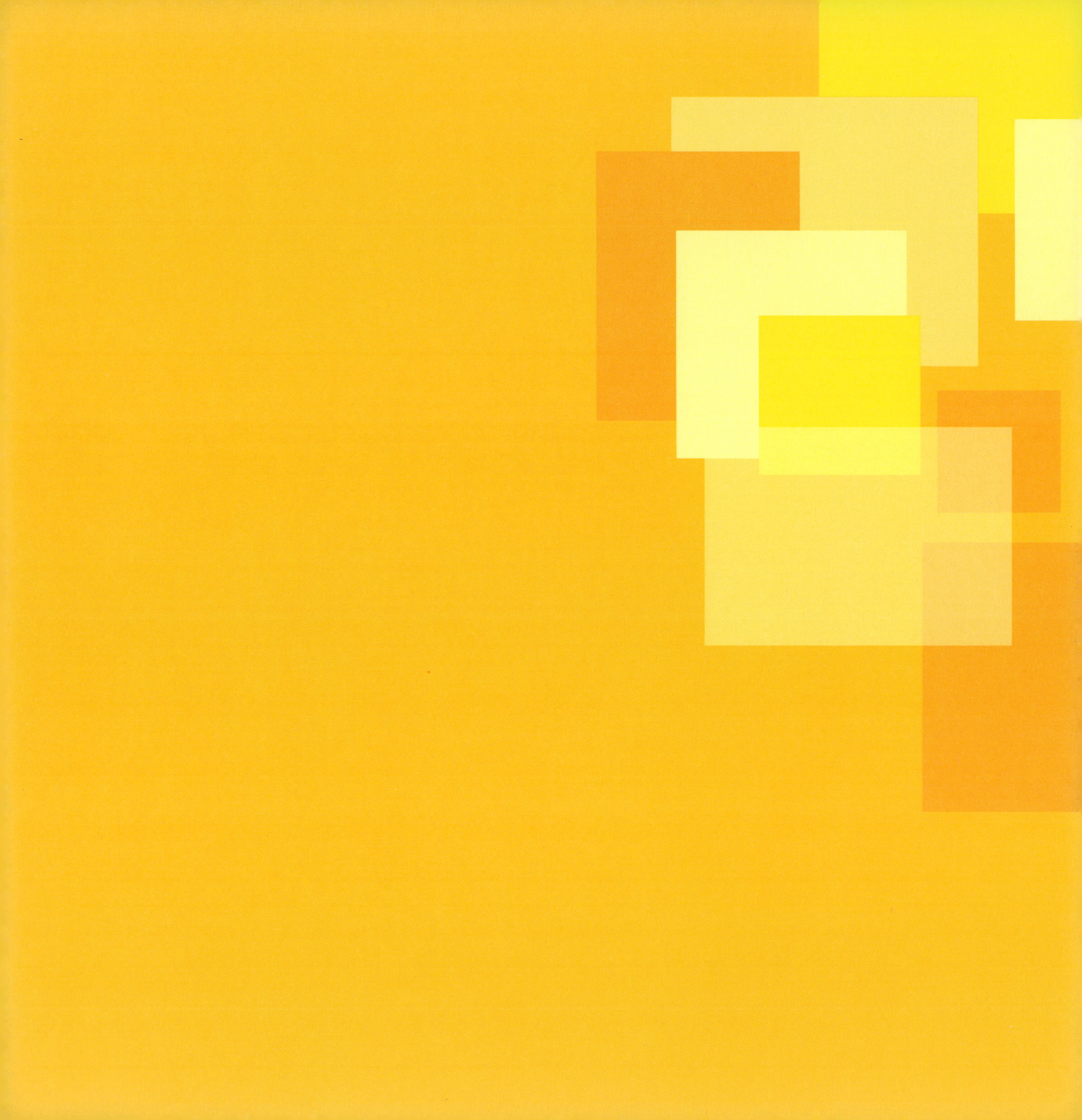

YELLOW

INTRODUCTION

What we call the 'yellow' or 'amber' light on a traffic signal has a clear enough meaning: it is a warning, a call to attention. Yet, it is not without a certain ambiguity, for while the rules of the road prescribe conduct, yellow leaves us with a choice – to stop or go on. In many fields – for example, in rating threats – yellow is associated with an initial level of attention ('yellow alert'), requiring a decision as to how to proceed.

In fact, even the origin of yellow's name is ambiguous, deriving from a Latin word meaning 'light green'. Yellow's symbolic value is twofold, with some artists employing it in a morbid, even paranoid way: Van Gogh and Munch are telling cases. Yet yellow is also distinguished. Along with blue (cyan) and red (magenta), it is one of the three primary colours. It is the first colour the human eye perceives in the rainbow. One of the colours most favoured by children in their drawings, its importance on the palette of artists is inarguable.

The obvious association of yellow with the sun is shared by widely divergent cultures, along with that heavenly body's symbolic characteristics of warmth, strength, power, royalty, the ripening of the harvest, and vital energy. Bright yellow inspires infectious happiness: the Beatles' song 'Yellow Submarine' is unforgettable. For decades, yellow was also the colour of taxis in New York and many other cities.

However, there is a completely different side to yellow. When it appears on a human being's face, it is seen to be caused by fear, illness (particularly jaundice and other liver ailments) or even death. Yellow suggests the pallor of ill health or a negative mood, while a rosy, or better still bronze, complexion is associated with positive values. The devastating Neapolitan epithet *faccia gialluta* ('yellow face') equates an unhealthy appearance with meanness and shabbiness. A sallow face indicates that it is being eaten away by the deadly sin of envy, just as the emaciated appearance of someone suffering from scurvy is associated with an unsociable, scorbutic character. Westerners long related the 'yellow' colour of Asians to impenetrability, cynicism and dissimulation. The French expression *rire jaune* refers to the forced – or perhaps jaundiced – laugh elicited by apprehension.

In some cultures, especially the Far East, yellow is the symbol of the highest, most restrictive social elite and so was reserved for the clothing and table service of the imperial court. China's longest river, the Yang-tze, is in fact the Yellow River. On the other hand, in the West and the Mediterranean basin, yellow was used to identify and disparage social outcasts for thousands of years. In ancient Greece, madmen were required to wear a yellow tunic; in the Middle Ages, a lugubrious yellow flag was raised on ships with an outbreak of the plague; during the Renaissance in cities like Rome and Venice, prostitutes had to make themselves known by wearing yellow clothes; and a visible yellow accessory (such as a hat or, in uncomfortably recent times, a Star of David sewn to the clothing) identified Jews and became a bitter symbol of anti-Semitism. This led to the complete overthrow of the symbolic message: the colour combines the resplendent divine sun and the flames of hell, gold and sulphur, and there is no lack of yellow images of the devil. Notorious traitors like Judas and Ganelon, the latter in the *Chanson de Roland*, wore yellow, an obvious attribute of their unpardonable perfidy.

All in all, yellow is not an ordinary, neutral colour, but one to be handled with care.

BETRAYAL

Giotto
The Kiss of Judas
c. 1303-1306
fresco, 200 x 185 cm
Scrovegni Chapel, Padua

The ambiguous value of the colour yellow is shared by many Mediterranean people, both Christian and Muslim. Glorious golden yellow sits in contrast to the negative significance of paler tones. As sulphur burns without a flame, yellow is associated with falseness, lying and treason. One of the three faces of Lucifer in the depths of Dante's inferno is yellow. In medieval Europe, Jews were required to wear a yellow hat or yellow clothing, a symbol that reappeared most appallingly under Nazism, which obliged Jews to display a yellow Star of David on their clothes.

Certainly not coincidentally, in many paintings of Christ's Passion, Judas, the traitor par excellence, wears a yellowish cloak. In the dramatic scene of the Arrest of Christ painted by Giotto in the Scrovegni Chapel (one of the earliest examples of a nocturnal setting, with torches and sticks waving against the night sky) Judas approaches Jesus to bestow the kiss of betrayal, and his voluminous yellow cloak seems to enfold both figures.

The contrast between the miserable figure of Judas and the profile of Christ is underscored by the colours: the traitor's pale yellow contrasts with the gold of the halo around Jesus's head. In iconographic tradition St Peter, too, often wears a yellow cloak, perhaps recalling his moment of human failing in the night of Good Friday, when he thrice denied that he knew Christ.

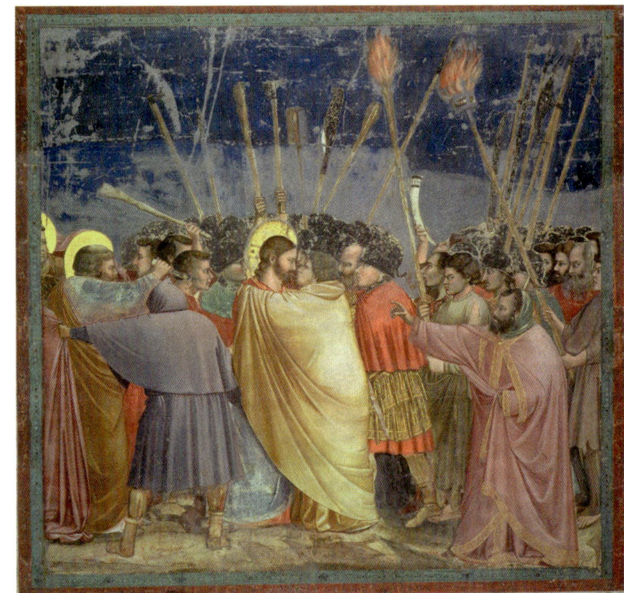

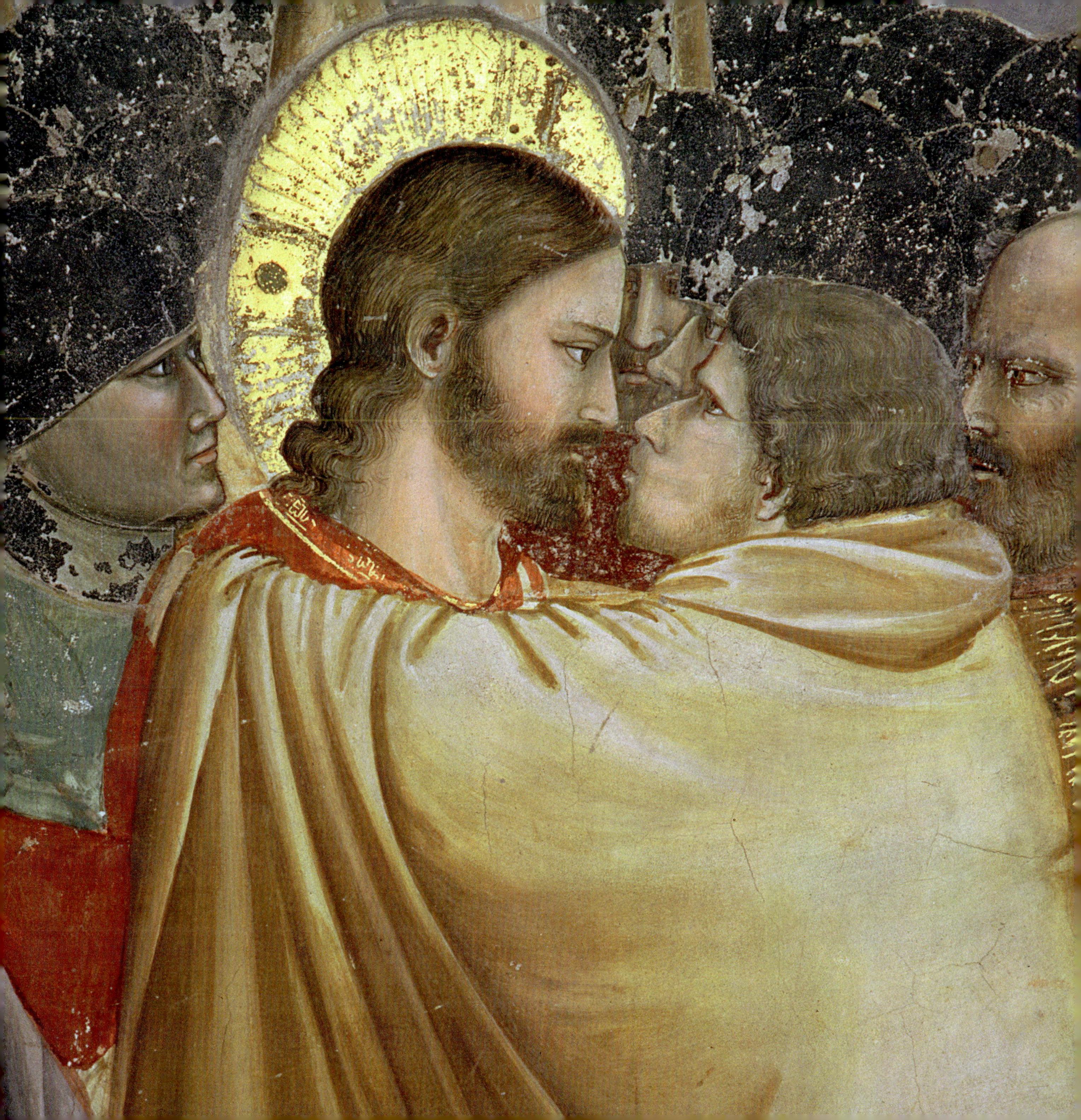

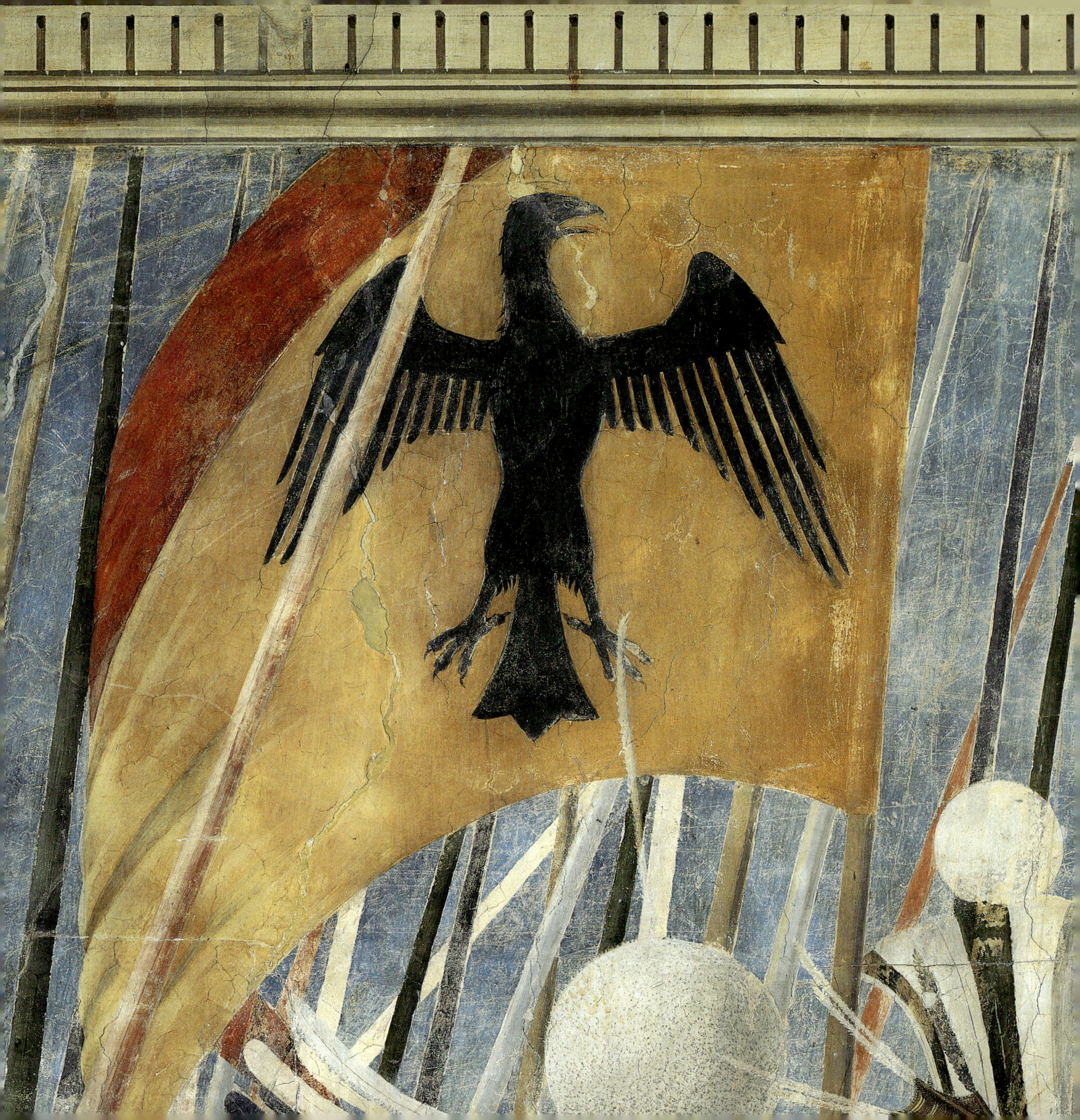

EMPIRE

Piero della Francesca
Constantine's Victory over Maxentius
1452-1466
fresco, 322 x 764 cm
San Francesco, Arezzo

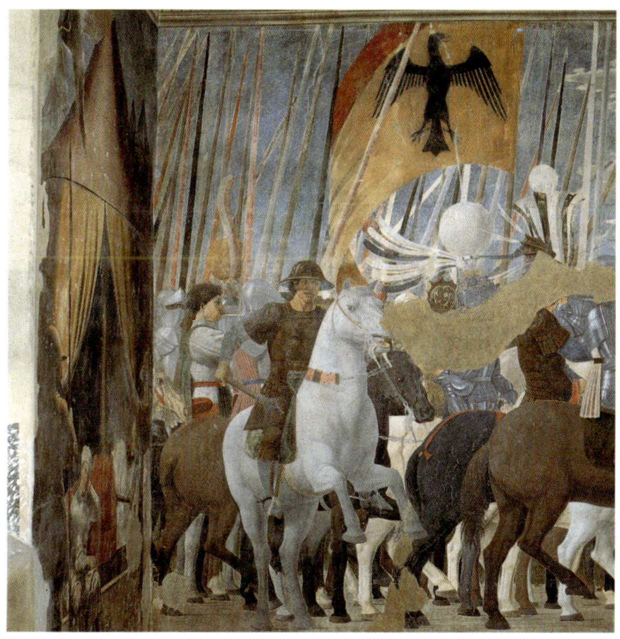

Yellow is a traditional colour of the emperors of China: the sun is the centre of the universe, and the emperor is the 'unmoved mover' of his people and realm. The roofs of the Forbidden City of Beijing and the porcelain used exclusively by the court were yellow, and a particular type of marble quarried in China is generally called 'imperial yellow'. Among the Japanese emperor's prerogatives is the use of yellow insignias. And in the West in the last thousand years, golden yellow gradually replaced purple as the colour of absolute imperial power.

Beginning with the Comnenus dynasty in the 11th century, the Byzantine emperors adopted the insignia of the two-headed black eagle on a yellow background. Shortly before, starting with Otto II, the Holy Roman Empire too had adopted the black eagle on a yellow ground for its arms. The Habsburgs and the Romanovs bore this millennial shield until the beginning of the 20th century, when they were overwhelmed by the First World War and its consequences.

In art, banners and shields with the device of the black eagle on a yellow ground make it possible to recognize the imperial army without hesitation. A famous example is the fresco by Piero della Francesca depicting Emperor Constantine's victory over Maxentius. In some Crucifixions and other scenes of martyrdom, a poisonous scorpion on a yellow background replaces the noble eagle to identify the soldiers of the still-pagan Roman Empire.

Hieronymus Bosch
The Seven Deadly Sins
c. 1480
oil on panel, 120 x 150 cm
Museo Nacional del Prado, Madrid

ENVY

In traditional Chinese theatre, when actors appear on stage with their faces coloured yellow, it signifies that they are envious or jealous. The unmistakable sign of inner turmoil, a deathly sallow face betrays a physical uneasiness caused by effusions of bile due to nerves. Envy is considered one of the most serious evils and sins. Condemned in the Ten Commandments, covetousness lay at the root of what the ancient Greeks considered to be the most grievous fault of all – hubris, a proud human's challenge to the gods. The Latin poet Horace left a memorable portrait of envy in the famous *Satire* in which he encourages balance and good sense. Dante repeatedly mentions envy as the ruination of humanity.

In a remarkable early work originally conceived as a table top, Hieronymus Bosch depicted the Seven Deadly Sins in scenes from everyday life around a sunburst with rays emanating from Christ. The inscription reads *Cave cave, Deus videt* (Beware, God sees [you]). It is a unique document not only of the great Dutch painter's talent, but also of the world at the close of the Middle Ages. The sins are matched with corresponding infernal punishments.

The scene representing envy is set in the quiet of an ordinary middle-class town in front of a merchant's shop. While a passer-by tries to seduce the merchant's wife with a flower, the pale, thin shop owner casts a sidelong glance at an idle elegant gentleman who is amusing himself with a falcon. The merchant is holding a bone that is coveted by a hungry dog that already has other bones to gnaw. Bosch seems to be saying that envy is not exclusive to human beings.

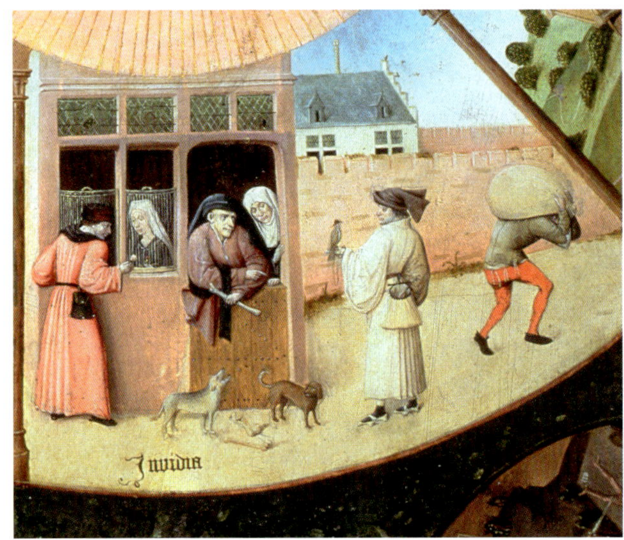

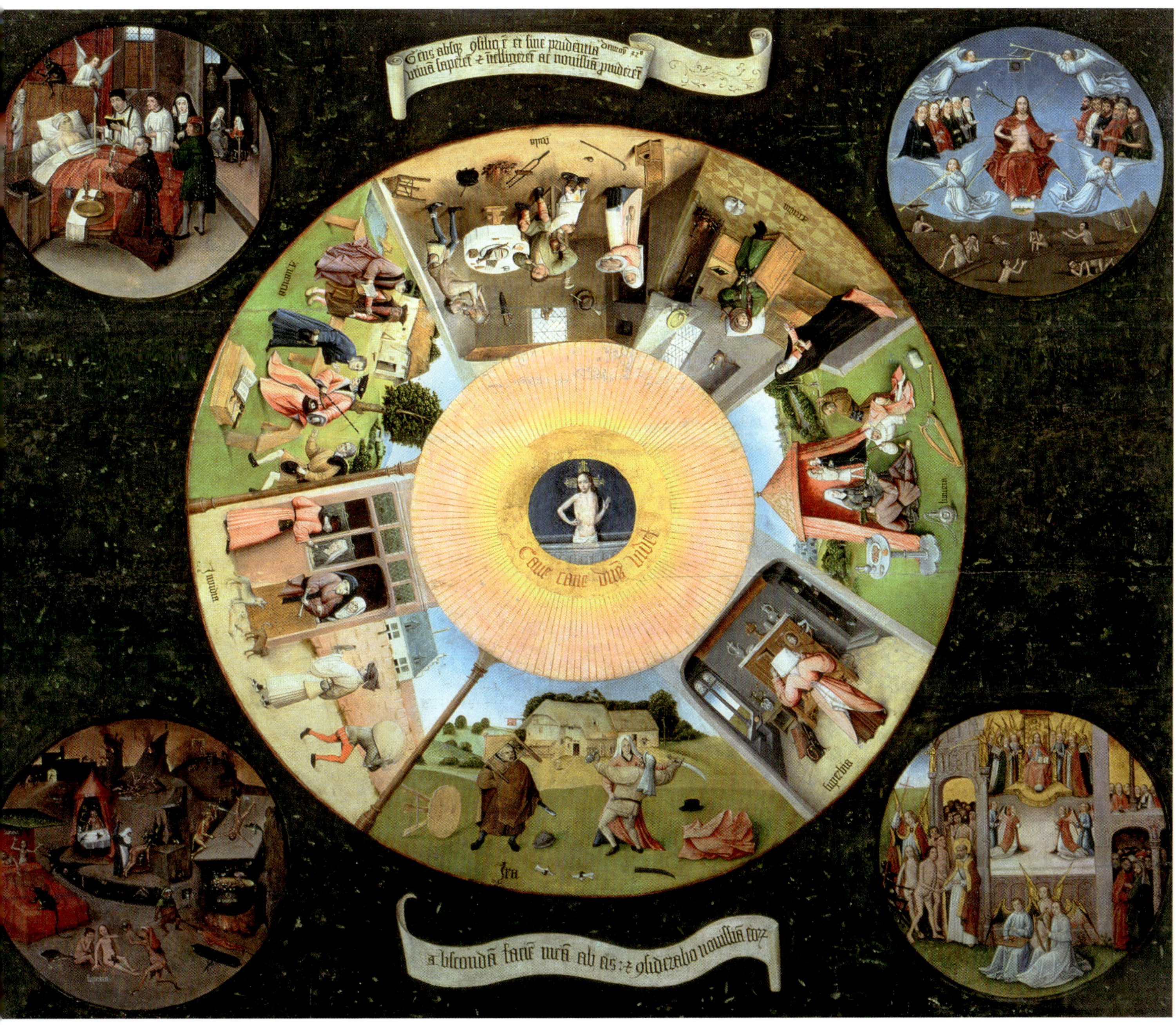

SPLEEN

▸

Albrecht Dürer
Self-portrait
c. 1512-1513
pen and ink with watercolour on paper, 11.8 x 10.8 cm
Kunsthalle, Bremen

▾

Pieter Codde
Young Scholar in His Study: Melancholy
c. 1630
oil on canvas, 46 x 34 cm
Palais des Beaux-Arts, Lille

The word 'spleen' refers to both the anatomical organ and the feeling of melancholy, an analogy that has singular importance in art. In 1503, Dürer was afflicted by an illness of the spleen. An effusion of bile convinced him he was suffering from melancholia. Throughout his career, Dürer illustrated and propounded the widely held doctrine of the Four Humours to the point of verging on hypochondria. According to this theory, four liquids flow through the human body: blood, phlegm, yellow bile and black bile (*melan cholè* in Greek). A balance among the fluids accounted for one's good physiological health, and an excess of one of them signified illness.

Dürer considered himself of a melancholy temperament, dominated by the influence of Saturn. Therefore, the great German painter considered that he came under the pathological and astrological sphere of those who achieve great works through trials and tribulations. The theory of the Four Humours implied by Dürer's engraving *Adam and Eve* (1504) and the famous *Four Apostles* (1526) is the key to understanding many of the master's works. In this self-portrait, the artist points to the area of his abdomen between the liver, spleen and gall bladder. The inscription above it reads, 'Where the yellow spot is, and where my finger points, is where it hurts.'

The association between yellow and melancholy held fast in art and psychopathology for a long time. Interior decorators still consider yellow a 'risky' colour. If walls are a brilliant, luminous yellow, they predispose us to creative activity (and for this reason are recommended for the kitchen). But if they are pale or greenish yellow, as in the painting by Codde, they can lead to depression.

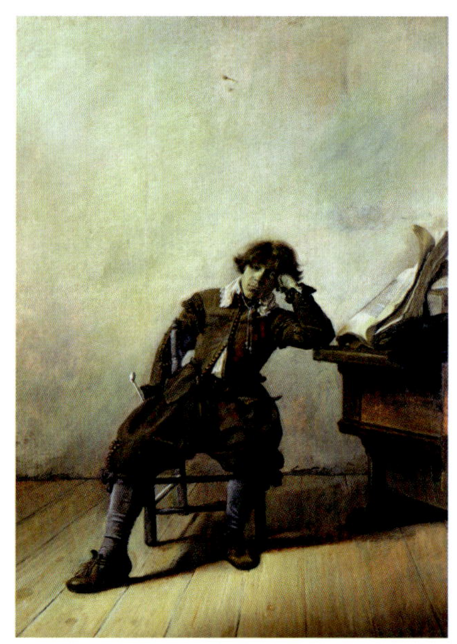

Do der gelb fleck yst vnd mit dem
finger drawff dewt do yst mir we

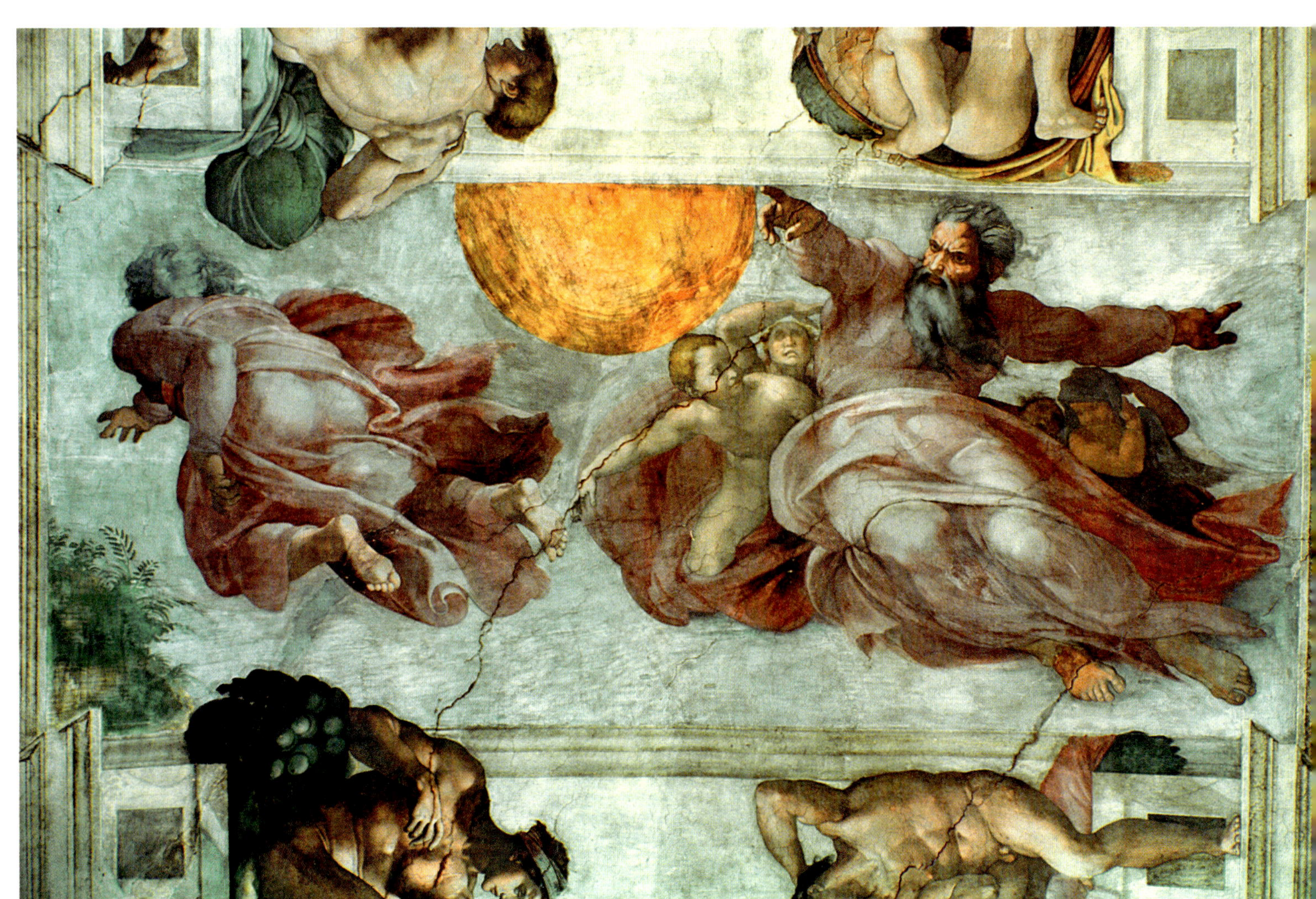

POWER

Heat, truth, light, creation: the sun is the world's vital principle, and the most positive values of the colour yellow are associated with its rays. 'The sun is God,' Turner exclaimed – and this analogy can also be found in the Creation scenes Michelangelo painted in the Sistine Chapel. The splendour of the solar disc is placed in direct relation with one of the most powerful images of God the Father in Western art.

It is the beginning of the world. After the first scene, with God separating light from darkness, Michelangelo included God twice in the second painting on the ceiling: at the right, he is creating the major heavenly bodies; at the left, seen from behind, he is giving life to the plants. God is in flight in both representations, but there is a strong contrast between the astonishing creative will in the image at the right, with the index finger pointing to the sun, and the secluded calm at the left.

In executing the frescoes, Michelangelo proceeded in reverse order with respect to the narrative sequence depicted. When the scaffolding was removed halfway through the work, he realized that the episodes painted first – for example *The Great Flood* – contained many figures that were too small to be seen clearly from below. For this reason, he drastically simplified the scenes painted later (including this one), accentuating the finality of the gestures and the colour contrasts.

Michelangelo Buonarroti
Creation of the Sun, Moon and Plants
1511
fresco, 280 x 570 cm
Sistine Chapel, Musei Vaticani, Rome

APOLLO

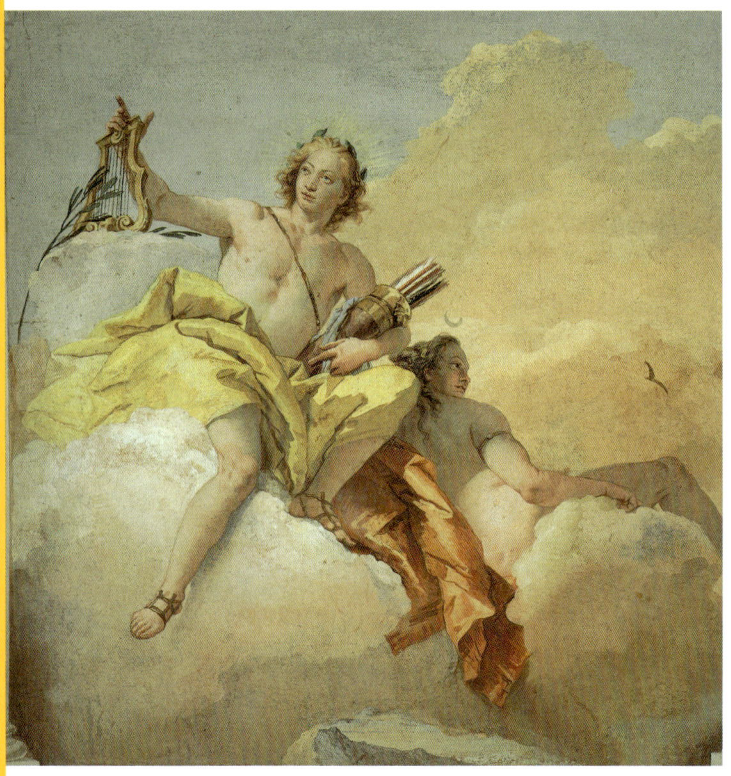

Giambattista Tiepolo
Apollo
1757
fresco, 200 x 185 cm
Sala dell'Olimpo, Villa Valmarana, Vicenza

In Greek mythology, the handsome Apollo is the god of the sun and as such often appears in art bathed in a golden gleam. The son of Zeus and Latona courses through the sky in a chariot every day bringing daylight. Like the other inhabitants of Olympus, he is often involved in love affairs, but more than any other god he loves music and song. His attributes include the laurel crown (a souvenir of his unhappy love for Daphne), arrows (which recall the fiery sun's 'darts') and the lyre, the musical instrument invented by Hermes (the obtaining of which cost Apollo his famous herd of oxen).

In the mid-16th century, Apollo's sun chariot frequently coursed across the ceilings of villa and palazzo halls. Giulio Romano intensified the virtuoso effect of foreshortening seen from below with horses galloping over the clouds and a resplendent sun surround the god's head. Diana, goddess of the night, follows Apollo, in keeping with the customary symbolism of day-sun-male as opposed to night-moon-female.

In the Baroque period, the splendour of the sun and the mythological figure of Apollo were disseminated most impressively in the festivities of Louis XIV of France, the incomparable 'Sun King'. But this success continued through the entire 18th century ('Enlightenment' refers to the light of reason). Apollo is the favourite god in the fantastic mythological allegories painted on the ceilings by Giambattista Tiepolo. After his 'solar' victory at Austerlitz, Napoleon Bonaparte was quick to have his monogram inscribed within a radiant sun.

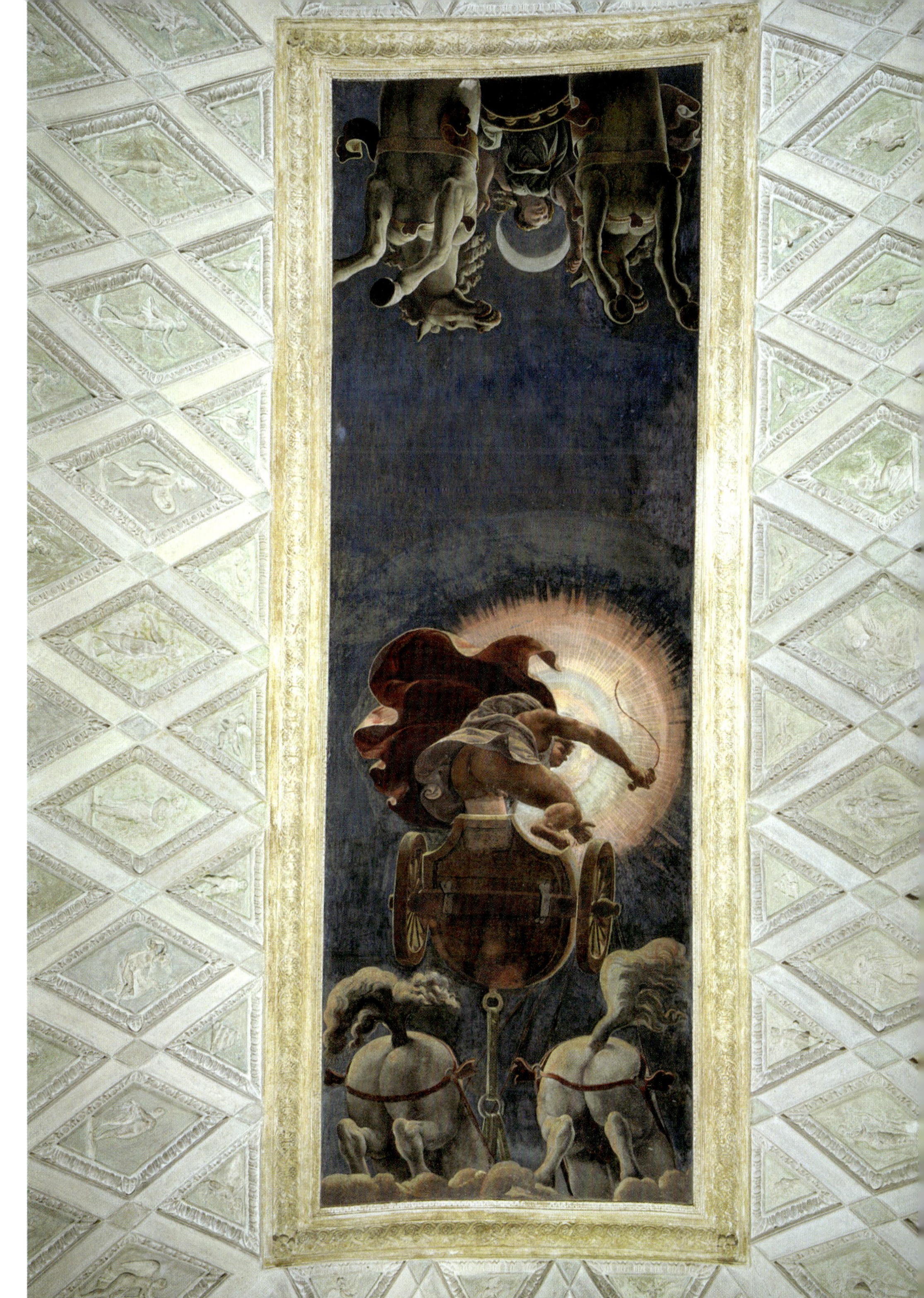

Giulio Romano
Chariot of the Sun
1526
fresco
Stanza del Sole, Palazzo Tè, Mantua

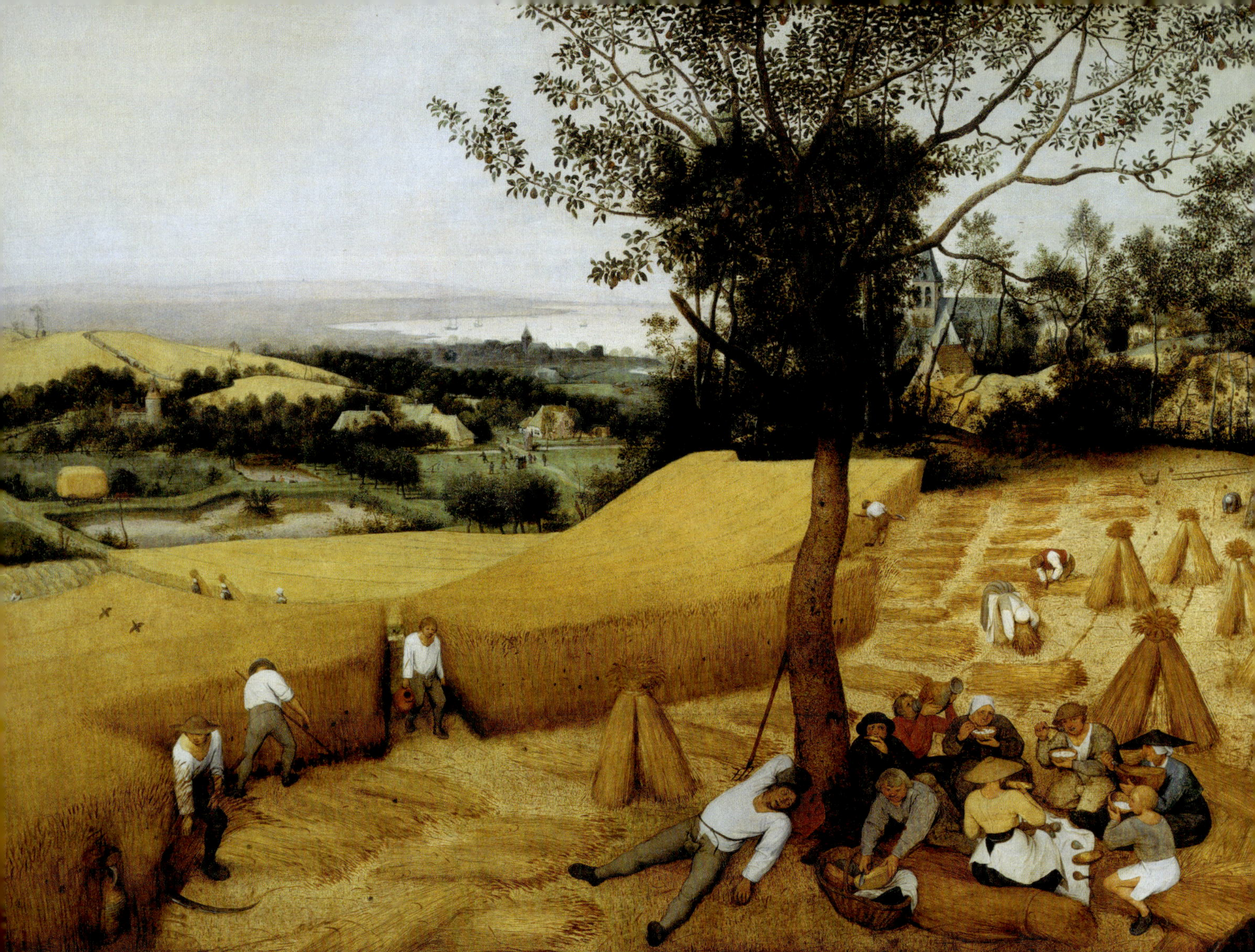

Pieter Bruegel
The Harvesters
1565
oil on panel, 119 x 162 cm
The Metropolitan Museum of Art, New York

WHEAT

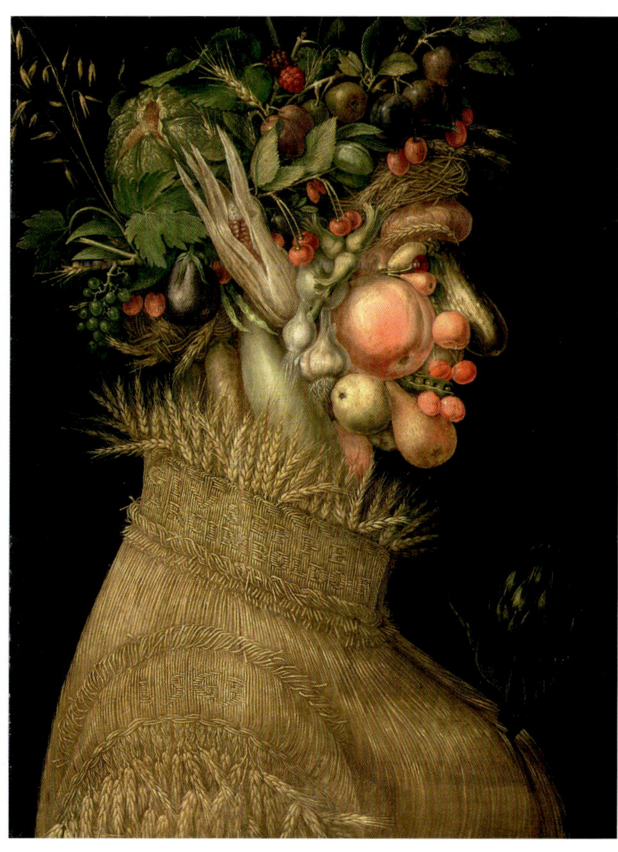

Giuseppe Arcimboldo
Summer
1563
oil on panel, 67 x 51 cm
Kunsthistorisches Museum, Vienna

The yellow of ripe wheat ready for harvest is the predominant colour of fields at the height of summer. Wheat is one of the strongest Christian symbols, and the Gospels abound with similes and references to the fields, from sowing time to harvest: 'Behold, I say unto you, Lift up your eyes, and look on the fields; for they are white already to harvest. And he that reapeth receiveth wages, and gathereth fruit unto life eternal: that both he that soweth and he that reapeth may rejoice together.' (John 4:35–36).

The famous image of harvest workers at rest, dominated by the warm colour of the wheat, is the summer episode in the cycle of the months), a masterpiece by Pieter Bruegel, commissioned by the Antwerp merchant and collector Nicolaes Jongelinck. The feeling of sultriness, scorching heat and the exhaustion of the peasants taking their break contrasts with the flaxen colour of the crops, while the gaze moves on to discover details like the cart loaded with grain, and then a panoramic vista of moving depth.

At more or less the same time that Bruegel was painting his months, Giuseppe Arcimboldo was also producing an interpretation of the four seasons for the imperial court in Prague. His version, however, takes the bizarre virtuoso form of 'composed heads' – ingenious combinations of nature's produce. *Summer* is wrapped in wheat and yellow straw.

VERMEER'S 'TINY PATCH OF YELLOW WALL'

Johannes Vermeer liked and used yellow more than any other 17th-century painter. Women in various paintings are dressed in an unmistakably yellow fur-lined dressing gown. The milkmaid at the Rijksmuseum, the lacemaker at the Louvre and the young prostitute in Dresden are wearing the same lemon yellow corset. The famous girl with a pearl earring is wearing a blue and yellow head cover. Vermeer's use of yellow is celebrated by Marcel Proust's description of the *View of Delft*, from *Remembrance of Things Past* (The Captive, 1923). In the famous passage, Proust describes the fatal emotion of the writer Bergotte before the painting on exhibition in Paris: 'At last he came to the Vermeer which he remembered as more striking, more different from anything else that he knew, but in which, thanks to the critic's article, he remarked for the first time some small figures in blue, that the ground was pink, and finally the precious substance of the tiny patch of yellow wall.'

The episode of the death of Bergotte is one of literature's most famous references to a painting. Proust seems to describe Vermeer's masterpiece with meticulous and passionate accuracy. Nevertheless, there is no agreement as to which yellow wall Proust refers: the small building behind the fortified gate, immediately to the left, or the wall behind the drawbridge, at the right.

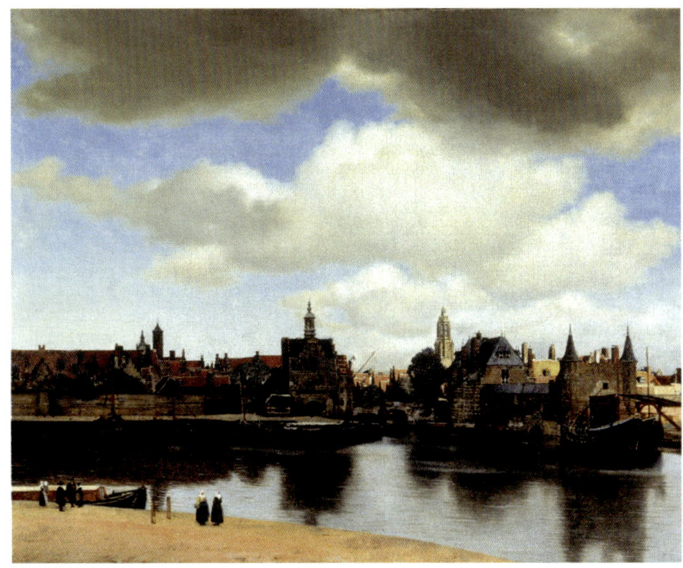

Johannes Vermeer
A View of Delft
c. 1661-1663
oil on canvas, 96.5 x 115.7 cm
Koninklijk Kabinet van Schilderijen Mauritshuis
The Hague

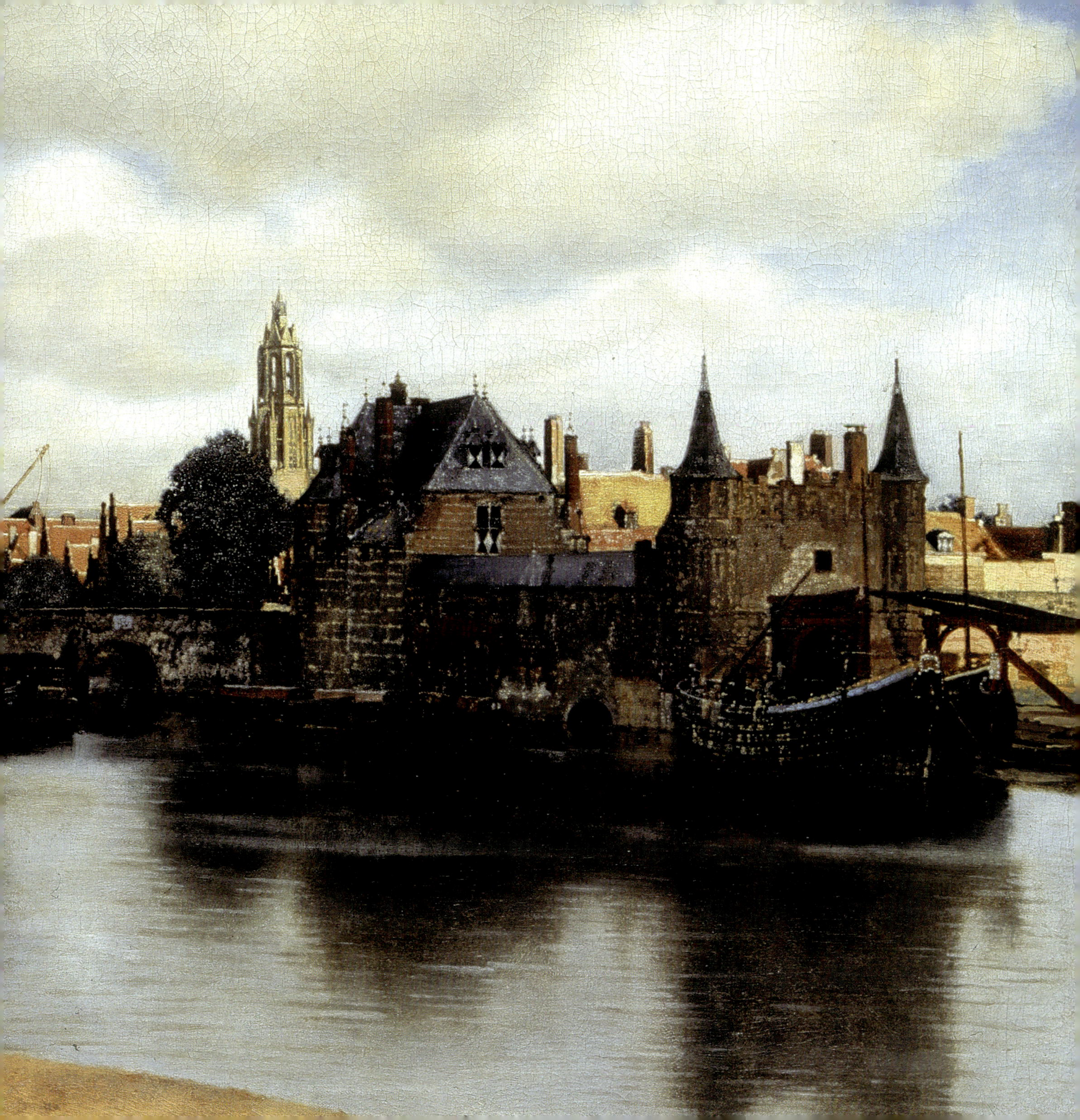

BAROQUE CONTRASTS OF LIGHT AND SHADOW

The contrast between light and shadow is a predominant theme in 17th-century European culture. In painting, night scenes are very frequent. Developed by Caravaggio, they met with favour among collectors in the 17th century and often became displays of pure virtuosity. On the other hand, the night theme found a singularly effective psychological motif in the precarious light of a candle. The contrast between the deep black of night and the candle's faint yellow glow became the expression in paint of solitary doubt, a moment of reflection.

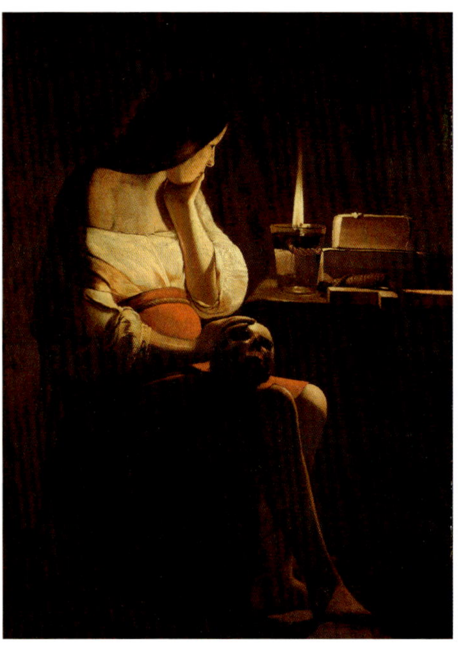

In French painting of the first half of the 17th century, the intimate nocturnal poetry of Georges de La Tour contrasts with the radiant intellectual classicism of Nicolas Poussin. Little or nothing is known about the training of de La Tour, which likely took place in Nancy. After a probable stay in Italy, which would have introduced him to Caravaggio, from 1620 on de La Tour lived in his wife's hometown of Lunéville. From the early paintings set in daylight, de la Tour progressed to the intense nocturnal compositions of his maturity, in which candlelight illuminates calm, well thought-out compositions with a few figures absorbed in intimate meditation.

The candle flame is a symbol of precariousness, for it may go out at any moment and is inexorably consumed. The politics of French splendour and the absolute power of the Sun King communicated a sense of omnipotence and control over the fate of the world. And yet, in 17th-century French culture there is a fear of a fragile world that often seems on the verge of collapse. René Descartes went so far as to doubt whether the things around us really exist. However, doubt assures us of the existence of ourselves and the world (*Dubito ergo sum*).

Georges de La Tour
Magdalene with the Nightlight or *The Penitent Magdalene*
1640-1645
oil on canvas, 128 x 94 cm
Musée du Louvre, Paris

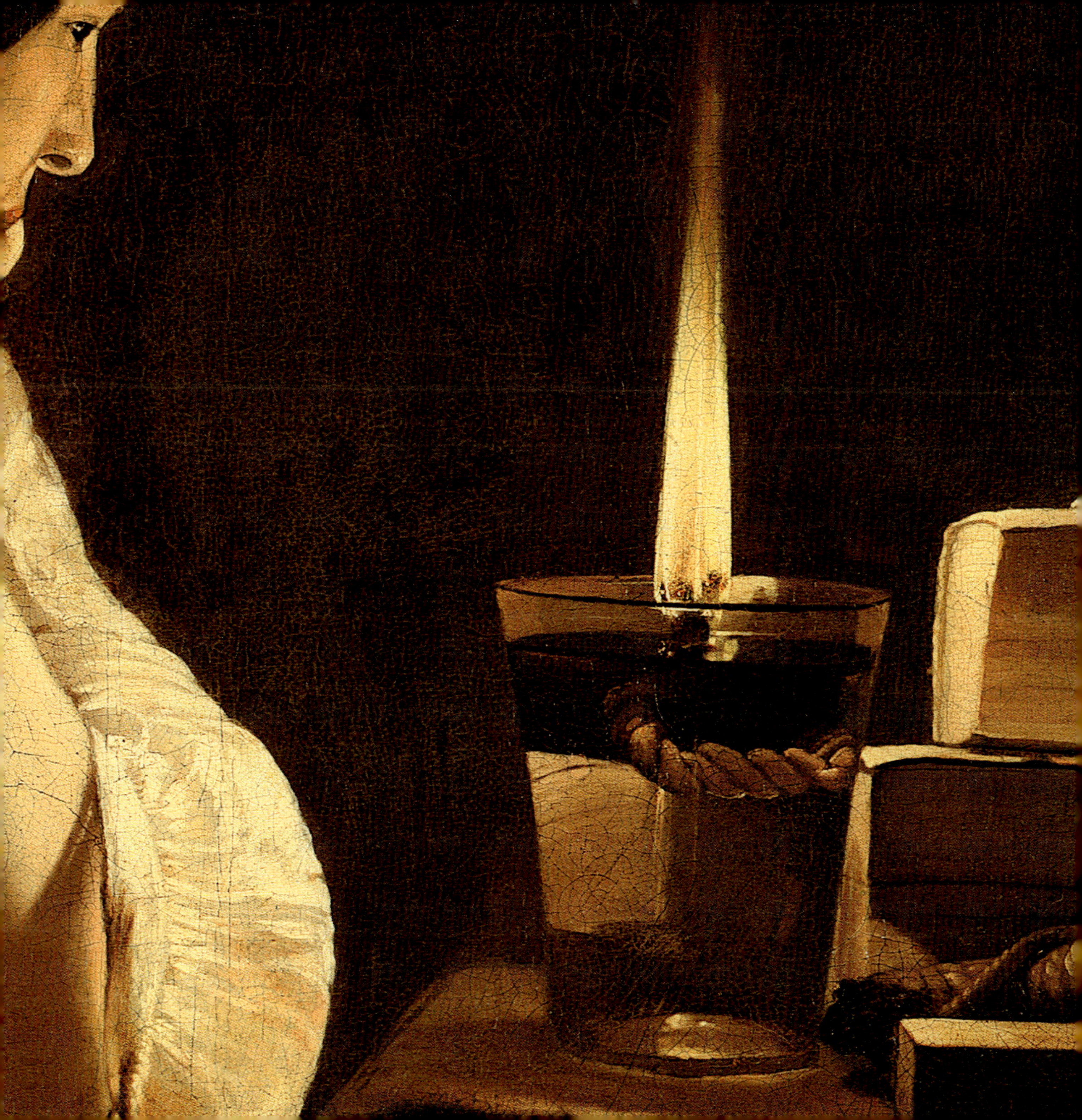

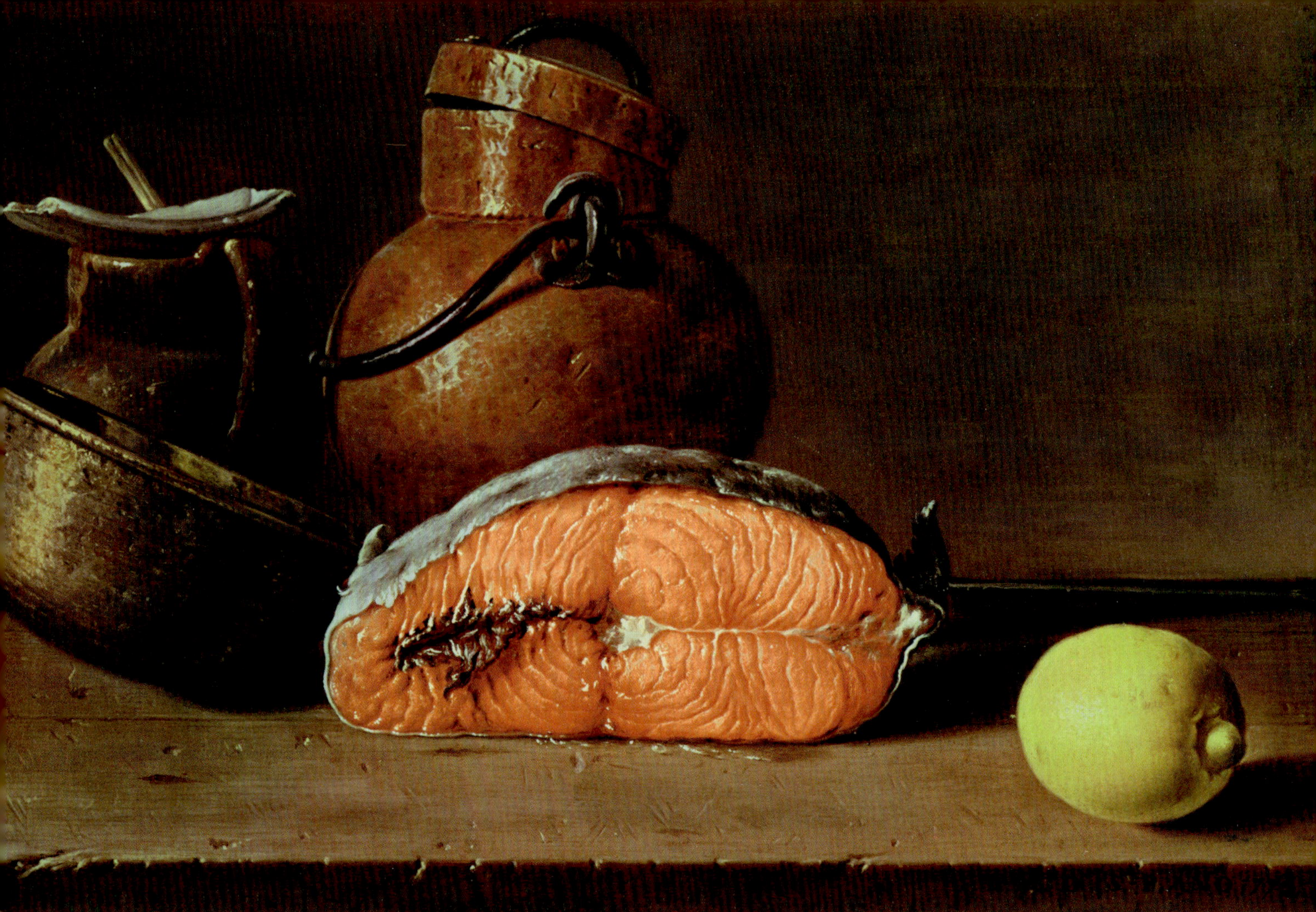

Luis Egidio Meléndez
Still Life with a Piece of Salmon, a Lemon and Kitchen Utensils
1772
oil on canvas, 41 x 62.2 cm
Museo Nacional del Prado, Madrid

LEMON

The frescoes of Pompeii demonstrate that the Romans knew of lemons, but their preferred citrus fruits were citrons and bergamots. The lemon's great popularity in the Mediterranean world and commercial diffusion in Europe as a prized aromatic fruit is the result of plantations introduced by the Arabs, who probably imported the lemon from India – and indeed India is still the world's largest lemon producer. The root of the word 'lemon' derives from the Persian language.

Lemon yellow, one of the brightest colours in the painter's palette, has been exploited frequently since the Baroque period. But while for Southern European painters the lemon was a familiar fruit, found in every kitchen, in Central and Northern Europe it was more exotic. Except for a few prize examples sheltered in greenhouses, it was imported from warm, sunny climates and suggested a taste beyond the everyday. For this reason, in Northern painting a peeled lemon is often combined with precious porcelain.

The analogy between the lemon's colour and the heat of the sun is recalled in one of Eugenio Montale's most beautiful poems:

When one day through a gate left open
there appears among the trees in a courtyard
the yellow light of lemons;
and the icy heart melts
as in the breast roar
their songs,
the gold trumpets of solarity.

Eugenio Montale, 'The Lemons', 1925

Willem Kalf
Still Life with a Porcelain Bowl and a Nautilus Cup
1660
oil on canvas, 64.1 x 55.9 cm
Museo Thyssen-Bornemisza, Madrid

FROM GLORY TO DISASTER

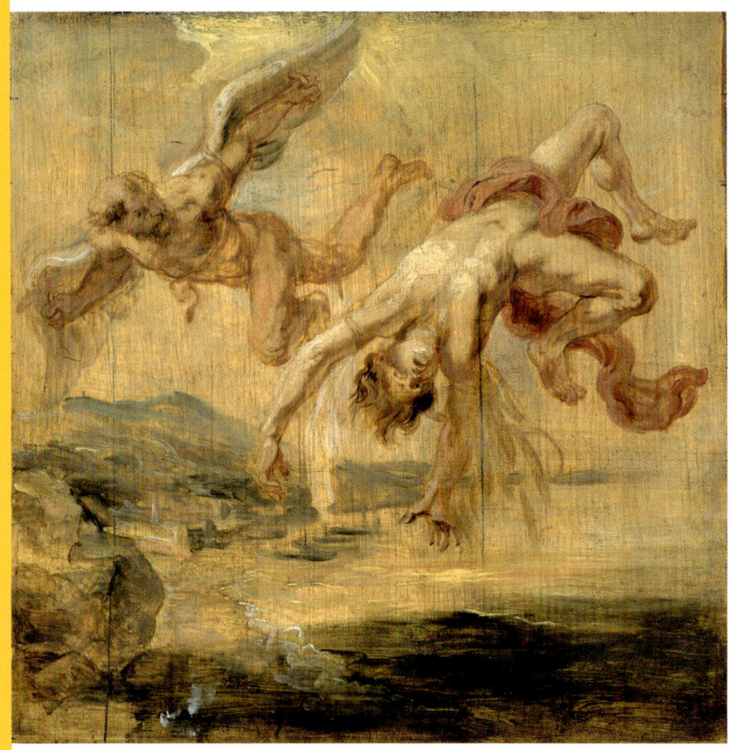

▲
Peter Paul Rubens
The Fall of Icarus
1636
oil on panel, 27.4 x 26.8 cm
Musées Royaux des Beaux-Arts de Belgique, Brussels

▶
Joseph Mallord William Turner
War, the Exile and the Rock Limpet
1842
oil on canvas, 79.5 x 79.5 cm
Tate, London

For Turner, light is the prime regulator of the world because it reveals the nature of things through colours. Colour becomes the supreme manifestation and thus the very spirit of the world, an assertion Turner encountered in an essay by Arthur Schopenhauer, 'On Vision and Colours' (1816). In the painter's last works, colours dominate the space, obliterating the limits imposed by drawing and allowing him to render his Romantic concept of nature.

Napoleon's solitary exile on St Helena provides the occasion for an allegory of the sunset of glory. In the glaring light of the sun shining on the beach, the defeated Napoleon, watched over by a guard, contemplates a mollusc – apparently insignificant but free to go where it will. This allegory draws an analogy between Napoleon's rising and falling 'star' and the trajectory of the sun.

The theme of the fall is expressed many times in classical mythology and the art it inspired. Phaeton tried to control the sun's chariot, but failed and plummeted to his death, while Icarus perished after flying too close to the sun. In the sketch by Rubens (an unforgettable little masterpiece), the whole sky is inundated with the sun's golden heat, which melts the wax of Icarus's artificial wings as his anguished father, Daedalus, looks on.

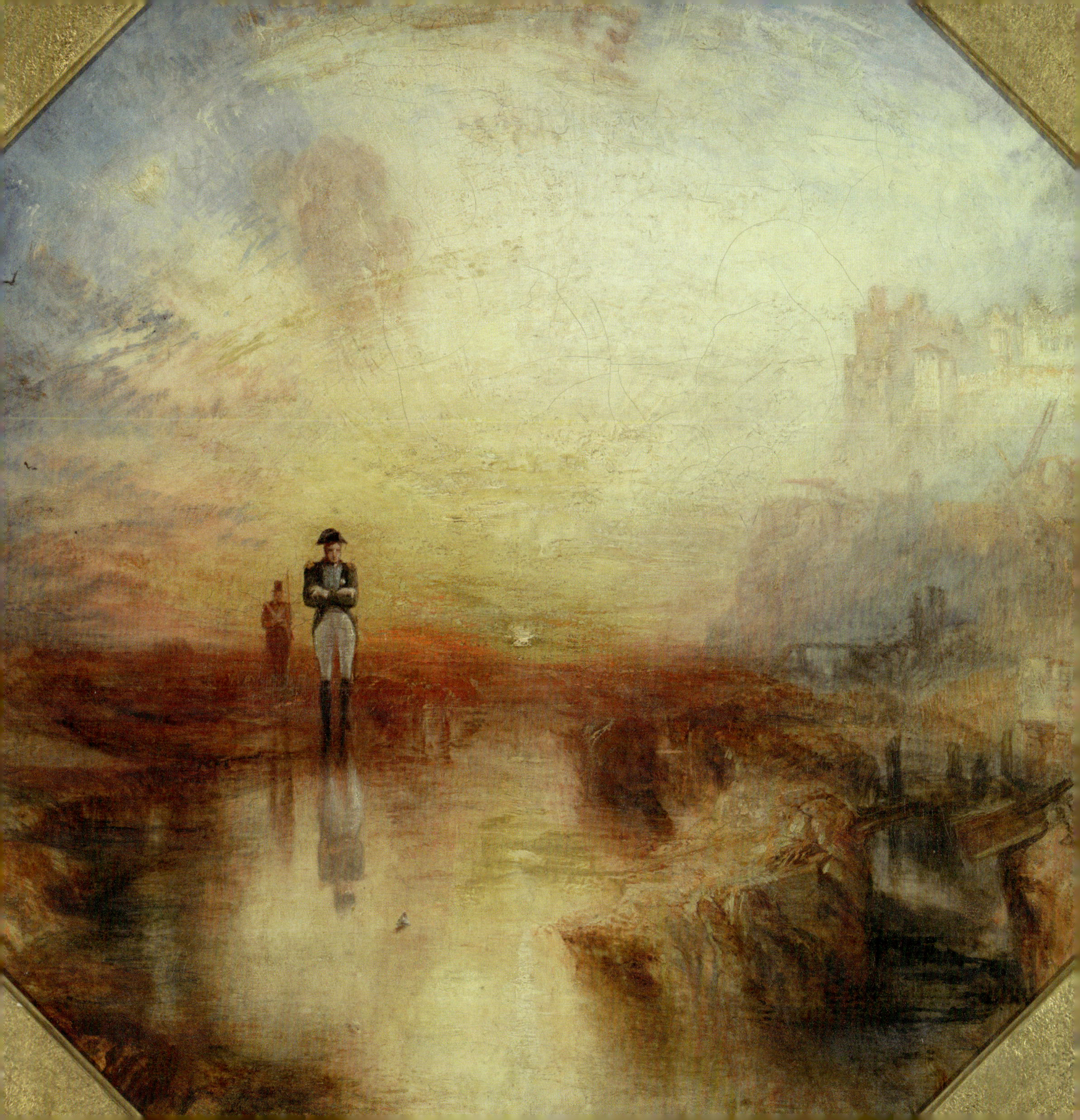

SUNFLOWER

▸

Vincent van Gogh
Sunflowers
1888
oil on canvas, 95 x 73 cm
Van Gogh Museum, Amsterdam

▾

Sir Anthony van Dyck
Self-portrait with a Sunflower
c. 1632
oil on canvas, 60 x 73 cm
private collection

While in Arles, Van Gogh frequently – and perhaps even obsessively – painted sunflowers. In his eyes, they transmitted the sun's strength and energy, emanating a light of their own; they also reflected his deep and sincere love of life. By insistently repeating the same subject, Van Gogh laid the foundation for his own unique style: the few colours used are then modulated using white and black; the light is intense, devoid of shadow and chiaroscuro; the drawing is rapid, without hesitations or reworking; and the composition has little depth, a feature learnt from Japanese prints and through contact with Gauguin.

Van Gogh squeezed colours directly from the tube – he is one of the first artists to use commercially prepared paints. He may even have been in the habit of tasting them. The yellows on his palette are yellow ochre, chrome yellow and cadmium yellow, along with other warm colours like orange, vermilion and the earth tone sienna.

The sunflower's large blossom is an appealing subject for painters. Another example can be found in an unusual self-portrait painted by Van Dyck at the peak of his career. The artist from Antwerp, who had settled in London, intended to pay homage to the King of England, Charles I. As the sunflower follows the course of the sun, so is Van Dyck reflected in the monarch's glory. The optimistic painter could not have known that his life would be unfortunately brief or that the king would be overthrown by Cromwell's revolution.

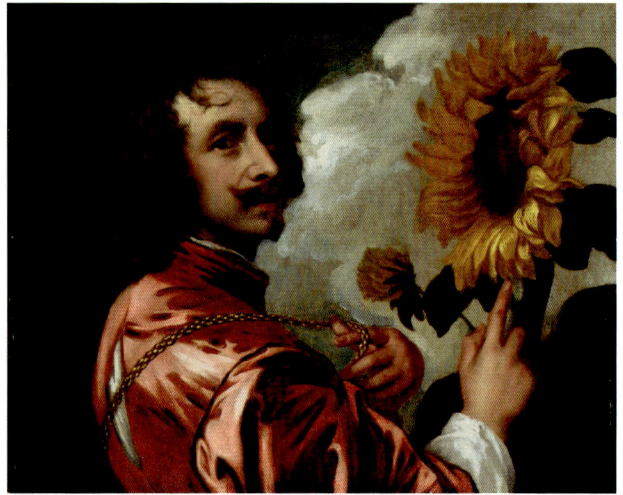

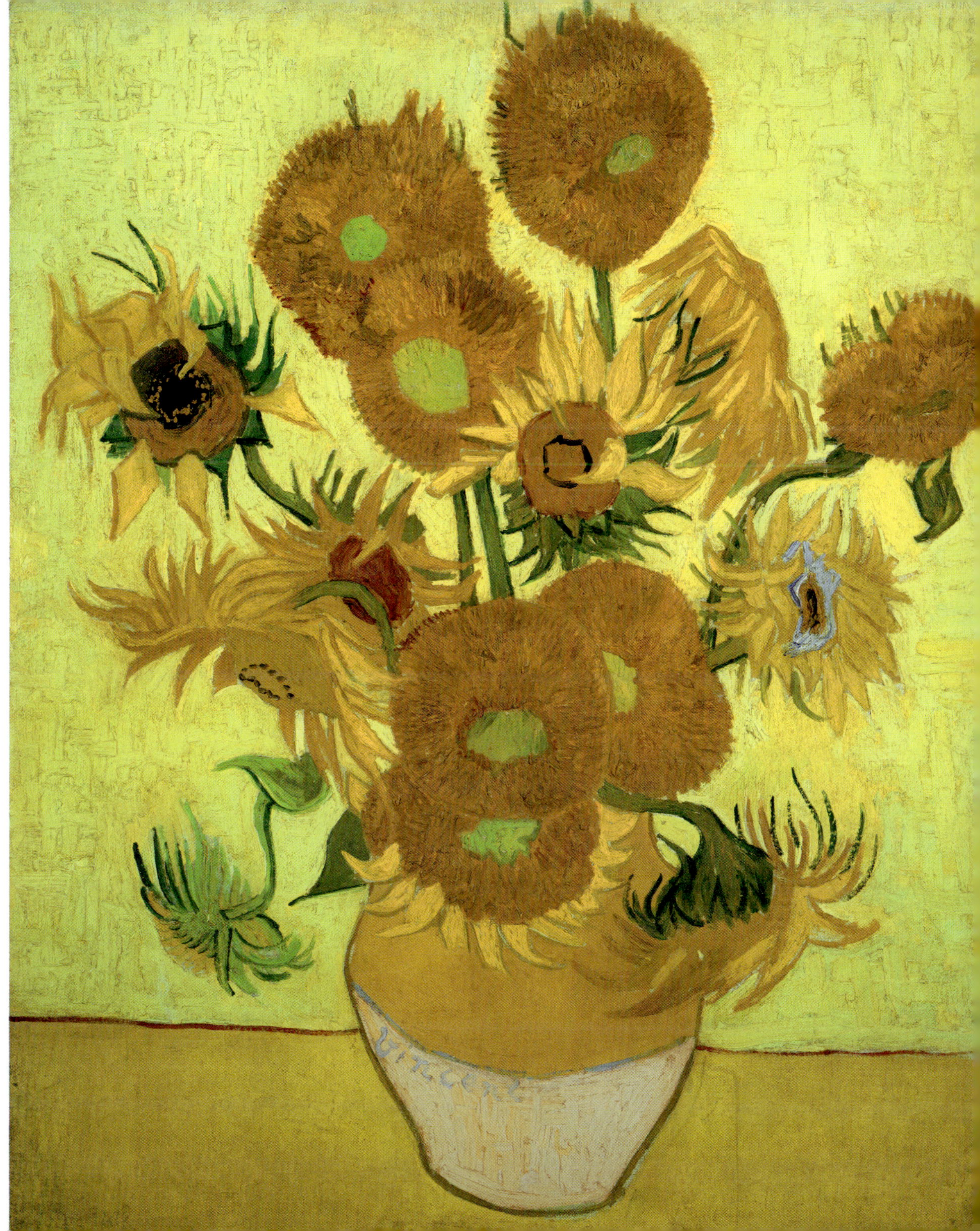
Vincent

VAN GOGH AND GAUGUIN: THE YELLOW HOUSE

'The outside of my house here is painted buttery yellow and has green shutters. It is in full sun on a square that also faces a park with oleander and acacia trees.' In the modest house he rented in Arles, at 2 Place Lamartine, Van Gogh dreamed of founding a new aesthetic current (the École du Midi). It was the site of his few months' turbulent cohabitation with Paul Gauguin, which ended abruptly on 23 December 1888. With a haunted look on his face, Van Gogh attacked Gauguin with a knife. The robust Gauguin punched him and left. Falling prey to delirium and despair, Van Gogh cut off one of his own earlobes.

'As soon as possible I want to go to the South, where there is still more colour and more sun,' Van Gogh had written to his sister Willemien in early 1888. Having arrived in Provence from Paris, he was thrilled by the light. In the spring, his love of yellow exploded: 'Now we are having beautiful warm windless weather that is very beneficial to me. The sun, a light that for lack of a better word I can only call yellow, bright sulphur yellow, pale lemon gold. How beautiful yellow is!'

One of the best-known results of the two artists' association in the yellow house is the portrait Gauguin made of Van Gogh intently painting his beloved sunflowers. Done from an unusual violent angle, the portrait is a masterpiece. Vincent found the portrait a good likeness but also revealing of his mental state: 'It is me,' he wrote, 'but gone mad.'

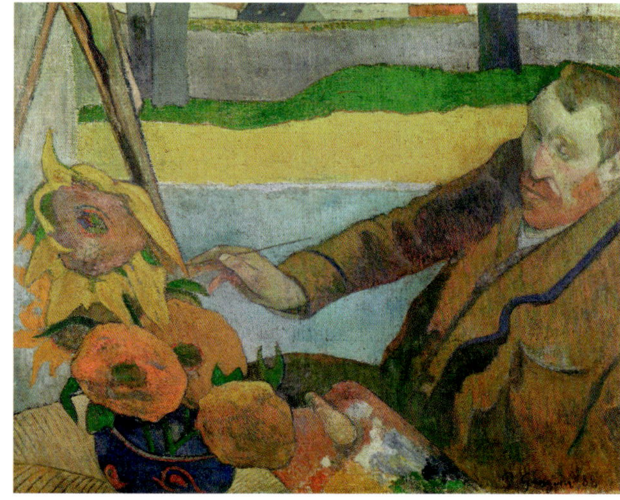

Paul Gauguin
Portrait of Van Gogh Painting Sunflowers
1888
oil on canvas, 73 x 91 cm
Van Gogh Museum, Amsterdam

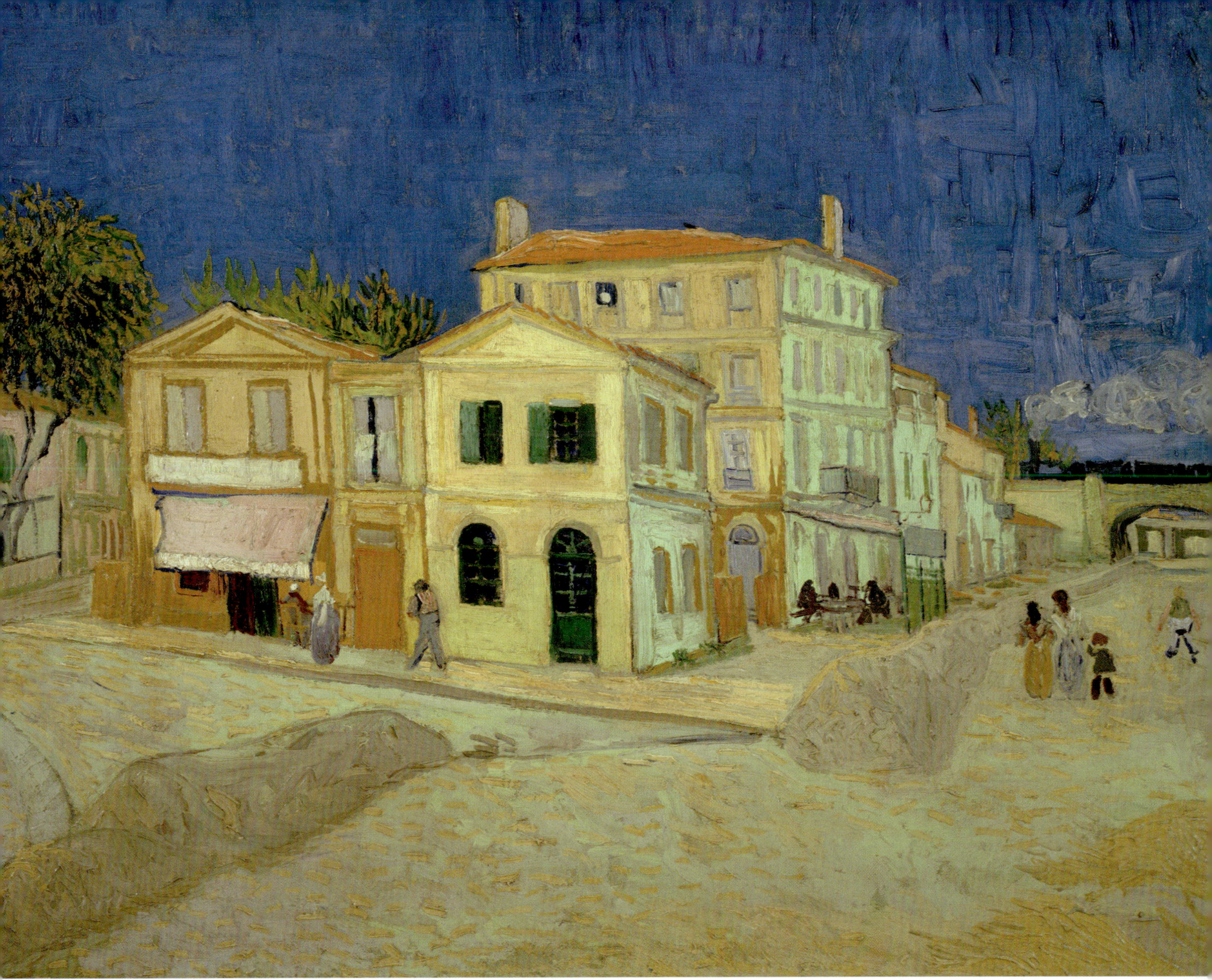

Vincent van Gogh
The Yellow House (The Street)
1888
oil on canvas, 72 x 91.5 cm
Van Gogh Museum, Amsterdam

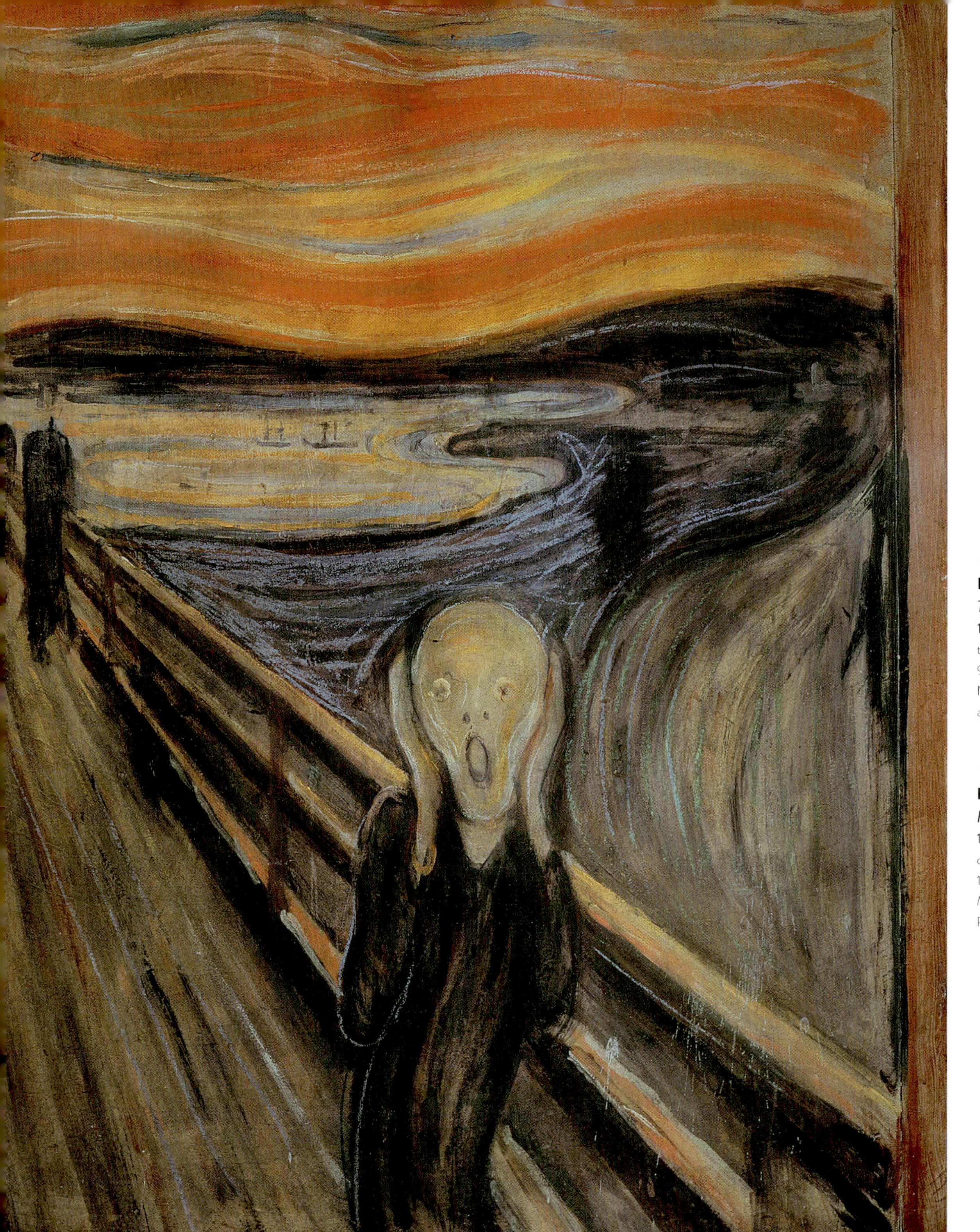

◂

Edvard Munch
The Scream
1893
tempera and crayon on cardboard,
91 x 73.5 cm
Nasjonalmuseet for kunst
arkitektur og design, Oslo

▸

Frederic Leighton
Flaming June
1895
oil on canvas,
120 x 120 cm
Museo de Arte de Ponce
Puerto Rico

BETWEEN LIFE AND DEATH

'Then the Sun set – all at once the sky became blood red. I felt a great, unending scream piercing through nature.' Thus Munch himself described the state of tension from which this famous work – a symbol of the artistic and cultural transition from the 19th to the 20th century – arose. Munch used a continuous undulating line, wrapped around things in an ineluctable, suffocating grasp. The scene is set on a bridge as an unprecedented sunset inflames the colours, altering their natural tones, with a prevalence of flaming reds and yellows. The atmosphere is dramatic, anguished and even deafening in the frustrated violence of the colours. The figure of the screaming man who covers his ears is reduced to a skeleton, a simplified sign of a body and human features. It is a tense painting, pushed to the limit, in clear anticipation of the relentless synthetic current of German Expressionism.

Although living and working in Norway, Munch was not an isolated artist but maintained contacts with the brightest painters of his time, in addition to taking a keen interest in the progress of psychoanalytical studies. Also inspired by the plays of his fellow countryman Ibsen, in the last decade of the 19th century Munch embarked upon a course of taut intensity, descending into the dramas of the psyche and projecting onto his painting an acutely tormented inner sensibility. Many moments in Munch's work may be interpreted in light of his disturbed psychological state. The present is confused with memory, and with a yearning nostalgia that anticipates Scandinavian theatre and cinema.

Working at the same time as Munch, but in a different vein of symbolism, Lord Leighton offered this diametrically opposed image of early summer colours. However, the sunny peacefulness is only an appearance. The poisonous leaves of the oleander in the background suggest the thin line between sleep and death.

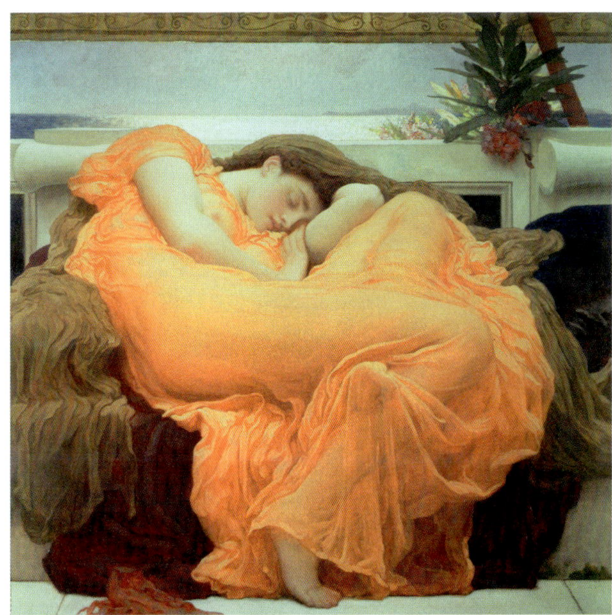

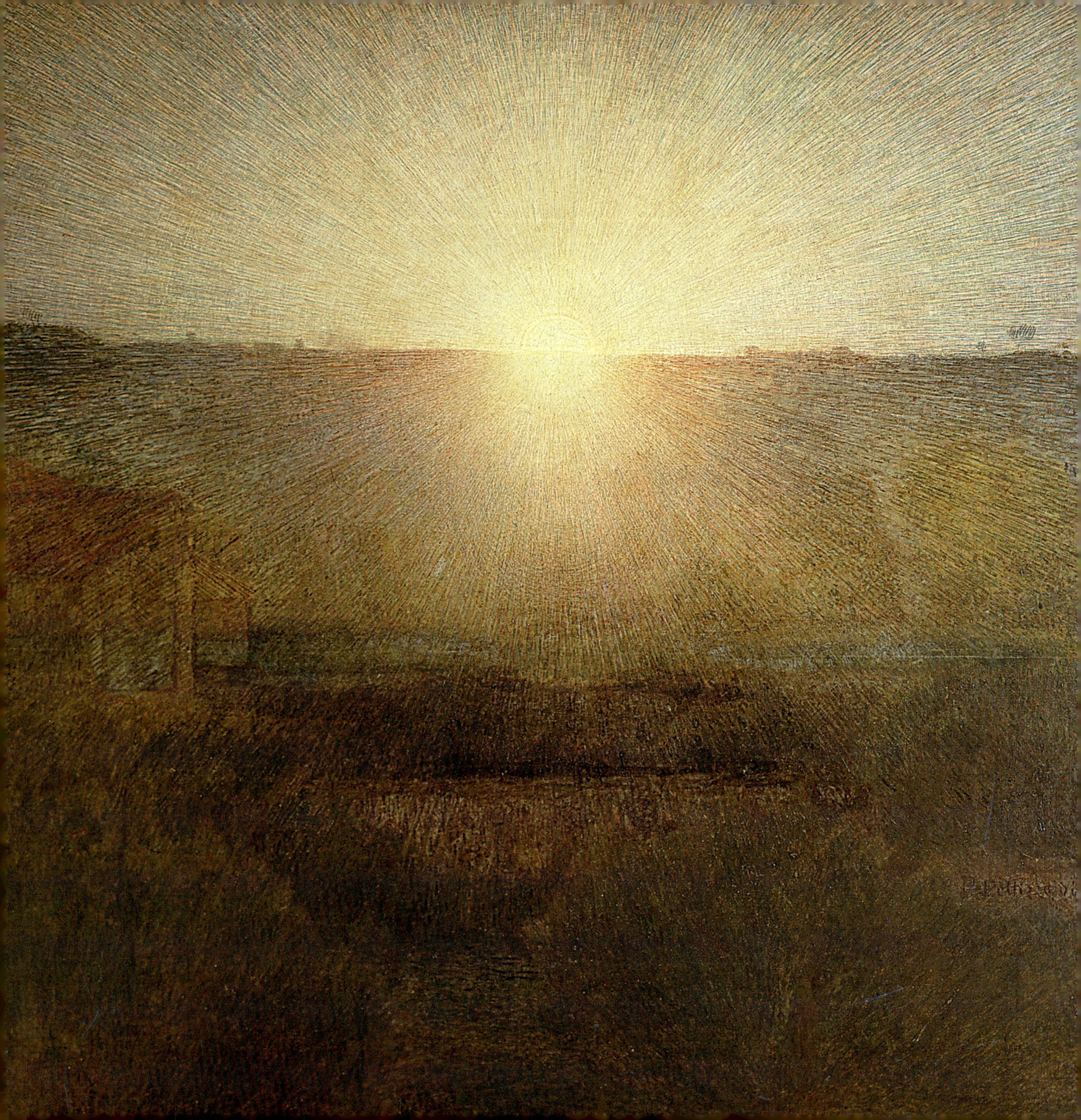

THE SUN

It is not easy to paint the sun. According to Picasso's famous statement, 'Some painters transform the sun into a yellow spot, others transform a yellow spot into the sun.' Yellow, orange or red, setting or rising, resplendent or veiled, dazzling at the beach or shining pleasantly over Impressionist Paris, the sun is often featured in 19th- and early 20th-century painting.

In dramatic contrast with the shadows, the sun's intense light is the main interest in this painting by Giuseppe Pellizza da Volpedo, a prominent figure in Italian art across the 19th and 20th centuries. His most significant paintings are steeped in a diffuse light, radiant as gold dust, and based on a symbolically charged antithesis between light and dark. This approach culminates in *The Rising Sun* of 1904, which the artist described as follows: 'The rising sun enchants, dazzles and invades nature, subjecting it completely to its influence. To tell the truth, this great and powerful spectacle escapes our meagre means of reproduction, but it seemed to me that painting might tackle it – not with the intention of reducing it to a detached scheme but ... to imprison a ray of its light in the coloured material itself.'

Moved by impulses of solidarity and genuine political commitment, Pellizza was certainly also thinking of the 'sun of the future' extolled by international movements and socialist parties, auguring a radiant future for the working classes. In the same period, another Italian artist, Gaetano Previati, in turn adopted the technique of Divisionism (an original and independent answer to French Pointillism) to represent the radiant chariot of the sun, a symbol of progress in business and industry, like a fiery furnace and as rapid as the ways of modern commerce.

◂
Giuseppe Pellizza da Volpedo
The Sun, or *The Rising Sun*
1904
oil on canvas, 155 x 155 cm
Galleria Nazionale d'Arte Moderna, Rome

▾
Gaetano Previati
The Chariot of the Sun
1907
oil on canvas, 127 x 185 cm
Camera di Commercio, Milan

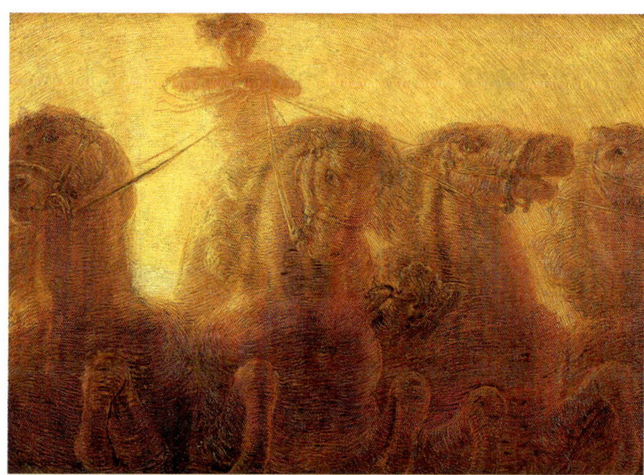

KANDINSKY AND 'DER GELBE KLANG'

Kandinsky repeatedly explored the expressive boundaries between painting and music. In his famous essay 'Concerning the Spiritual in Art', he proposes an analogy between the palette and the piano: 'Colour is a means of exerting direct influence on the soul. Colour is a keyboard, the eye is the hammer that strikes it, the soul the instrument with a thousand strings.' This approach reached its peak between 1908 and 1914. With increasing gestural and chromatic freedom, Kandinsky simply left spots and streaks on the canvas. He also planned a series of theatrical spectacles based on interaction between colour, music and stage action. The only performance that took place was devoted to his favourite colour: *Der gelbe Klang* (The Yellow Sound), staged in New York in 1982.

In Munich on 2 January 1911, Kandinsky had attended a concert with compositions by Arnold Schoenberg – the String Quartet, Op. 10, and the *Drei Klavierstücke,* Op. 11, to be exact. The Russian painter was struck by this music, which he felt to be very close to his painting: neither sought to describe reality, but attempted instead to express the inner life and most intimate emotions of humankind. In subsequent years, Kandinsky and Schoenberg had the opportunity to become acquainted and see each other often, forming a close personal and professional relationship.

Arnold Schoenberg, the father of twelve-tone music, was also an accomplished painter. His relationship with Kandinsky underscored the strong connections between the two disciplines and the common quest for new forms of expression. It is not by chance that the painters of Der Blaue Reiter often used the term 'vibration' to describe the visual effect created by colours, which parallels the effect of sound and conveys emotions through images.

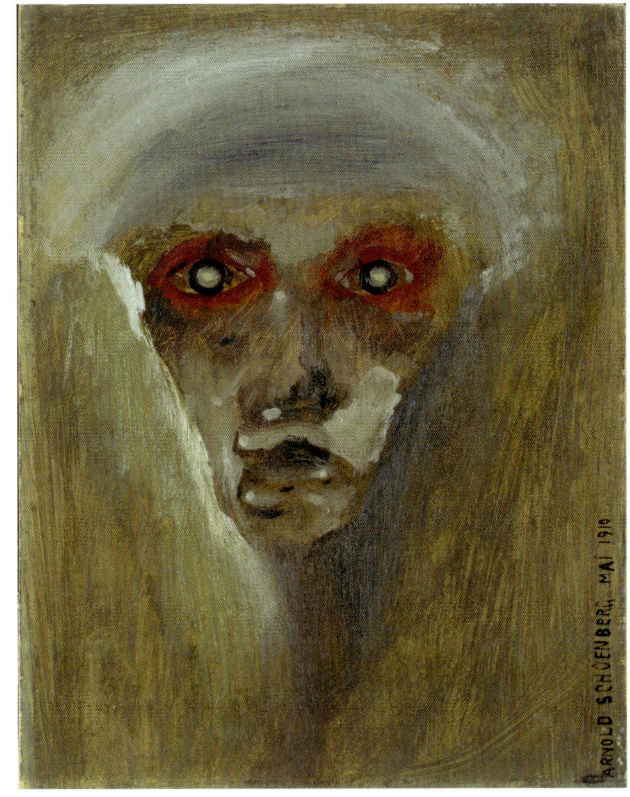

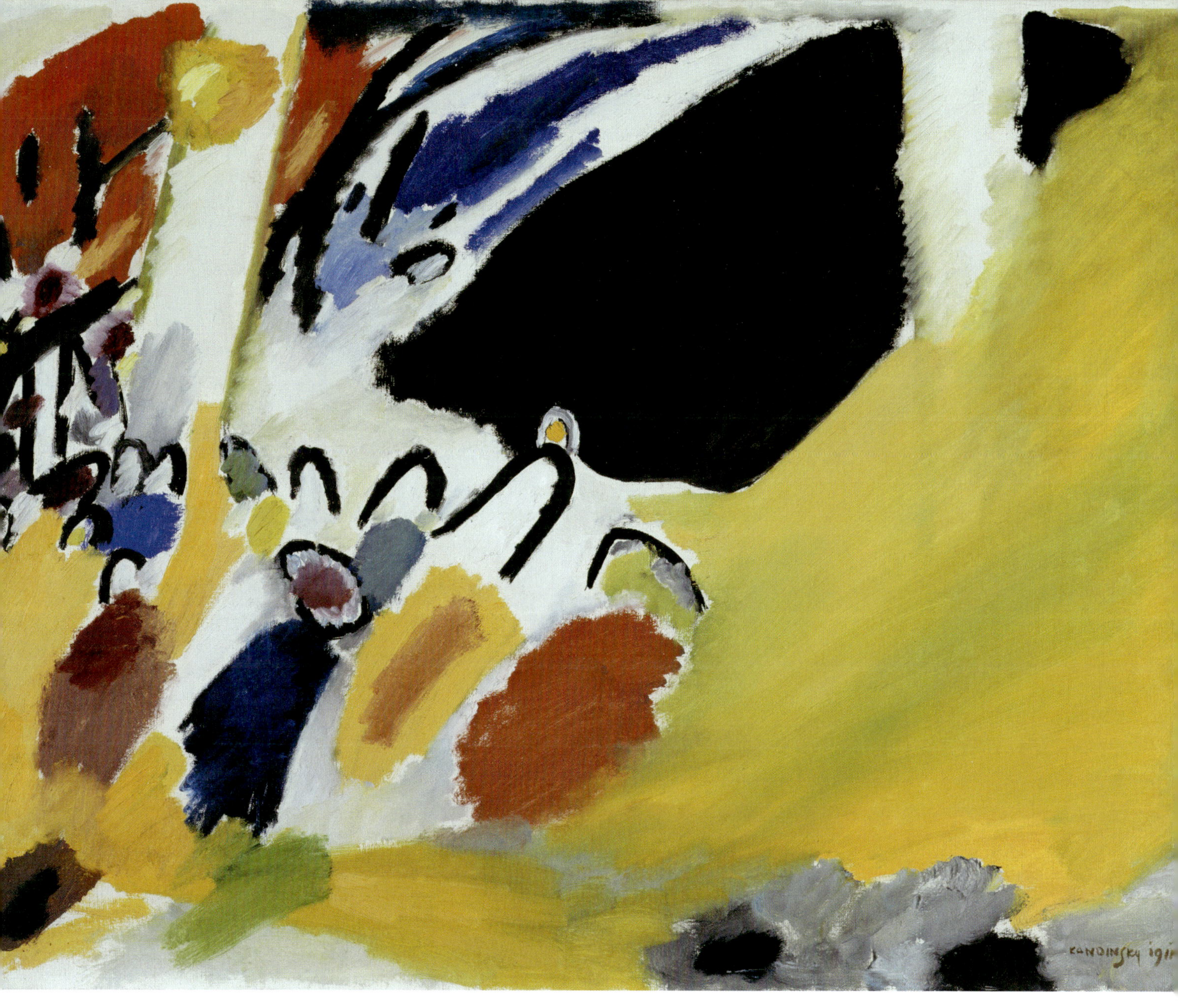

Arnold Schoenberg
Der rote Blick
1910
oil on card, 32.2 x 24.6 cm
Städtische Galerie im Lenbachhaus, Munich

Wassily Kandinsky
Impression III (Concert)
1911
oil on canvas, 77.5 x 100 cm
Städtische Galerie im Lenbachhaus, Munich

STRAW HAT

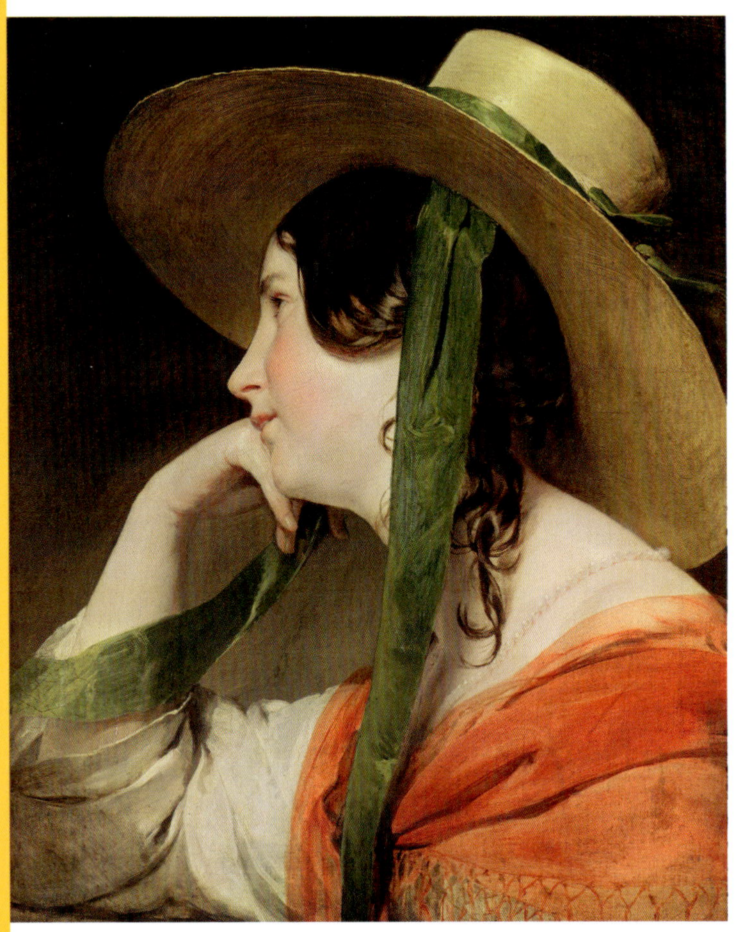

In the 19th century, light, wide-brimmed straw hats offering protection from the sun – a necessity in rural peasant life as we can see from medieval art – became a fashion accessory synonymous with summer. Men's rigid straw hats were especially popular, while women's hats had long ribbons and soft, gently curved brims. The natural colour of straw blends with the characteristic tones of seaside localities: the scorching sun, hot sand, light-coloured clothing and, starting in the 20th century, golden suntans.

It is significant that the title of this masterpiece of American painting is *Summer Sunlight*: it is light that dominates the scene, which records a summer holiday in Maine. In the centre of the painting, wearing a wide yellow hat, is the painter's eldest daughter, to whom a friend is offering a banana (a further note of yellow, against a green towel). Despite the vivid light and bright colours, a subtle disquiet permeates the painting, reminiscent of the atmosphere of a famous murder mystery by Agatha Christie, *Evil under the Sun* (1941).

Even before social conventions and the tenets of health fanatics made it acceptable for men and women to bathe together at the seaside, exposing ever larger areas of the body, the straw hat was a typical summer accessory, worn gracefully by young ladies of polite European society. It was particularly prevalent in the Biedermeier period (1815–1848).

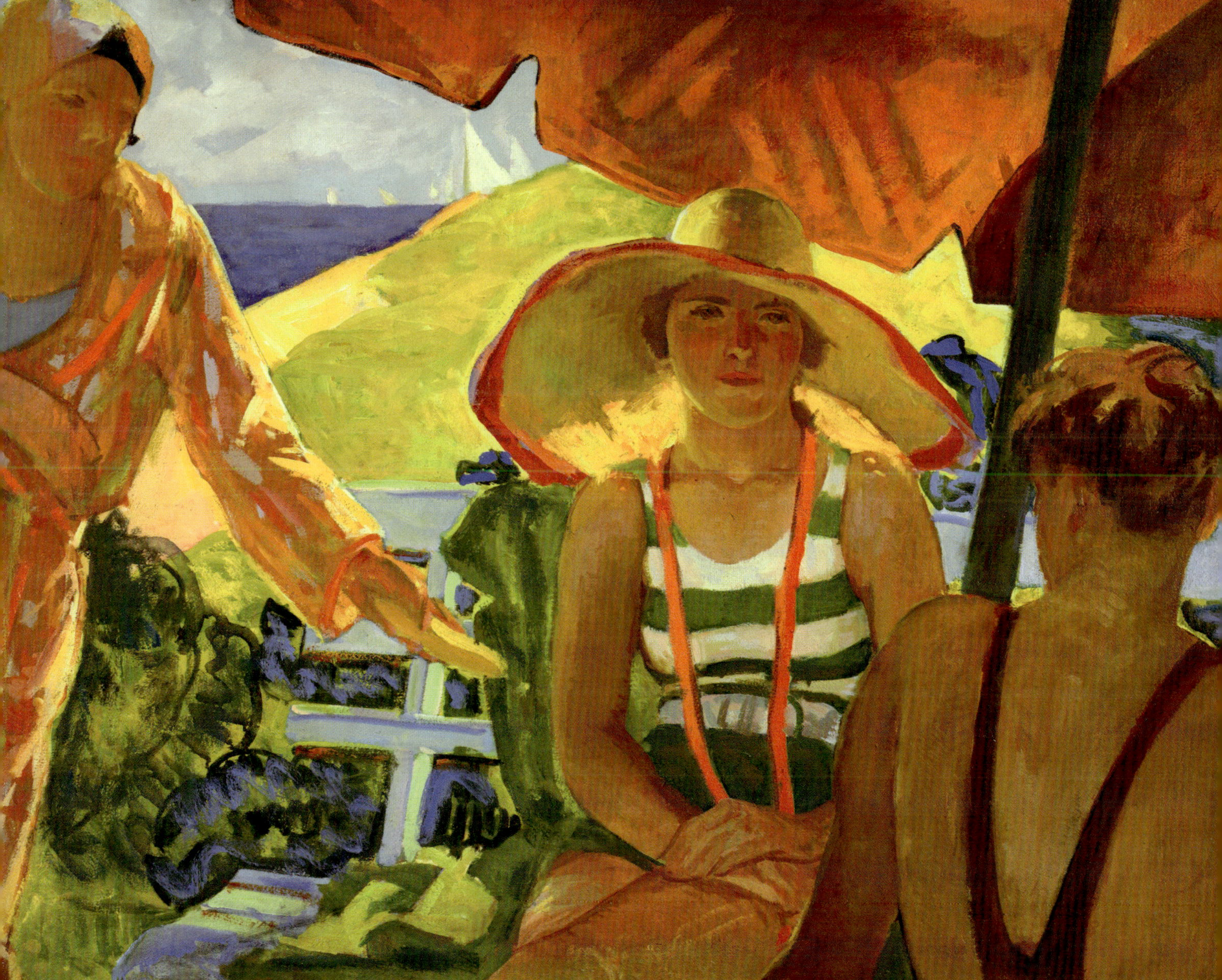

◄

Friedrich von Amerling
Girl in Yellow Hat
1835
oil on canvas, 58 x 47 cm
Kunsthistorisches Museum, Vienna

▲

Beatrice Whitney Van Ness
Summer Sunlight
c. 1936
oil on canvas, 99 x 124.5 cm
National Museum of Women in the Arts, Washington D.C.

ROTHKO: COLOUR FIELD PAINTING

During a trip to Italy, Rothko had the opportunity to see the frescoes at Pompeii and those of Fra Angelico, and he was impressed by the way the light was distributed in them. He studied and adopted the technique, in use since antiquity, of applying colour in successive homogeneous layers in order to control its effects, sometimes denser and more opaque, sometimes liquid and transparent. He liked large-format, unframed canvases that give the viewer the impression of being submerged in the coloured space. The painter considered colours a universal language, like music, and he reflected his moods in them.

The result was a new way of painting that came to be called Colour Field. Rothko's paintings consist of coloured rectangles and squares with hazy outlines. He abandoned any connection with reality once and for all and, for titles, often simply used numerical sequences.

In the last years of his life, suffering from recurrent bouts of depression, Rothko tended towards dark, gloomy tones that create an atmosphere of tragic drama. His last major work, a kind of spiritual testament, is the group of large paintings for the De Menil Chapel (now known as the Rothko Chapel) in Houston. Rothko took his own life in New York on 25 February 1970.

Mark Rothko
Untitled
1968
oil on paper mounted on masonite
private collection

GENTLEMEN PREFER BLONDES

Andy Warhol
Marilyn
1964
acrylic on canvas, 101.6 x 101.6 cm

Dante Gabriel Rossetti
Monna Vanna
1866
oil on canvas, 88.9 x 86.4 cm
Tate, London

The movie *Gentlemen Prefer Blondes*, directed by Howard Hawks (1953), established Marilyn Monroe's reputation as a sex symbol, but also cemented the connection between 'dumb' and 'blonde'. Marilyn is the perfect symbol of stereotyped mythologizing and the dramatic dissolution of celebrity. Warhol has immortalized her in the style of a movie poster, in which actresses must always appear as seductive examples of feminine wile. Emptied of their inner nature, Andy Warhol's figures are offered up as models for a globalized society, where all is levelled and uniform.

The forced use of colours blatantly accentuates Marilyn Monroe's feminine features: the perfect platinum blonde curls, the heavy make-up, the prominent eyebrows, the mole on her left cheek, the half-closed, full lips, the sensual, seductive expression and the enigmatic smile all add up to something like a 20th-century *Mona Lisa*. As in Byzantine icons, the neutral background places the image outside of real time and space. Marilyn Monroe, who committed suicide at the age of thirty-six, became a universal symbol of beauty and seduction, a new Venus and at the same time a tragic heroine whose fairytale existence was the short-lived dream of a girl who rose from nothing to become a star.

The predilection for blondes is firmly entrenched in art, from the 15th-century Florentine painters' stylized profiles of young girls of good family to the full-figured young women of the Venetian Renaissance and the affluent Antwerp of Rubens. Golden-blonde hair exercised its irresistible fascination on the Pre-Raphaelites as well.

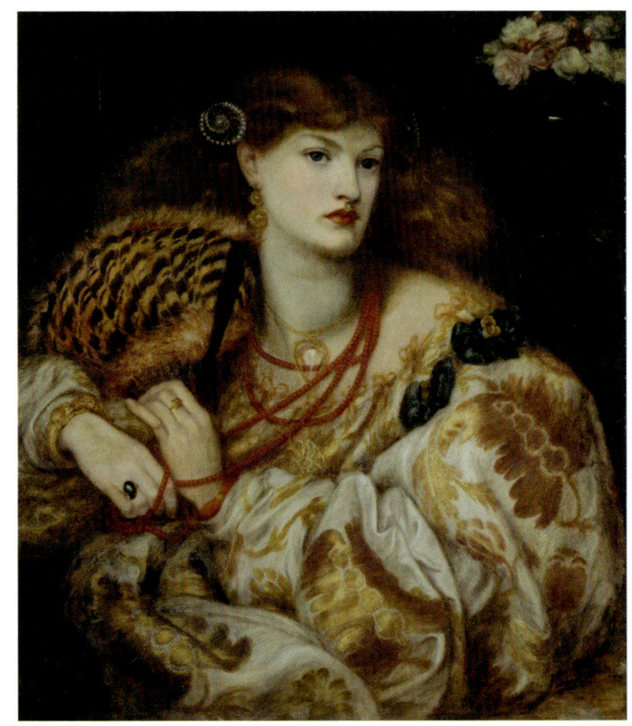

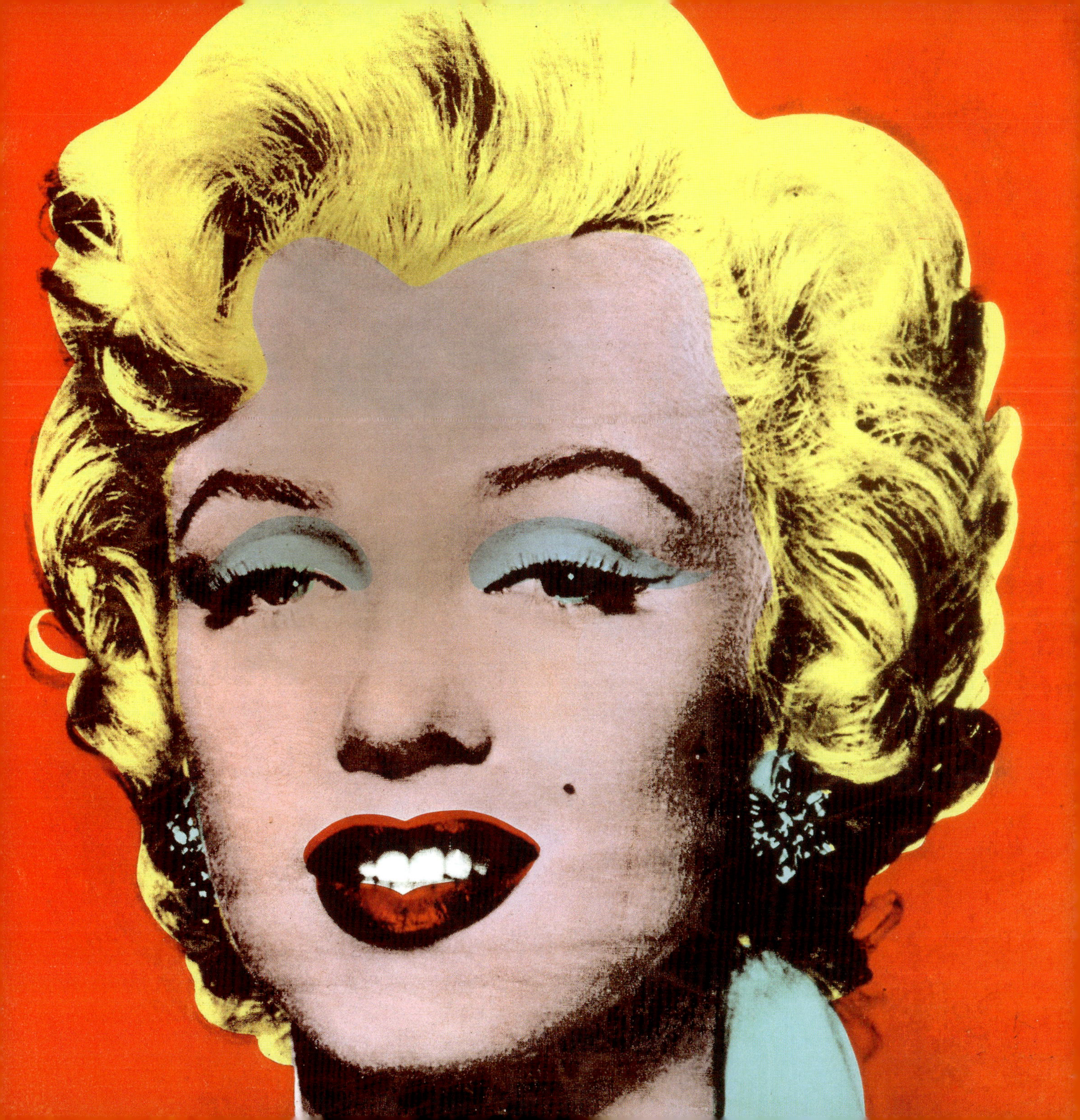

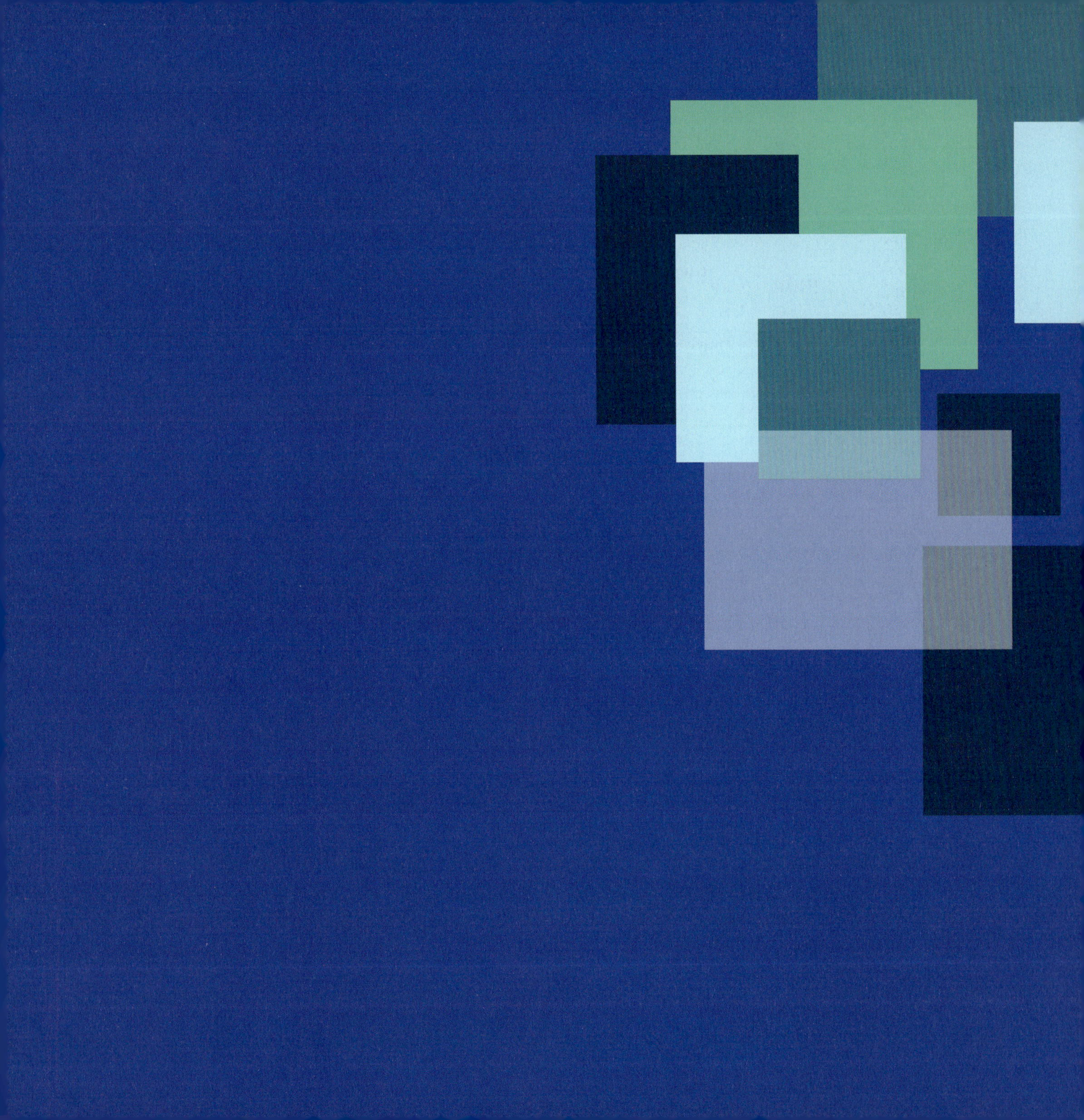

BLUE

INTRODUCTION

Owing to the refraction of the wavelength of light, blue is the colour of the infinite spaces of the sky and the sea, of unattainable horizons and unfathomable depths. The Italian for 'sky blue' – *celeste* – is also an adjective describing divine beings and heavenly settings. The great German poet Friedrich Hölderlin (*Hyperion*, 1793) incomparably described the sense of transport, spiritual elevation and aspiration to higher than human spaces and heights inherent in blue: 'Often lost in the wide blue, I look up into the ether and down into the sacred sea, and I feel as if a kindred spirit were opening its arms to me.'

Blue suggests peacefulness, serenity and calm, and perhaps for this reason, the colour is often used for the uniforms and vehicles of police and peacekeepers. Furthermore, blue has a political connotation related to the concept of stability and security. It is the colour of the United Nations and the European Community, and traditionally of conservative political parties, as opposed to the progressive red. But blue is not always synonymous with the institutional values of the right. The word 'blue' derives from the French *bleu* (and not from classical languages) and can take on ambiguous connotations. It is one of the three primary colours, the inescapable basis of human vision, and yet for many ancient civilizations blue seems to have been indefinable, barely distinguishable from green (as is the case with the Maya and the Aztecs) or black (as occurs in Sanskrit). The Latin term *caeruleus*, meaning 'sky blue', is a very pale, whitish tone. As its etymology explains, it is the colour of the wax (*cera*) that candles were made of. The Greek word *cyan*, still used in printers' jargon to name a stage of printing (the cyanotype, or blueprint), indicates an extreme unhealthy pallor – someone whose face and skin are bluish because of illness or oxygen deficiency is said to be cyanotic. In German, *blau sein* (to be blue) describes the altered appearance of someone who has had too much to drink.

It might seem strange that the same word is used for a range of shades from a tenuous, nearly white light blue to the deep, nearly black hue of the night. It was perhaps this ambiguity, along with the 'degenerate' excesses of the avant-garde, that disturbed Adolf Hitler, prompting him to exclaim, 'Whoever sees and paints a green sky and blue fields should be sterilized!' We must not forget, however, that the German dictator considered himself above all an artist, notwithstanding having twice failed the entrance exam for the Academy of Fine Arts in Vienna. The small, youthful landscapes that have come down to us do not indicate any creative talent but only a prosaic observation of natural and architectural reality, with the commonplace tones of picture postcards and very predictable, lifelike colours.

In art, and Christian painting in particular, blue is a very important colour: Jesus's cloak is often blue and that of the Virgin Mary almost always so. The colour of the vast sea becomes the 'lap' of Mary, protector and salvation of humanity. For this reason, the most expensive pigment – the blue of powdered lapis lazuli – was frequently used for the Virgin's cloak in medieval and Renaissance painting.

However, blue can also take on the opposite role. The sea, the infinite fountain of life, is also a place of the mystery and anxiety of the unknowable, of what is found below the surface – the monstrous Leviathan swims in its depths. Blue is tinged with the idea of a dark inhuman force: Deep Blue is the name of the IBM computer that challenged world champion Garry Kasparov to a memorable chess game in 1996. The machine-against-man tournament was fascinating: Kasparov eventually won, four to two. The origin of the word 'depression' derives from the dark vortex of the deep water – *depressus* means 'deep' in Latin. In everyday Italian, it is customary to speak of *una paura blu, una fame blu* to indicate the intensity of a sensation like fear or hunger. In English 'feeling blue' means to feel sad, and the nostalgia of the Afro-Americans gave rise to the musical genre of the 'blues'.

In other words, even though sober and calming, blue has a soul!

DIVINE BLUE

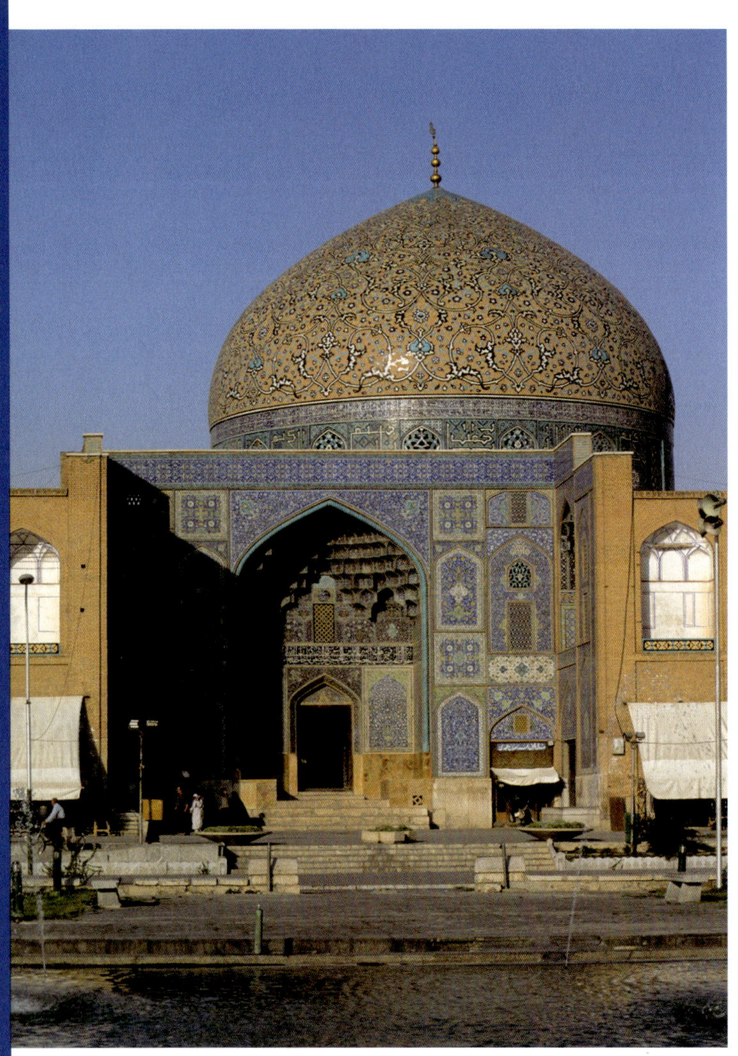

The Islamic religion considers creation to be a manifestation of the divine will, present in all things and knowable by each individual through faith and reason. Therefore, it is necessary to seek an understanding of the rules that govern existence and strive to comply with their logic. Every work of art and architecture must aim to respect and reproduce this invisible spiritual mechanism. Mohammed himself railed against the erection of architecture that did not evoke the presence of Allah among his worshippers. Sacred buildings should express an almost immaterial lightness, conveying the idea of limitless space all the way to the dissolution of the walls, so as to reveal divine closeness in human creations. The absence of animal and human images is offset by extraordinary ornamental displays based on calligraphic verses from the Koran or repeated plant forms. The filtered light and the colours used play a specific symbolic role in bringing worshippers closer to the spiritual dimension.

Islam's characteristic colour is green, but blue has considerable importance as well, representing the sky, seat of the unknown and the divine, and recalling the ancient Bedouin spirituality that grew up amid the desert's torrid heat and the calm starry night. Precious ceramics of a particularly intense blue cover the walls of the Friday Mosque, built between the 11th and the 15th centuries in Isfahan, Iran, during the rule of the Seljuk dynasty. The sight upon arriving in front of the four iwans (porticoed areas that give access to the main building) is arrestingly beautiful. Ceramic plant decorations accentuate the blue and gold, symbolizing the unity of the religious edifice and the divine will that inspired its construction.

The Sultanahmet Camii, or Blue Mosque, built in the 17th century at the behest of Sultan Ahmet I, is one of the most beautiful and striking in Istanbul. Flanked by six minarets, the central space is covered by an enormous dome supported by a series of lateral half-domes, enlivened with windows of coloured glass that create a striking play of light. Inside, walls, columns and arches are covered in majolica (tin-glazed earthenware) painted with floral motifs in which blue tones predominate.

▸

The Blue Mosque
17th century
Istanbul, Turkey

◂

The Friday Mosque
11th-15th century
Isfahan, Iran

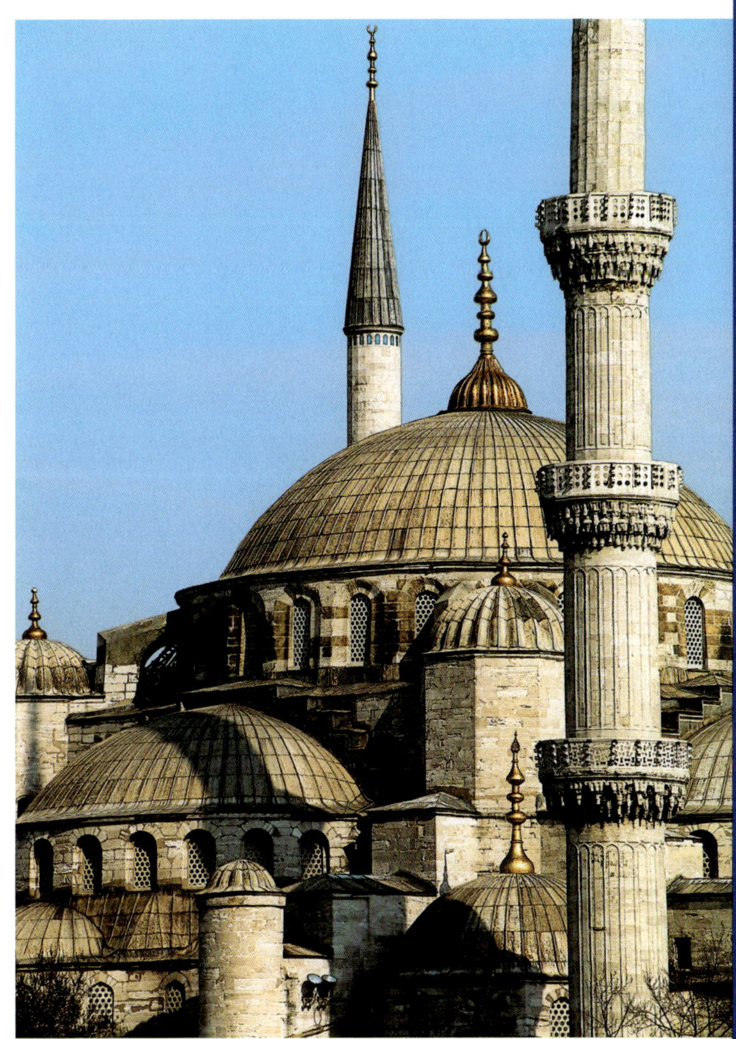

STAINED GLASS

Already used in the Romanesque churches of Central Europe, polychrome glass assumed a decisive role in Gothic architecture – that of the constant glorification of 'light', understood as the 'image' of the divine in the human.

In Chartres Cathedral, the colour effects created by the light are enhanced by 176 medieval stained-glass windows, almost all of which remain intact today. The windows at Chartres present two special qualities: they gleam with the same intensity at all hours of the day; and despite a surprisingly varied range of colours, the most striking colour is without doubt the blue. This blue is obtained by colouring the glass paste with cobalt oxide. An outstanding example is the Romanesque window known as *Notre-Dame-de-la-Belle-Verrière*, depicting the Virgin and the infant Christ, in the south ambulatory.

The procedure for making stained-glass windows is described by the German writer Theophilus in the second book of his *Schedula diversarum artium* (12th century), a collection of technical recipes.

The process is undertaken in several stages. First comes the design, which progresses from a simple planning sketch to a full-scale drawing executed with a lead point or a tin point on a wooden panel covered in gesso or chalk. (Over the years, the impractical panel was replaced successively by easier-to-handle materials like cloth, parchment and finally paper.) On this preparatory cartoon are placed pieces of glass of various colours – obtained by adding earth or metal oxides to the incandescent glass paste – to be cut into the desired shapes with red-hot iron tools. The pieces are generally arranged and fastened over a slab of supporting glass in a frame that is then raised onto an easel.

At this point, details like facial features and drapery are painted on the glass in grisaille, or else using an additive colour (green, brown or black) obtained by kneading glass powder and iron oxide into hide glue. When the painting is finished, the glass is subjected to a second firing on an iron panel covered with quicklime and ash. It must be allowed to cool extremely slowly to prevent the crystallization of the silicates in the mixture, so as to avoid a noticeable reduction in the transparency of the glass, which makes it opaque and liable to break or crack. In the last step, the individual pieces are joined together by being inserted into double-channelled lead strips, called cames, that have been soldered together with tin to form a large irregular lattice making up the structure of the stained-glass window. These are then inserted into an iron armature that is finally placed in the window opening.

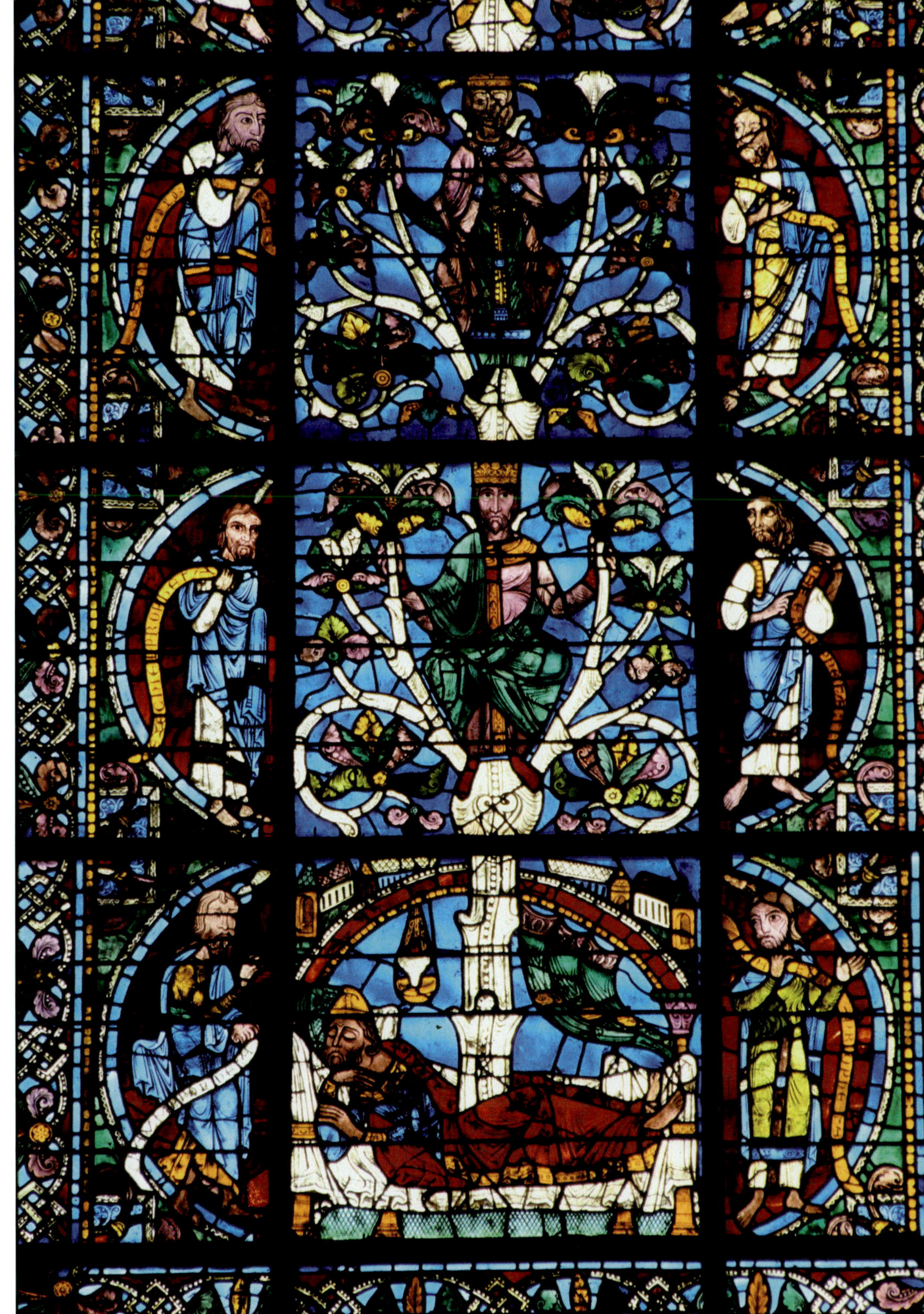

The Tree of Jesse (detail)
1150
stained glass
Chartres Cathedral

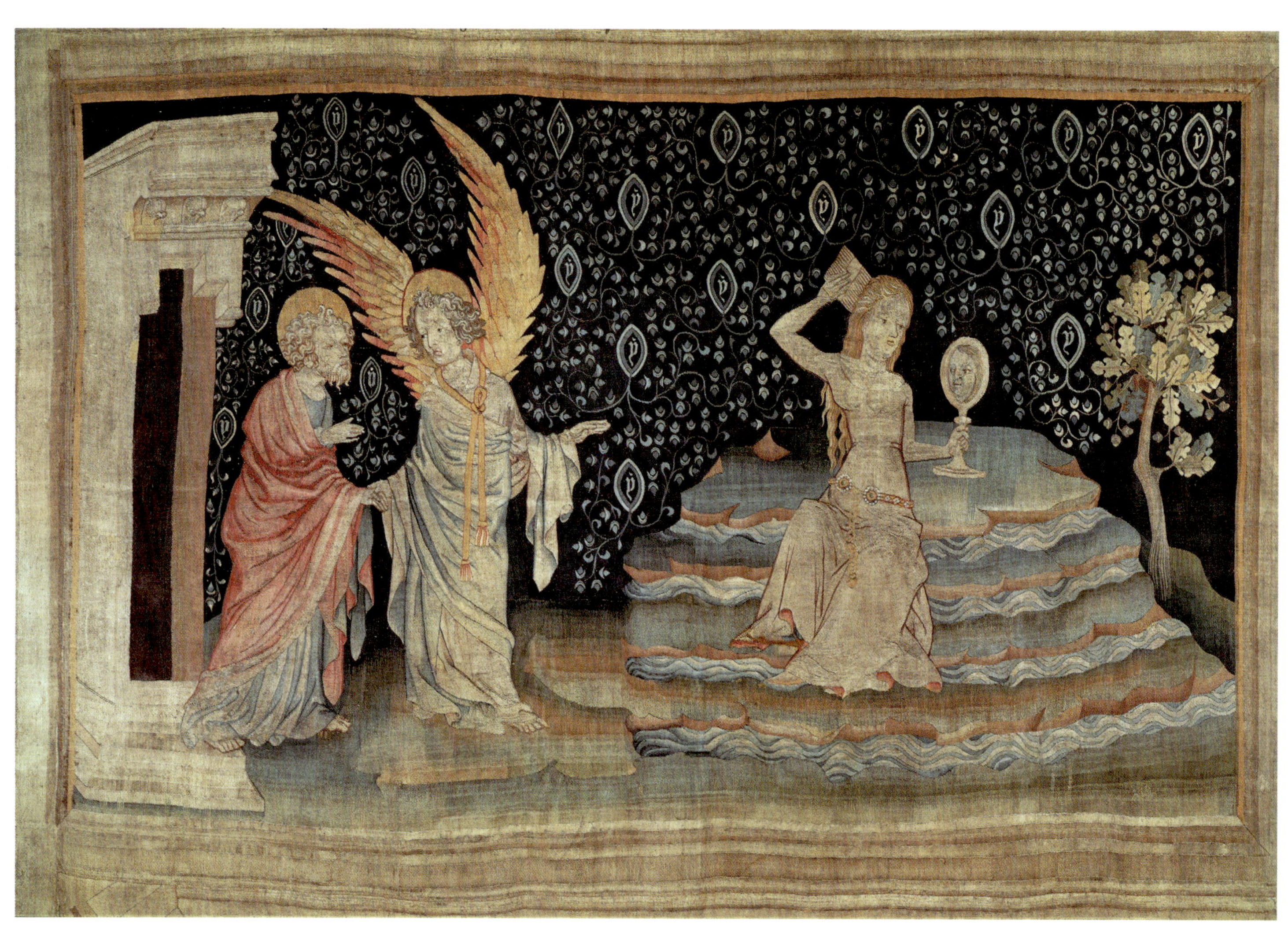

BLUE WOAD: THE TAPESTRIES OF THE APOCALYPSE

The Tapestries of the Apocalypse, executed between 1373 and 1382, are supreme masterpieces of medieval weaving. Rather than individual hangings, one must speak of a cycle, since together they extend to some 150 metres. Today 70 scenes remain – about two-thirds of the original quantity (98 or perhaps 105) – extending to 107 linear metres. The tapestries' excellent state of conservation, despite some mishaps, is due to the choice of colours for the costly, durable fabric. The blue, in particular, was obtained by steeping in the leaves of the woad plant (*Isatis tinctoria*), widespread in many areas of Europe, especially in the Languedoc, the Maritime Alps, and Thuringia. It produces a blue very similar to indigo.

Louis I, Duke of Anjou, the youngest son of the King of France John the Good, commissioned the painter and miniaturist Jan Boudolf, known as Hennequin de Bruges, to produce the cartoons (preparatory drawings at a scale of 1:1) for the weavings. Hennequin reworked, adapted and expanded the scenes of the Apocalypse treated in 12th-century illuminated manuscripts with a Gothic imagination full of invention, *drôleries*, splendours and discoveries. The Parisian tapestry weaver Nicolas Bataille worked on the colours for the layout, choosing to alternate blue and red for the background and reducing the tints of the threads to a dozen. This artistic and technical simplification made it possible to keep execution time to a minimum. The entire cycle was completed in about nine years, with dozens of individual hangings being undertaken simultaneously.

The Angers Apocalypse transforms the illuminated miniature into an overpoweringly grandiose form. Heavenly armies and infernal legions of almost life-size proportions fill our visual field. They create a vertical 'wall' from which the episodes seem to spring with an inescapable force. The Middle Ages – generous and chivalrous, romantic and terrible, imaginative and devout – find deeply fascinating expression in the tapestries of Angers.

Robert Poinçon and Jan Boudolf
The Great Whore that Sitteth upon Many Waters
Tapestry from the *Apocalypse of Angers cycle*
1373-1382
227 x 317 cm (approx.)
Musée de la Tapisserie de l'Apocalypse, Angers

BLUE ANGELS

Jean Fouquet is the greatest French painter of the 15th century. His paintings and extraordinary miniatures contain a fascinating mixture of accurately observed reality and aristocratic symbolism. One of his masterpieces is the diptych executed for Etienne Chevalier, treasurer of the King of France, today divided between museums in Berlin and Antwerp. The left panel (in Berlin) includes the portrait of the patron who commissioned the work, protected by his saint, Stephen. The right panel (in Antwerp) is an unusual image of the Madonna *lactans* (that is, nursing the infant Jesus), against a background densely populated by angels.

The essential nature of the figures' geometricized shapes (the Virgin's breast, a perfectly round sphere; the squared head of the Christ Child) reveal contact with Italian humanism, in particular Piero della Francesca, while the meticulous rendering of the gems on the throne and the crown adhere to the figurative culture of northern Europe. Mary's oval face, as smooth as if it were carved in ivory, is defined by an intense direct light. Her eyebrows are barely suggested, and the forehead is high and plucked, according to 15th-century custom. The Madonna's face is recognizable as the idealized features of Agnès Sorel, the mistress of Charles VII. She died in 1450 and the Chevalier was the executor of her will. Perhaps the extreme pallor of Mary is a reference to the lady's premature death.

The background is made up of an unusually dense army of little nude angels of the day (red) and night (blue). According to another interpretation, blue represents purity, associated with the cherubim, and red the fire of passion, associated with the seraphim. A reading based on alchemy is also possible: the red seraphim would represent the element of fire; the cherubim, the blue of the air.

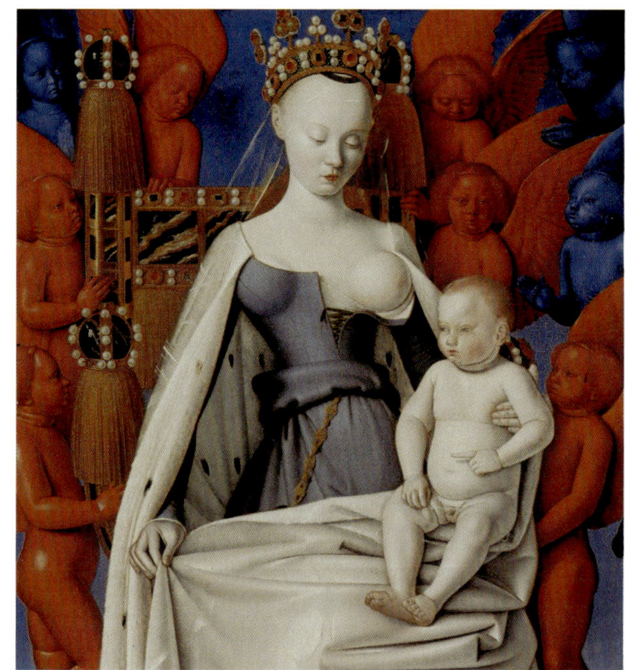

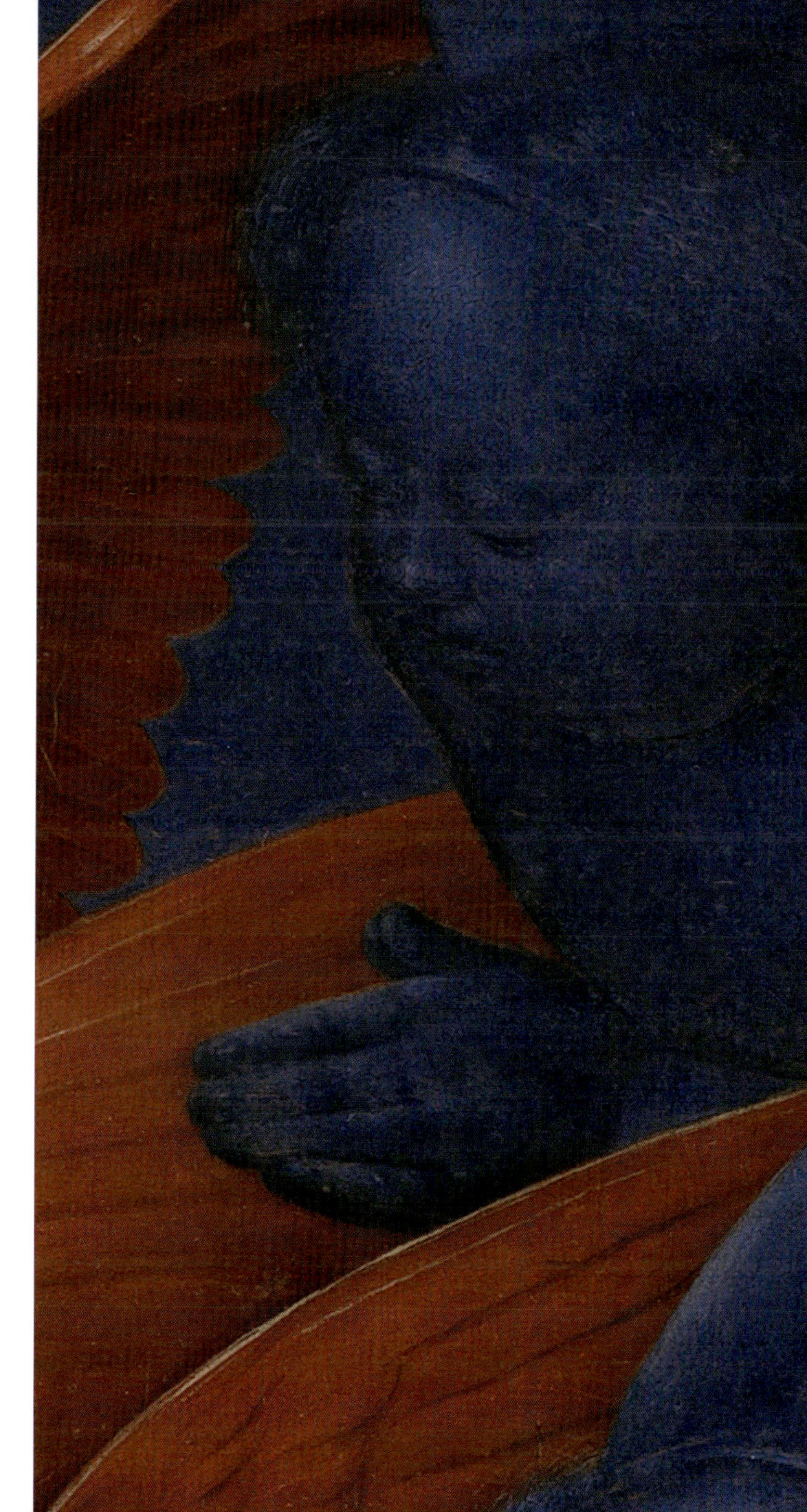

Jean Fouquet
Madonna and Child
with Seraphim and Cherubim
1451–1452
oil on panel, 94.5 x 85.5 cm
Koninklijk Museum voor Schone Kunsten,
Antwerp

DELLA ROBBIA TERRACOTTAS

Blue and white are the basic colours of the enchanting glazed terracottas produced by the Della Robbia workshop beginning in the mid-15th century. Luca della Robbia, the family's founder and leading figure, started out as a marble sculptor, but competition from Donatello spurred him to turn to a new medium. Combining his exquisite sensitivity with incomparable technical competence, Luca della Robbia invented an innovative method for colouring and enamelling the surface of terracotta sculptures. The contrast between the white of the figures and the intense but soft blue of the backgrounds is unmistakable. Highly successful between the 15th and early 16th centuries, these glazed terracottas found applications in a wide variety of fields: images for domestic devotion, heraldic arms, full relief sculptures, large relief altarpieces.

The initial steps in the production of Della Robbia's majolica are the same as for ordinary terracotta sculpture – hand-modelled or moulded, then fired at a temperature between 750 and 950 degrees. Meanwhile, the glaze is prepared. The mixture – a silica base with tin, ash, lead and metal oxides – is finely ground and mixed with water and egg white, then brushed onto the sculpture. A second firing melts and fixes the glass powder. The porous terracotta is now completely covered with a glossy layer of glaze.

Different colours are obtained by varying the mixture's chemical ingredient. The colours that resist the high heat of the firing are white, blue, green and yellow. The milk white of the figures is produced with tin oxide. The uniquely captivating blue is made with cobalt. Green, used for grassy meadows, leaves and plants, is obtained from copper oxide, while the yellow of some details (especially the fruit in ornamental garlands) is made with antimony oxide. Black, used for the figures' eyes, and the occasional brown are rare.

Luca della Robbia
Madonna of the Rose Garden
c. 1450–1455
glazed terracotta, 83 x 63 cm
Museo Nazionale del Bargello, Florence

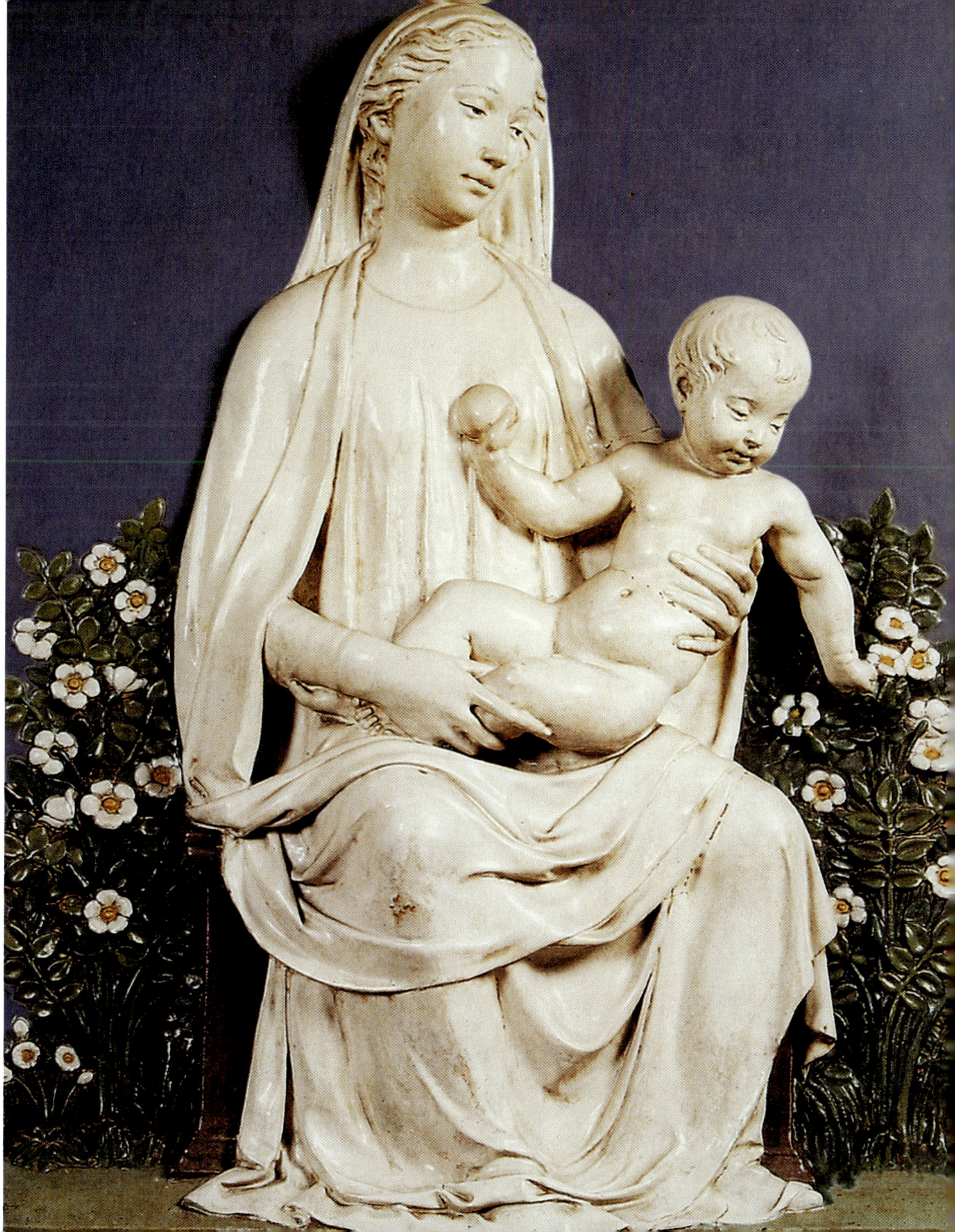

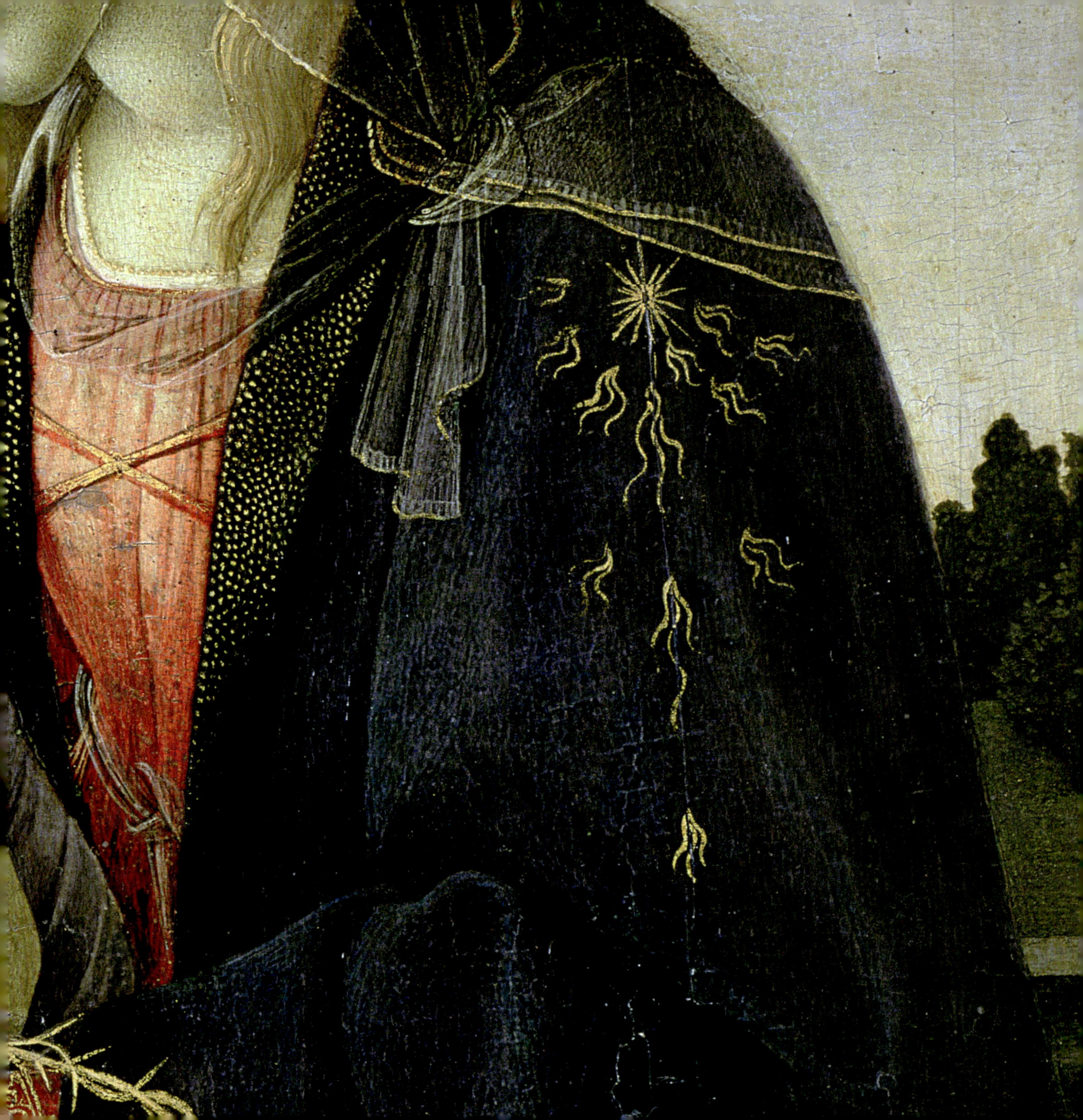

ULTRAMARINE BLUE

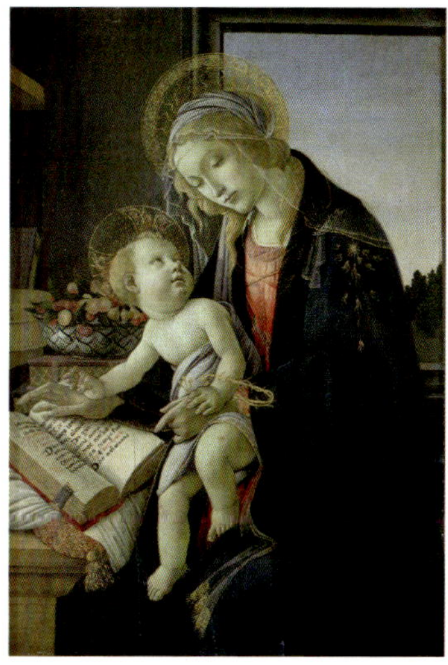

Sandro Botticelli
The Virgin Teaching the Infant Jesus to Read
1480-1481
tempera on panel, 58 x 39.6 cm
Museo Poldi Pezzoli, Milan

In the second edition of the *Lives of the Artists*, Vasari reports an episode at the Jesuit convent in Florence, where Perugino was executing some frescoes. The prior of the convent had requested the use of prestigious and costly ultramarine blue, and wanting to be sure of the proper use of this precious pigment, the friar personally oversaw its application by the painter. But he was unaware of Perugino's clever ruse. Every time the painter dipped his paintbrush in the pigment diluted in water, he secretly squeezed the bristles into a small basin, so the prior would think that much more ultramarine was being consumed than was actually being used in reality. Like any number of passages in Vasari, this anecdote seems to owe more to the author's inventive imagination than to facts. Nonetheless, the supposition upon which it is based – the prior's economic concerns – appears more than justified.

Ultramarine blue was the most expensive pigment of all. Obtained from lapis lazuli (a very hard, intensely blue stone from modern-day Iran and Afghanistan), its high cost was due not only to its distant origin but also to the difficulty of extracting and working it. Transforming lapis lazuli into pigment was a long, complicated process of eliminating the mineral's many impurities. This process, which was not perfected until the Middle Ages, mixed the ground lapis lazuli into melted wax, resins and oils before immersing it in a solution of diluted lye. Lapis lazuli enabled painters to obtain various intense bright blues that were particularly resistant to light. Its exorbitant cost, as well as its limited covering power, meant that ultramarine blue was applied only to small surfaces corresponding to the most important figures and iconographic motifs.

Occurring frequently in religious images in Italy from the late Middle Ages onward, ultramarine blue was the pre-eminent colour of Mary's robe – a highly symbolic choice because it associated the figure of the Virgin with the celestial realm and confirmed her central role in Christian iconography.

THE ALLURE OF BLUE EYES

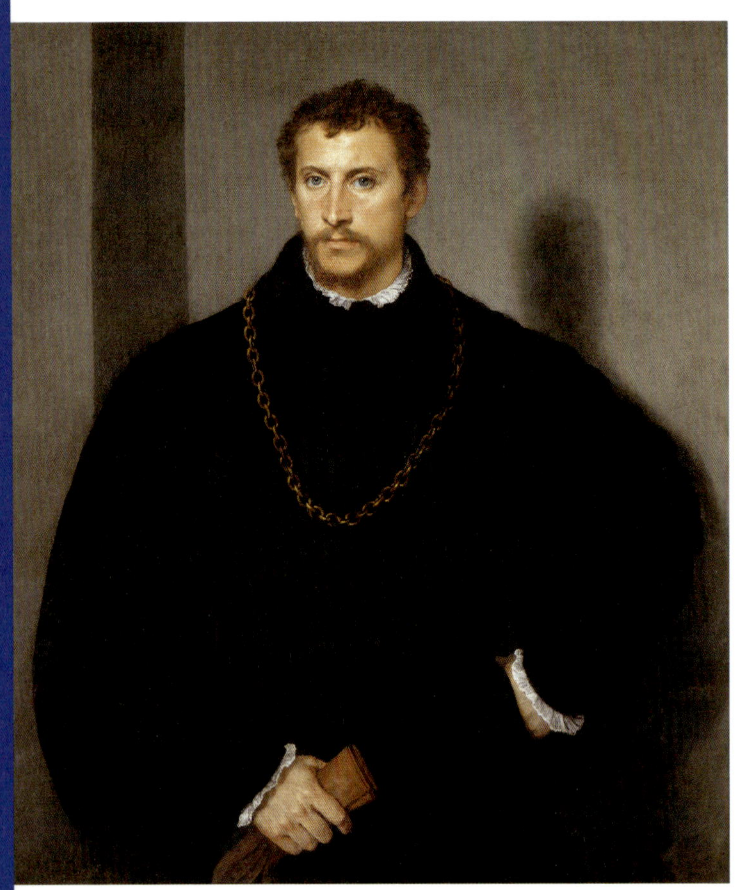

The Greek adjective *glaukos* means 'gleaming, silvery'. It usually refers to the sea and, according to Homer, is a property of Athena's eyes. It is not actually a colour but a particular brilliance, the vivid glint of intelligence. The ancient Greeks tended to mistrust people with light eyes, who usually came from the north and were therefore considered 'barbarian'. When taken into Latin, however, *glaucus* referred to an eye colour that varied from bluish to greenish grey.

Magnetic 'gleaming' eyes provide the title for one of Titian's most mysterious male portraits, whose sitter historians have long failed to identify. Because of the blue-grey eyes and reddish-blond highlights of the beard, the figure has traditionally been considered a 'young Englishman'. An attempt to identify him with the Duke of Norfolk proved impossible because of the sitter's age. The work is usually dated to the early 1540s. In comparison with the rich lighting of the early portraits, here Titian has used a reduced range of colours, remarkably effective in heightening the transparency and intensity of the entrancing young gentleman's eyes.

In Titian's painting, the blue eyes of the energetic young man convey a sense of decisiveness and lucid detachment. Especially in geographical areas where they are a rarity, blue eyes are normally associated with three feelings: purity, innocence, sincerity. These are the characteristics expressed in the portrait of *Doge Leonardo Loredan*, a masterpiece by Giovanni Bellini. Elected by surprise in 1501, at the age of sixty-five, Loredan had to face a series of wars and difficult situations in the twenty years of his dogeship. After his death, he was accused of embezzling, so that his heirs had to pay a hefty 2,700-ducat fine. Nevertheless, the refined range of blues and greys in Bellini's portrait make his image serene, calm and reassuring.

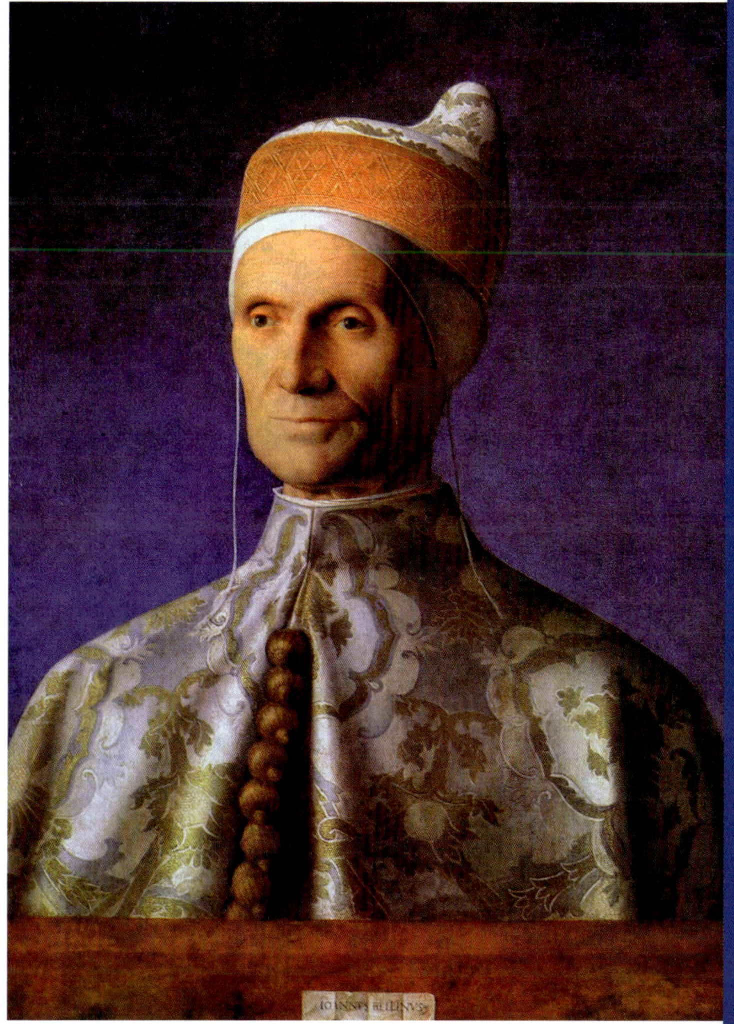

◂
Titian
Portrait of a Man ('The Englishman')
c. 1540–1545
oil on canvas, 111 x 96.8 cm
Galleria Palatina, Palazzo Pitti, Florence

▸
Giovanni Bellini
Doge Leonardo Loredan
1501-1502
oil on panel, 61.6 x 45.1 cm
National Gallery, London

Pieter Bruegel the Elder
Proverbs
1559
oil on panel, 117.5 x 163.5 cm
Staatliche Museen zu Berlin, Gemäldegalerie

BLUE CAPE

One of the most amusing and astonishing paintings of the Northern Renaissance was long known as *The Blue Cloak*, after the scene near the centre of the composition: a woman is arranging a blue cape on the shoulders of a man with an obtuse and absent look. According to a Flemish saying, 'putting a blue cape on one's husband's back' was synonymous with marital infidelity.

A telling work from the Antwerp painter's early period, partly inspired by the *Adages* of Erasmus of Rotterdam, the painting today in Berlin illustrates more than eighty Netherlandish proverbs and sayings, some still current, others now forgotten. Figures, episodes and paradoxical situations merge in the apparently normal surroundings of an animated village. Only in looking attentively does one discover how absurd the combinations are. Many provide examples of human stupidity and credulity, and yet the general atmosphere is permeated with a sense of disenchantment with the essentially inalterable reality of rustic life.

The culture of Bruegel, like that of his 'spiritual master' Bosch, is largely based on popular traditions, proverbs and sayings. Within the unified landscape of this extraordinary painting, Bruegel arranges illustrations of over eighty proverbs, mainly dealing with human simplemindedness and inspired by peasant life. He works on several registers, including moral and religious cautions. However, the prevalent attitude is that of amused and disillusioned participation. The vices, defects and touches of folly belong to everyday life, and the painter does not assume the role of critic.

Beyond the virtuoso composition of the Berlin painting, Bruegel offers an 'anthropological' image of vices, manias and timeless human situations. The 'blue cape' episode was also painted by Bruegel in a cycle of twelve Flemish proverbs on round supports with reddish backgrounds mounted in a single frame, today at the Mayer van den Bergh Museum in Antwerp.

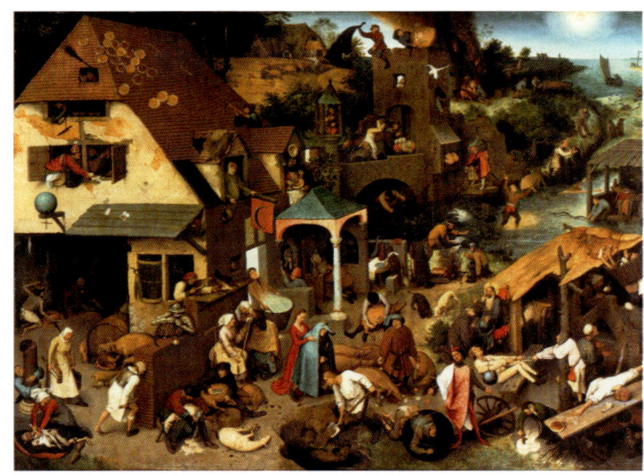

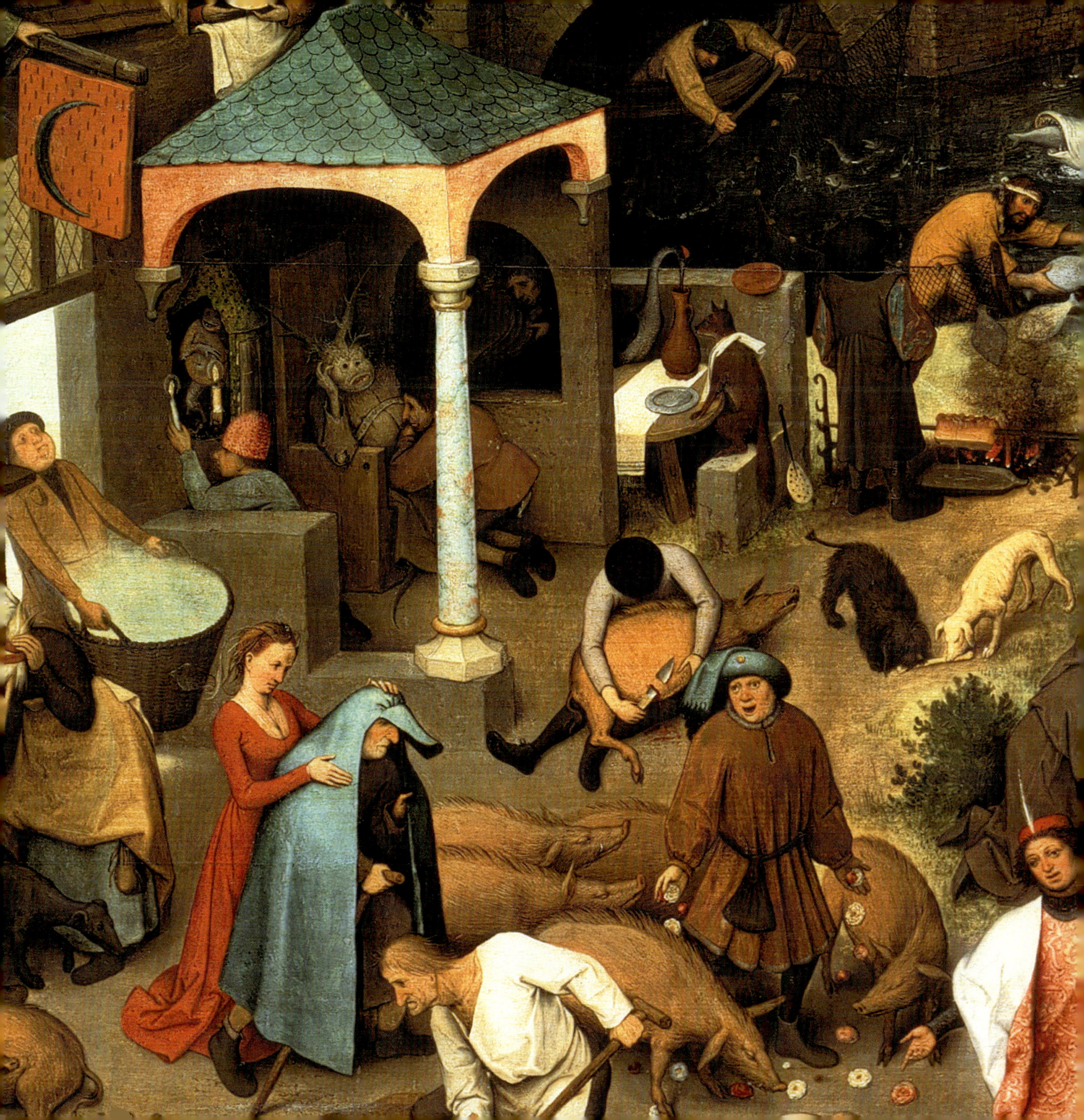

BLUE BLOOD

Diego Velázquez
Philip IV on Horseback
c. 1628-1634/35
oil on canvas, 301 x 314 cm
Museo Nacional del Prado, Madrid

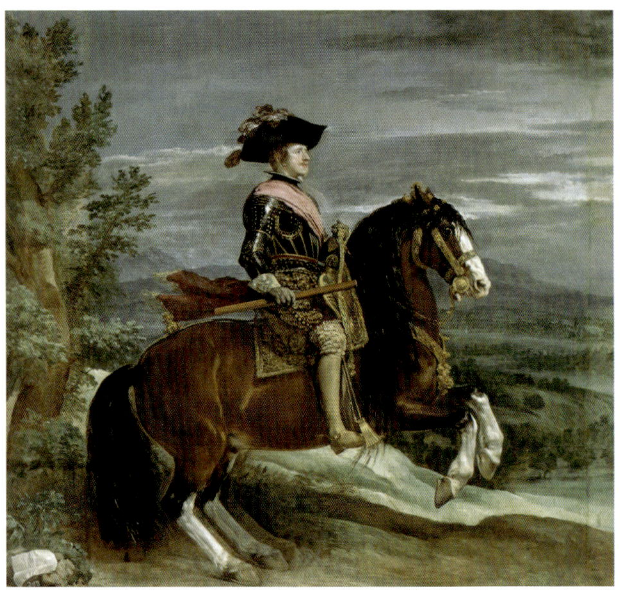

While it is often said that aristocrats have 'blue blood', blue is also used by convention in anatomy manuals to depict the veins of the circulatory system – red being reserved for the arteries.

The belief that nobility has a different colour of blood from the 'plebes' originated in Spain. After the Reconquista and the expulsion of the Moors from southern Spain, it was considered indispensable for the nobility to demonstrate that they had no Arab ancestors or kin – and this was done by exhibiting very light skin. Veins (bluish, and hence the notion of 'blue blood') showing through beneath pale skin was an unmistakable sign of distinction.

The severe black clothing worn by Spanish gentlemen from the mid-16th century onwards accentuated the delicate white skin of their faces and hands. The pinnacle of nobility was obviously the sovereign: Philip IV, with his blond hair and light complexion, offers a characteristic example of the aristocratic ideal. Even a hereditary imperfection like the displeasing protruding lower jaw was considered a sign of pure 'dynastic' blood and a trait of the Habsburgs' genealogical distinction, uniting the Spanish and Austrian branches of the family.

Later, in the late 19th century, when the benefits of exposure to the sun's rays were being cautiously revealed, it was characteristic of the well-to-do to protect themselves carefully from any sign of a suntan. A darker colouring was considered an indication of manual labour performed in the sun – an activity considered indecorous for a gentleman. With the 20th century (and the transformation of the great mass of the working class from outdoor peasants to indoor shop workers), the situation was reversed, and a suntan became a sign of good health and the leisure to spend one's holiday in the sun.

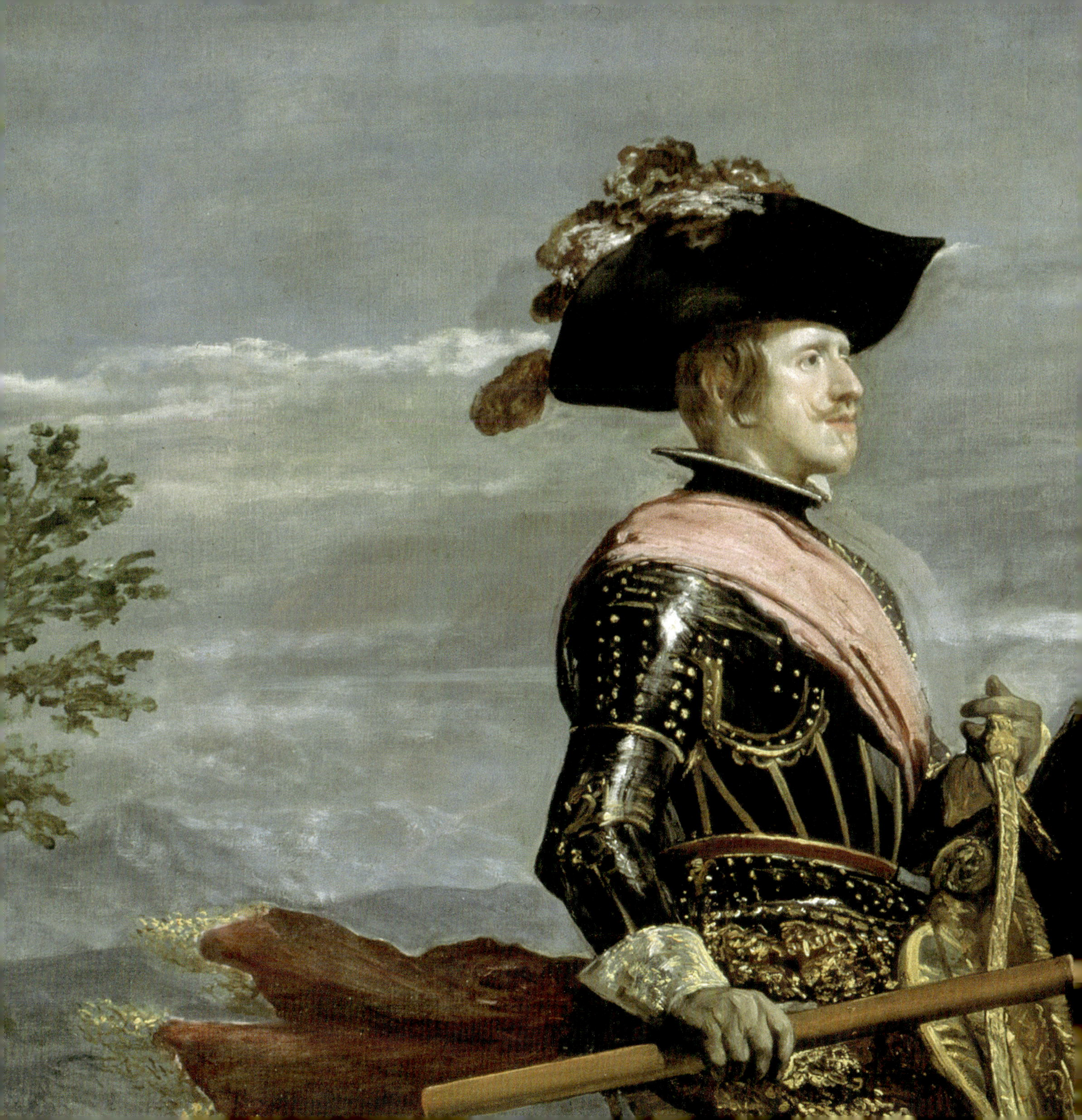

PRUSSIAN BLUE

Paul Cézanne
Bathers
c. 1890
oil on canvas, 60 x 82 cm
Musée d'Orsay, Paris

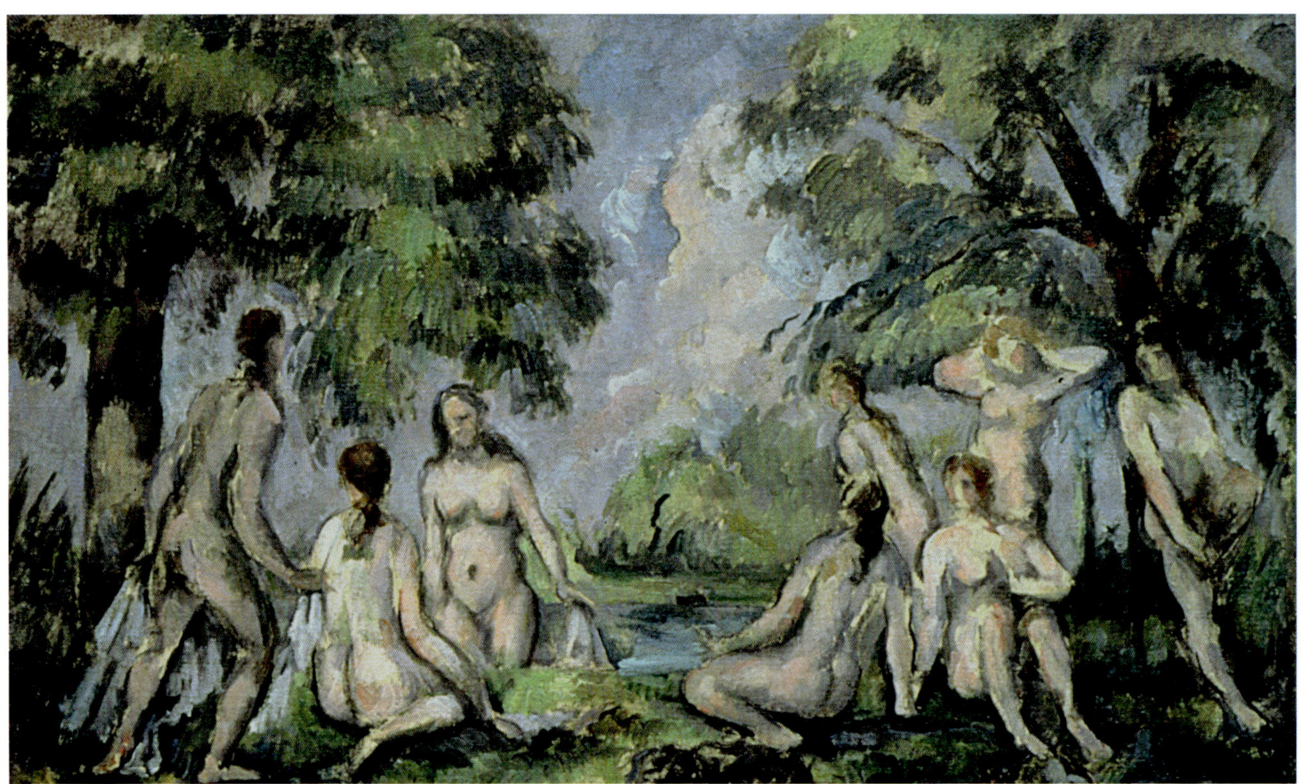

One of the most accurate and simplest chemical analyses that can be performed to help establish a painting's date and authorship is to check for the presence of Prussian blue. Among the oldest synthetic colours, it was first obtained by the Berlin chemist Johann Jacob Diesbach around 1706 by oxidizing ferrocyanide salts. Originally called Berlin Blue and used as a fabric dye, it was first used in painting by Pieter van der Werff, in a *Deposition of Christ* now in the picture gallery at the

Katsushika Hokusai
The Great Wave at Kanagawa
(from a Series of
Thirty-six Views of Mount Fuji)
c. 1831–1833
polychrome ink and colour on paper
25.7 x 37.9 cm
The Pushkin State Museum of Fine Arts, Moscow

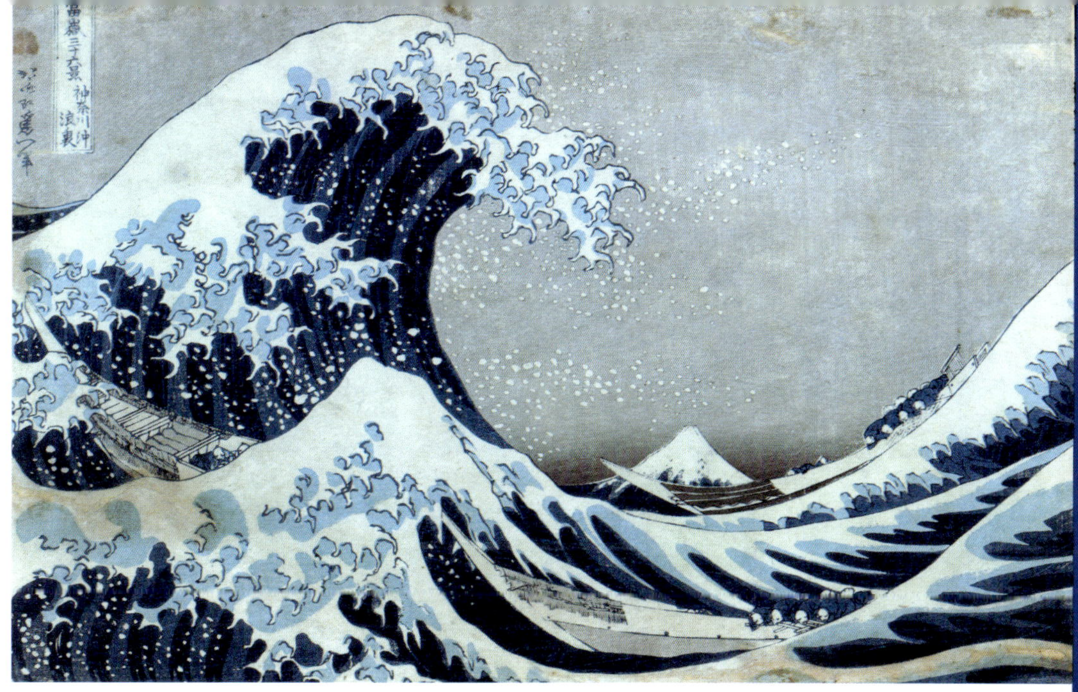

Sans Souci castle in Potsdam. Within a few years, the formula for Prussian blue was published and discussed by chemists, and the colour became available throughout Europe, retaining the name of its place of origin.

Stable, inexpensive and nontoxic (although poisonous Prussic acid is produced during its preparation), Prussian blue met with rapid success among artists. Soon after 1710, it was being used by Watteau, Lancret and Pater, especially for skies. During the 18th century, it was also widely adopted by Canaletto and Gainsborough. Tubes of Prussian blue were regularly included in the Impressionists' paintboxes, and the colour was given full and varied application by Cézanne, who frequently used it in skies and shadows. Prussian blue is the basic colour of the series of 'Bathers' that typifies the production from the last years of the painter's life.

Around 1820, Prussian blue reached Japan where it had great influence. In colour woodcuts from the Edo period, the printing block was coloured with vegetable pigments, among which blue is rare and unstable. The importation of chemical dyes enabled *ukiyo-e* artists to produce an extra-ordinary range of chromatic effects. A striking use of Prussian blue is Hokusai's famous print *The Great Wave at Kanagawa*, from his 'Thirty-six Views of Mount Fuji' series, published between 1831 and 1833.

BLUE SUIT

From jeans to dress suits to navy gala uniforms, blue is surely one of the most frequent colours in modern Western dress. Yet what is today one of the dominant colours of our wardrobes was for many centuries considered unsuitable to wear. Associated with the people of northern Europe, blue was a 'barbarian' colour to the Romans, synonymous – for whoever wore it – with a low social background. In ancient Rome, blue was also a colour of pain and death, an association that persisted in the Christian West into the early Middle Ages. Paradoxically, it is this very association with death and mourning that freed blue from the ostracism to which it had been subjected by the Greeks and Romans. Worn by the Virgin as a sign of mourning, from the 13th century onwards blue increased in popularity with the spread of the Marian cult. From the dark tones of the first images of the Virgin, artists began seeking lighter, more luminous shades by introducing new precious materials. Once an ill-regarded colour, blue became symbolic of Mary's royal and heavenly nature, and was adopted as the colour of the French monarchy.

From the early 16th century on, with geographical discoveries and new trade routes, commerce with the lands across the ocean opened new horizons to a colour that had now become the epitome of elegance and distinction. Among the products imported from the Americas and Asia was indigo, a more economical, stronger dyestuff than woad, and from it new intense shades of particularly durable blue were obtained. In the 18th century, blue made its way into 'polite society', from the upper nobility to the middle class. If dark blue dominated the most fashionable wardrobes in the first half of the century, in the second half, light blues had their turn – a true novelty in both men's and women's clothing.

Painted in the 1770s, Gainsborough's famous portrait shows a young man with a promising future, dressed in blue from head to toe, in step with the latest trend. Today we might consider him a 'fashion victim', were it not for the fact that the suit is cut in the style of the previous century (a clear reference to the great portrait tradition of the 17th century, especially Van Dyck). Keenly current, however, was the rivalry between Gainsborough and Reynolds. *The Blue Boy* demolished once and for all Sir Joshua Reynolds' theory that blue was ill suited to the foreground, and should only be applied in the background.

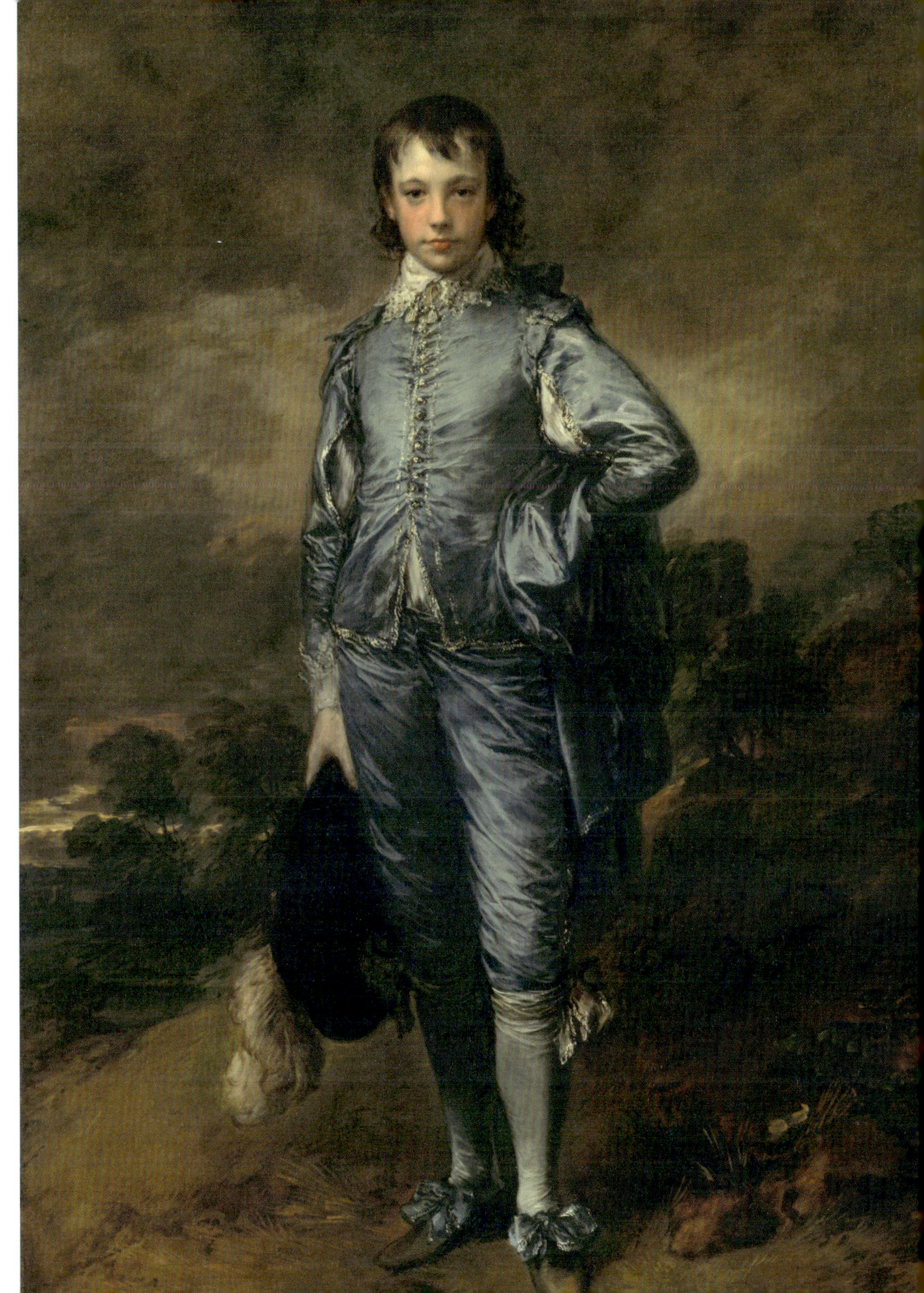

Thomas Gainsborough
The Blue Boy
c. 1770
oil on canvas, 177.8 x 112.1 cm
Huntington Library, San Marino, California

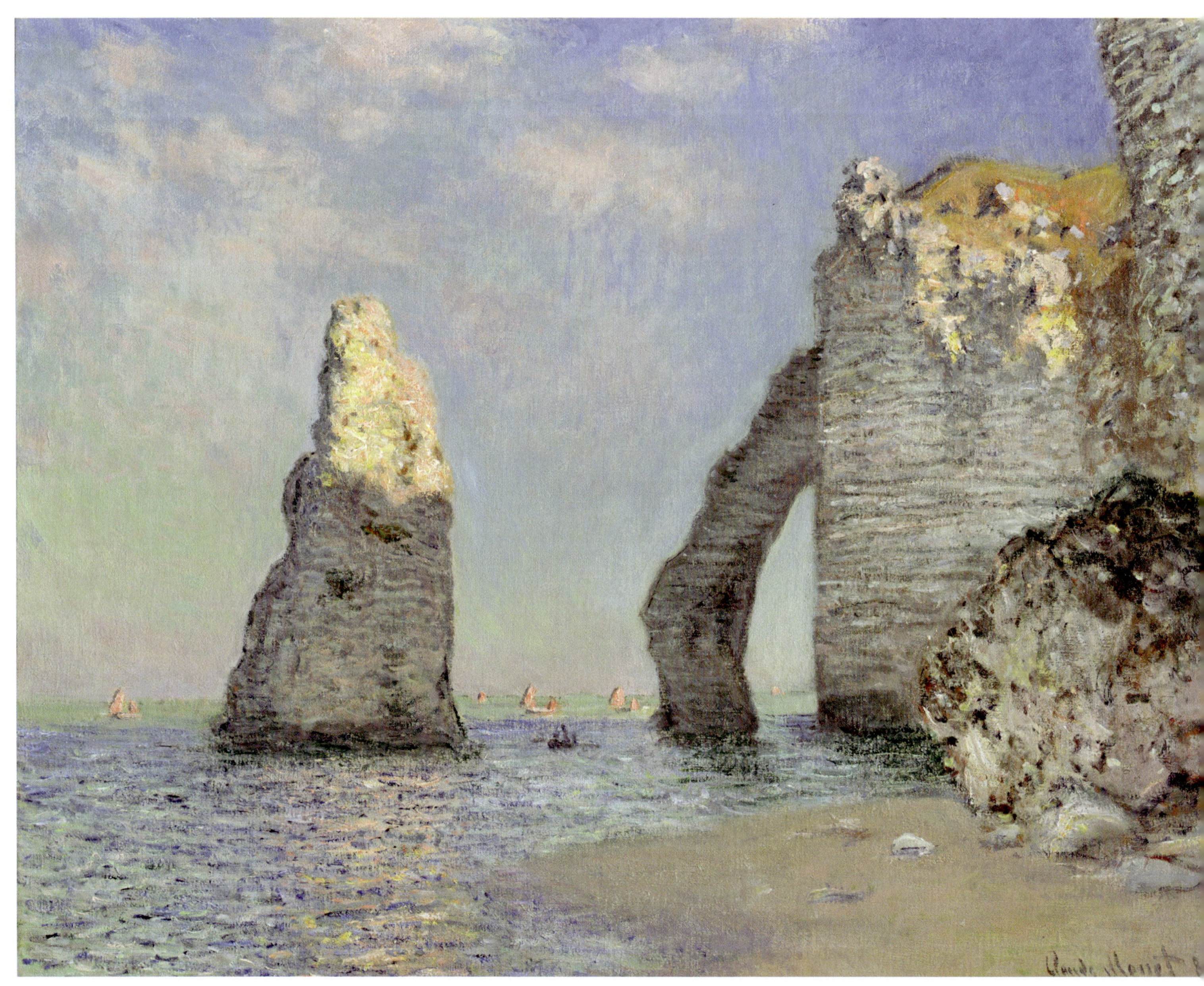

THE SEA

Blue and azure immediately make us think of the colour of the sea. In a famous poem of 1857, Baudelaire celebrates the sea: 'Free man, you will always cherish the sea! / The sea is your mirror.' And in this mirror are reflected the deep passions of the Impressionist painters. *Plein air* (outdoor) painting left the forest and discovered the coast, capturing everything from the cliffs of the North Sea to the glistening Mediterranean, not to mention the oceans subsequently explored by Gauguin. The quivering light, the foam of the crashing waves, the activity of the boats, the remote horizons and variations of light and colour make the sea the protagonist of much of their art. And for a typically urban movement like Impressionism, the coasts, the water and the light falling on the azure expanse provided a vital antidote to life in Paris.

An important role was played by Jongkind, an artist of Dutch origin who, in the mid-19th century, updated the Low Countries' grand tradition of marine painting – this first step would be developed by Monet in an extraordinary way. Having grown up in Normandy, Monet had spent his life observing the infinite variety of water, the luminosity of summer resorts and stormy seas beating against deserted shores. From October to December of 1885, Monet worked on the Normandy coast. His teachers Boudin, Jongkind and Gustave Courbet had previously painted the sheer cliff and port of Aval at Étretat. Monet now felt mature enough to measure himself against his predecessors, giving the same subject an Impressionist treatment.

Using unmixed colours with a strong contrast of white and blue, Monet captured the fleeting effects of the light on the rocks and the crash of the waves against the craggy shore. Guy de Maupassant has left us a precise image of Monet painting at Étretat: 'Planted before the subject, he waited for the sun or shadows and, with a few strokes, fixed on the canvas a ray of light from the cloud passing through the sky ... I saw him capture a beam of light on the white cliffs.'

Claude Monet
The Cliffs at Étretat
1885
oil on canvas, 64.9 x 81.1 cm
Sterling and Francine Clark Art Institute, Williamstown

PICASSO'S BLUE PERIOD

Throughout the stages of a remarkable and long career, Picasso pushed the horizons of 20th-century art towards ever-new goals. One of his first self-contained stylistic phases was his so-called Blue Period.

The son of a respected artist and painting teacher, Picasso was born in Málaga on 25 October 1881. In 1897, he enrolled at the Royal Academy in Madrid but did not attend it regularly, preferring to visit the Museo del Prado in order to study old art. After some travels as a teenager, in mid-June 1901, not yet twenty years old, Picasso made his second trip to Paris. A Catalan industrialist, Pere Mañach, offered him a monthly contract of 150 francs, found him a studio and had him exhibit sixty-four works, including drawings and oils, at the Ambroise Vollard gallery.

In October 1901, Picasso was joined in Paris by Jaume Sabartés, to whom he would remain attached all his life. It was the beginning of the Blue Period, which continued until 1904. The paintings from these years are characterized by a prevailing blue tonality, and in them Picasso depicts figures on the fringes of society – melancholy scenes of nonetheless great human intensity, sustained by impeccable drawing.

Despite the recognition and esteem of colleagues and some critics, his works did not find buyers. It was a time of dire poverty. He shared a simple room with Max Jacob, taking turns sleeping in the only available bed and struggling to scrape together just enough money to eat. When winter arrived, his circumstances were no better, and it is said that he burned a great many drawings to keep warm. He was forced to return to his parents' house in Barcelona, where he developed and explored the themes of his Blue Period.

Picasso returned to Paris in April 1904. He found lodgings in a hovel in Montmartre: the famous Bateau-Lavoir ('boat-washhouse'), as Max Jacob called it, a hotbed of creativity where Picasso studied and worked in close contact with other artists. He lived here until October 1909.

Picasso's friendship with the poets Max Jacob and Guillaume Apollinaire stimulated him to deepen the subject-matter of his paintings, bringing them closer to Symbolism. Little by little, the pained, distressed humanity and cold, dull tones of the Blue Period gave way to more fluid use of line and brighter, more colourful compositions. In early 1905, he entered what came to be called the Rose Period, which consisted of about 130 to 150 works, including some masterpieces. The Rose Period ended with the transition to his next phase, analytic Cubism.

Pablo Picasso
Life
1903
oil on canvas, 197 x 127 cm
Cleveland Museum of Art

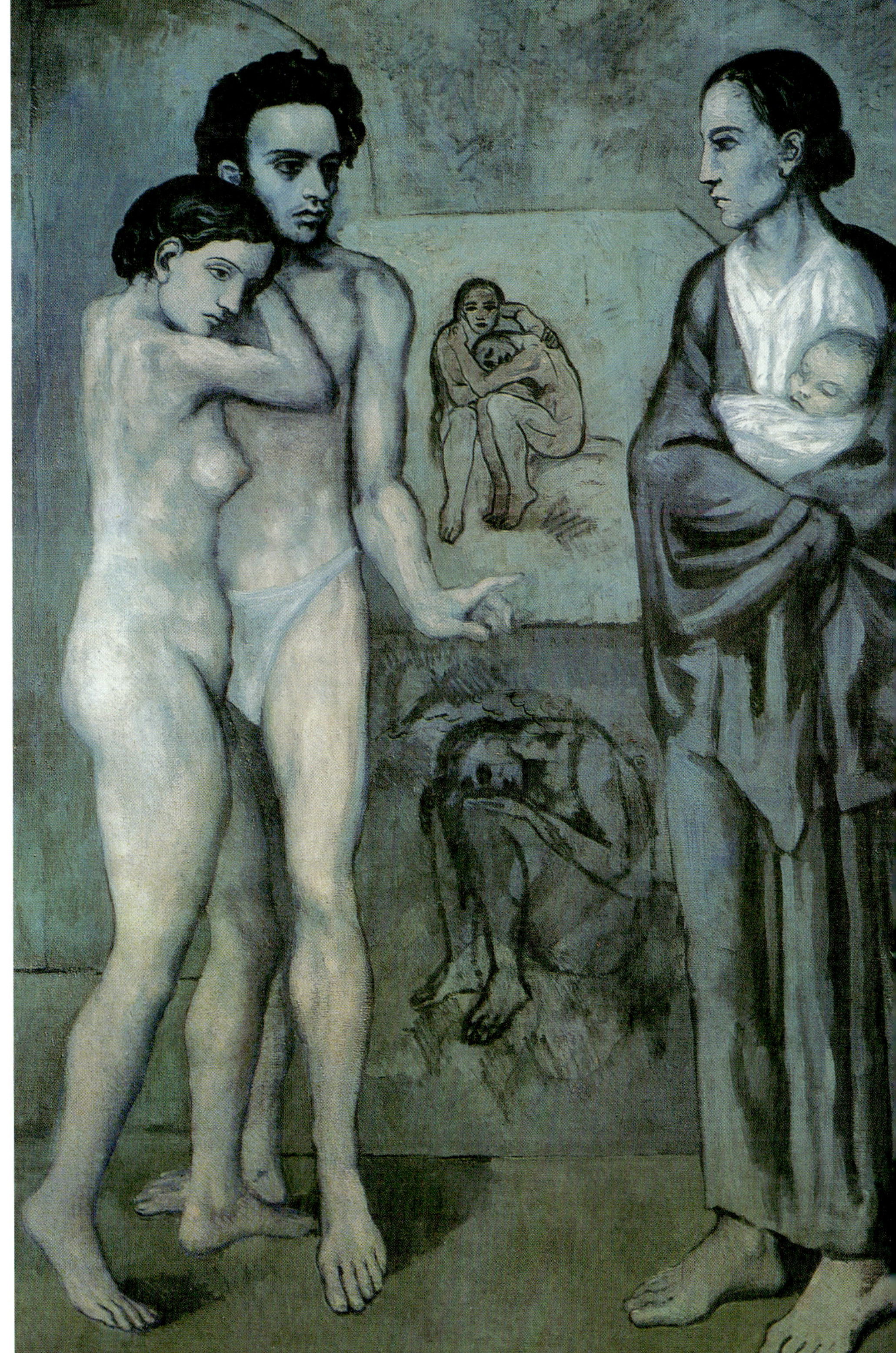

Wassily Kandinsky
The Blue Rider
1903
oil on canvas, 52.5 x 55 cm
Buhrle Collection, Zurich

DER BLAUE REITER

In 1911, Wassily Kandinsky, Franz Marc, August Macke and Gabriele Münter founded an artist group called *Der Blaue Reiter* (The Blue Rider). On 18 December of that year, they inaugurated their first exhibition at the Thannhauser Gallery in Munich; it remained on view until 1 January 1912 and then travelled to Cologne and Berlin. From 12 February until 2 April, the group held a second exhibition of 315 works on paper in the Munich bookshop and art gallery of Hans Goltz. Despite the exhibition's title Black White, many of the compositions were in colour. In May of the same year, the publisher Reinhard Piper brought out *Der Blaue Reiter Almanach*, a large-format volume with many colour illustrations and critical essays on contemporary painting and music. Its publication confirmed the birth of one of the most important German art movements of the early 20th century.

With the name Der Blaue Reiter, Marc and Kandinsky wanted to express poetically two themes close to their hearts. The first was the predominance of colour – especially blue – over drawing. The second element, the rider, is the symbol of the contemporary artist, who saw art as an ethical and spiritual duty, a mission to defend and spread the values of beauty and truth. Other front-rank personalities who worked more or less regularly with Kandinsky, Macke and Marc included Alexei von Jawlensky and Paul Klee. Some musicians also participated in their meetings, foremost among them Arnold Schoenberg, the main founder of dodecaphonic music, as well as a painter of some merit, which attests to the close connection between the two disciplines and the common quest for new expressive forms. It is not by chance that the Blaue Reiter painters often used the term 'vibration' – a reference to sound vibrations – to indicate the visual effect created by colours and to translate emotions into images. Kandinsky painted with increasing gestural and chromatic freedom, streaking and spotting the canvas. He accompanied this pictorial production with a flurry of theoretical writings and continuing relations with other artists and avant-garde groups.

The Blaue Reiter's goal was to demolish the doctrines and privileges of the authorities. Kandinsky and his friends claimed total freedom of expression for the individual through works rife with symbolic figures and intense, bright colours. The group's last exhibition was held in April 1914 at the Der Sturm Gallery in Berlin. The First World War put an end to their activity. Kandinsky returned to Russia, while Macke and Marc enlisted and went to the front. Macke died on 26 September 1914 in the Champagne region at the age of twenty-six. Marc was killed near Verdun on 4 March 1916.

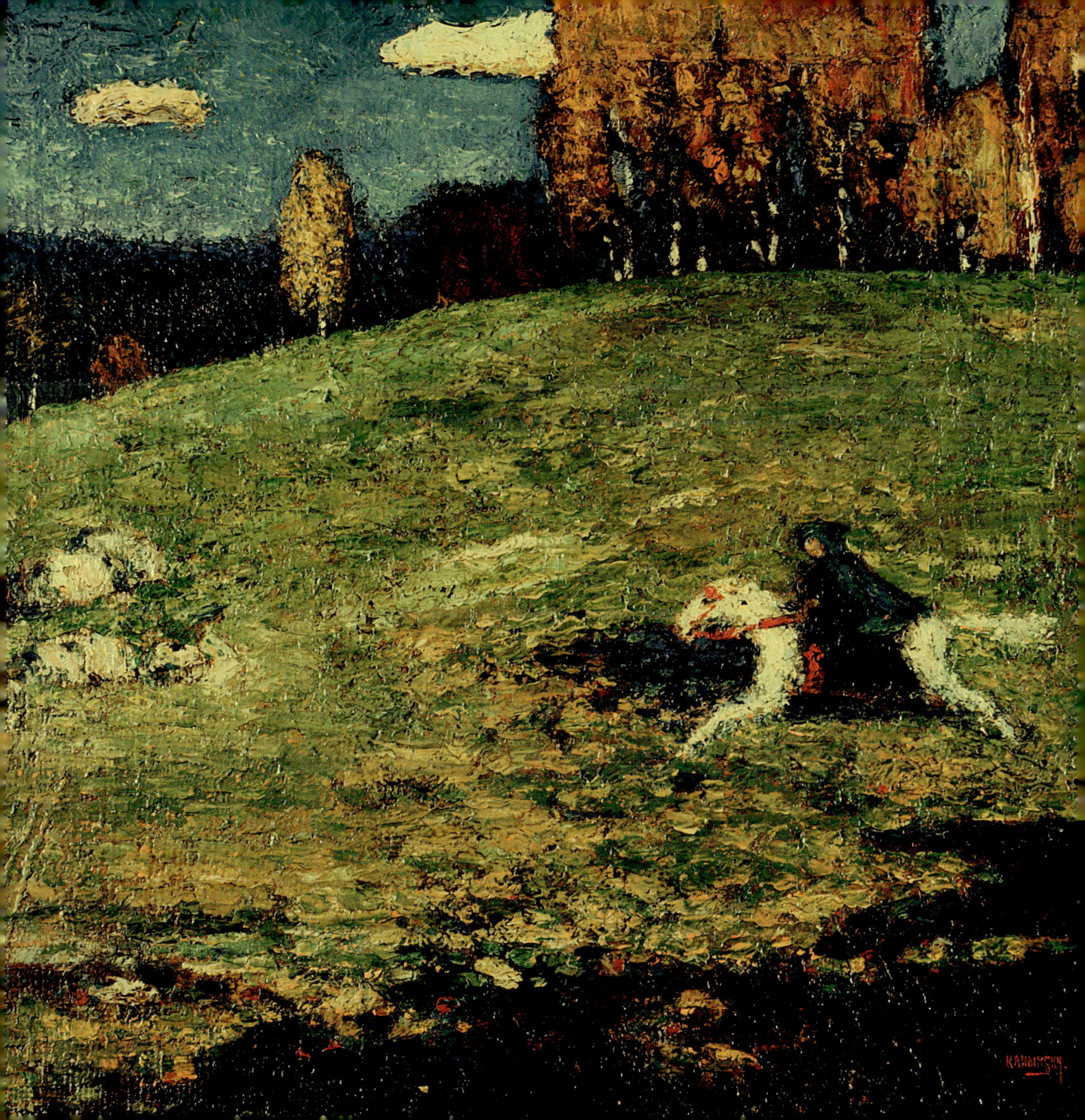
KANDINSKY

YVES KLEIN
PATENTED BLUE

Many painters have had an intense love of blue. One of them even patented a shade of blue: Yves Klein. Klein, who died prematurely of a heart attack, was one of the leading figures of Nouveau Réalisme, an expressive movement in France in the 1950s. Klein had been frustrated by the way colours change, how once they are laid down on the canvas they tend to lose their lustre. In 1955, after various attempts with various hues, he began to use Rhodopas, a synthetic resin particularly effective in fixing ultramarine blue, as a binder. This is the origin of the beautiful colour known as International Klein Blue (IKB). It remained the artist's exclusive property and was not produced commercially.

From the first experimental works in 1955, Klein systematically adopted blue for his paintings, which were subsequently interspersed with increasingly frequent performances and happenings. The colour was used, for example, in the 'Sponges' series, in which blue-soaked sponges of various sizes and shapes were attached to a solid blue background. The insistence on a single colour is typical of the perseverance of Klein, who stated, 'The painter must constantly create a single, unique masterpiece: himself.'

One of the most significant uses of International Klein Blue is the 'Anthropométries', pioneering examples of 'body painting' first done in 1958. Klein covered the nude bodies of his models with his favourite colour and asked them to lie down on the canvas to leave an imprint, thus transforming them into 'living paintbrushes'. The result is reminiscent of palaeolithic cave paintings – prehistoric humans decorated their caves with hunting scenes and the simple impression of their hands on the rock walls. The female body (the models followed Klein's instructions) thus became a symbolic transfiguration of the strength and magical powers of the Earth Mother.

◀

Yves Klein

Untitled Blue Monochrome (IKB 46)

1955

dry pigment in synthetic resin
on fabric on wood
66 x 46 cm
private collection

▶

Yves Klein

Anthropometry: Princess Helena

1960

dry blue pigment in synthetic resin
on paper mounted on wood
198 x 128.2 cm
The Museum of Modern Art
New York

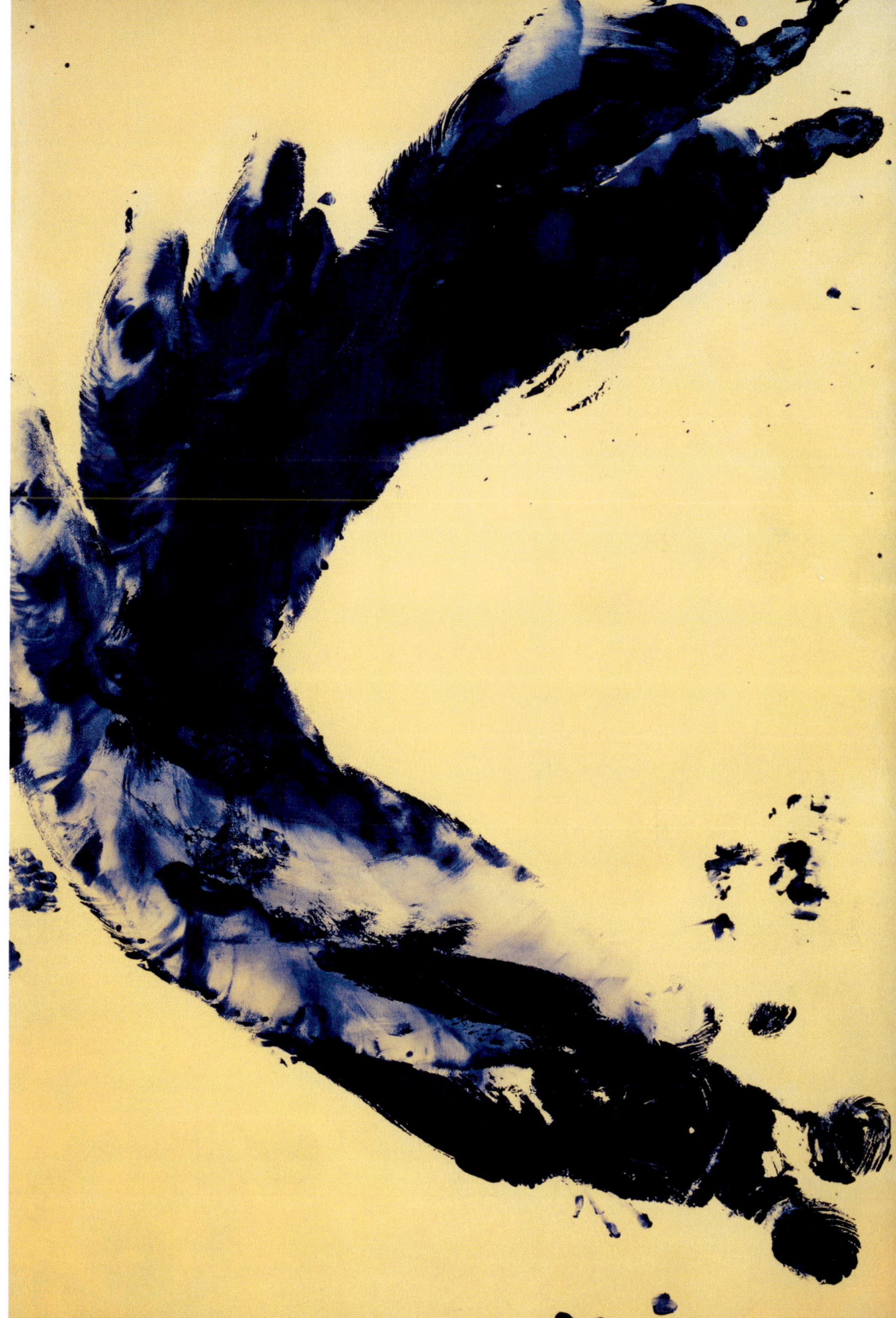

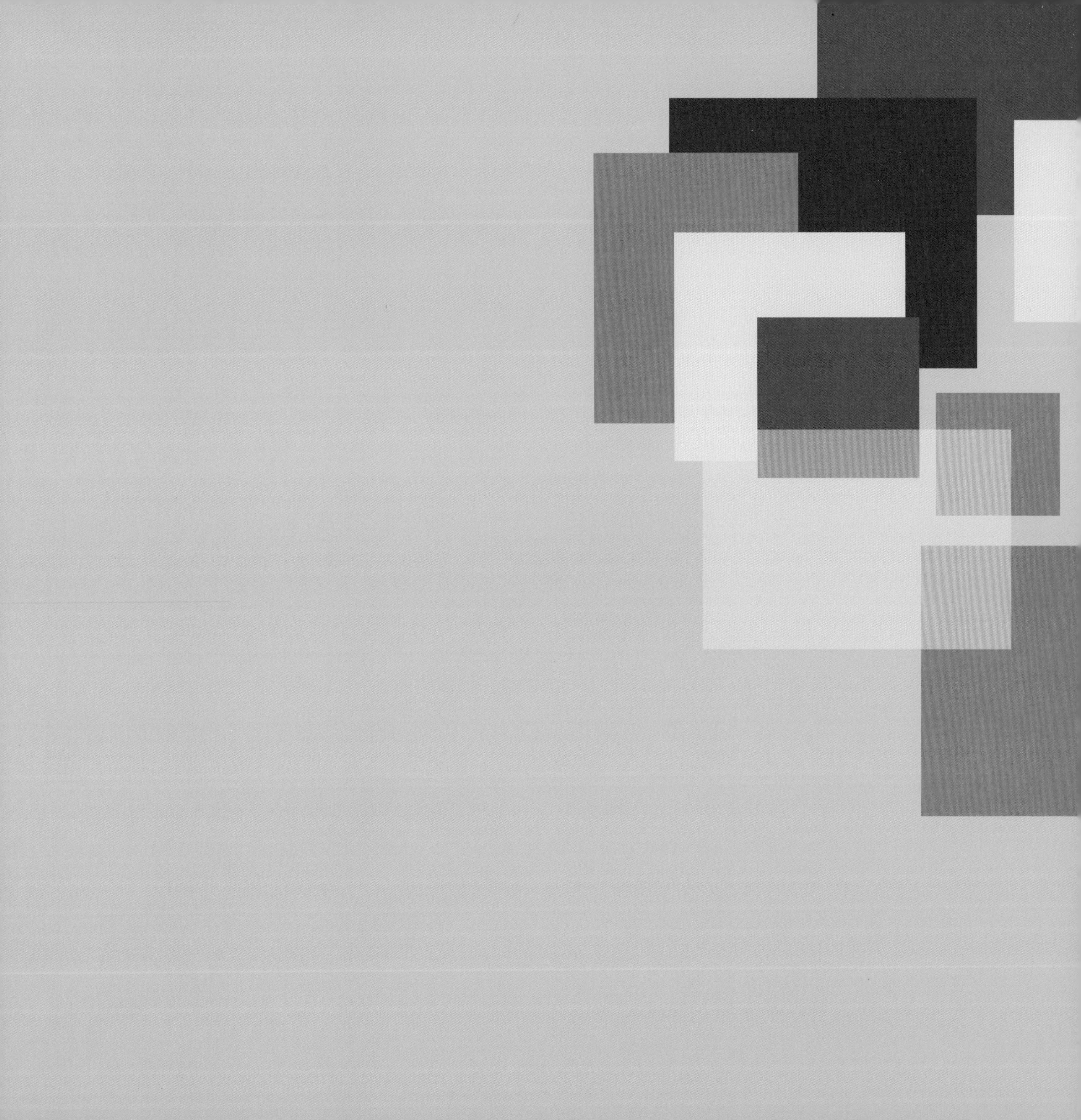

GREEN

INTRODUCTION

Voltaire concluded his novella *Candide* with an invitation to 'cultivate our garden'. Watteau inaugurated a new painting genre, the *fête galante* (garden party), a significant precedent for the Impressionists' 19th-century country outings. In *Emile*, Jean-Jacques Rousseau extols education through contact with nature. The English garden architect Lancelot Brown earned the nickname 'Capability' Brown due to his innovative attention to the 'opportunity' offered by the natural landscape. According to Goethe's *Theory of Colours*, green is restful, ideal for wallpapering an apartment, even the bedroom. These are all examples of the 'rediscovery' of green in the 18th century, beginning with the Enlightenment – a comeback initiated after a thousand years' neglect.

After being subsequently tarnished in the late 19th and 20th centuries – coinciding with positivism and industrial development – green has come back into style today as a symbol of ecology, health (continental European pharmacy signs and surgeons' gowns are both green), unpolluted nature, faith in the future, serenity, youth, the arrival of spring and for that matter financial prosperity – the expression 'greenback' is widely used to designate the American dollar. Christian iconography clothes the personification of Hope in green, one of the three Theological Virtues along with Faith (white) and Charity (red). Easter coincides with the reawakening of spring: Christ is resurrected as the fields again flourish with green grass and leaves. On road signs, green means 'All clear, go ahead!' In every possible shade, it is obviously one of the world's most prevalent colours, since the chlorophyll in plants absorbs the wavelength of all the colours except green. It is also venerated as the emblematic colour of Islam. The Muslim religion, which arose in an arid region, sees the image of coolness and paradisiacal bliss in the green of gardens and oases, and the green flag is a strong shared symbol. In Chinese tradition, a green dragon represents the yin – one of the two original principles that regulate nature's laws – and is carried in procession during boisterous annual festivals.

A positive and pleasing colour all in all. As Goethe wrote, 'All theory is grey / And green the golden tree of life.' But it was not always so, and green still bears the burden of unpleasant connotations. The classical languages and many present-day Asian languages have no word to distinguish blue (or generic 'dark') from green. The etymological roots in Western languages (the Latin *viridis*, the Old English *growan*) have a similar meaning: in either case, they indicate growth, development, and are thus linked with the natural cycle of growth and blossoming. Green is also the colour of unripe fruit, and widely diverse languages abound in expressions and sayings that associate green with immaturity and lack of experience.

Strictly from the point of view of figurative art, until the advent of industrial colours in tubes, green was the colour that deteriorated the most rapidly. Unless produced with costly materials like malachite, it tended to fade or turn brown in tempera painting and even disappear from frescoes. Oil paint fared a bit better, but when protective varnishes oxidize, it is always green that suffers the most.

The present praiseworthy status of green, understood as a healthy natural space as opposed to the insalubrious grey of the cities, is quite recent. Apart from the fascinating late humanistic parenthesis of the town Palladio designed for the fertile countryside of the Veneto, at least until the advent of English landscape architecture in the second half of the 18th century the countryside was viewed with detachment by city dwellers. Previously, Italian- and French-style gardens were the fashion, where trees, grass, hedges and flowers were considered architectural materials to be used according to the will of the designer: green was subjugated, programmed and organized.

Moreover, the very colour that symbolizes nature can be viewed conversely as a decidedly unnatural colour. Fresh, tender green shoots turn to the rotten green of putrefaction and death. A greenish coloration in the human face is a clear indication of disease or worse. In ancient Egyptian papyri and wall paintings, it symbolizes the face of the dead, beginning with the god Osiris, and shades of green are still widely used in horror movies for vampires' and zombies' faces. In keeping with a persistent superstition in England, a bride's wedding garments, theatrical costumes and cars of the colour green are still regarded with consternation.

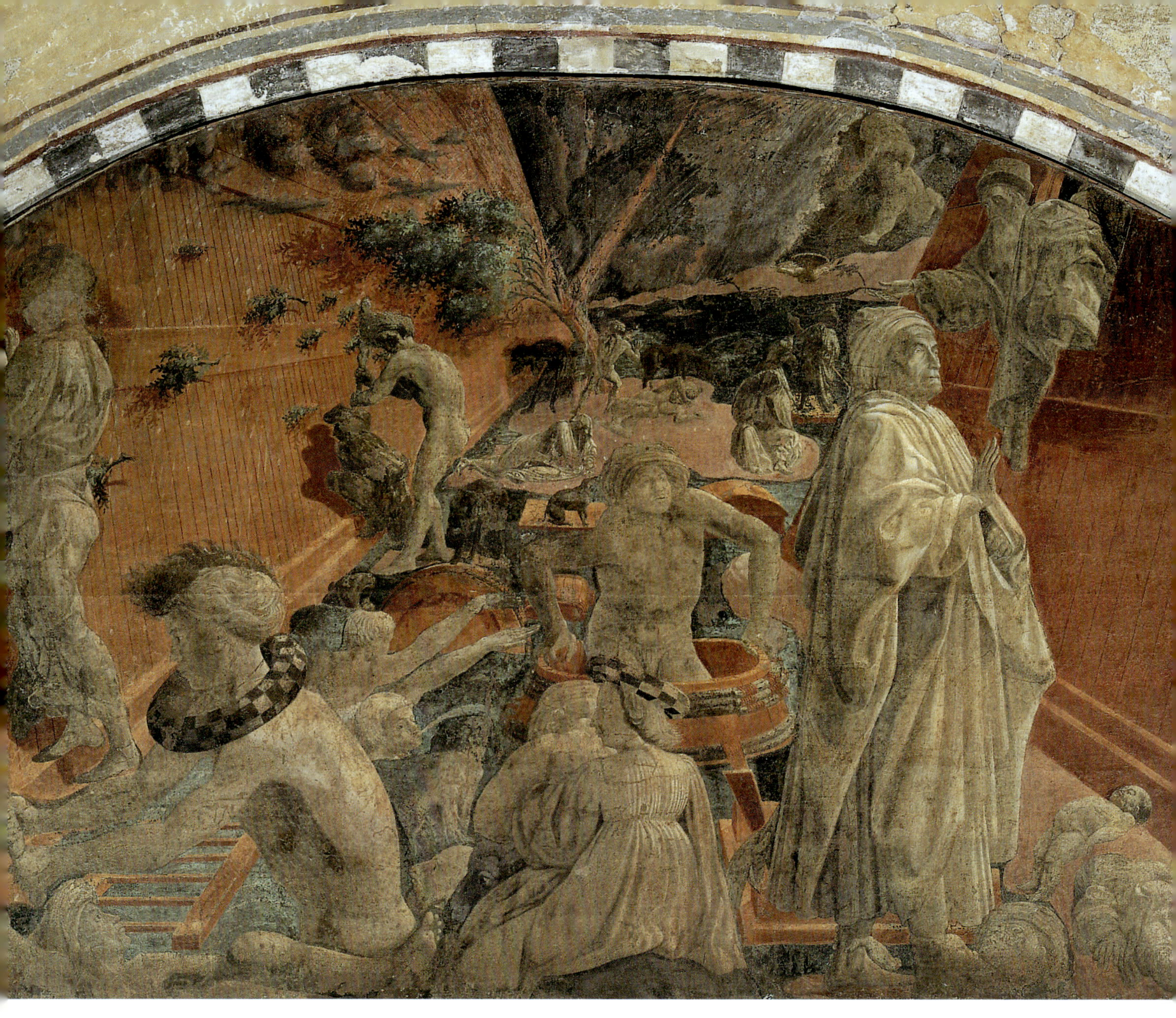

VERDACCIO

According to Vasari, the 14th-century painter Spinello Aretino was the first to experiment with monochrome paintings in 'earth green', a pigment with an iron oxide or silicic acid base. This colour, which lends itself to elegant combinations with grisaille or red-orange, had a limited distribution in the late Gothic period and from the early days of humanism to the mid-15th century, being limited above all to Tuscany and the courts of northern Italy. But it then fell into disuse.

Paolo Uccello used the technique of earth-green fresco for the equestrian monument of the mercenary captain Sir John Hawkwood (1436) in Florence's Duomo. The use of monochrome accentuates the innovative perspective adopted by the painter: horse and horseman are seen perfectly side-on, while the sarcophagus and the console shelf are seen from below, where the observer is located. However, the best-known application of monochrome is found at the Dominican church of Santa Maria Novella, also in Florence. The characteristic colour of the lunettes, frescoed several times by Paolo Uccello and collaborators, has led to this setting being known as the 'Green Cloister'.

Paolo Uccello
Noah and the Flood
c. 1430-1437
fresco
'Green Cloister', Santa Maria Novella, Florence

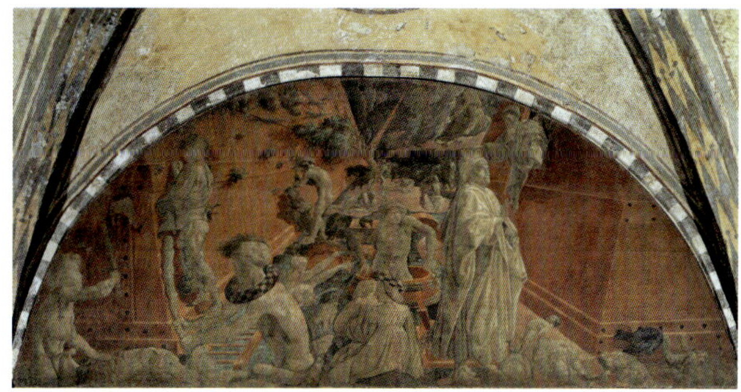

The frescoes at Santa Maria Novella, which are not in a perfect state of preservation, depict Old Testament episodes. Noah is calmly approaching the steep side of the Ark as the rest of humanity desperately seeks to escape the flood in any way they can. One man is lowering himself into a barrel; others are clinging to the trees. The woman in the centre and the man in the left foreground are wearing, respectively, a white-and-black checked headpiece and collar – a typical means of displaying mastery of perspective.

Michael Pacher
The Devil holding up the Book of Vices to St Augustine
c. 1480
oil on panel, 103 x 91 cm
Alte Pinakothek, Munich

GREEN DEVIL

Associated with the sin of Envy and feared reptiles such as snakes, in the popular imagination green came to be associated with witches, fairies and elves. The Grimm brothers even collected a folktale in which the devil and his followers wear green jackets. A famous appearance of the devil in art history is on a side panel of the *Altar of the Early Church Fathers*, a masterpiece painted by Michael Pacher for the Abbey of Novacella (not far from Brixen). In the unusual scene in which St Augustine forces the demon to hold up his missal, the contrast between the green colour of the devil and the Benedictine bishop's red-and-white liturgical vestments is striking.

Trained in the humanistic atmosphere of Padua but obviously in direct contact with Germanic culture, the Tyrolese Pacher sets the scene in the main street of a typical Gothic city in the Alps with sloping roofs and projecting balconies. The archways in the background give a sense of depth to the urban perspective, suggesting a pleasant place to stroll. The monstrous devil's unnatural, displeasing presence is heightened by the setting – the serene simplicity of a Tyrolean town on a sunny afternoon.

The devil as imagined by Pacher has human dimensions but the appearance of a dragon. Large, scaly wings grow from the bony shoulder blades, the head is horned, the mouth sprouts twisted boar-like tusks and a long red tongue, and the cross-eyed bloodshot eyes seem to dart from their sockets. The thin arms and deformed hands with twisted black nails seem to strain to hold up the heavy missal; the thin legs end in cloven hoofs. But the most peculiar detail is without question the 'second face' that peers out from the buttocks, with a tail for a nose!

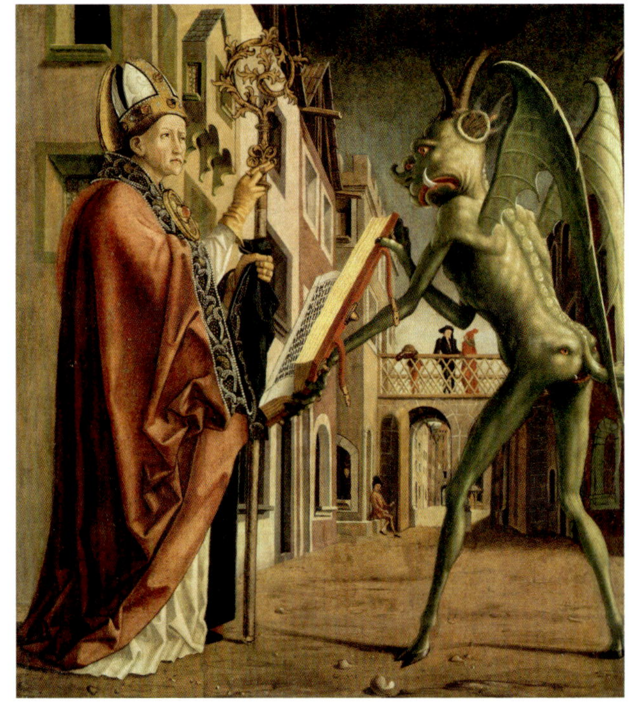

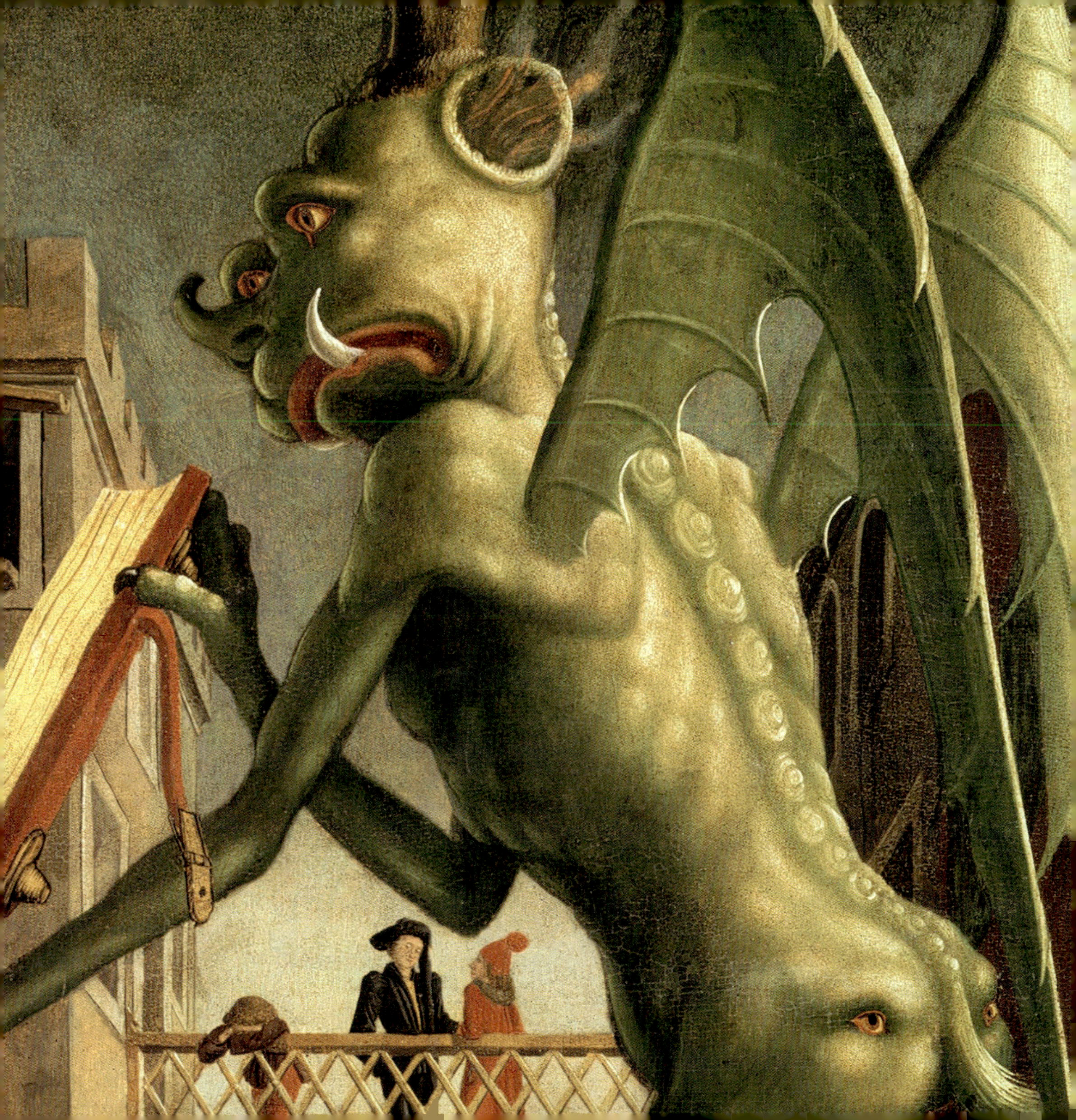

GREEN DRAGON

Vittore Carpaccio
St George and the Dragon
1504-1507
tempera on canvas, 141 x 360 cm
School of San Giorgio degli Schiavoni, Venice

Palaeontological research seems to demonstrate that dinosaurs' skin was not green, and yet in Hollywood's re-creations, dinosaurs are often portrayed in this colour, like traditional dragons and monsters. From classical mythology to the deeds of Christian saints, mortal combat between the good hero and the dragon is a metaphor for the eternal struggle between good and evil. In classical mythology (Perseus, Cadmus, Odysseus), the monstrous dragon symbolizes the savage bestiality and chaos that can be defeated by human wit and disciplined strength. Christianity considers dragons and basilisks to be incarnations of the devil because they resemble the tempter-snake. For this reason, they are often represented as spewing fire.

St George is the epitome of the Christian hero. The kingdom of England chose him as its patron, and the city of Stockholm has made him its symbol owing to the presence of a 15th-century masterpiece sculpted by Bernt Notke. The original story runs something like this: a monstrous dragon was terrorizing the Libyan city of Silene, forcing its inhabitants to provide animals and humans for it to eat. After sacrificing many youths to appease the insatiable beast's hunger, at last came the turn of the king's daughter. At this moment appears St George, mounted on a white steed; he defies the terrible dragon, pierces it with his lance and frees the princess. All in all, it makes for a wonderful medieval legend with the feel of chivalric poetry. Many images of the clash between St George and the dragon appear in Gothic and Renaissance art. A good example is the scene from the cycle of panels executed by Vittore Carpaccio between 1504 and 1507 for the School of San Giorgio degli Schiavoni in Venice.

The painting depicts the saint lancing the dragon to free the princess. The threatened city stands out in the background. The dark green, with some reddish and greyish veining, used by Carpaccio to depict the beast's skin and terrible wings assumes a diabolical value, the animal's raw violence standing for untamed nature.

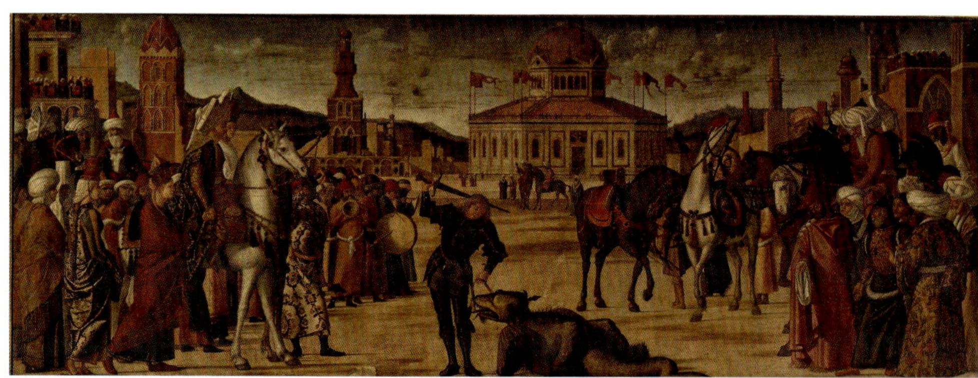

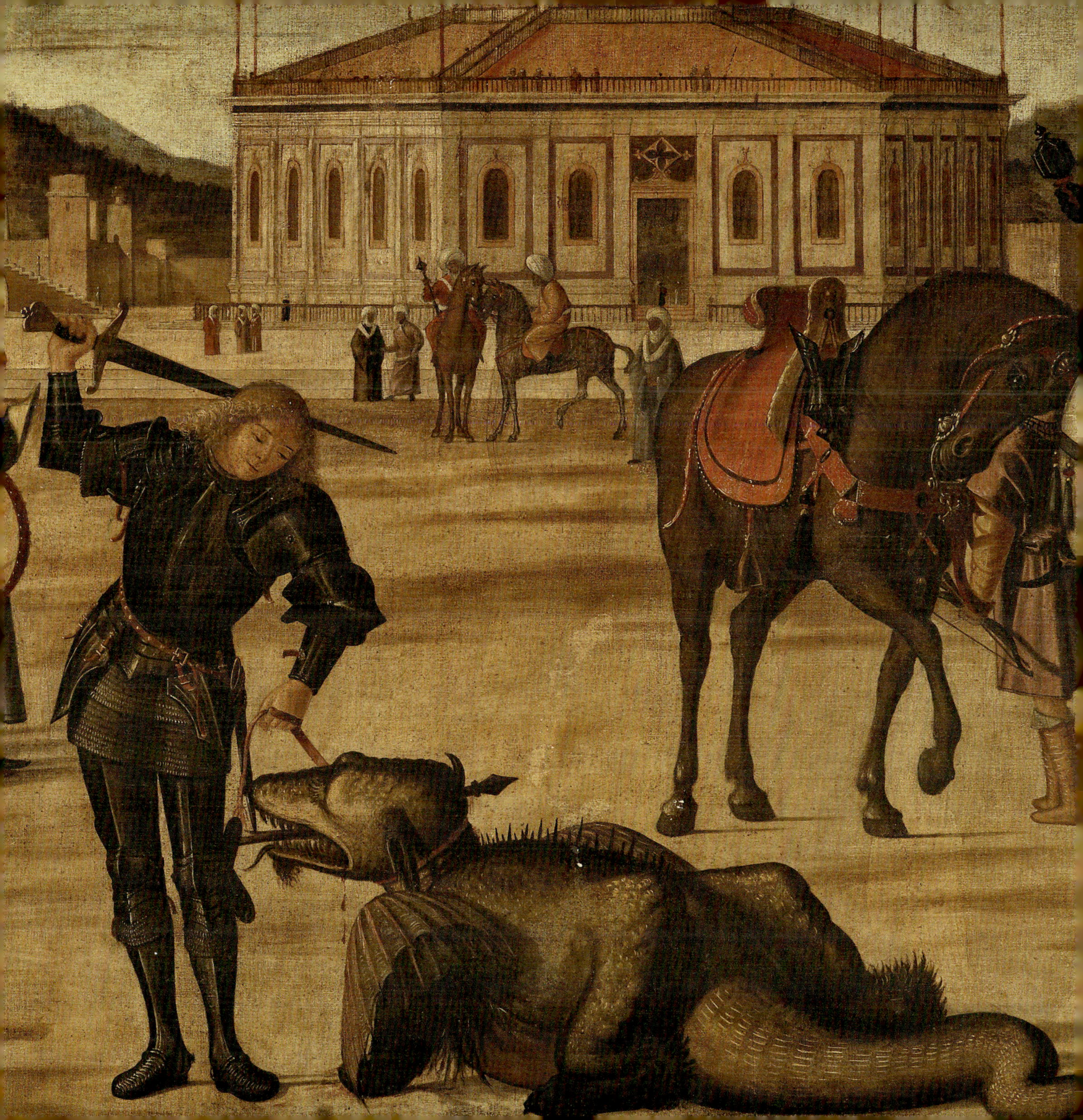

'GREEN' HANS

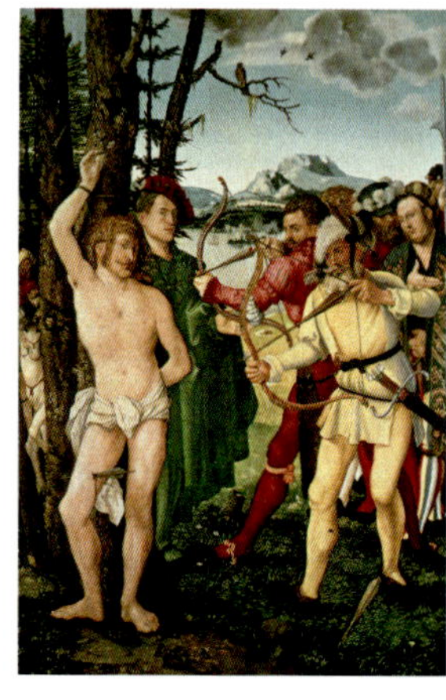

Hans Baldung Grien
The Martyrdom of St Sebastian
(centre panel)
1507
121.4 x 78.7 cm
Germanisches Nationalmuseum, Nuremberg

The German Renaissance master Hans Baldung was so fond of the colour green that he appended Grien (Old German for 'green') to his name. In some paintings – for example, the centre panel of the dazzling *Martyrdom of St Sebastian* – he included a portrait of himself wearing an eye-catching bright green cloak. His artistic path – large religious commissions, admiration for Dürer's genius and eventually the crisis of faith of the Reformation – effectively sums up the enthusiasm and troubles of early 16th-century Germany.

For a few brief years, Baldung Grien struck a delicate balance between the German Gothic heritage – legendary, disturbing and knightly – and a compound monumentality inherited from Italian humanism. He was born in Swabia about 1485 and moved to Strasbourg as a child. He was trained in that city in the Rhineland, which remained his favourite place to live. In 1503, Baldung Grien went to Nuremberg, where he came in contact with Dürer, becoming not only his most trusted assistant but also one of his closest friends. In fact, he was left in charge of Dürer's workshop when Dürer went to Venice. Baldung Grien identified with the style and mentality of the greatest genius of the Northern Renaissance, learning from his multifaceted techniques (including engraving and preparing cartoons for stained glass), inventiveness and universal vision.

When Baldung Grien returned to Strasbourg about 1510, he devoted himself to depictions of the female body, from monstrous and seductive witches to allegorical figures. In 1512, simultaneously with Grünewald's activity in nearby Alsace, he began executing a large winged altarpiece for the cathedral of Freiburg-im-Breisgau. The centre of the main view depicts the Coronation of the Virgin, flanked by two paintings of the Apostles; the lateral wings contain four episodes from the Life of Mary; and on the back is a large Crucifixion. In this masterpiece, one of the most important of the German Renaissance, Baldung Grien eschewed his favourite colour green in favour of a white with bluish reflections. In 1517, the year after finishing the polyptych, he returned permanently to Strasbourg. The climate had changed, and the painter was among the first to heed Martin Luther's urging. From then on, works on sacred subjects became less frequent. Their place was taken by allegories and moralistic subjects, along with book illustrations and excursions into his favourite subject-matter of witches. He died in Strasbourg in 1545.

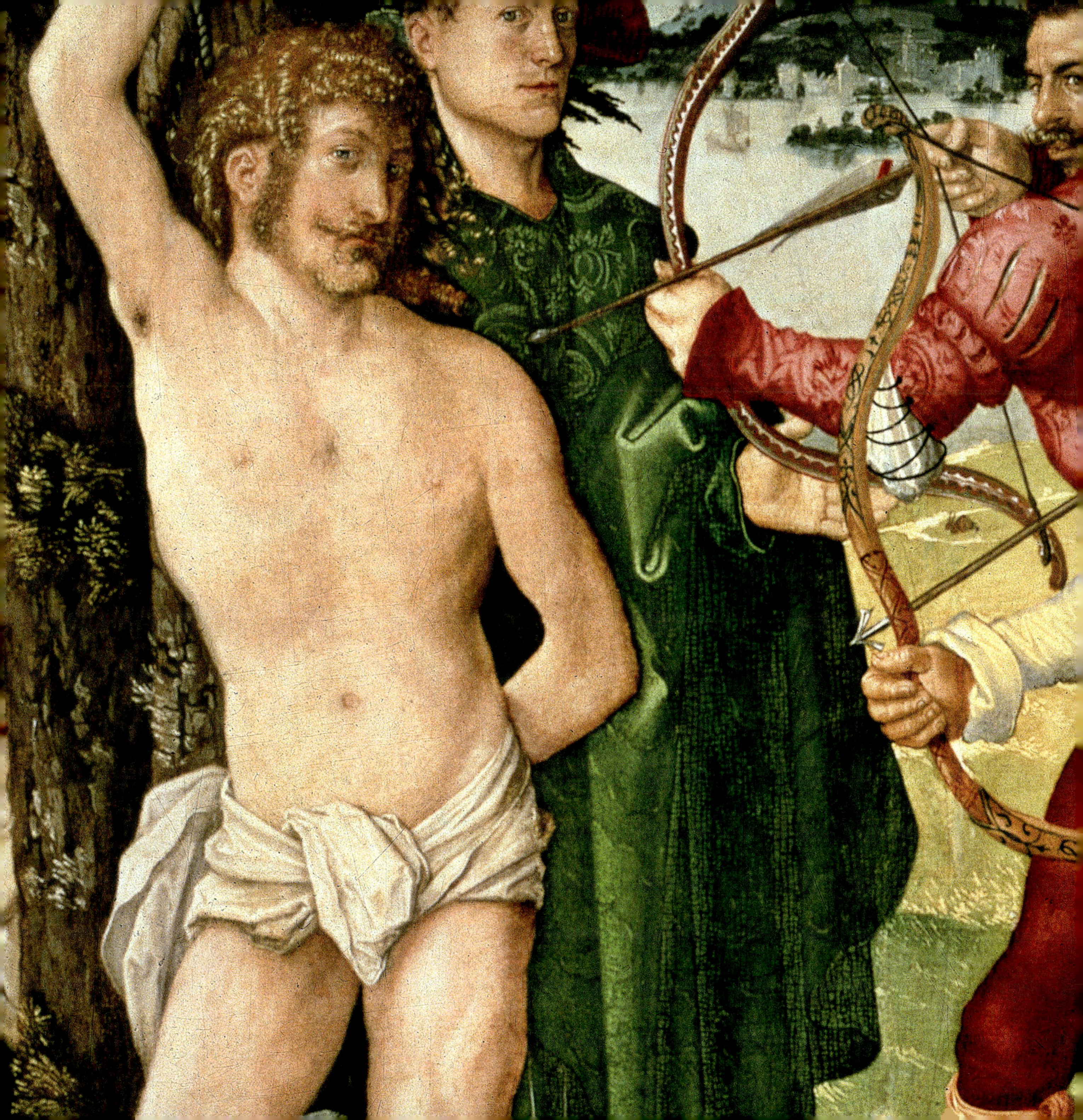

THE GREEN ROOM

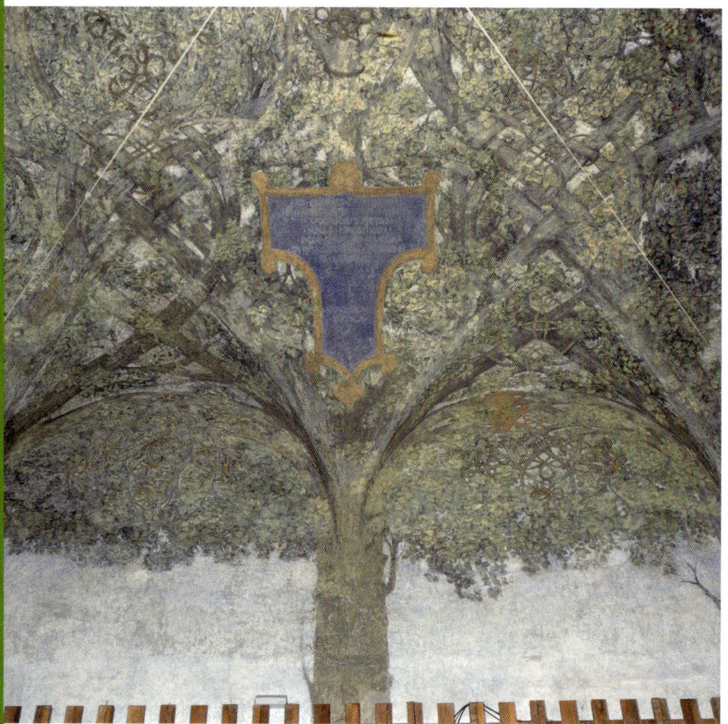

Immediately after finishing *The Last Supper* in the refectory of Santa Maria delle Grazie, Leonardo da Vinci turned to another commission for the Duke of Milan, Ludovico il Moro. Inside the Castello Sforzesco, in the huge Sala delle Asse ('Room of Wooden Panels', immediately beneath the duke's bedroom), Leonardo painted a fantastic tangle of branches, trees, foliage, knots and coats of arms. The complicated story of its deterioration and restoration notwithstanding, Leonardo's fresco is the earliest accomplished Renaissance example of naturalistic illusion, magically transforming the building into a dream forest. Along the walls, Leonardo painted tree trunks down to their roots, which seem to make their way with difficulty between boulders and rocky outcroppings.

Leonardo was also a key reference for the Emilian painter Antonio Allegri, called Correggio after the town where he was born. But thanks to his intelligent mediation of other important influences, and above all his individual contribution of innovative stylistic features, during the 1520s Correggio made some of the most significant works of the entire Renaissance, and not just in the Po region.

Commissioned by Abbess Giovanna Piacenza to host literary meetings, the so-called Camera della

▲
Leonardo da Vinci
The Sala delle Asse
1498
fresco
Castello Sforzesco, Milan

▶
Correggio
The Camera di San Paolo
1518-1519
fresco
convent of San Paolo, Parma

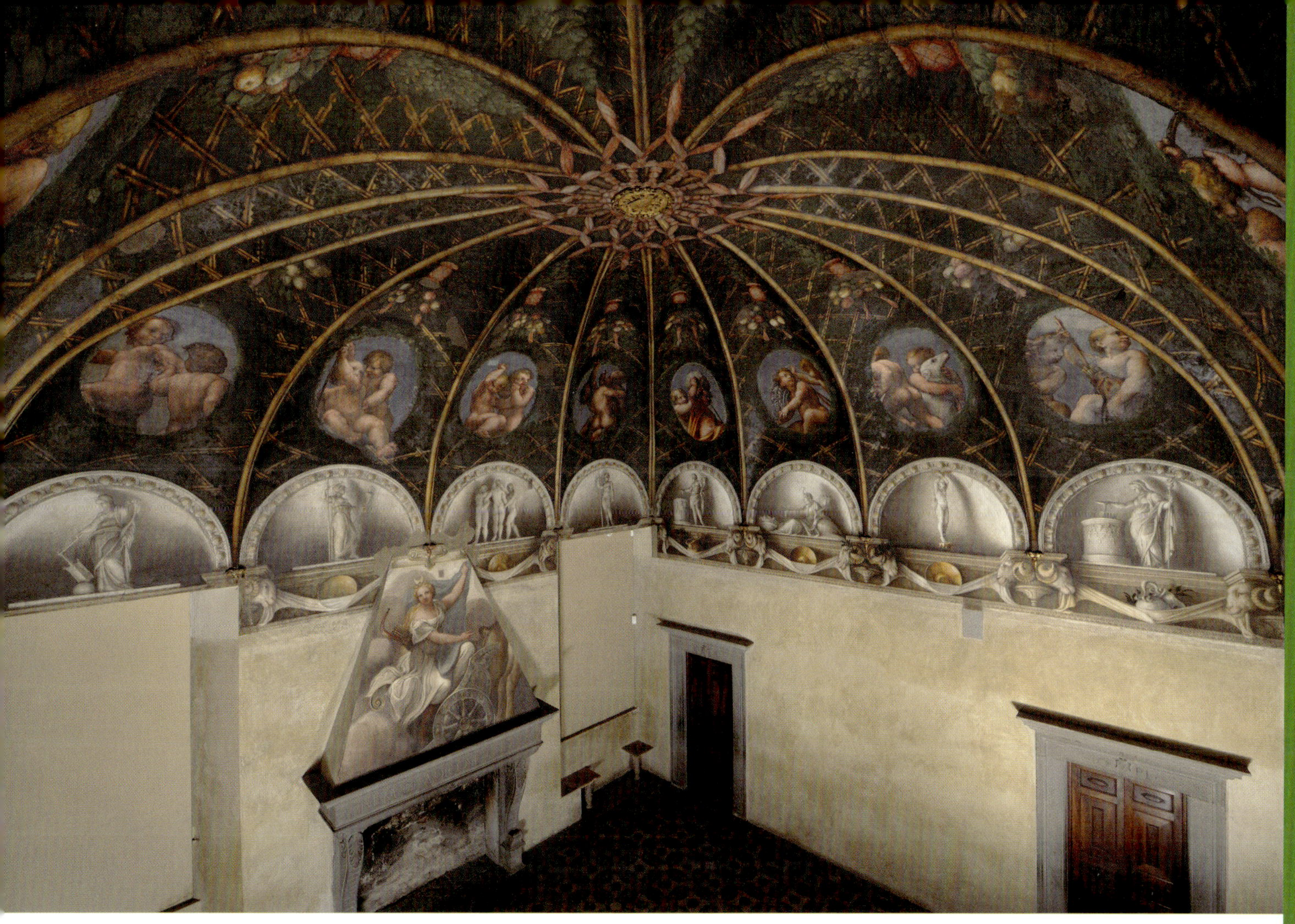

Badessa (also known as the Camera di San Paolo, 1518) presents a profane mythological iconography within the convent of St Paul. Correggio developed the motif of the naturalistic perspective ceiling by simulating a pergola with oval openings. Smiling putti of fresh, childlike liveliness peer out between the branches. Along the walls, instead of the trees of Leonardo's prototype, is a series of monochrome lunettes that imitate delicate ancient low reliefs, offering a perfect harmony between nature and the myths of the classical world.

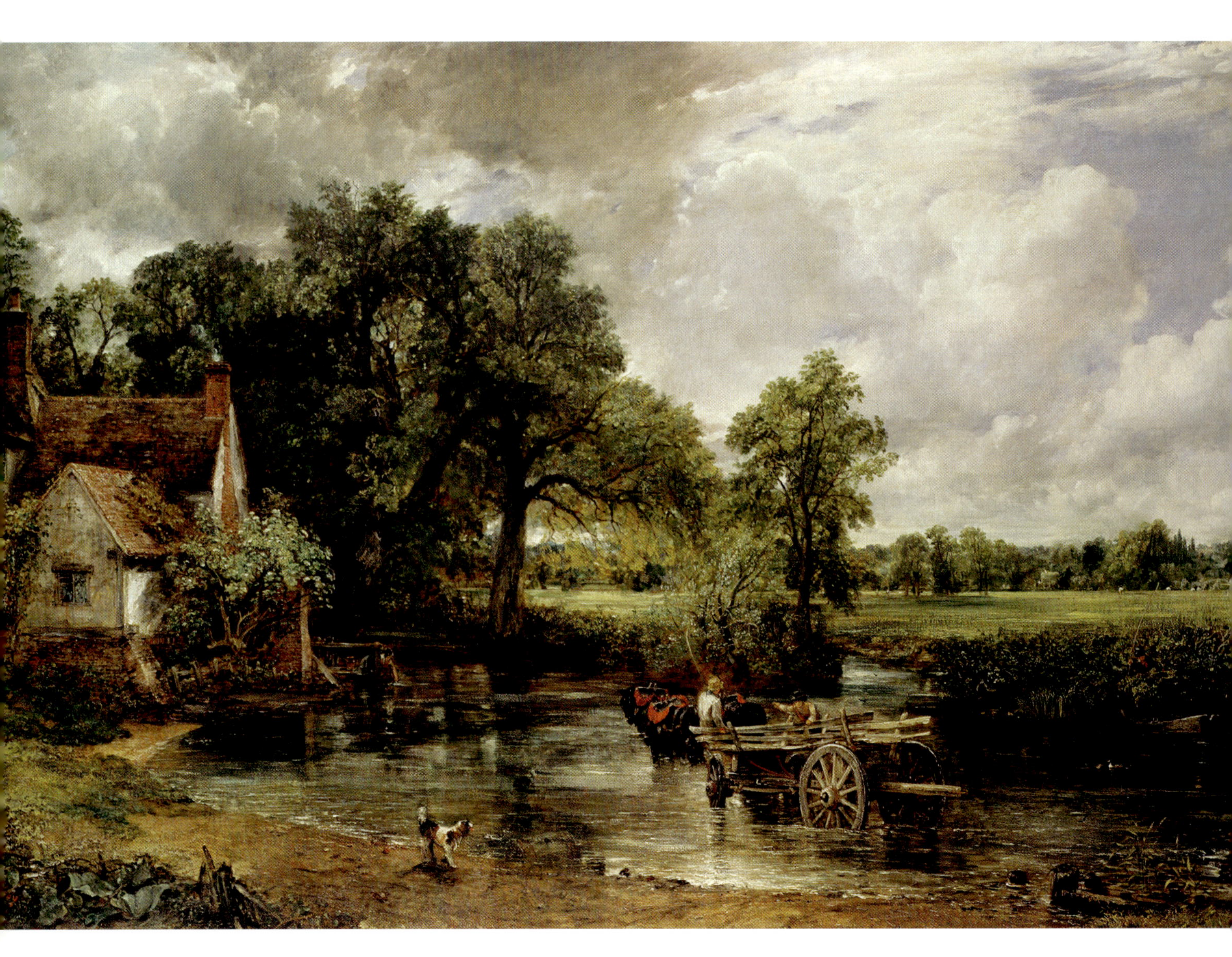

CONSTABLE

John Constable
The Hay Wain
1821
oil on canvas, 130.2 x 185.4 cm
The National Gallery, London

At the close of the 18th century, an increasingly widespread dissatisfaction with classical rationalism and generic Enlightenment cosmopolitanism began to be felt in Europe. A faithful reflection of the transformation afoot is *plein air* landscape painting, with its technical innovations of small format and rapid brushstroke. In the late 18th century and the early 19th century, the English scene was thronged with landscape painters, many of whom – for example the refined Bonington – continued the tradition of Italian travel. Others, however, pursued the landscape in Britain. The most important of these is no doubt John Constable, who arrived in London from Suffolk's green rural vistas in 1799.

A model student at the Royal Academy, Constable started out in the recent tradition of the idealized classical landscape but developed a new approach within a few years. Quite opposed to classicizing idealism and the contemplation of the sublime, Constable depicted his familiar rustic world exactly as it appeared to his eyes, in an unending quest for 'natural painting'. To achieve the greatest possible adherence to nature, he adopted a fresh, spontaneous touch in laying on colour, which emphasized the impression of immediacy. As in early Romantic English poetry, Constable sought and found nature's harmony, investigating it with patient care and intense involvement, deciphering hidden signs in the landscape and seeking to restore an objective image of it. It was furthermore a utopian poetry: Constable's landscapes, though reproduced with absolute fidelity, are still a touching and subjective image of beloved places he identified with.

From the 1810s on, Constable approached the landscape in a scientific frame of mind. Having chosen particular places (Salisbury Cathedral, Hampstead Heath, the pastures of Dedham Valley), Constable repeatedly analysed their characteristics in various seasons and the changing hours of the day, always working from life. He produced marvellous sketchbooks with cloud studies that look like fascinating abstract compositions and *plein air* paintings that profoundly influenced other European schools, beginning with the group of French painters who gathered at Barbizon. And yet, Constable did not meet with the success he deserved in his homeland, owing to his reserved, reluctant character as a lover of the countryside rather than London society. Constable finally obtained a teaching post at the Royal Academy in 1829, when his painting had begun to lose the clarity of the preceding years.

Jean-Baptiste-Camille Corot
Rocks at Fontainebleau
1842
oil on canvas
Narodni Galerie, Prague

THE GREEN FOREST OF FONTAINEBLEAU

The decision to paint out of doors, 'from nature', taking easel, canvas and colours into the open, was a great advance, and not an easy one. There were various precursors to Impressionism, from the 18th-century Italian *veduta* painters to the English landscape artists of the Romantic period, but the determining impulse came from the group of artists who gathered in the town of Barbizon, on the edge of the magnificent forest of Fontainebleau. Around the middle of the 19th century, the influence of the great master Corot, and the hospitality of Théodore Rousseau, incited not only painters but also critics and the general public to look upon painting executed directly in the bosom of nature with increasing favour. Initially, subject-matter consisted mostly of the majestic trees in the forest surrounding Barbizon. Then thanks to Monet, Sisley, Renoir and Pissarro, the natural settings became increasingly varied and diversified. Painting in the open air was not limited to depicting vistas and the forms of objects, but aimed to capture variations of light, atmosphere, weather, and the physical and emotional sensations experienced in direct contact with nature. The variety of greens in a wood is the subject that offers the greatest range of chromatic values within a single hue.

The village of Barbizon, a few kilometres from Paris, was frequented by artists from the mid-18th century. In the 1830s, the so-called School of 1830 or Barbizonniers (sometimes referred to as the 'Painters of Fontainebleau') came together there. Though often working side by side, they did not form a proper school, nor did they attempt to give themselves a unifying poetic or establish hierarchical relationships. Their common denominator was the desire to reject academic teaching in the name of a direct connection with reality and nature. They painted landscapes and scenes of rural life, often of small dimensions, in which nature is the main figure. In general they liked to work in the open air, but unlike the Impressionists later, they preferred to complete and refine their creations in the calm of the studio. They greatly admired the English landscapists, in particular John Constable, from whom they borrowed his use of colours and attention to natural details.

The main exponents of the Barbizon group were Jean-François Millet, Constant Troyon, Camille Corot and Charles-François Daubigny. Théodore Rousseau, considered the most representative and influential exponent, reached the peak of his success when he shared a gallery with Alexandre Gabriel Decamps at the Paris World's Fair of 1855. Besides painters, realist writers were also drawn to these sites: in 1867, Edmond and Jules de Goncourt set their novel *Manette Salomon* in the inn of Mère Ganne. Two other villages associated with

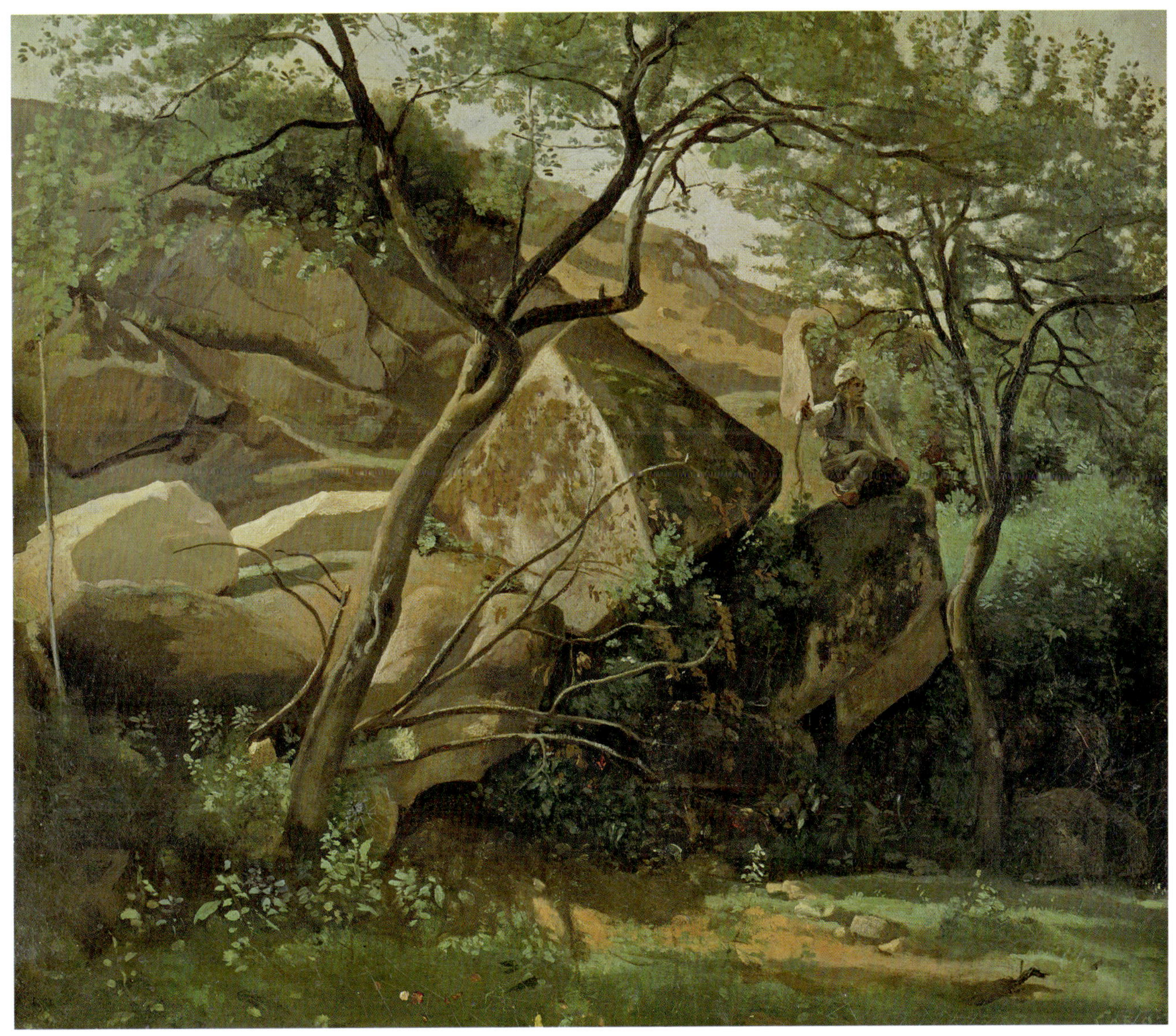

Barbizon are Pontoise, on the banks of the Oise, and Marlotte, where the Cabaret de la Mère Anthony was located. Among its regular customers were Courbet, Pissarro, Sisley, Monet and Renoir, who depicted it in a painting in 1866.

GREEN MALACHITE

One of the most precious green pigments is made from malachite. This stone possibly takes its name from the Greek *molochitis*, meaning 'mallow', because of its characteristic green colour, changing from light to dark, creating a subtle play of shades and colours. Ground to a powder, malachite is used as a pigment in painting and is known by various names: Hungarian green, mineral green, mountain green, copper green, green bice and green verditer. Malachite is ascribed beneficial properties. In ancient times it was used to make amulets that provided protection from misfortune. The stone's relative softness makes it hard to work, adding to its commercial value.

In czarist Russia, widespread use was made of malachite as a covering for lavish furniture (as at the Hermitage) and even in architecture. For this purpose, a complicated mosaic technique was employed, carefully fitting flakes of mineral so as to exploit the ornamental designs of the veining. The cathedral of St Isaac in St Petersburg was built for Czar Alexander I, who announced a competition in 1816 that was won by the French designer August Ricard de Montferrand. Constructed between 1818 and 1858, the church is one of the finest examples of Russian Neoclassical architecture, surmounted by a huge dome covered in strips of gilded copper. A vestibule with eight red granite columns leads to the interior, with its magnificent malachite columns of a striking green.

Inside the sumptuously decorated cathedral, a frame supported by gilded brackets runs along the entire volume, surrounding the columns, which have gilded Corinthian capitals. The striking chromatic interplay of the veined green malachite with the gold decorations and architectural mouldings transforms the church into a sacred treasure chest.

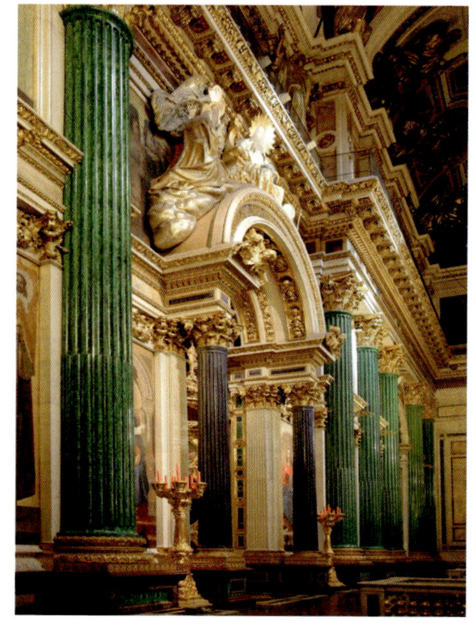

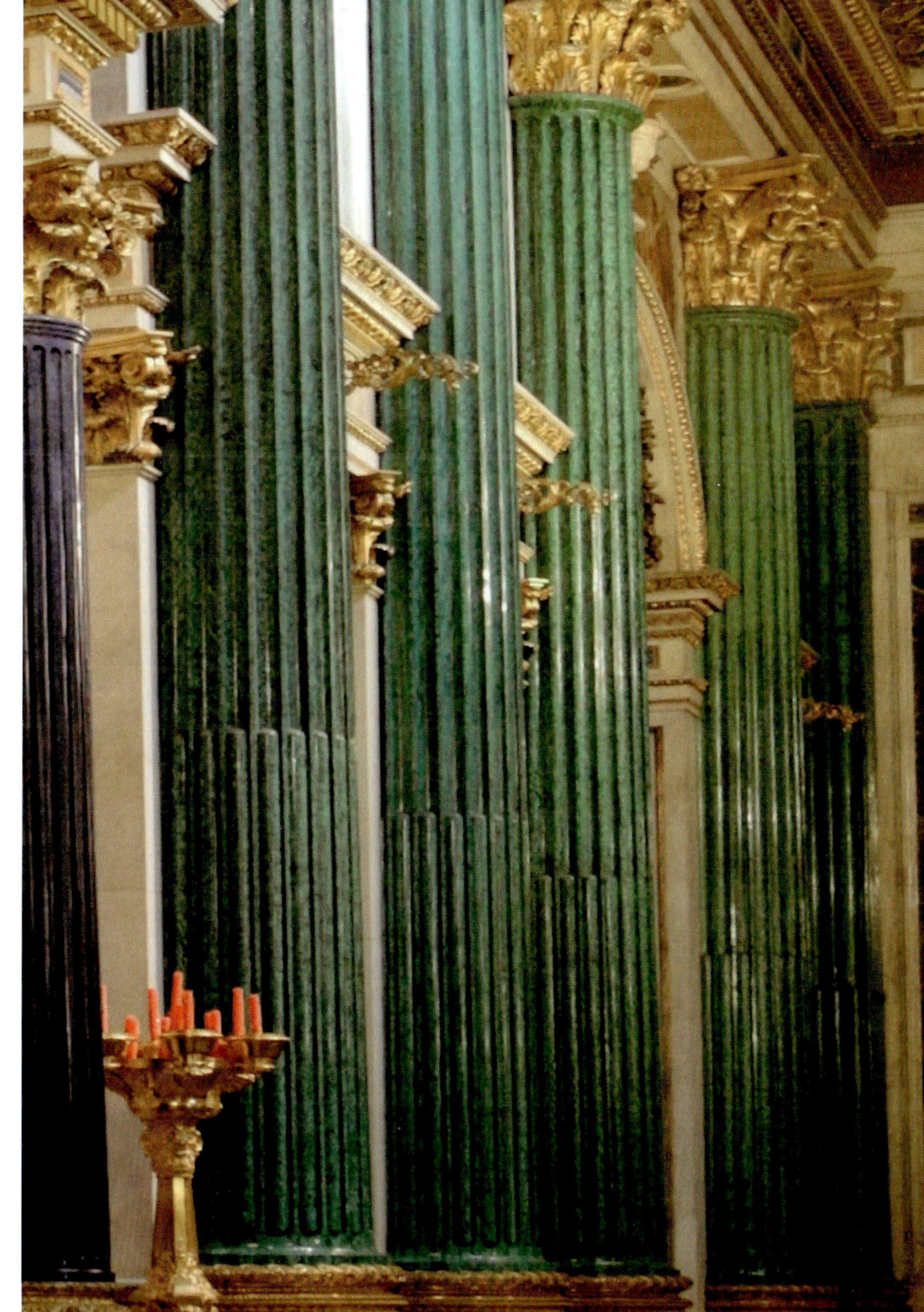

Malachite column
Cathedral of St Isaac
1818–1858
St Petersburg

A CONTROVERSIAL LUNCH ON THE GRASS

The son of a well-known Paris judge, the refined and well-to-do Manet became the prime example of the 'accursed painter' in the 1860s. His paintings were the butt of rejection, scorn, derision, invective and caricatures – particularly bitter indictments for a painter whose social rank and culture put him far from the cliché of the artist as eccentric misfit. On the contrary, Manet had wanted to earn acceptance and success, entering the art market and even museum collections by the front door. He even inserted Renaissance references in his paintings. But the official bourgeois art scene, perhaps because it felt it had been betrayed by one of its own, reacted with particular violence to Manet's unintended 'provocations'.

Manet submitted three canvases to the selection committee for the Salon of 1863: *Young Man Dressed as a Majo*, *Mademoiselle V dressed as an Espada* and *Le Déjeuner sur l'herbe*. All three were rejected, along with paintings by many other artists. The protests of those who were excluded convinced Napoleon III to concede the possibility of allowing the public to evaluate their work, which was then exhibited in what came to be called the Salon des Refusés. However, the judgement of the public and the critics was as harsh and cutting as that of the Salon's jury. The press took delight in publishing a great number of satirical vignettes. Foremost among the works lashed out at was Manet's *Déjeuner sur l'herbe* (exhibited as *Le Bain* – The Bath), which was considered an offence to morality, logic and the most elementary rules of painting. The artist had based his work on figures from *The Judgement of Paris*, an engraving by Marcantonio Raimondi after an image by Raphael. He furthermore reinterpreted in a modern vein Titian's *Pastoral Scene*, which he had seen at the Louvre.

The scene depicts the Sunday-afternoon diversion of a group of friends in a park in the outskirts of Paris. The four figures sit in a grassy glade, surrounded by the green of the trees. The picnic is depicted in the foreground, partly on the abandoned clothing of the woman in the centre. The obvious erotic implications of a nude woman between two completely clothed men are mitigated by the natural setting, its cool shadows alternating with the sunlight filtering through the trees. The woman in the foreground, who unleashed a tremendous scandal with her brazen nudity, is Victorine Meurent. Beside her is Manet's brother, Gustave, and in front, the Dutch sculptor Ferdinand Leenhoff, the brother of the artist's wife, Suzanne (who almost certainly posed for the woman in the background).

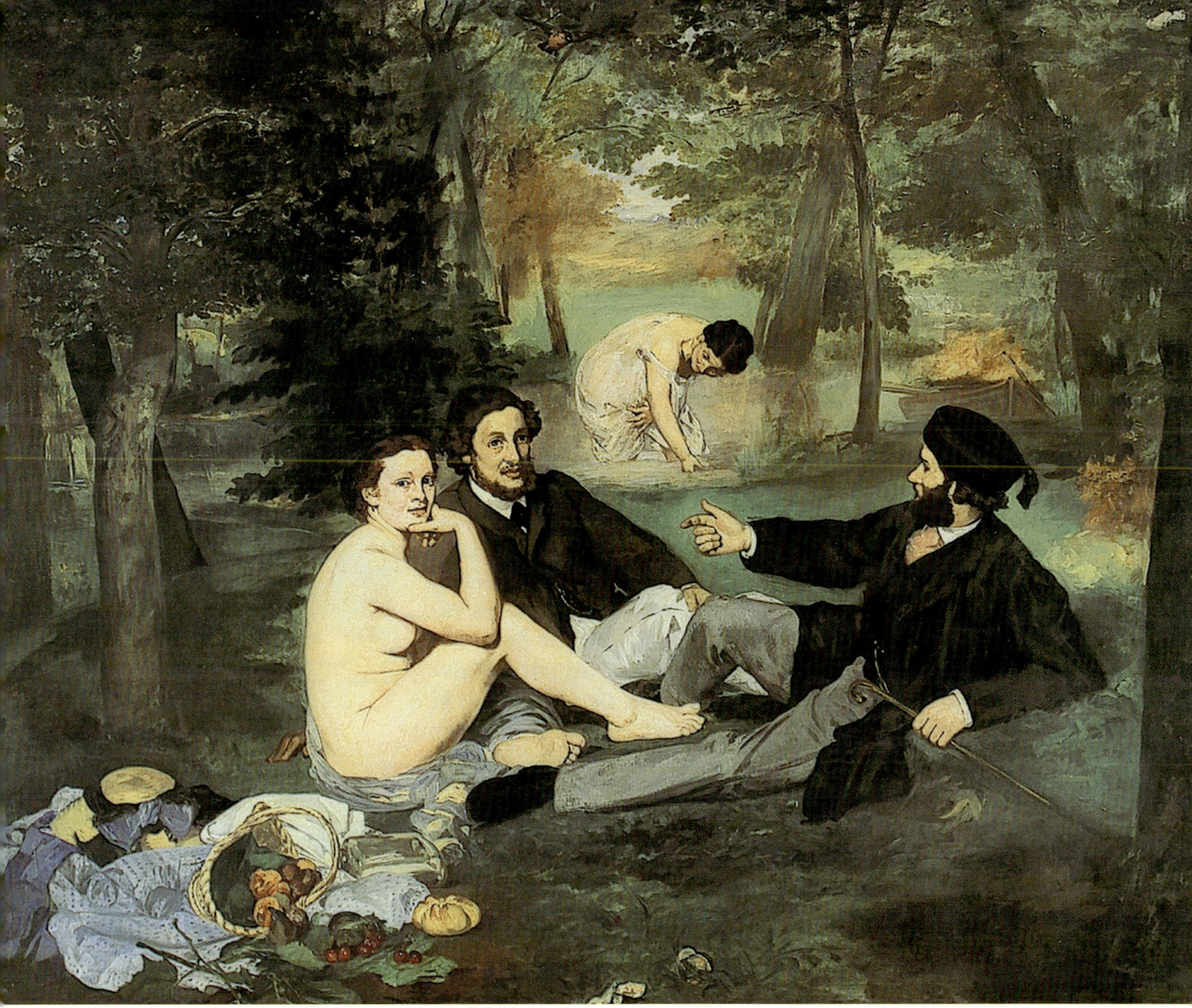

Edouard Manet
Le Déjeuner sur l'herbe
1863
oil on canvas, 208 x 264 cm
Musée d'Orsay, Paris

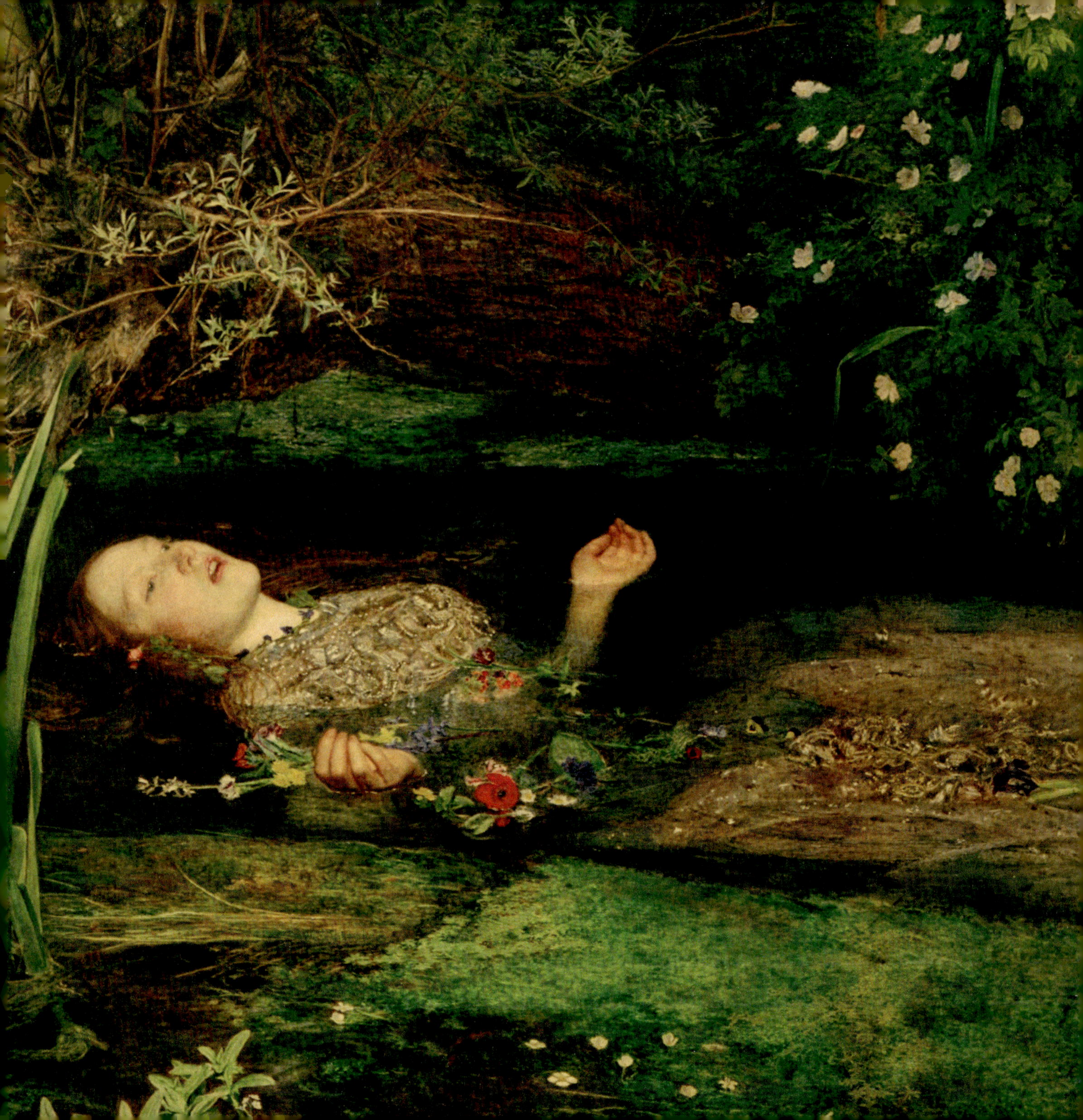

MILLAIS'S OPHELIA

John Everett Millais
Ophelia
1851–1852
oil on canvas, 76.2 x 111.8 cm
Tate, London

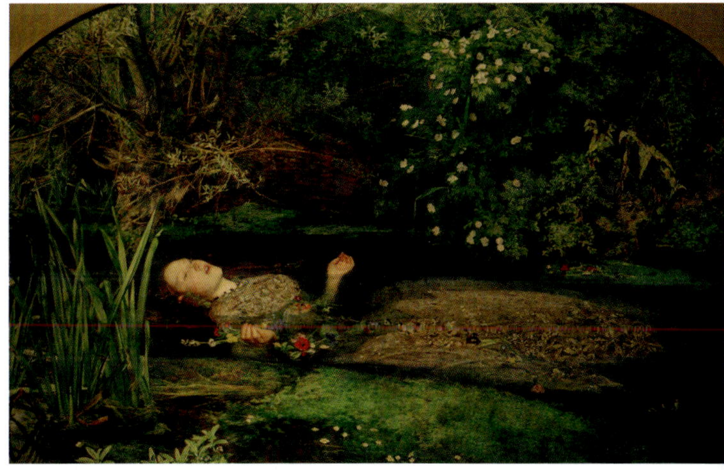

Nature's green frames the death of Ophelia. Although the tender, melancholy young woman does not occupy a foreground role in Shakespeare's tragedy *Hamlet*, she has nevertheless been the play's favourite character among artists, especially for her silent death. In the aesthetic climate of the early Victorian period, the Pre-Raphaelite Millais painted the fragile, drowned young woman as a mysterious, sensual water plant, floating among the reeds and waterlilies on a pond's clear surface. The young woman – who according to Shakespeare lay 'mermaid-like' in the water and was pulled under by the weight of her drenched clothing – still clutches the flowers with which she was wont to weave garlands. We seem to hear the last notes of a song of longing love issue from her half-closed mouth.

For his model, Millais chose Elizabeth Siddal, known as Lizzie. She subsequently married Dante Gabriel Rossetti but was herself destined to suffer an unhappy early death. But the figure of Ophelia gliding towards death was not the main concern of the painter, who must have finished the painting by October 1852. In order to reproduce the plant setting accurately, Millais went to stay in Ewell, Surrey, in June. Painting out of doors the whole summer, waiting for the optimal blossoming of each species of flower, the artist had to cope with swarms of insects, swans and other fenland birds, as well as the weather. The effort to depict the natural setting exactly seems like the work of a botanist, but it soon reveals itself to be full of symbolic allusions.

The willow, nettles and daisies, associated with innocence, come directly from Shakespeare. Other plants, however, are the painter's additions: the poppy alludes to the eternal sleep of death; a symbol of love, youth and beauty, the rose also has a funereal connotation, connected with ceremonies devoted to the cult of the dead; the forget-me-not is obviously the flower of memory; and the pansy, which signals unhappy love, is also tied to the symbolism of early death.

BILLIARDS

The customary game table covered with a green cloth appeared in France and England in the 18th century. According to an unconfirmed report, the first billiard table was made by an English cabinetmaker for King Louis XIV, and the green covering was meant to recall the colour of meadows. The habit of covering surfaces in green on which to play games of chance or skill (cards, billiards, backgammon, roulette) spread rapidly through the aristocratic circles in all of Europe. From there it penetrated the 'professional' environment of gambling parlours and casinos.

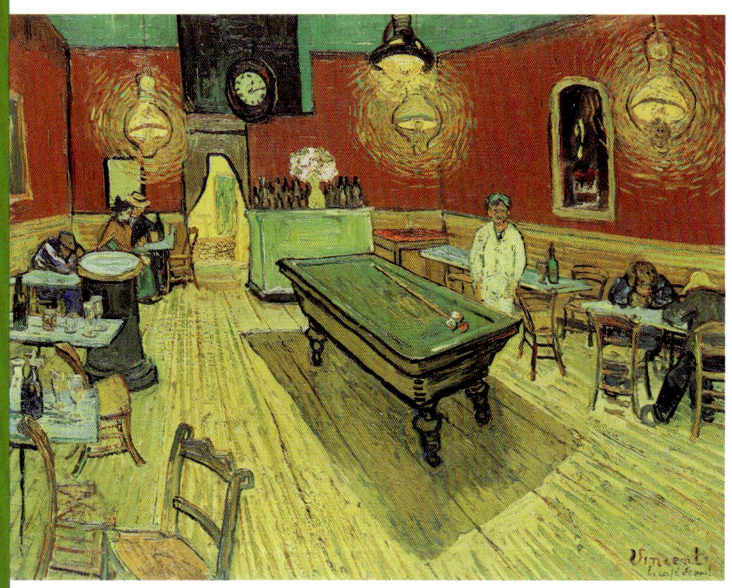

The green of the playing table could be seen simply as a restful colour for the eyes, against which cards, chips and billiard balls stand out distinctly. In roulette, the number zero has a green background, distinguishing it from the thirty-six other numbers, which alternate red and black. The green associated with games of chance is loaded with negative connotations as the colour of the 'poison' that intoxicates inveterate gamblers and brings them to ruin.

The most famous billiard table in art history is without doubt that of the café at the train station in Arles, painted by Van Gogh. He describes the scene in an often-quoted letter to his brother Theo in September 1888: 'I have tried to express the terrible passions of humanity by means of red and green. The room is blood red and dark yellow with a green billiard table in the middle; there are four lemon-yellow lamps with a glow of orange and green. Everywhere there is a clash and contrast of the most alien reds and greens.' Vincent added that the discord of red and green inside the café had a harmful psychological effect.

Vincent van Gogh
The Night Café
1888
oil on canvas, 70 x 89 cm
Yale University Art Gallery, New Haven

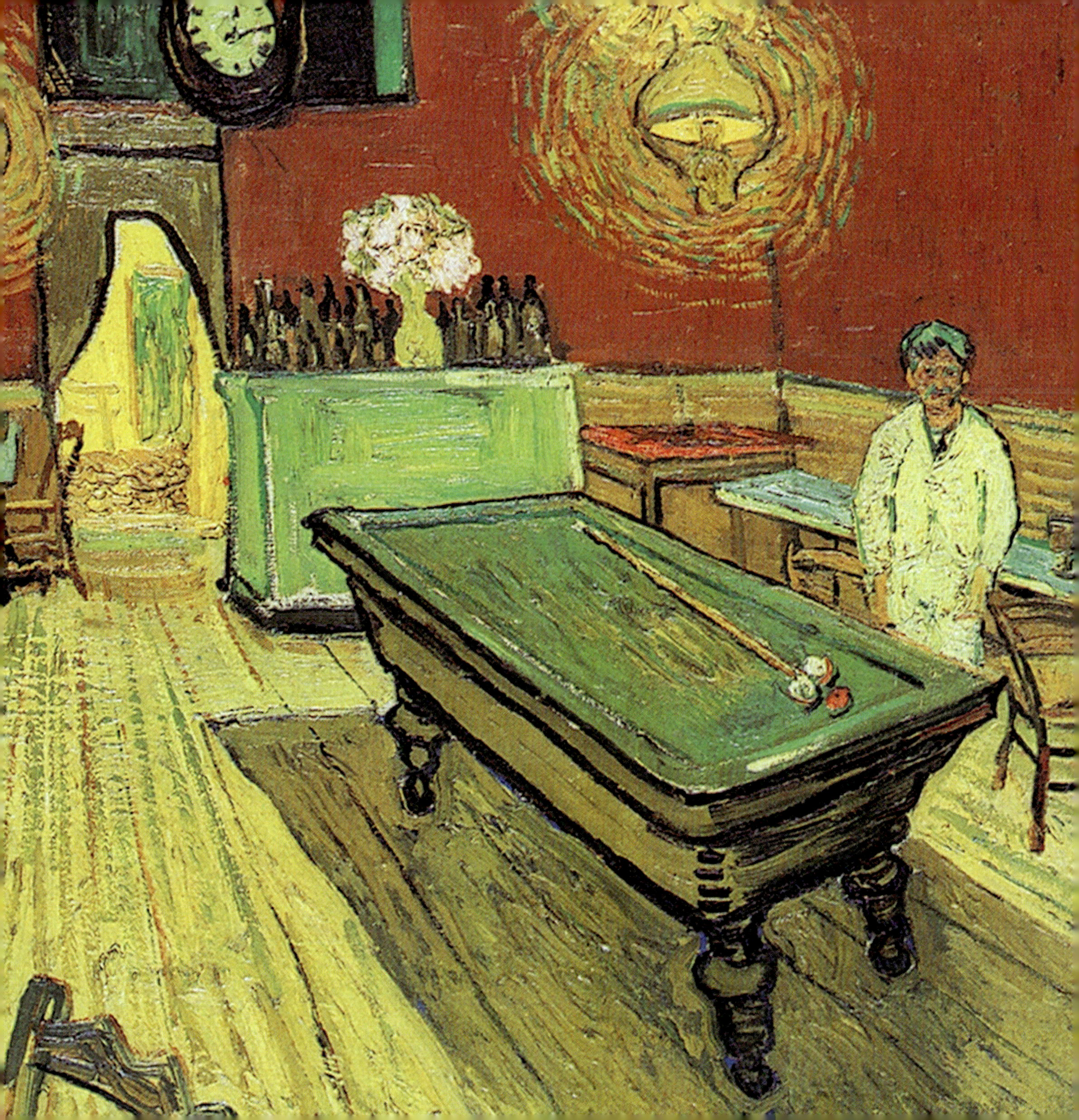

GREEN DECONSTRUCTED

A cultivated, refined intellectual, Seurat painted only a few works, owing to the extreme slowness required by the technique he used, the huge dimensions and the protracted working out of each painting. This large, memorable canvas is one of the radical turning points in the conception of colour in painting. An open-air scene set in a park on the Seine, attention is concentrated mainly on the green shades of the lawn and trees, between the shadow and the afternoon sun. Presented at the eighth exhibition of the Impressionists in 1886 and at the Salon des Indépendants the same year, the painting provoked an immediate uproar, due to its visual impact and expressive force. The critic Félix Fénéon considered it the manifesto of Pointillism. The colour is applied in an entirely innovative way, decomposed in an infinite series of separate little dots. Seurat's artistic career and life were cut short by his untimely death in 1891, at the age of thirty-one.

As with all Seurat's paintings, execution was long and laborious, since he wanted to put his study of optics into practice. Thirty-three studies and twenty-eight preparatory drawings for the final painting are known. In the morning, Seurat would go to the site, a wooded islet along the Seine, and paint *en plein air*. In the afternoon (and sometimes all night), he reworked his sketches in the studio, decomposing the colours and applying them to the canvas with separate brushstrokes. In addition, as in some of his other works, Seurat painted the frame with little dots. In doing this, he used colours complementary to the ones nearby on the canvas, in order to increase the visual effect in keeping with the theory of contrasts.

The large canvas – measuring three metres across – depicts Parisians strolling and resting on a Sunday afternoon on the island of the Grande Jatte in a park on the Seine. To the left and above, the river flows, no less populated than the shores. The figures have been arranged on the grass and in the shade of the trees after careful study of the masses and spaces, along compositional lines the artist established geometrically. Seurat does not seek a psychological characterization of the figures but an analysis of their poses and attitudes. Even if the figures are in motion, they are crystallized in a dimension outside time and space so that their faces, having lost a great part of their individuality, become symbols of an era and its way of life.

Georges Seurat
A Sunday on La Grande Jatte
1884-1886
oil on canvas, 207.5 x 308 cm
Art Institute of Chicago

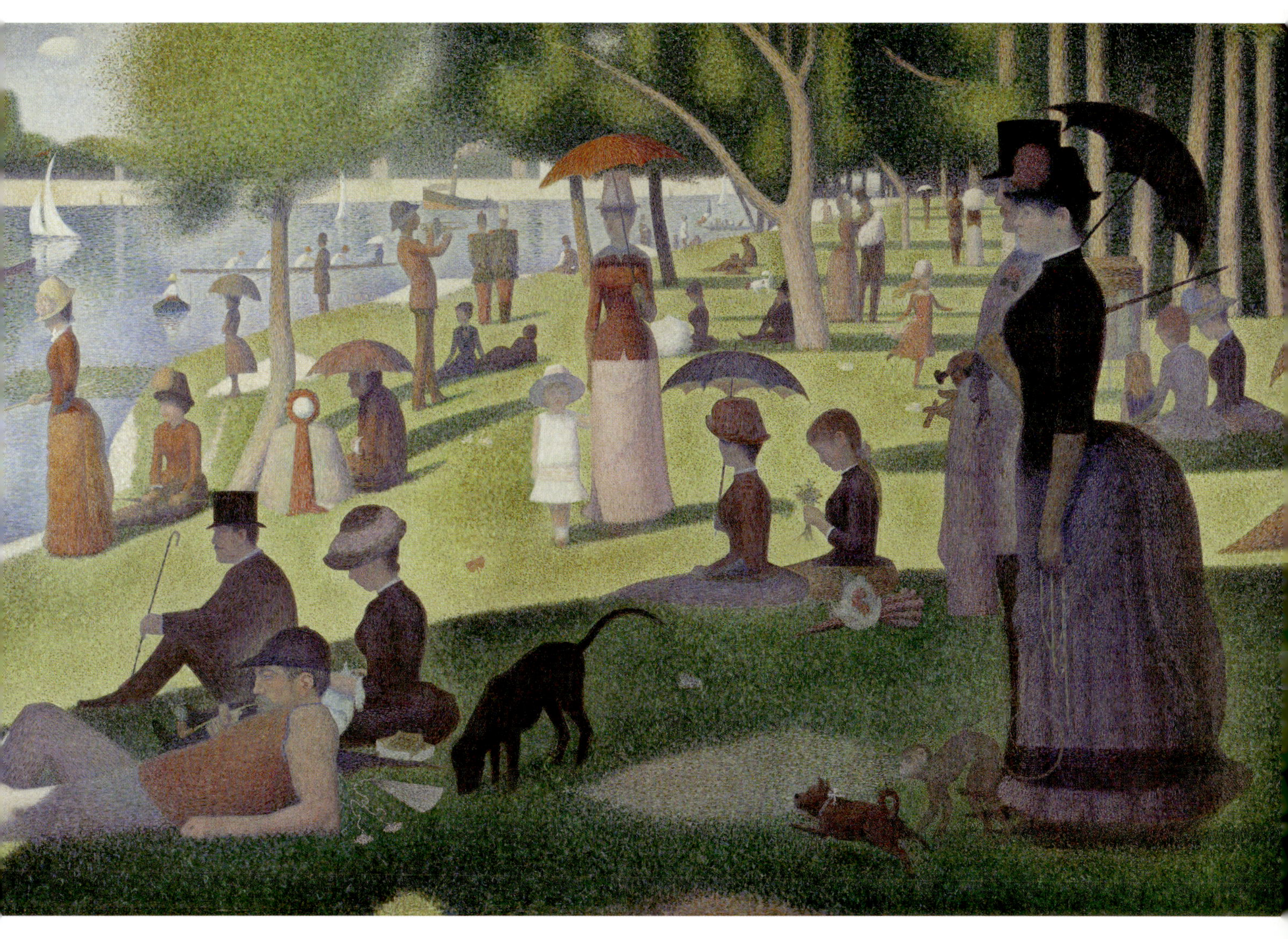

ABSINTHE

Until it was banned in 1915, absinthe – the 'green fairy' – was one of the muses of art and literature in the late 19th century. Absinthe was usually drunk in ice water, sometimes with sugar, making it cloudier but reducing the alcohol content, which was quite high (between 45 and 75 per cent) in order to stabilize the chlorophyll. There were four varieties: 'ordinaire', 'demi-fine', 'fine' and 'supérieure'. The best-known brand was Pernod Fils. After absinthe was prohibited, Pernod developed *pastis*, with a star anise base replacing the green anise seeds and liquorice.

Absinthe was produced by the maceration and distillation of various herbs, and the green from the chlorophyll could be more or less intense. In addition to absinthe leaves, it contained green anise seeds and the seeds of fennel, hyssop, lemon balm and sage, as well as other ingredients that varied from distillery to distillery (but including angelica, mint, genepy, camomile, coriander). While some imitations from clandestine distilleries are known (beverages cut with copper or indigo to obtain a green colour), the addition of opium or laudanum, suggested by the effect of somnolence and oblivion from drinking excessive amounts, is unconfirmed.

Glasses of cloudy green liquor appear in a number of paintings by Toulouse-Lautrec, but the image of absinthe in art is indelibly linked to one of the bitterest masterpieces by Edgar Degas, who created an ingenious effect with the cropping of the image from bottom to top and irregular framing. A shabby couple sits without talking at the table of a deserted bar where nothing remains but human solitude and the devastation of relationships and consciousness around a glass of absinthe.

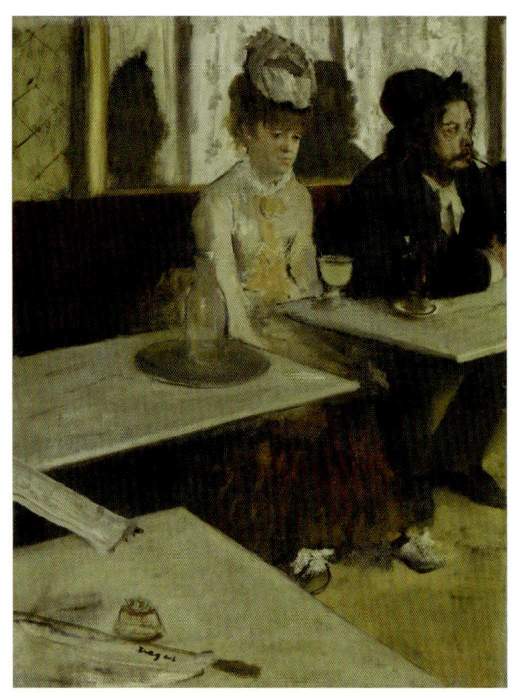

Edgar Degas
In a Café (L'Absinthe)
1875-1876
oil on canvas, 92 x 68 cm
Musée d'Orsay, Paris

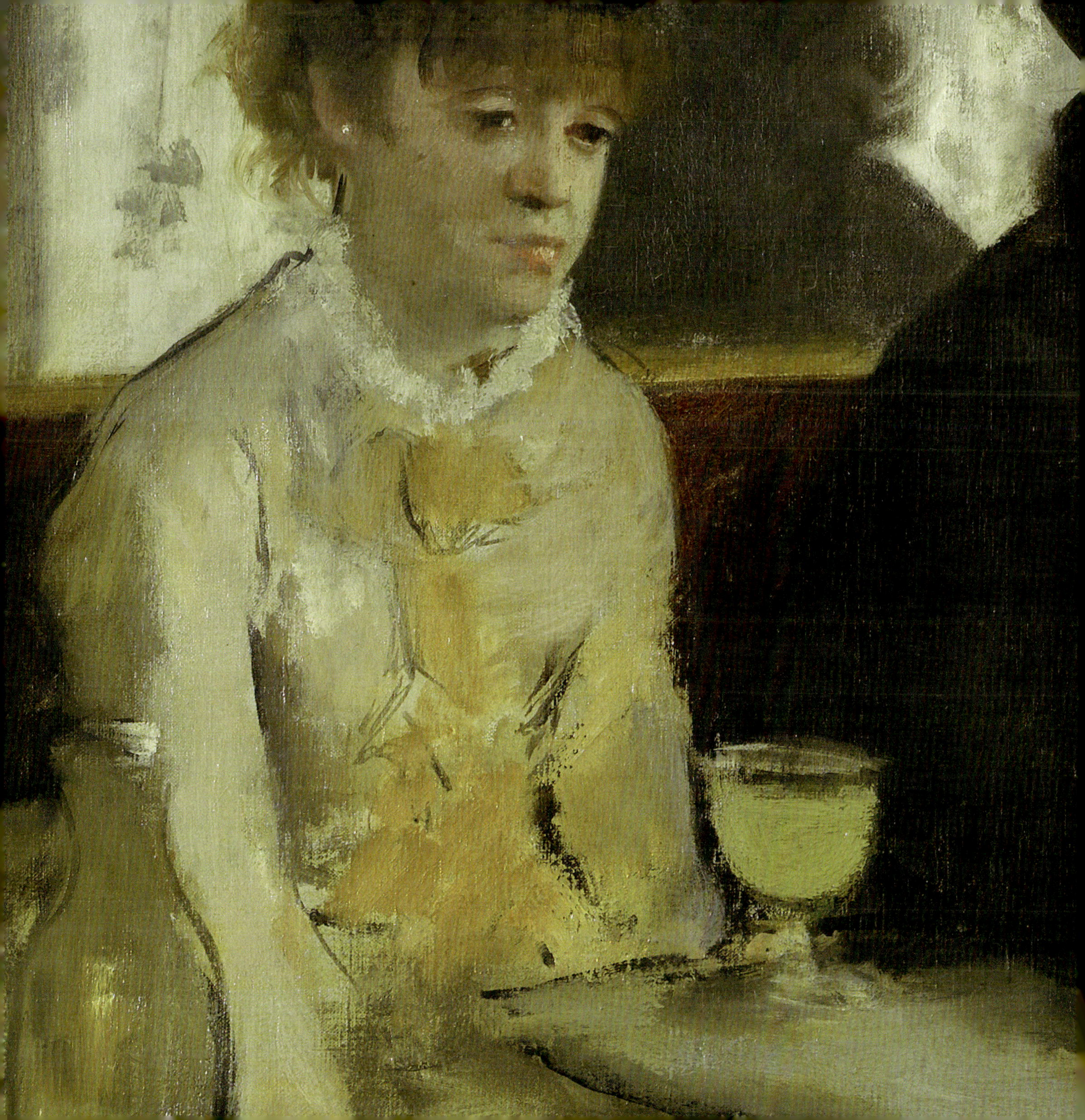

JUNGLE

Henri Rousseau, called Le Douanier because he worked for the Paris customs office, is one of the most surprising artists of the early 20th century. With no academic training, he approached art as a self-taught painter. He began painting as a dilettante, executing awkward copies of famous paintings at the Louvre. After the age of forty, he advanced to independently conceived canvases of great compositional simplicity, with figures and landscapes delineated in an ingenuous and immediate way. His highly stylized forms, cool colours and deceptively simple images depict a fantastic world where traditional patterns collapse. In the years bridging the 19th and 20th centuries, when the taste for ethnic art and a pure and simple 'primitivism' was spreading, the innovativeness and originality of Le Douanier Rousseau's painting won the esteem of other artists. Picasso and Matisse saw a return to the very sources of art and expressiveness in Rousseau's simplified images.

The forms are stylized, the colours cold (a good example is the series of varied greens expressing impenetrable tangles of leaves, creepers and jungle vines), and the images represent a fantastic world where logical links fail. Today, it is hard to discern the lack of an academic 'foundation' in Rousseau's apparent ingenuousness or an actual intention of renewal. His art, which is often singled out as the main source for naive painting, belongs to a cultural period that opened itself to exotic, fantastic worlds laden with mystery and magic. In France one thinks of the novels of Jules Verne, and in English literature, those of H.G. Wells.

Rousseau alternated commonplace scenes in the outskirts of Paris with images of fabulous landscapes and inextricable jungles populated with exotic wild animals and disturbing characters, where the most incredible adventures can occur. Unlike Gauguin, Rousseau never set foot outside France, and these evocations of enchanted landscapes, savage beasts and mysterious plants belong entirely to the world of the imagination.

Henri (Le Douanier) Rousseau
The Snake Charmer
1907
oil on canvas, 167 x 189.5 cm
Musée d'Orsay, Paris

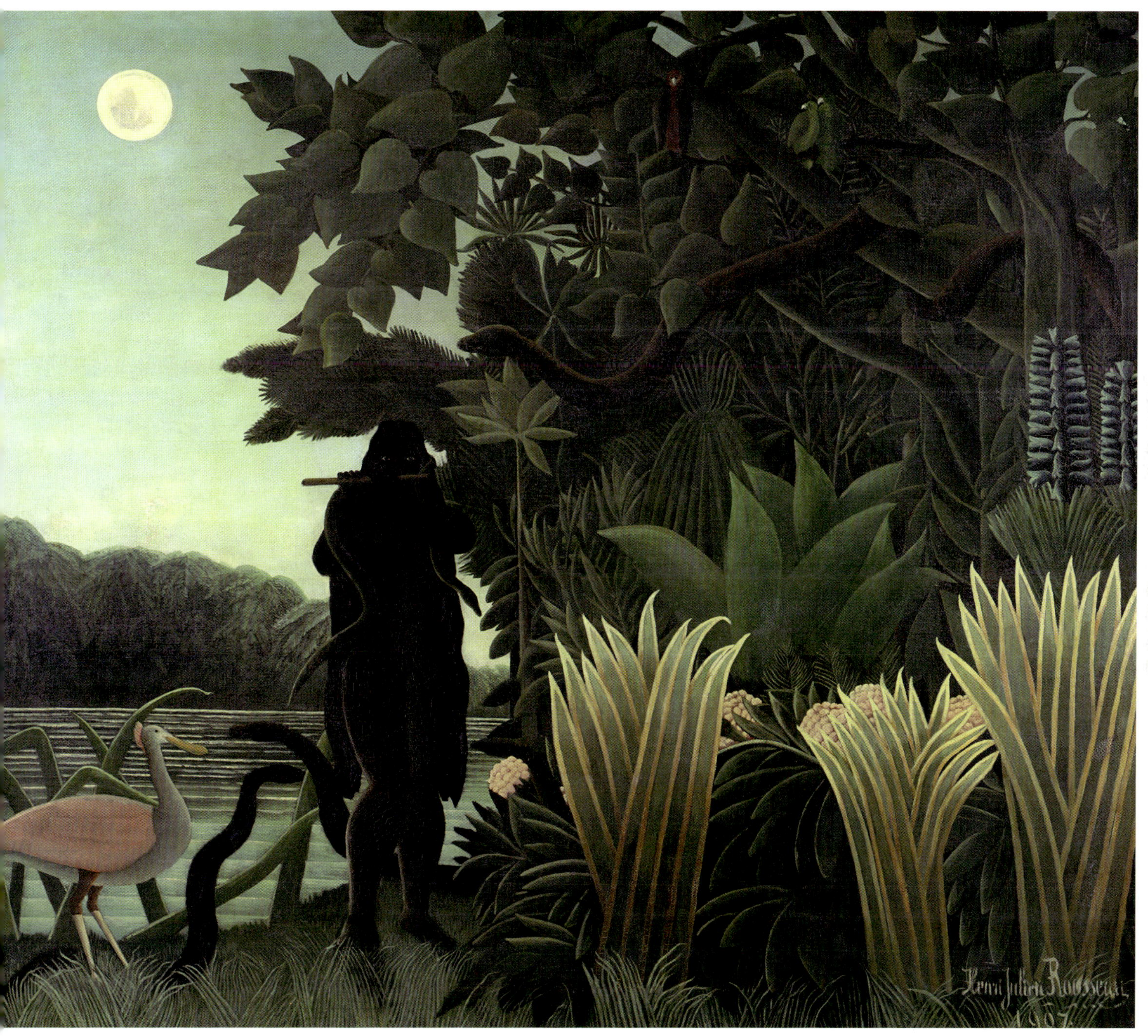
Henri Julien Rousseau
1907

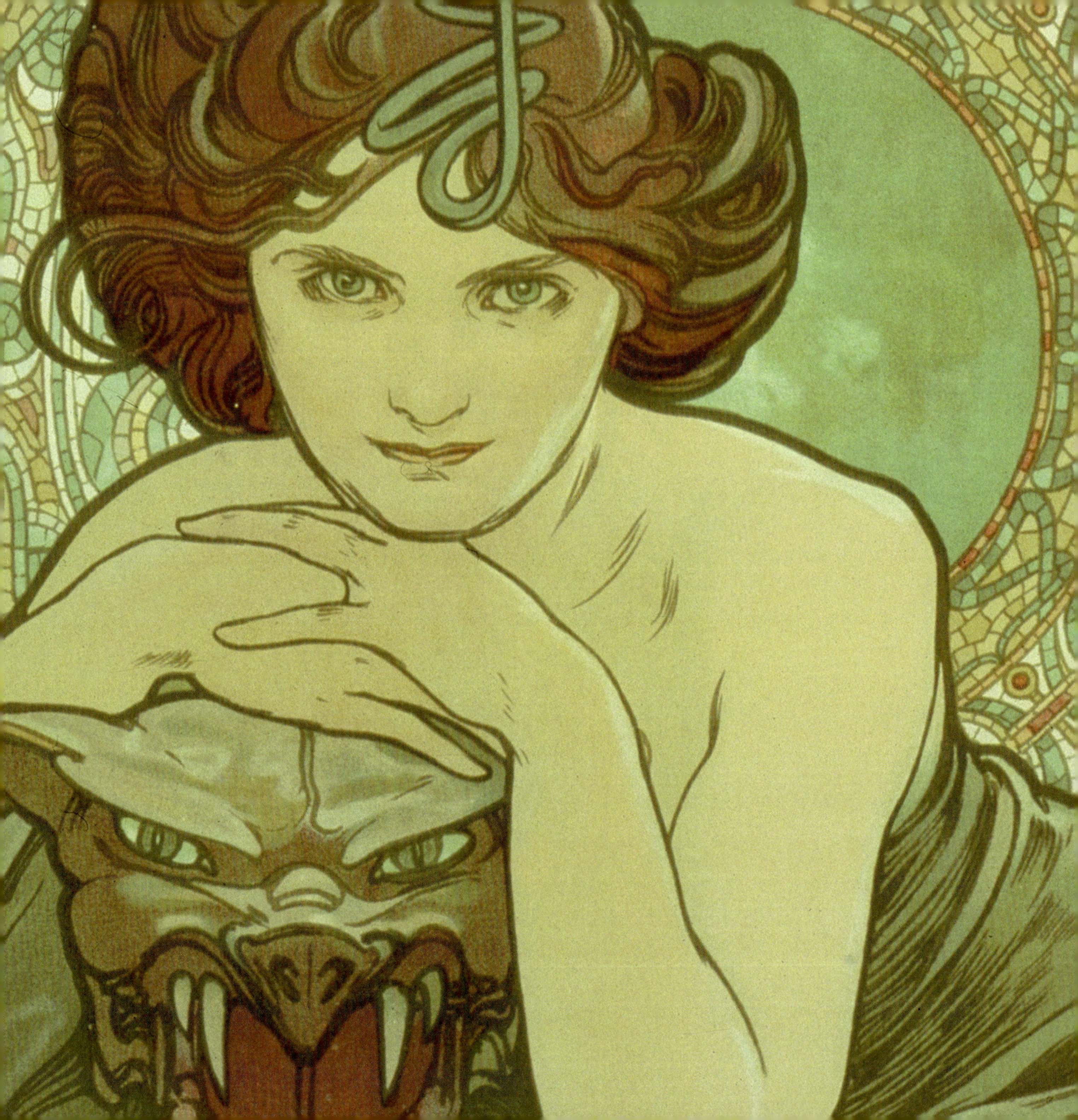

EMERALD GREEN

The emerald derives its name from the Greek *(s)maragdos*, probably from the Semitic *maragata*, meaning 'green'. Due to its green colour and nature, ancient popular belief attributed to the emerald water and rain symbolism – for example, believing that it could keep storms away. On the other hand, the emerald also carries negative associations and has rarely been depicted in art.

Nonetheless, Alphonse Mucha devoted a lithograph to the emerald in his cycle on the precious stones, emblems of international taste during the Belle Époque. The Czech artist refers allegorically to the precious stones' colours and virtues through charming female figures in Neoclassical garb surrounded by floral motifs that form geometric frames. In the emerald lithograph, a young woman comfortably ensconced in a seat with an unusual arm stares at the viewer with a riveting gaze. Her face is set against a circle decorated with geometric motifs, while flowers and leaves, perfectly blended with the figure, occupy the foreground at the foot of her thickly draped dress.

In the medieval era, it was thought that gemstones came from Hell, taken from Lucifer's crown, and for this reason, they were an effective tool for withstanding the forces of the devil. The woman's bewitching gaze could allude to such a legend. She wears a serpentine diadem in her hair and rests her crossed hands on a feline *protome* with a frightful gaping mouth showing sharp teeth.

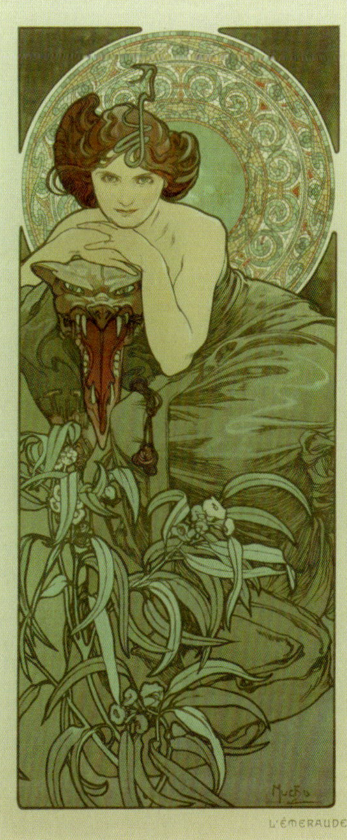

Alphonse Mucha
Emerald
1902
lithograph from the series 'The Precious Stones'
107 x 47.5 cm

GREEN APPLE

'My painting consists of clear images that hide nothing, that evoke mystery. Mystery in turn means nothing, it is unknowable.' In a dispassionate, polished, meticulous style, René Magritte painted a disturbing reality, filled with commonplace objects distorted by alterations or gigantic dimensions. This resulted in enigmatic images that, as he himself stated, are meant to evoke mystery – like the works of De Chirico, they are alienating and frightening at the same time. Some of Magritte's recurrent subjects have become icons of a world where logic is overthrown by a paradoxical vision that is open to various interpretations.

In the Zurich painting, the green apple that often appears in Magritte's paintings – for example, hiding the face of the famous man in a bowler hat – expands to fill an entire room, saturating it, making it cramped and claustrophobic despite the presence of a window at the left. It is an apparently ordinary object that intrusively assumes a threatening meaning here; and this is made even more disturbing by the perfect monochrome, modulated only by the play of shadow created by the light coming in the window.

The fruit of a tree of the Rosaceae family, or *pyrus malus*, the apple is often associated with the sin of seduction because of the resemblance of the Latin words *malus* (apple) and *malum* (evil, wicked). In this case, the object's convulsive hugeness instils a sense of anxiety in viewers, leading them to detect a negative significance in the image. The shrill colour of the fruit's skin refers at the very least to a state of unripeness. Nevertheless, the interpretation of such an image – that is both commonplace and visionary, at the fluid boundary between dream and reality – depends on the sensitivities of the person who is looking at it.

René Magritte
The Listening Room (La Chambre d'écoute)
1958
oil on canvas, 38 x 46 cm
Kunsthaus Zürich

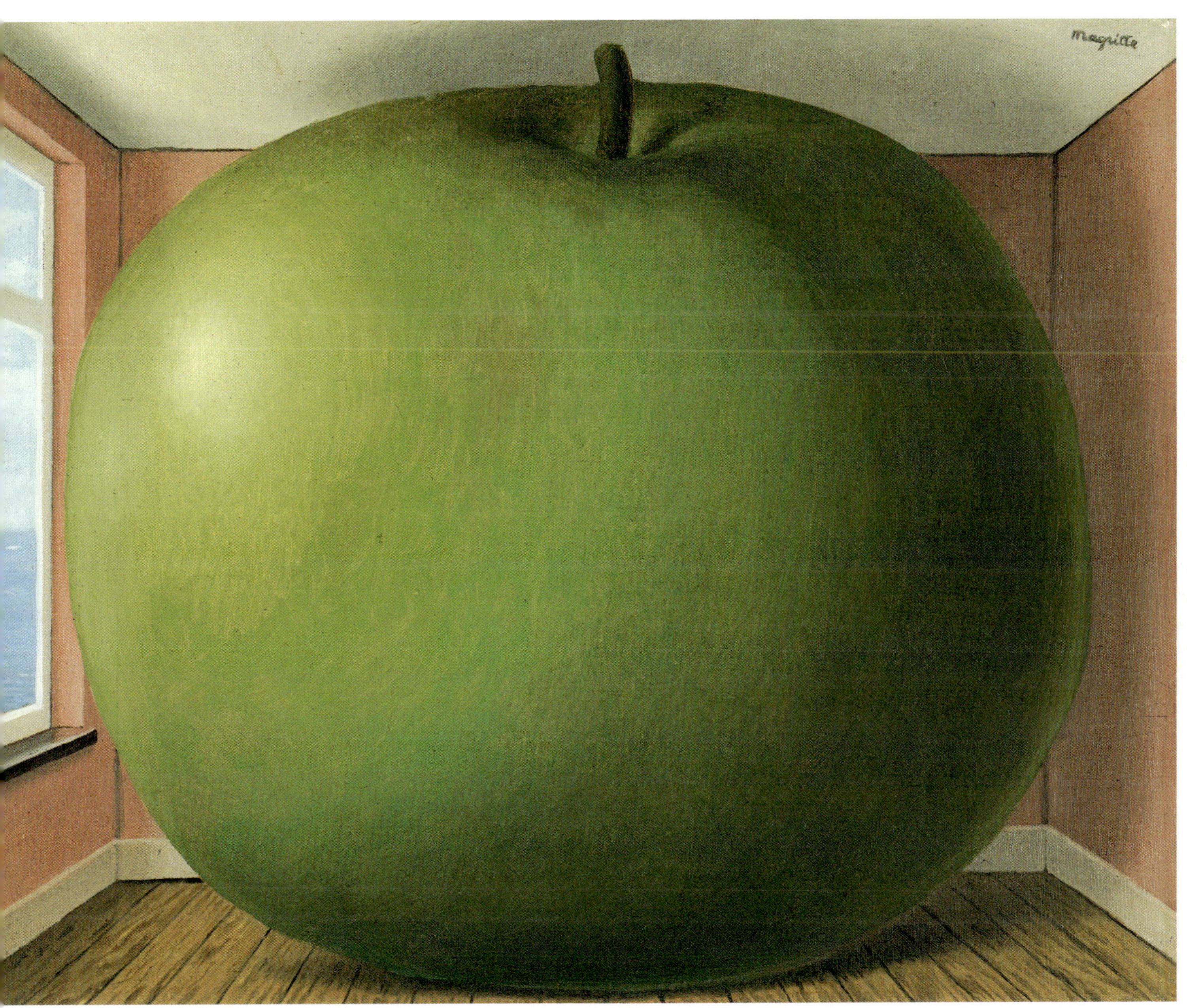
magritte

GOLD

INTRODUCTION

In the Old Testament, the word 'gold' occurs over four hundred times. This alone underlines the strong historical, symbolic and social importance of this precious metal. The characteristics of gold – its resistance to corrosion, brilliance, 'warm' colour and economic and exchange value – have fascinated people on all continents for millennia. Gold seems eternal; it can be continually melted and reshaped without losing any of its value. It is estimated that all of the gold now present on our planet would fit in a cube less than thirty metres on each side – a relatively small volume in which to contain so many cultures and civilizations. Gold jewellery and decorations exist from over six thousand years before the birth of Christ, and the word or ideogram for gold appears in the very earliest written documents, in the first linguistic expressions in Sumerian cuneiform script and Egyptian hieroglyphics.

This chapter refers to some of the countless myths, legends, historical memories and social phenomena connected with gold. In Greek mythology alone, there is the Golden Fleece of Colchis, the golden apple of the Judgement of Paris, the golden fruit in the garden of the Hesperides, the goldwork executed by Hephaestus in his forge beneath Mount Etna, the gold and ivory statue of the goddess Athena in the Parthenon, and the Golden Shower that appeared to Danaë.

The Gold Rush does not concern only the Klondike and Alaska: it has been a constant preoccupation over thousands of years. The pharaohs of Egypt invented complicated ways of preventing the gold in their tombs from being plundered by thieves – all in vain. In their funeral *kurgans*, the chieftains of the nomadic peoples of the steppes buried the gold of the Altai Mountains, whose mines were said to be guarded by gryphons. The Vikings of Scandinavia, although they had no monetary system, used old imperial Roman gold coins for commercial transactions (there are many specimens in the vaults of the National Historical Museum in Stockholm). Adventurers in South America dreamed of reaching Eldorado, and the coffers Spanish galleons transported along Atlantic routes gave rise to raids by pirates of the Caribbean and, today, expeditions in search of sunken treasure. Beyond all consideration of economics and the active circulation of the physical metal, the expression 'golden age' is still used to describe the period of a civilization's greatest flourishing. The 'gold medal' is the most cherished prize – even if in many sports, even the Olympics, the reference is purely chromatic and symbolic. And for centuries, alchemists sought to transform base metals into gold.

Produced and worked since prehistoric times, gold has a high status in art because of its inherent symbolic value of nobility and divinity. Gold is suited to everything sacred: in the Christian world we find it applied to chalices, patens, monstrances, reliquaries, altars, the covers of Gospel Books, ecclesiastical robes and liturgical accessories, and sometimes even the word of God is written in gold. However, the relationship between gold and the Church is a conflicted one. The objection has often been raised that the Church should use its gold to help the poor. In the 11th century, Abbot Suger of Saint-Denis summarized the meaning behind the use of precious furnishings: 'I confess it always has seemed right to me that the most expensive things should be used above all for the administration of the holy Eucharist ... It is proper to have vessels of gold, priceless stones and all that is considered most precious in Creation to receive the blood of Jesus Christ. Those who criticize us object that all that is required for such a celebration is a holy spirit, a pure soul, an intention of faith. I admit this is most important of all but also assert that we must serve with the exterior ornamentation of sacred vessels, and above all else in the holy sacrifice, with absolute inward purity and outward nobility.'

Gold is not only a 'valuable commodity': it is the intimation of a place, space and time beyond the human. Sacred Byzantine art elevated this concept to the level of mysticism. The gold used in icons and in the covering of domes, apses and other parts of a church helps the transcendence of the earthly level, transferring it to a higher context. Enraptured by the contemplation of gold, worshippers in turn raise their spirits and prayers above the simple sphere of human reality.

THE TREASURE OF TUTANKHAMUN

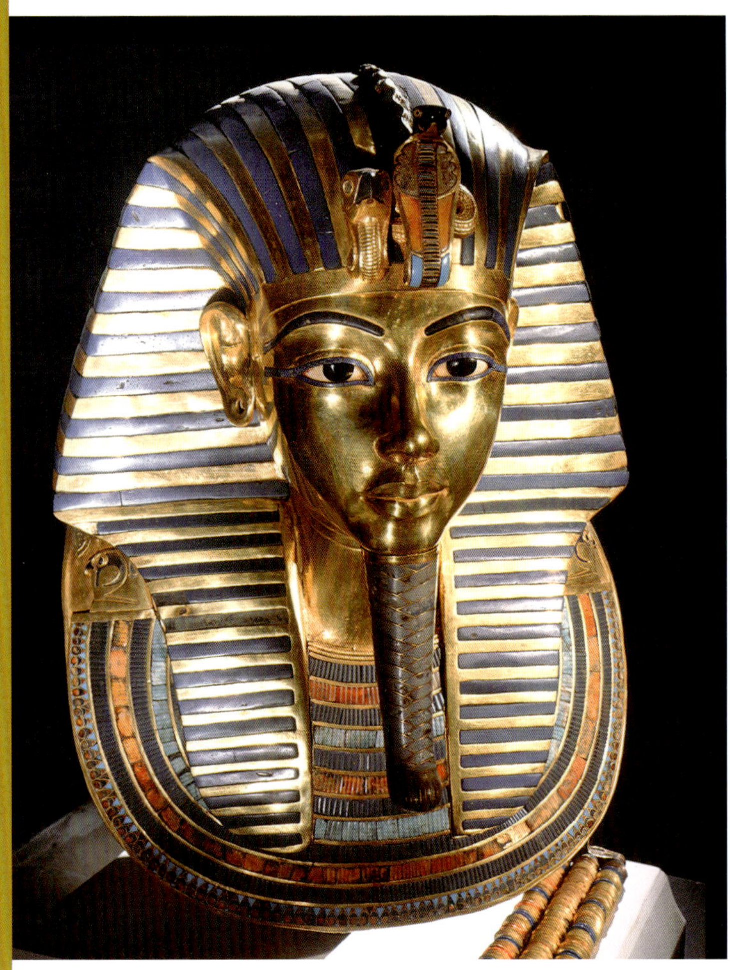

Burial Mask of Tutankhamun
gold, lapis lazuli, carnelian, quartz, obsidian, turquoise and coloured glass, 54 cm (h.)
Egyptian Museum, Cairo

Tutankhamun, 'living image of Amun', ascended to the throne in 1336 BC at the age of nine and died ten years later. During his reign, he repudiated the cult of Aten and reinstated that of Amun, moving the capital to Thebes. Tutankhamun was buried in the Valley of the Kings with sumptuous grave goods consisting of about 5,500 objects. When discovered by Howard Carter in 1922, the tomb had been violated but very little had been plundered, so it provides a historical and artistic record of inestimable value. The treasure constitutes the largest example of goldwork from any time or civilization.

The burial chamber was occupied almost entirely by an enormous gold-laminated casket (measuring 275 x 508 x 238 cm) inside which was a wooden structure covered in linen. This contained a third structure, again laminated with gold decorated in relief, and finally a fourth (190 x 290 x 148 cm), on which the funeral procession was depicted. This contained a quartzite coffin with a granite lid, inside which was a gold-clad wooden sarcophagus in the shape of a mummy that contained a third mummiform sarcophagus, again in gold-clad wood, encrusted with glass paste and semiprecious stones. This protected the spectacularly beautiful solid-gold mummy-shaped sarcophagus, weighing over 110 kg, similar in shape to the preceding one but of impressive technical and artistic quality, skilfully shaped and inlaid with lapis lazuli, carnelian, zirconium, malachite and faience. When this innermost sarcophagus was opened, it revealed, as a final protection for the mummy, a dazzling golden mask with the youthful features of the pharaoh – fleshy lips, eyes of lapis lazuli and white and black stones, a royal vulture and serpent headdress – and a spectacular pectoral.

The most valuable piece in the adjacent treasury was the canopic shrine, guarded by a statue of the jackal-headed god Anubis in stuccoed and gilded wood. Inside that, an alabaster shrine contained four canopic jars, also of alabaster and sealed with images of the pharaoh's face, containing small gold sarcophaguses that held the pharaoh's stomach, intestines, liver and lungs, which had been removed during embalming.

Among the other finds, which were almost all of extraordinary value and superb artistic quality, were a ceremonial cart, three funerary beds with frames in the form of animals, refined alabaster objects, an inlaid ceremonial seat, *ushabti* (statuettes representing 'answerers' – that is, those who will work in place of the deceased in the afterlife), various images of the pharaoh, an exquisite chequerboard, ceremonial daggers and swords, and countless gems and jewels of stupefying beauty, including the Horus pectoral with its spectacular plumage in glass paste. Special mention should be made of the stuccoed-wood casket painted with Tutankhamun on the war carriage to rout the enemy hordes and the magnificent gold-covered wooden throne inlaid with silver, semiprecious stones and glass paste, on whose back the young pharaoh is represented in a scene of everyday intimacy with his wife.

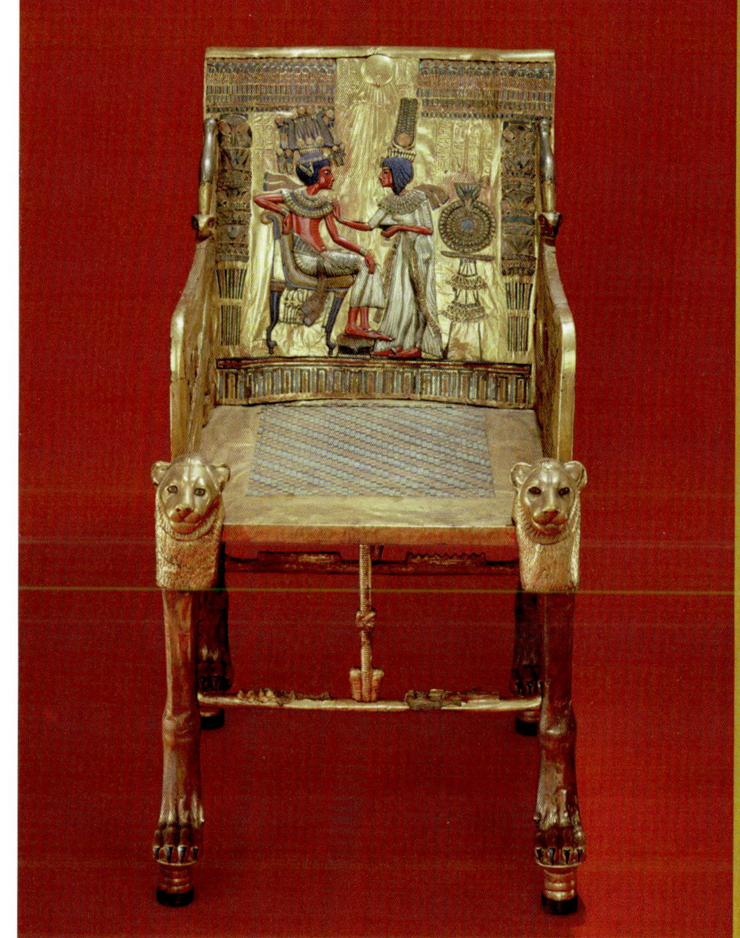

Royal Throne, Reign of Tutankhamun
c. 1336-1327 BC
wood, sheet gold, silver, semiprecious and other stones
faience, glass and bronze, 100 cm (h.)
Egyptian Museum, Cairo

GOLD OF THE STEPPES

Gold is almost the only testimony remaining of some peoples who have otherwise fallen into oblivion. The ancient Scythians and Sarmatians lived in the area between the Crimea, the Caucasus and the Russian plains, in the heart of Eurasia – that single continent that successive historical events have divided into two, creating a rift between East and the West. Our main source of information about these peoples is the Greek historian Herodotus, who collected valuable information (while also including outlandish fantasy and blood-curdling details). The pages Herodotus devotes to the Scythians gleam with gold; even the skulls of their enemies killed in battle were gilded inside and used as ceremonial cups.

Proud of their identity (they considered themselves the descendants of a love between Hercules and a half-woman, half-serpent creature) but enriched by a multiplicity of cultural influences from many different groups, the nomads of the steppes were abruptly erased from history. In the 3rd century BC, they seem to have dissolved under the force of the Mongol invasions. Now, centuries later and thanks to recent finds of exceptional interest, these ancient peoples have re-emerged from their previous obscurity. They left no cities, monuments or written records. The vestiges of their culture are confined to a thin trace of precious gold objects found in their only stable 'residences' – those of the dead. The panoramic view of the plains north of the Black Sea is occasionally broken by rounded funerary tumuli called *kurgans*. Inside these – sometimes of imposing size – are rooms in which these ancient peoples' important figures were buried along with sumptuous grave goods at the close of a ritual with bloody and dramatic implications.

Vessels, jewellery, relief sculptures, scabbards, brooches, appliqués, ornaments for clothing and horse trappings: the sparkle of gold adorns many objects from the daily lives of the people of the steppes. Their style ranges from the most refined Greek creations to obvious influences from Persia and even China. The dominant theme is animals: the fascinating bestiary that emerges from the tumuli is dominated by the figure of the deer but also includes horses, fish, wolves, lions, panthers, wild boar, camels, eagles and rams. In general, the artistic production of these groups dwells on the essence of nature, the body and the movements of animals. An ingenious stylization, in which the synthesis of form follows the lines of force, brings the animals' aggressive character leaping to life. Following the thread of this expressive distortion, the most typical characters of an animal are exaggerated beyond proportion. The deer's antlers, for example, far surpass natural proportions to become pure ornament, a stylistic effect of sophisticated, almost hypnotic beauty.

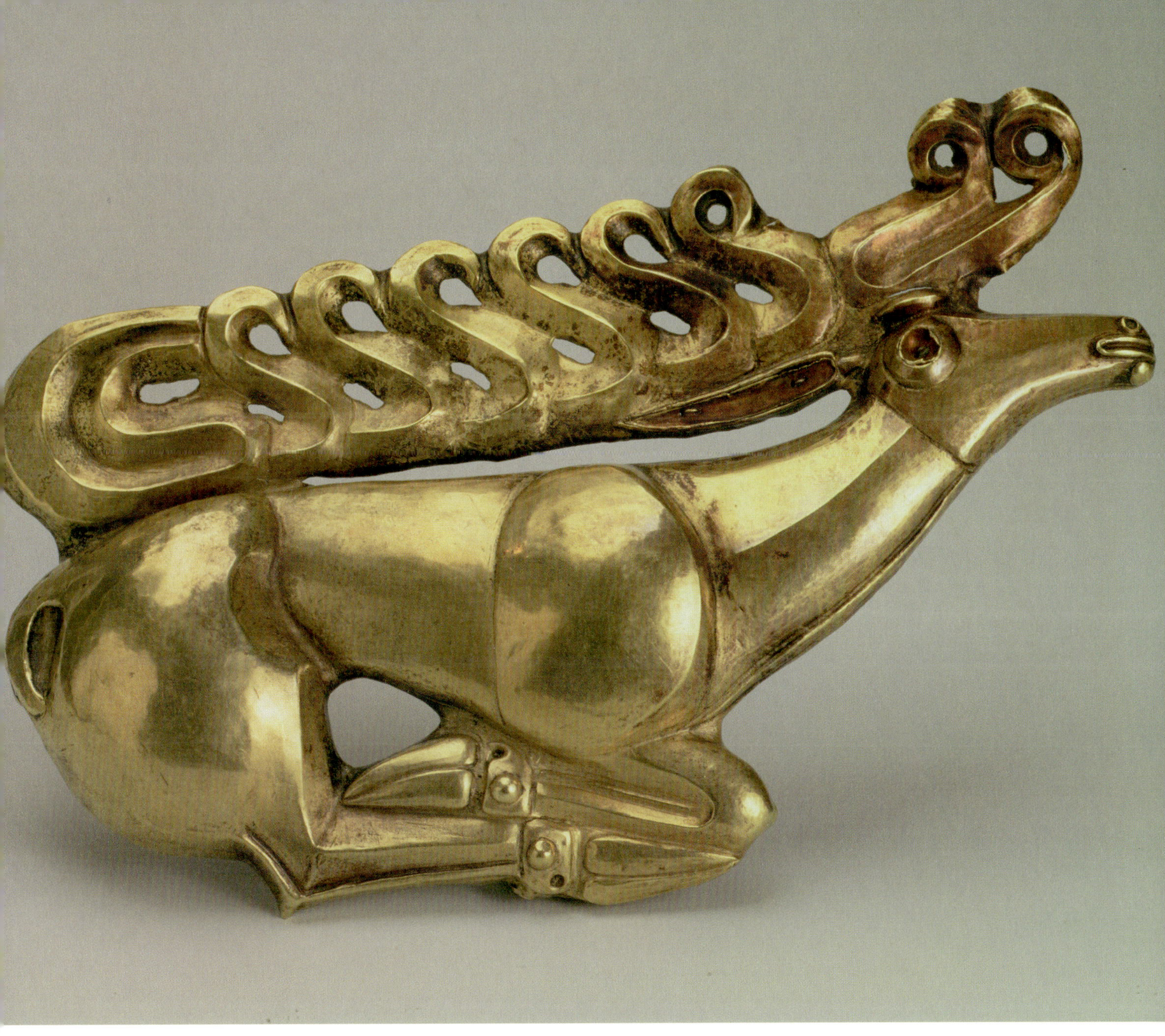

Scythian Shield Emblem in the Form of a Recumbent Stag
late 7th-early 6th century BC
gold, 19 x 31.7 cm
Hermitage, St Petersburg

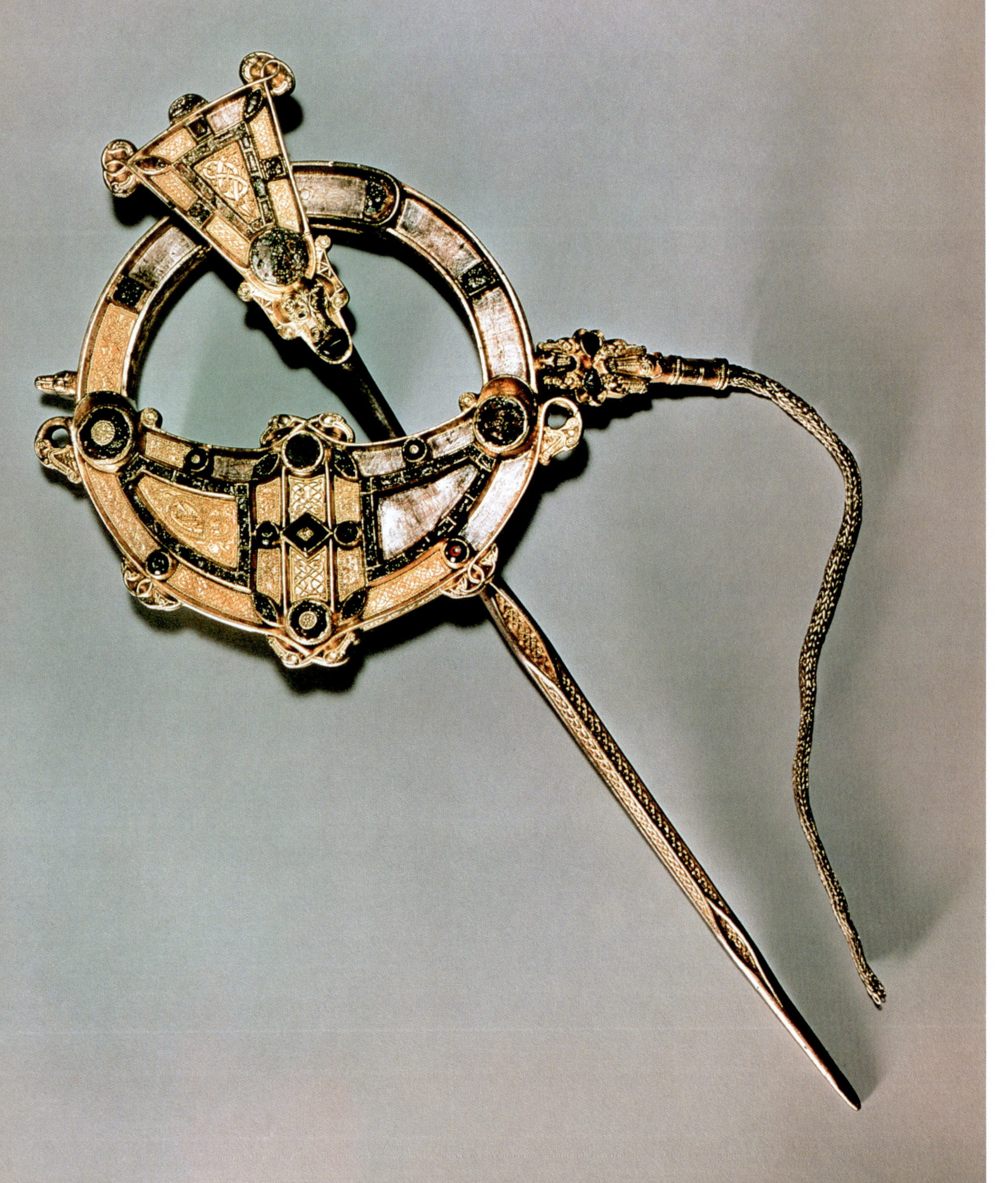

THE GOLDSMITH'S ART
THE LEADING ART OF THE EARLY MIDDLE AGES

Humanist historical writing, beginning in the 15th century, gives a decidedly negative slant to the clash between the people that lived in the northern and eastern limits of Europe and the Roman Empire during its decline. The generic designation 'barbarian' means 'stammering', emphasizing a scant knowledge of language as well as a lack of 'civilized' manners and customs. Various barbarian kingdoms were founded at the fall of the Western Roman Empire (AD 476): the Anglo-Saxons in the British Isles, the Franks and Burgundians in Gaul, the Visigoths in Spain, the Vandals in the Roman provinces of Northern Africa, and the Ostrogoths in Italy.

The rise of the 'barbarians' coincided with the decline of monumental artistic forms such as architecture, large-scale sculpture, and painted and mosaic wall decoration. On the other hand, other art techniques, related to the traditions of the new peoples, who were skilled in working transportable materials like wood, metal and leather, underwent strong growth. Moreover, in the second half of the 5th century, these peoples began converting to Christianity, transferring the features of their previous art into Christian liturgical objects and iconographical subjects. The goldsmith's art took its place as the most important artistic technique throughout the entire early Middle Ages, producing highly original results. The ornamental qualities of gold leaf clearly inspired stone reliefs, miniatures and book decoration (for example, by skilled Irish monks), while the capitals of columns show the influence of the cell-like decoration found on fibulas and jewellery.

Roman art, seeking a perfect imitation of reality, had developed the portrait genre and employed perspective to create the impression of depth. On the other hand, meaningful objects in the nomadic peoples' expressive formal language reduced human figures, animals and plants to flat shapes, emphasizing ornamental lines derived from goldwork, geometry and, most often, symbolic references. The Celts, the Lombard kings and then the Carolingian and Saxon emperors concentrated on the quest for easily recognizable symbols to express their rule. Thus, Christian themes (for example, the fish and the bunch of grapes) were no longer approached as imitations of nature but through a code of symbolic communication, simplified yet enormously powerful.

The Tara Brooch
8th century
silver gilt, amber, polychrome enamel, glass and pearls, diam. 8.7 cm
National Museum of Ireland, Dublin

THE TREASURY OF AACHEN

Lotharkreuz (Cross of Lothair)
with an Antique Gem of Emperor Augustus
c. 1000
gilded copper with gems, 49.8 cm (h.)
Treasury, Dome, Aachen

After the arrival of the magnificent gold artefacts plundered from Byzantium in 1204, the treasury of the Basilica of San Marco in Venice never again saw additions of the same quality; the Sack of Rome in 1527 brought about the dispersal of St Peter's treasury; the devastation of the French Revolution in 1789 reduced the treasury of the royal basilica of St Denis to a few fragments. Thus, today the largest surviving treasury in Western Christendom can be found at the prestigious ancient imperial seat of Aachen. Founded by Charlemagne at the dawn of the 9th century, the Palatine Chapel was conceived as a living memorial and the inheritor of the Roman Empire. It includes extraordinary late Roman bronzes and other classical finds, such as columns from Ravenna.

According to the wishes of Otto I, in 972 Aachen was proclaimed the coronation city. Imperial investiture took place there until 1531. With the renewal of travel and trade after the year 1000, Aachen became the focus of a kind of 'court pilgrimage', with donations and processions worthy of the Magi, solemnized by the proclamation of the sanctity of the founder Charlemagne. Upon the coronation of each new emperor, the Palatine Chapel was enriched with priceless gifts.

One of these gifts, from the early 11th century, was the cross given by Lothair. On the obverse it is decorated with pearls, cameos and precious stones, while the reverse has a Crucifix incised into the shining gilded surface, in which the skilful use of lines suffuses the figure with intense drama. Another key treasure was the golden frontal for the high altar, with sixteen relief carvings executed by Fulda and given by Otto III; and immediately after, in 1014, Henry II gave the ambo consisting of a dazzling parapet clad with metal strips and supported by a stone base, its decoration including inserted precious objects of various kinds, periods and origins (6th-century ivory strips, Egyptian crystal, even chess pieces made in the East).

More than a century later, Frederick I Barbarossa gave an imposing hanging chandelier, executed by Master Wibert soon after the middle of the 12th century, and later came an early 13th-century golden reliquary for the remains of Charlemagne. Following the emperor's canonization, his remains were transferred to this reliquary from the 2nd-century AD marble sarcophagus (called the Proserpina Sarcophagus) in which they had been kept previously. Later, the treasury received another typical product of early 13th-century Rhenish goldwork, the case for the so-called relics of the Virgin Mary (they are actually fragments of fabric and other personal objects).

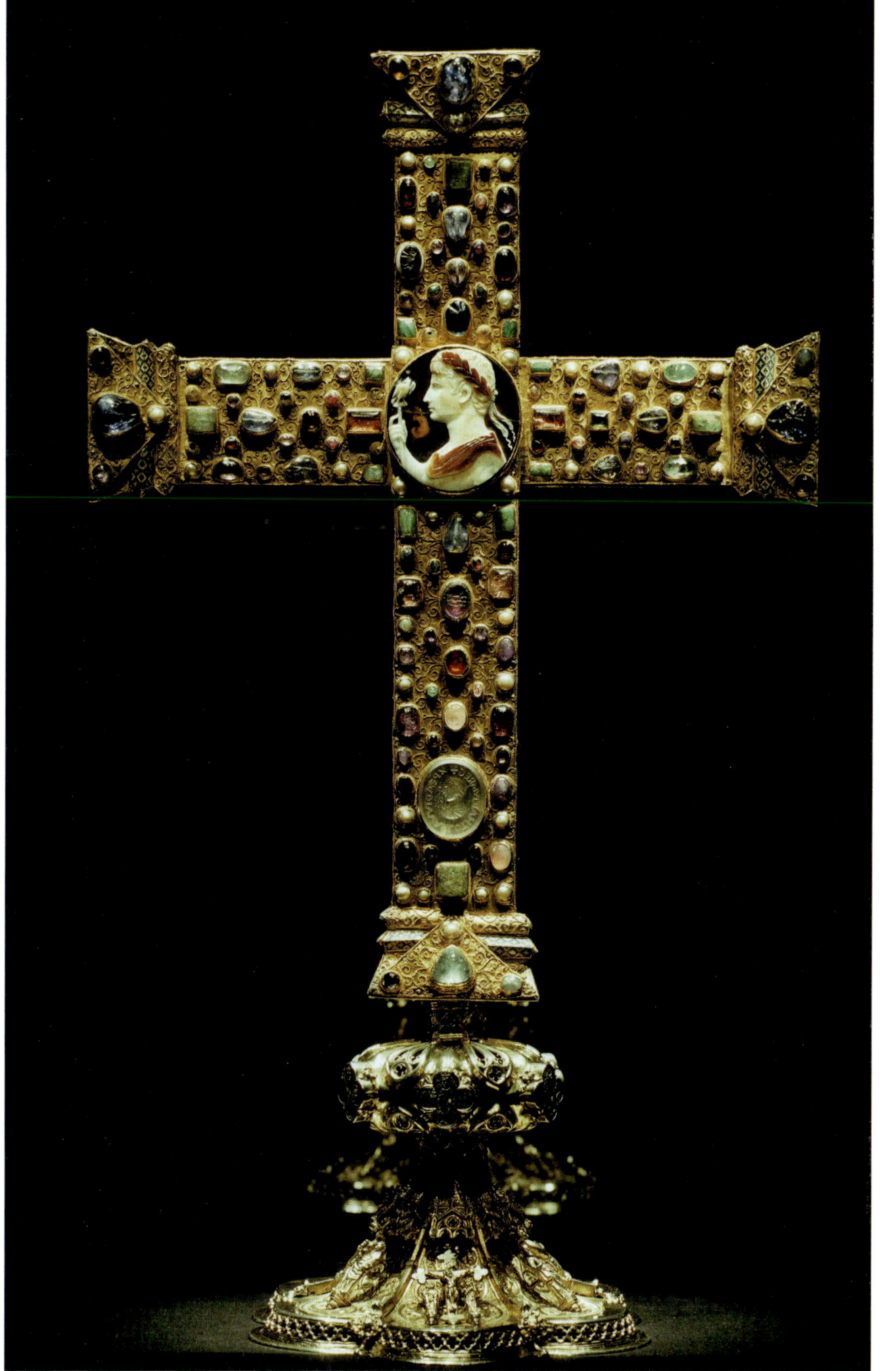

THE GOLDEN TEMPLE
THE CATHEDRAL OF MONREALE

The cathedral of Monreale, called the Golden Temple, was built at the wish of the Norman king William II of Altavilla as the symbolic centre of his glory and power over Sicily. Its interior is covered in more than 8,000 square metres of mosaics with a gold background, virtually obliterating the architectural structure. Set ablaze by the Mediterranean light that filters through the large windows, gold seems to flood everywhere, at the tops of the walls, descending from the ceiling, inundating the apse, gliding under the arches, outlining the mouldings, penetrating the window jambs, embedding itself in most of the marble cladding.

The iconographic programme of the Monreale mosaics is particularly elaborate. Although it is not known who devised it, it was in all probability a Benedictine monk. The plan and choice of individual subjects in various sections reveals a true expert in the mysteries of religion as well as a precocious genius for interpreting the sovereign's wishes. William II appears several times, wrapped in precious garments of silk and gold, as he receives a jewelled crown from Christ and the Virgin. It was William's idea to transform his grandfather's hunting estate into the centre of Sicilian Christianity and build, in his words (written in 1183), 'a work that has not been done by any king since ancient times, that will make all who come to know it marvel'. William is buried at Monreale, in the tomb next to his father's. But perhaps he imagined he would be resting like God the Father, who on the seventh day, sat wearily in the Garden of Eden and 'saw everything that he had made, and, behold, it was very good'.

Executed in the few short years during which the cathedral was being built (1172–1176), the mosaics of Monreale represent a crossroads of Byzantine, Arabic and Latin-Western traditions: an immersion in the colour that takes form, in the Idea that becomes an image, in the figure that is transformed into action. When this ravishing covering was being installed, part of Sicily was still Arab. The worshippers of Allah could have been driven out, forced to convert or persecuted by the Normans, but William II chose another path. Muslims are not permitted to represent the face of God, but in the gold of Monreale, God (the Father and the Son) appears a full fifty-three times, including the gigantic image of the Pantocrator that occupies the entire apse. At the end of the world and history, in a blaze of gold, Christ holds a book in which the same sentence is written in Greek and Latin: 'I am the light of the world; he that followeth me shall not walk in darkness.' [John 8:12]

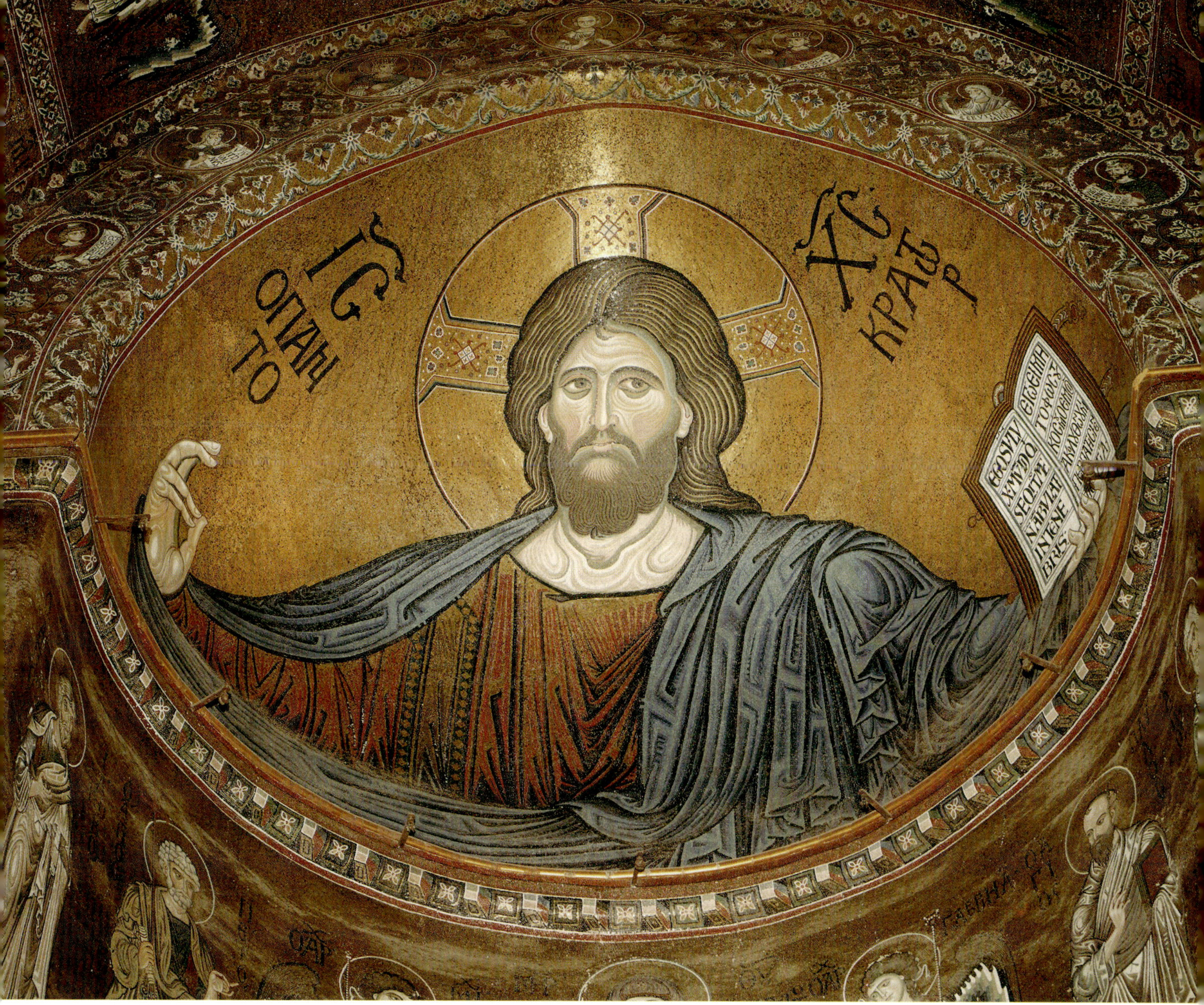

Christ Pantocrator
2nd half of the 12th century
mosaic
Cathedral of Monreale

Nicolas of Verdun
The Klosterneuburg Altar, Depicting Biblical Scenes
1181
gilded copper and champlevé enamel, 110 cm (h.)
Stiftsmuseum, Klosterneuburg, Austria

NICOLAS OF VERDUN:
FAR MORE THAN A GOLDSMITH

The Mosan goldsmiths of the 12th and 13th centuries were versatile artists, able to handle the pencil, burin and hammer with equal skill. They showed an outstanding sense of colour in their use of enamels and actually designed architectural models for their imposing, complicated reliquaries.

The undisputed master of Mosan-Lorraine goldwork, Nicolas of Verdun, is typical of the distinctive phase of the classical revival in Central European art on the eve of the 13th century, between the waning of the Romanesque period and the early burgeoning of the Gothic.

Because of the variety and complexity of the techniques Nicolas of Verdun used, to refer to him as a goldsmith might seem limiting: the plastic power of his figures, the technically impeccable use and combination of various materials, the ability to switch from graphic art to high-relief sculpture and the monumental feeling of the whole make him an artist of great and varied talents – certainly one of the greatest creative geniuses of medieval Europe.

The signatures on his masterpieces partly compensate for the lack of documents concerning his life. The stylistic influences in his works cover a wide cultural range, from Rheims-school sculpture to the classicism of Mosan ivories and miniatures, from the influence of the Rhineland to the Byzantine influence widely seen throughout the 12th and 13th centuries. Nicolas's production can be summed up by three masterpieces: the altar at the Abbey of Klosterneuburg, near Vienna (1181); the reliquary chest of the Three Magi in Cologne (1197); and the shrine of Our Lady of Flanders at the Cathedral of Notre-Dame in Tournai (1205). In addition to these there is the reliquary of St Anno, at the abbey church of St Michael in Seigburg (1184), in a somewhat poorer state of conservation.

The altarpiece at the Abbey of Klosterneuburg presents the most 'pictorial' aspect of Nicolas of Verdun's output. Commissioned by the Augustinian prior Werner in 1181 and originally meant for the decoration of an ambo, it was consequently damaged and dismantled, and then reassembled in its present form of an altar with winged panels. It has fifty-one plaques devoted to Old and New Testament subjects following a remarkably original iconographic system in which highly effective short texts are incorporated perfectly with the images. The plaques are held together by a frame and geometric ligatures into which allegorical figures and architectural elements are inserted at regular intervals. Nicolas uses the technique of champlevé enamel, achieving

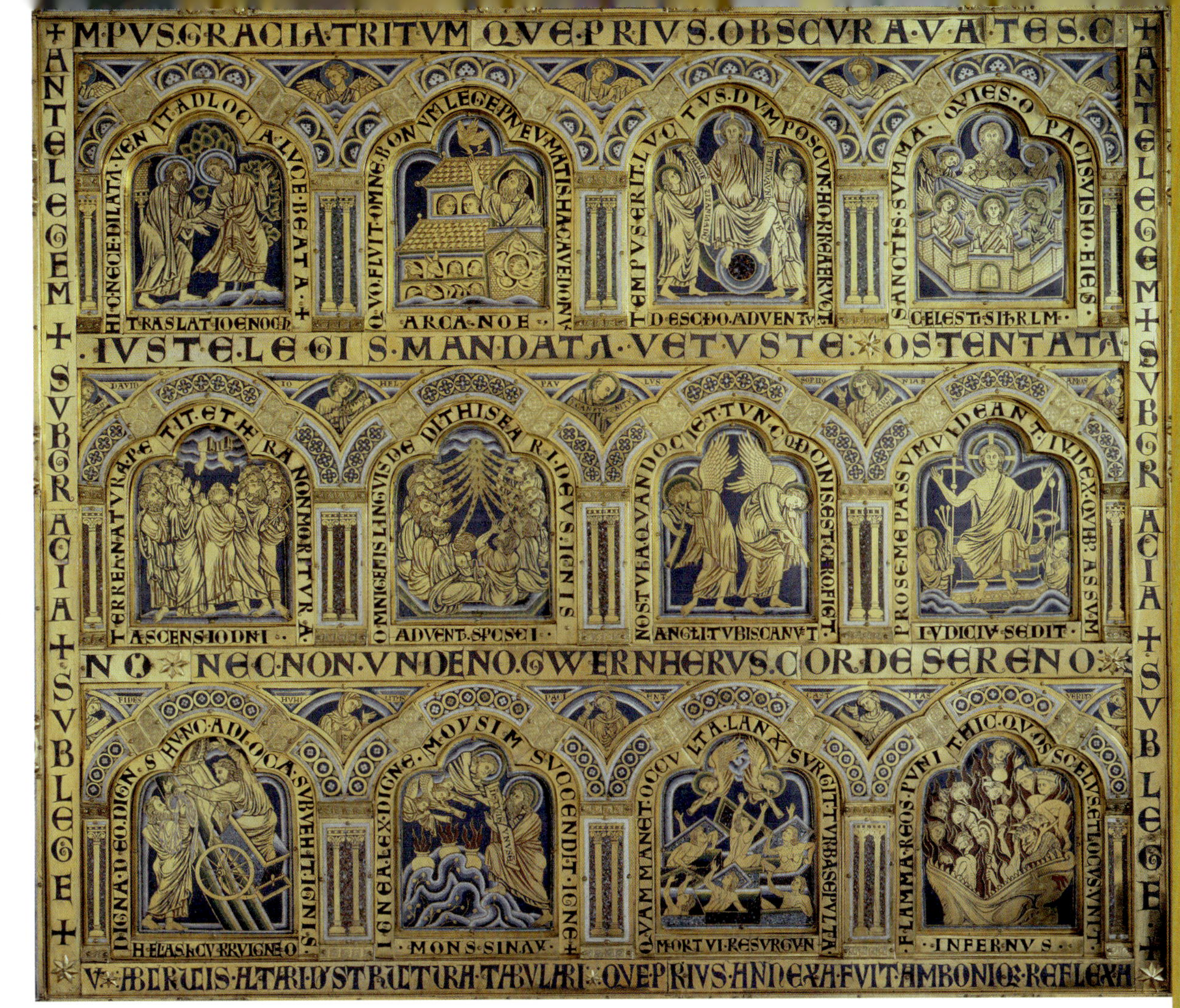

unsurpassed results in the monumental drama of the episodes, yet without relying on a particularly rich chromatic range. The elegant harmony of gold, blue and green confers upon the altar a characteristically measured tone. Another unmistakable element in the work of Nicolas of Verdun is the use of writing, already present in Mosan goldwork but brought by him to a level of great communicative and graphic prominence, with effective placement of the Latin words in a lettering style of surprising clarity and modernity.

PAINTINGS WITH GOLD BACKGROUND

The typical altarpiece from the late Middle Ages was a panel painting or polyptych with a gold background. Before the development of naturalistic perspective (and the consequent adoption of natural or architectural backgrounds), it was customary to set divine figures against a gleaming background of gold. The procedure for painting in tempera on wood panel is described in detail in Cennino Cennini's *The Craftsman's Handbook*, a practical treatise written in the vernacular Italian at the end of the 14th century by an artist with long experience in a workshop following the tradition of Giotto. The support for a painting is made up of one or more wood planks (for example, poplar, Scotch pine, oak or walnut) glued together; this is then braced at the back by shaped crosspieces, and held together in an outer frame closed with nails inserted from the front and bent at the back.

The artist must therefore plan the architectural arrangement of the whole, shape and prepare the panels, have the frame made, and design and execute the painting. When determining the composition, he must bear in mind the effect of the details versus the whole – that is, the pictorial quality of the individual panel, the alignment of the images and the shape of the frame.

The wooden panel, sometimes with strips of canvas glued to it, is primed with a mixture of gesso and animal glue (up to eight layers, the first rough and the last with the finest plaster powder) to form a ground. Once dry, the ground is smoothed and tinted with a coat of white or pale green tempera. At this point it is ready to be painted. Mainly tempera is used. The pigments are ground to a fine powder and then 'tempered' – melted with various binders that set solid when dry. The binders are organic: egg, milk, hide glue, wax and gums combined with water.

The panel's gold leaf background is a very thin layer obtained by hammering pure gold between two skins. Attached to the ground with the bolus (oily clay melted with water and egg white), the gold leaf is spread evenly with a flock of wadding on the portion not occupied by the figures and finally fixed with a punching tool. These tools may include elaborate decorative motifs and be prepared specifically for the halo of the Virgin Mary and saints. All the important artists in the late Middle Ages had their own punches, and comparative study of this detail can help in establishing an attribution.

The finished tempera painting is treated with various varnishes to give it lustre and protect the

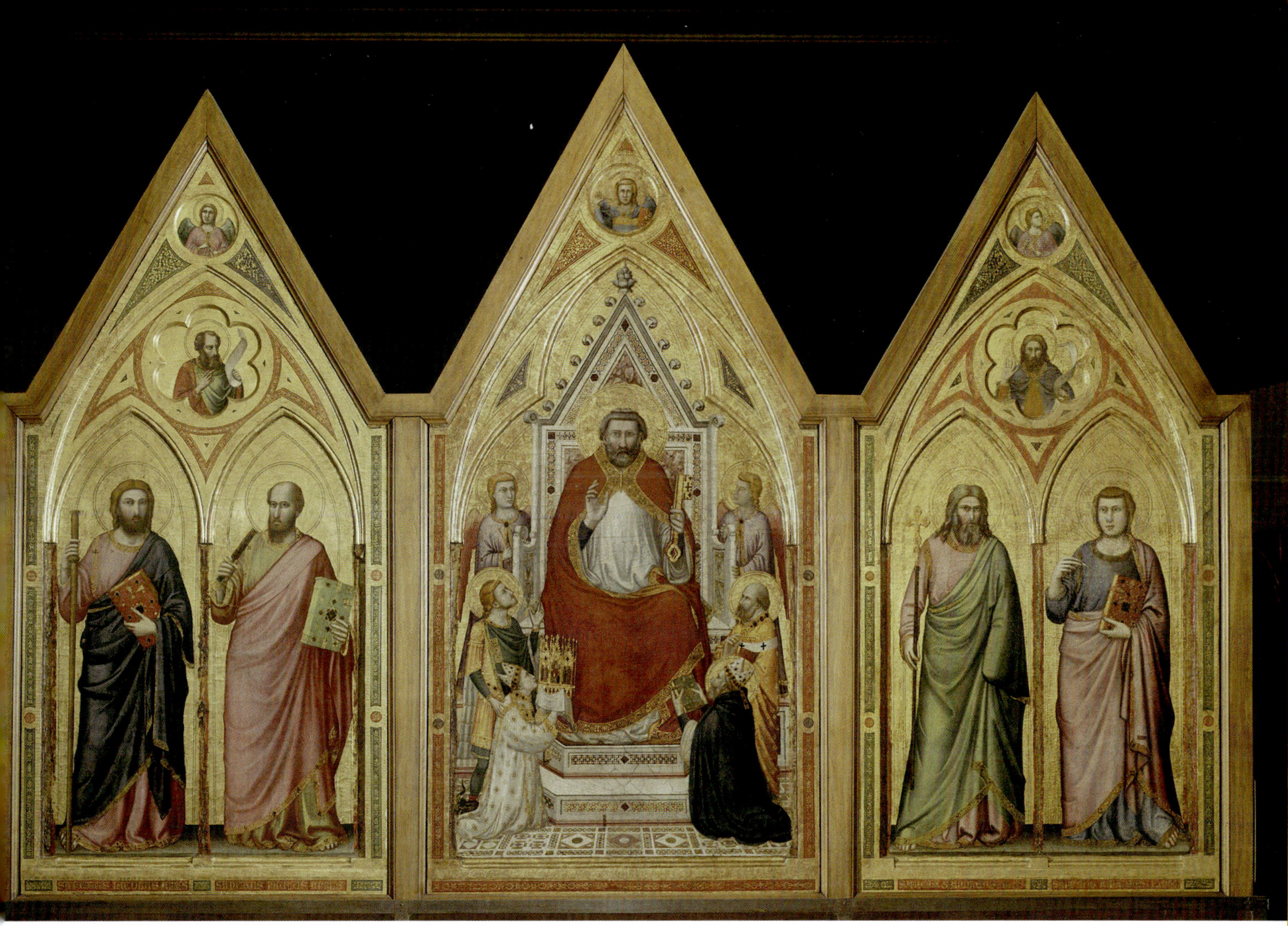

paint surface. It is these varnishes that deteriorate over time and collect lampblack from candles, dirt and in more recent years other atmospheric pollutants. In many cases, the cleaning and restoration of old paintings are limited mainly to the removal of oxidized or darkened varnishes.

Giotto
The Stefaneschi Triptych
c. 1320
tempera on panel
178 x 89 cm (centre panel); 168 x 83 cm (side panels)
Vatican Museums and Galleries, Vatican City

GIFTS OF THE MAGI

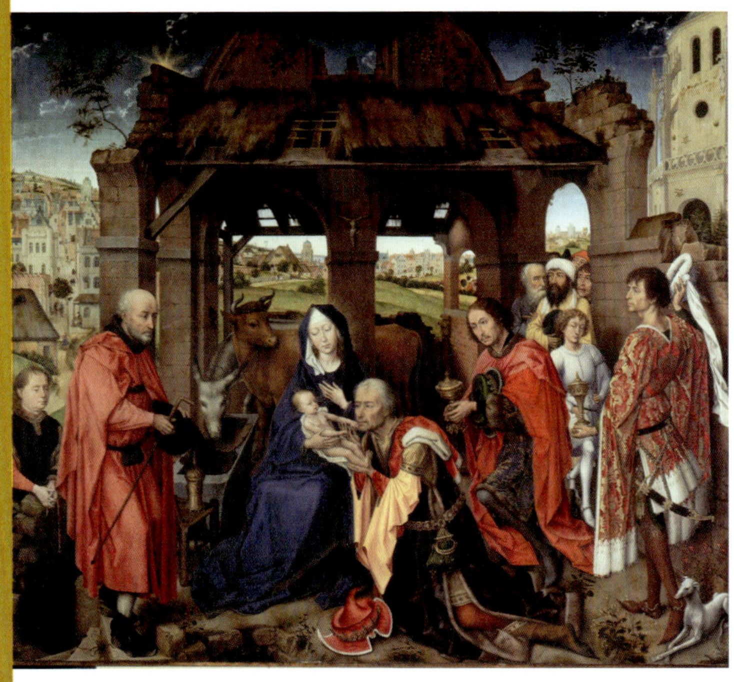

Rogier van der Weyden
The Adoration of the Magi
centre panel of the *Columba Triptych*
c. 1455
panel, 138 x 153 cm
Alte Pinakothek, Munich

Gold, frankincense and myrrh – according to the Gospel of Luke, these are the gifts brought to the new-born Jesus by the Wise Men (who have been identified as Persian astronomers associated with the Zoroastrian religion). In the countless depictions of the Adoration of the Magi, the boxes or bowls containing the frankincense and myrrh are almost always closed. However, the first king often places a glittering treasure chest of coins and jewellery before the Christ Child. It is one of the few occasions in Christian art where gold is represented with a positive value.

The Magi are not properly saints, and their widespread images often have a more profane than mystical tone. Extraordinarily popular figures, they are represented all around the world as kindly, exotic, rich sovereigns bearing precious gifts. Scenes of the journey, the procession and the Adoration of the Magi became favourite subjects of the International Gothic style and more generally in the late 14th and 15th centuries. The International Gothic period in particular saw sovereigns and nobles wishing to identify themselves with the Gospel's prototype of noblemen paying tribute to Jesus.

A memorable Flemish interpretation of the Adoration is the centre panel of the triptych by

Rogier van der Weyden from the church of St Columba in Cologne. In the Rhenish metropolis, the relics of the Wise Men are kept in Nicolas of Verdun's magnificent gilded shrine, and gold gleams profusely in Van der Weyden's painting as well. The king at the right, sumptuously dressed and accompanied by a greyhound, is probably an idealized image of Charles the Bold, Duke of Burgundy. And yet, despite the splendour of the costumes and the pomp of the retinue, the atmosphere of the painting appears predominantly focused, concentrated. The graphic and emotional tension that would characterize the painter's mature production begins to show itself. The figures' proportions become elongated and more sinewy, and the clearly outlined faces express a noticeable disquiet.

The son of a goldsmith of Hungarian origin, Dürer never missed an opportunity to depict, and sometimes design, elaborate pieces of goldwork. And certainly the containers for the Magi's gifts in the sumptuous Uffizi Adoration are spectacular. The German master painted himself in the guise of the most glamorous of the kings, covered in gold and priceless fabrics, with long curly hair. This autobiographical projection may be considered in light of other works in which Dürer goes so far as to compare his own image with that of Christ.

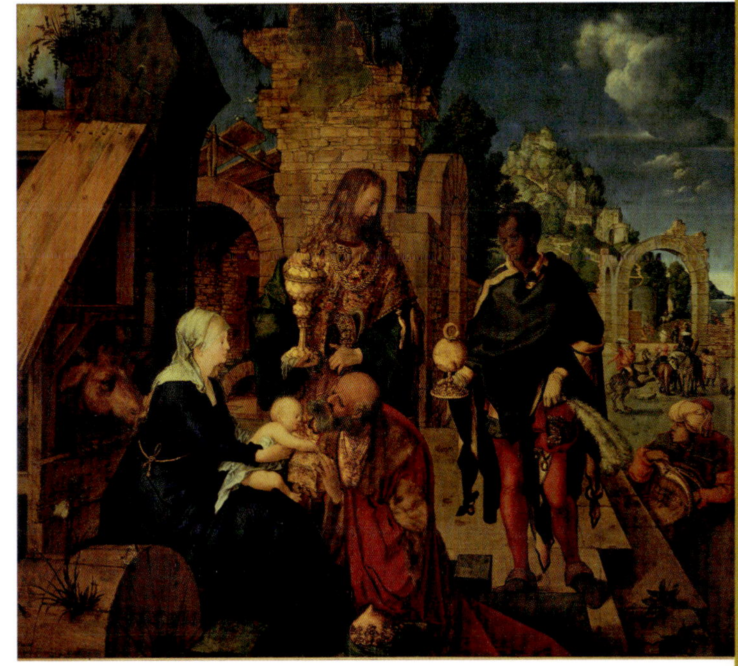

Albrecht Dürer
The Adoration of the Magi
1504
panel, 99 x 113.5 cm
Galleria degli Uffizi, Florence

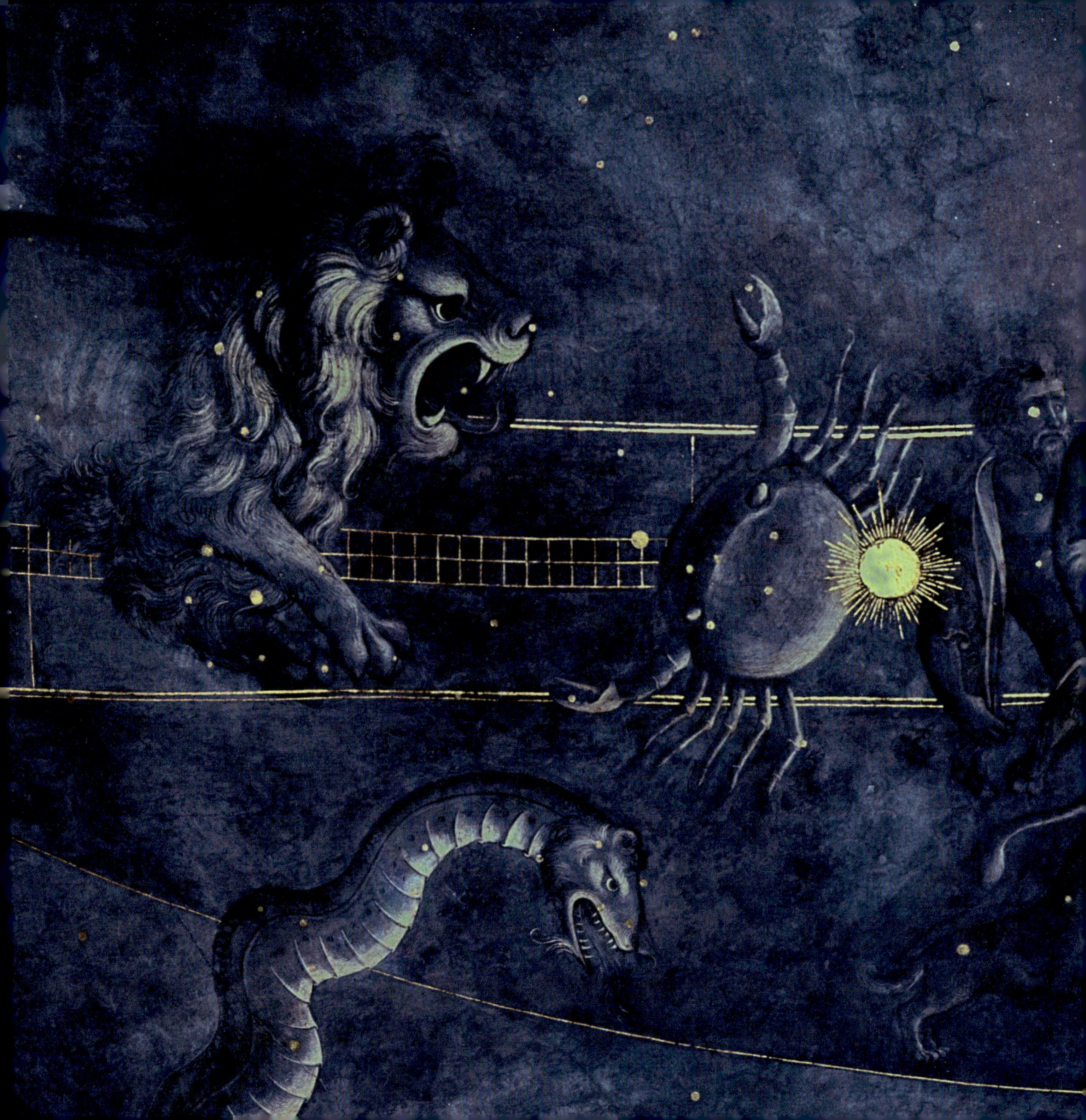

GOLDEN SIGNS IN A BLUE SKY

For thousands of years man has observed the sky, seeking in the stars answers to eternal questions, insights into what the future might hold, or, more prosaically, a stable way of measuring the passage of time. But the night sky changes every evening as the constellations pursue their unchanging circuit. A combination of science and fantasy has reduced the twinkling stars to a series of signs and images, arrangements of scintillating heavenly bodies against the background of the night. The belt of heaven that closely accompanies the apparent course of the sun in the annual cycle includes seven major heavenly bodies: besides the sun and the moon, Mercury, Venus, Mars, Jupiter and Saturn (the five planets visible to the naked eye). This zone comprises the zodiac, a term derived from the Greek for 'composed of living beings'. With an exceptional iconographic consistency, the twelve signs of the zodiac have come down through three millennia: from the Babylonian empire to Hellenistic Greece, from Egypt to Christianity, the name, sequence, representation, pairing with the planets and characteristics of the signs have remained the same.

A masterpiece of harmony designed by Brunelleschi, the dome over the altar of the Old Sacristy at San Lorenzo in Florence presents an accurate map of the heavens, including all the astronomical components from the sun's ecliptic with the constellations of the zodiac to the sun, the meridian, the North Pole, the paranatellonta and the planets in transit. Thanks to a recent restoration, and with the help of the astronomers at the Arcetri Observatory, it has been possible to pinpoint the date. the painting depicts the sky above Florence on 4 July 1442. The sun is positioned over the constellation Cancer, represented as the classic crab, between a threatening Leo and the two embracing adolescents of Gemini. The decoration of the dome is probably the work of Giuliano d'Arrigo, called Il Pesello, an artist still associated with the late Gothic miniature, who depicted the signs of the zodiac in gold leaf over a background of azurite. The position was undoubtedly calculated with the assistance of an astronomer, perhaps Paolo Dal Pozzo Toscanelli, a friend of Brunelleschi with ties to the Medici family.

While the dome of San Lorenzo is in a perfect state of preservation, the similar depiction in the Pazzi Chapel was less fortunate. Nevertheless, it has been possible to ascertain that it too represents the stars as they appeared in the night sky of 4 July 1442. It is not known what illustrious person or event may link these two images. Presumably, they refer to the arrival in Florence of King René of Anjou, who had been expelled from Naples when it was conquered by the Argonese. The alliance with the deposed Anjou king had aroused great expectations in Cosimo the Elder de' Medici, who commissioned the Old Sacristy of San Lorenzo. But his political hopes were in vain, which leaves one slightly sceptical as to the reliability of horoscopes.

Il Pesello (Giuliano d'Arrigo)
The Path of the Sun Through the Stars on the Night of the 4th July 1442
c. 1442
fresco
Old Sacristy, San Lorenzo, Florence

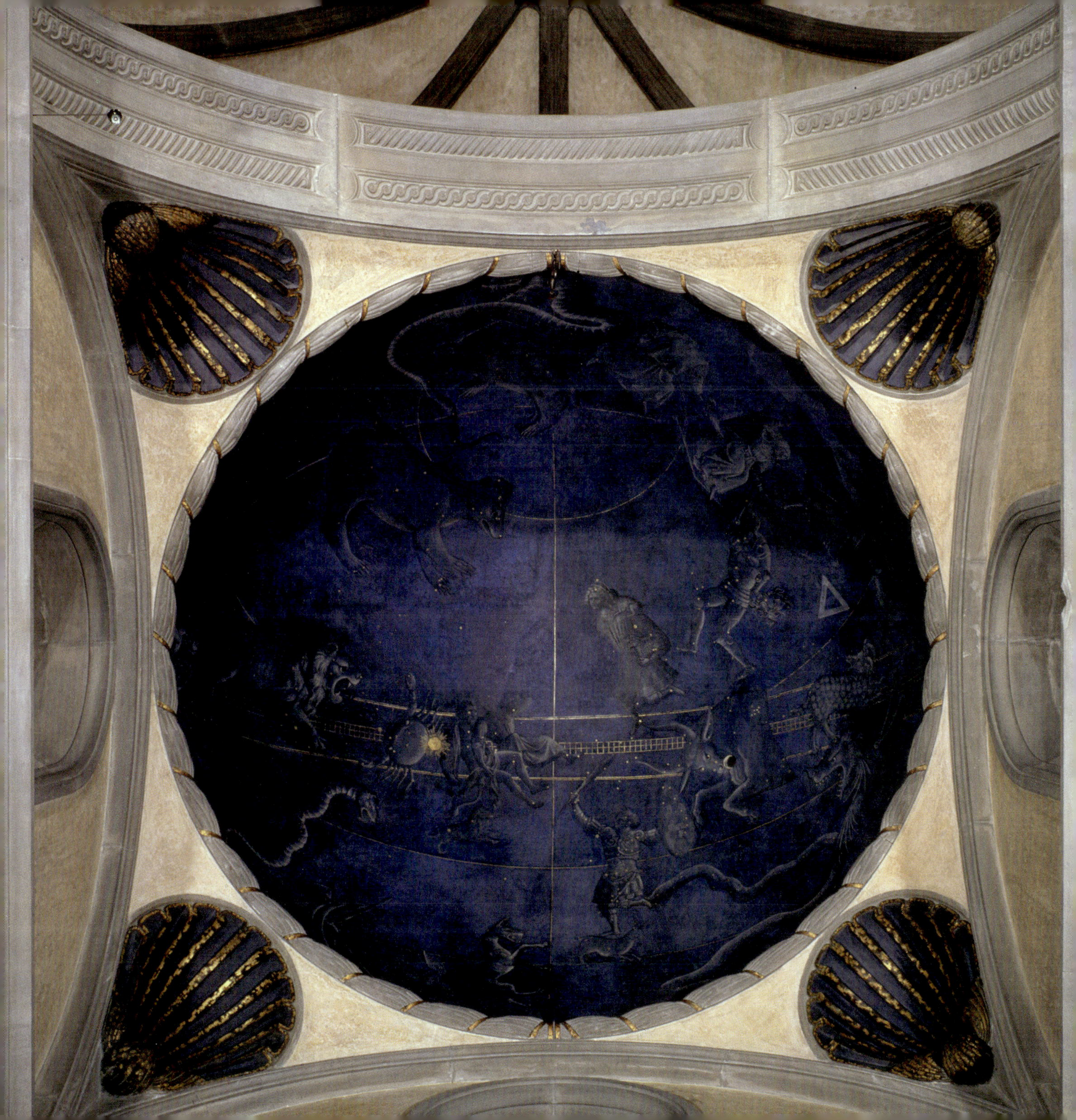

HALOS

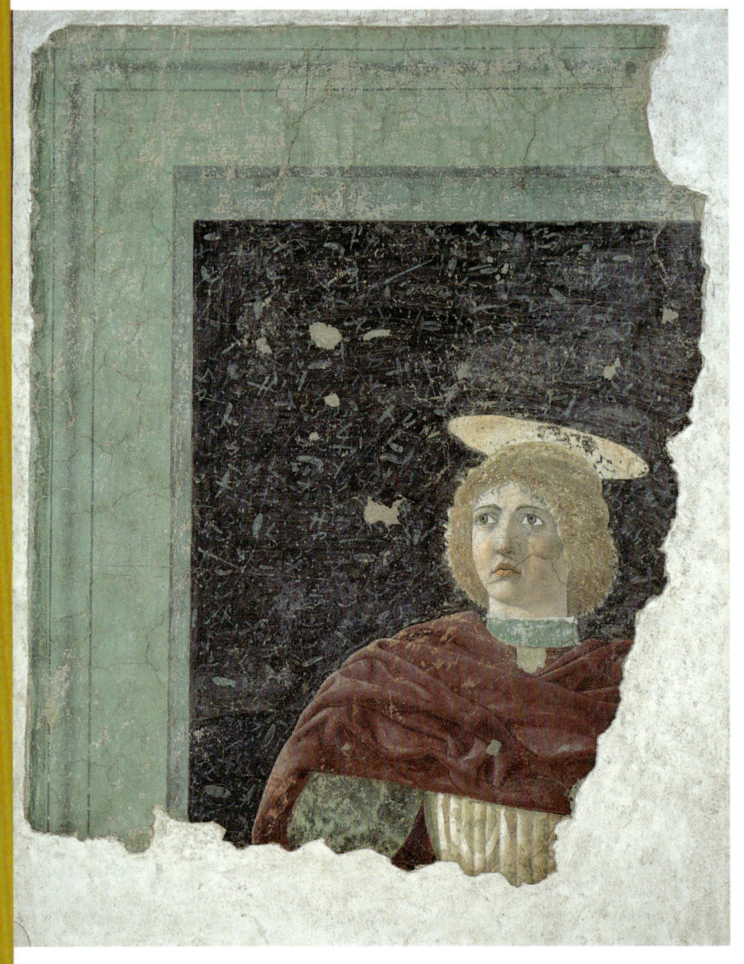

Piero della Francesca
St Julian
c. 1455
fresco fragment, 130 x 105 cm
Museo Civico, Sansepolcro

The word 'aureole' – referring to the radiant halo of light that often surrounds the head of Christ, the Virgin Mary and the saints – derives etymologically from the Latin *aureus*, meaning 'golden'. The presence of a glow or rays of light around the head of eminent or divine figures is not the exclusive prerogative of Christian art, however. The Romans, for example, represented the sun god Sol Invictus with rays that anticipate the unmistakable headpiece of the Statue of Liberty. And a warm golden irradiation also appears in some Buddhist images.

Besides a simple circle of gold – a very frequent attribute in images of the saints – various other types of halo may be recognized in Christian art. God the Father is sometimes represented with a triangular aureole, a symbol of the Trinity; the figure of Christ is often entirely surrounded by a glow of light (known as a 'mandorla'); a halo inscribed with a cross is reserved exclusively for Christ; in the Middle Ages, living persons or those not yet canonized appear with a quadrangular nimbus; and Judas is sometimes given a gloomy black halo. According to the vision of the mystic Hildegard von Bingen, the new-born Christ Child irradiated a bright glimmer. In the humanistic era of the Renaissance, however, the halo was 'reformed': Piero della Francesca represents it as a flat metal disc, foreshortened in perspective; Leonardo and Raphael favoured very fine gold lines.

On several occasions halos are transformed into a sort of rainbow, a symbol of the alliance between God and humankind as well as of the luminous concentric circles of the celestial spheres. One of the most spectacular of these occurs in a triptych commissioned by the Bourbon dukes from a painter who, because of this masterpiece, is conventionally known as the Master of Moulins. The central scene is still late Gothic in its compositional structure but quite up to date in its effort to achieve balanced geometrical proportions. The elongated figure of the Virgin and Child dominates the scene. She is surrounded by a great multicoloured halo, almost a mystical aura, with the moon at her feet (according to the iconography of the Immaculate Conception) and flanked by a choir of angels. The light of the luminous circle illuminates the absorbed faces of the two young angels who hold her crown.

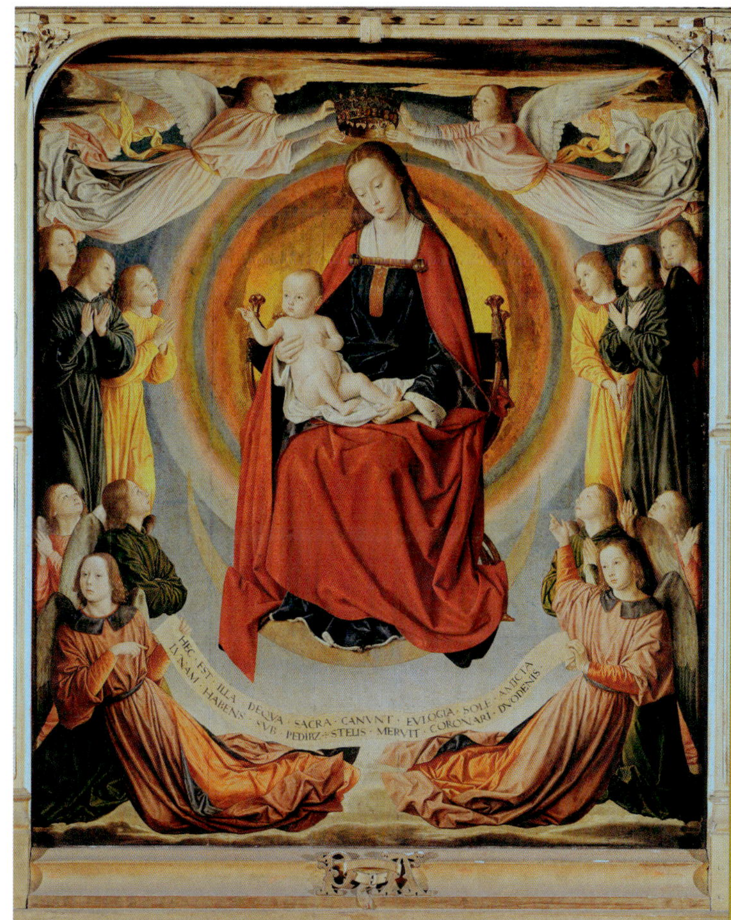

Master of Moulins
(identified as Jean Hey or Jean Prévost)
The Coronation of the Virgin
centre panel from the *Bourbon Altarpiece*
c. 1498
oil on panel, 157 x 136 cm
Cathedral, Moulins

'AURI SACRA FAMES'

Art, especially in the Catholic countries, often reinforced Virgil's classical condemnation of *auri sacra fames* (from the Aeneid, 3:56) – the cursed craving for gold that drives men to every wickedness. The evil that greed leads to is also well illustrated by the purse of thirty silver coins that Judas received for his act of betrayal. Coins poured into the traitor's hand or the purse itself appear not infrequently among the *Arma Christi*, the symbols and Instruments of the Passion. The image painted by Giotto in the Scrovegni Chapel in Padua is explicit: as Judas receives the sum agreed upon for betraying Christ, a demon behind him grimaces.

Hieronymus Bosch often depicted moral concepts with utterly original fantasy. His surprising paintings arise from the combination of popular sayings and elements of recent culture, as well as contact with humanistic painters of other religious beliefs, alchemy and science. According to an old Flemish proverb, 'the world is a hay wagon, and everybody grabs from it as much as he can get'. This popular tradition is probably the inspiration for one of the painter's earliest masterpieces, *The Haywain*. The centre panel is dominated by a huge cart loaded with hay, the golden colour of which refers to gold and lucre, functioning as an obvious symbol of the cupidity and vain desires of humanity, always in eager pursuit of earthly goods.

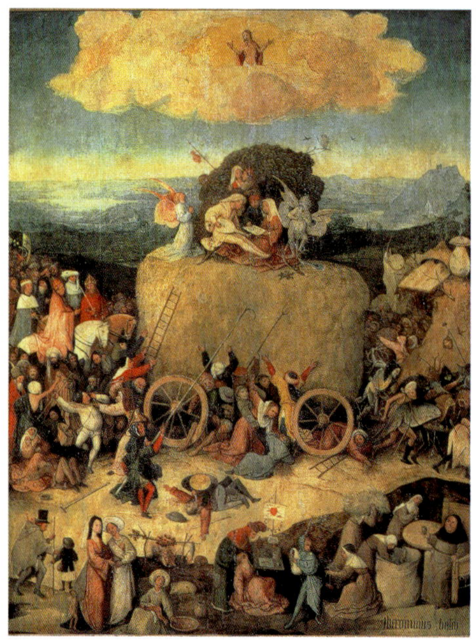

Hieronymus Bosch
The Haywain (centre panel)
c. 1516
oil on panel, 135 x 200 cm
Museo Nacional del Prado, Madrid

A mixed crowd throngs all around, coming to blows and getting themselves crushed under the wheels of the cart as they attempt to get closer. Even the pope and the emperor, splendidly dressed on horseback, indulge in the widespread folly by following the cart. On top of the hay, isolated as if in a dream, a group of lovers sing and dance – but it is the devil who is playing the pipe, while an angel directs a resigned prayer heavenward. Bosch lashes out with bitter humour at humankind's shared progress towards ruin in blind desire for money, goods and power. No one notices (at first not even the viewer) that the cart is being drawn by grimacing demons into the fires of Hell.

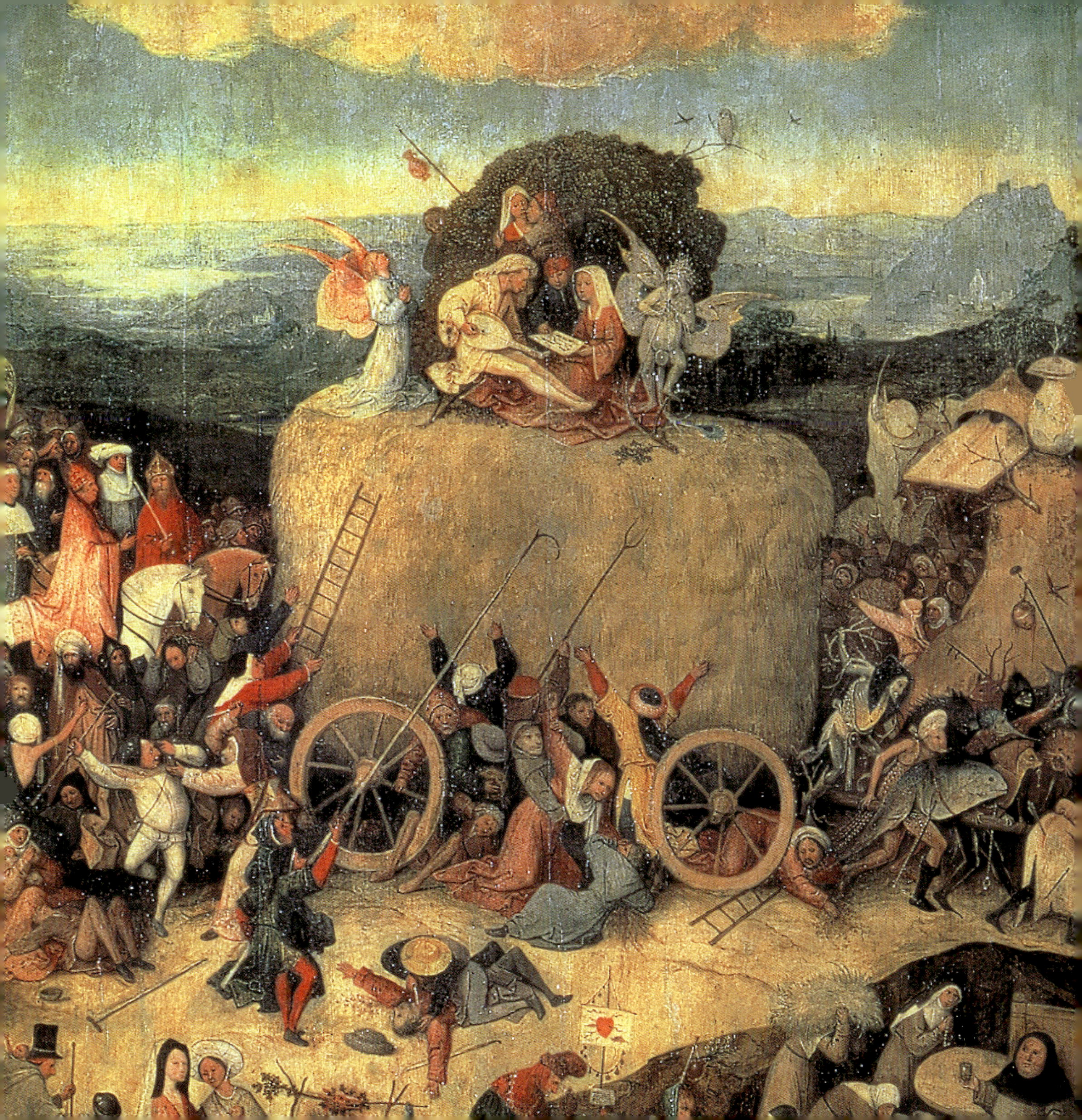

Rembrandt
The Money Changer (or the Parable of the Old Miser)
1627
oil on panel, 32 x 42 cm
Staatliche Museen zu Berlin, Gemäldegalerie

MONEY IN ART

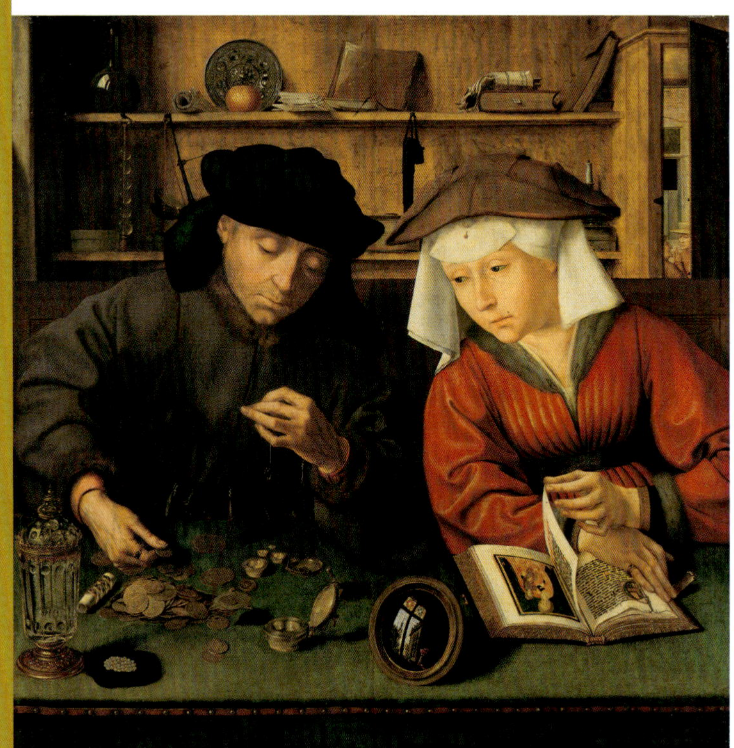

Quentin Massys
The Banker and His Wife
1514
oil on panel, 70 x 67 cm
Musée du Louvre, Paris

In religious art, the scene of Christ driving the merchants from the temple expresses condemnation of the sinful use of wealth. The money changers' benches are overturned, and coins are scattered on the ground, sometimes into the mud. Nonetheless, on the eve of the emergence of modern capitalism, a different image began to gain ground. The famous painting by Quentin Massys offers a characteristic portrayal of a 'professional dealer' in money. The mound of coins from various mints and the elegant objects in his shop indicate the increasing wealth of Antwerp as a commercial, cultural and financial centre. It is a painting of its time. The man casts a professional eye over the scale in which he is weighing coins. One of the most notable economic phenomena of the 16th century was the so-called 'price revolution', the inflationary thrust that coincided with the influx of precious minerals from South America and was partially responsible for the initial spread of paper money.

Massys's composition is not without a moral undertone. While the husband intently weighs and counts coins, his wife leafs through an illuminated book, the *Hours of the Virgin*, a collection of devotions to Our Lady. Yet, there is no hint of an ethical condemnation of money. Nothing in the calm, intimate image allows one to foresee the

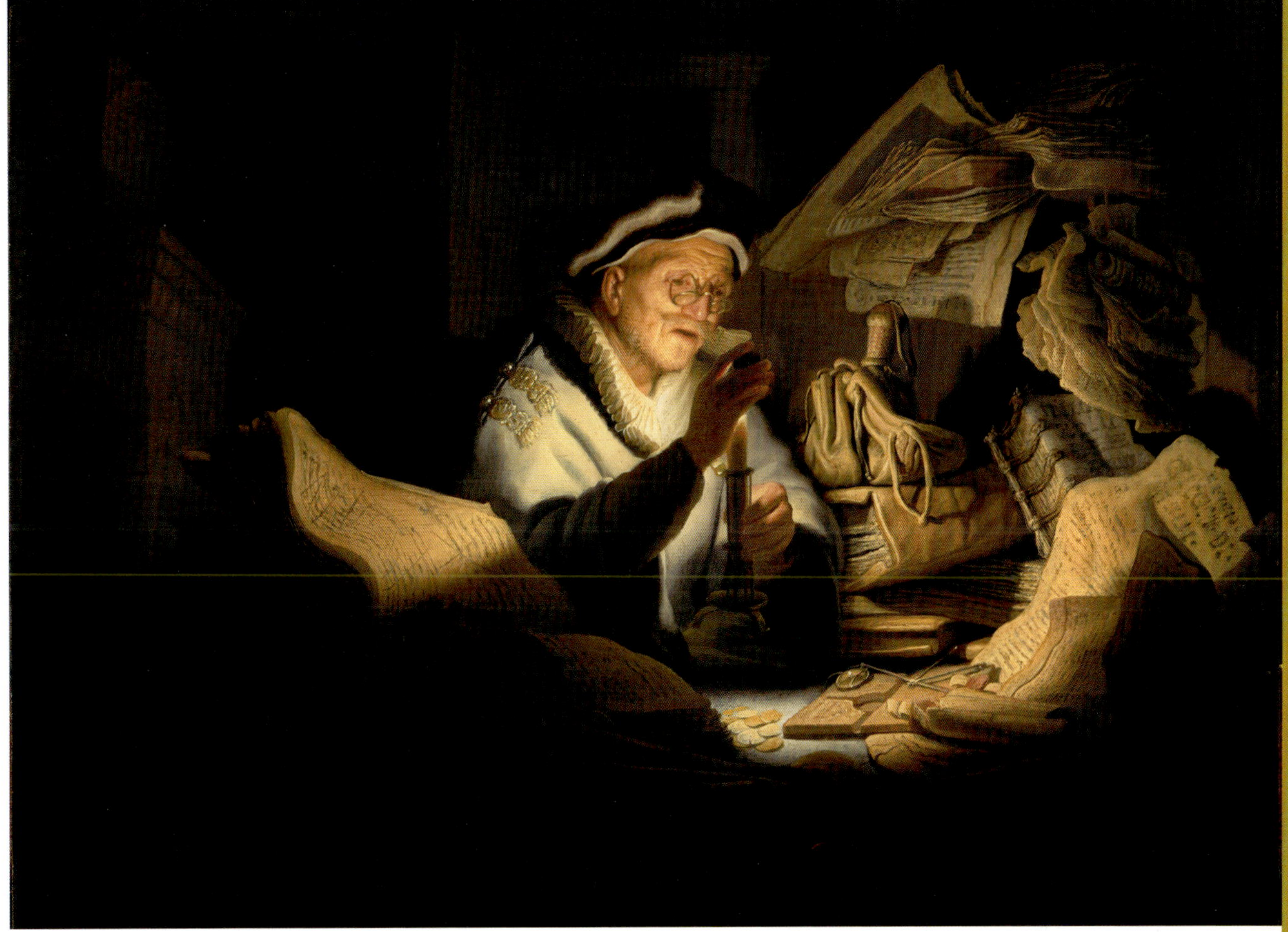

caricatures that would soon be derived from it. In various 16th-century Flemish and Dutch paintings – for example, works by Marinus van Reymerswaele – the sober, concentrated money lender becomes a mean usurer with greedily grasping hands.

More than a century after Massys, Rembrandt treated the theme of inspecting money in an early painting, a precocious example of the Caraveggesque style imported to the Low Countries by a group of painters from Utrecht. Immersed in a dark, disorderly interior heaped with books and objects scattered in confusion, an old man examines a coin by candlelight through the thick lenses of a realistic pair of glasses. The precise subject depicted is debated, and the interpretations that have been offered suggest radically different readings: the Gospel parable of the miser, a portrait of a money lender or an allegory of Avarice.

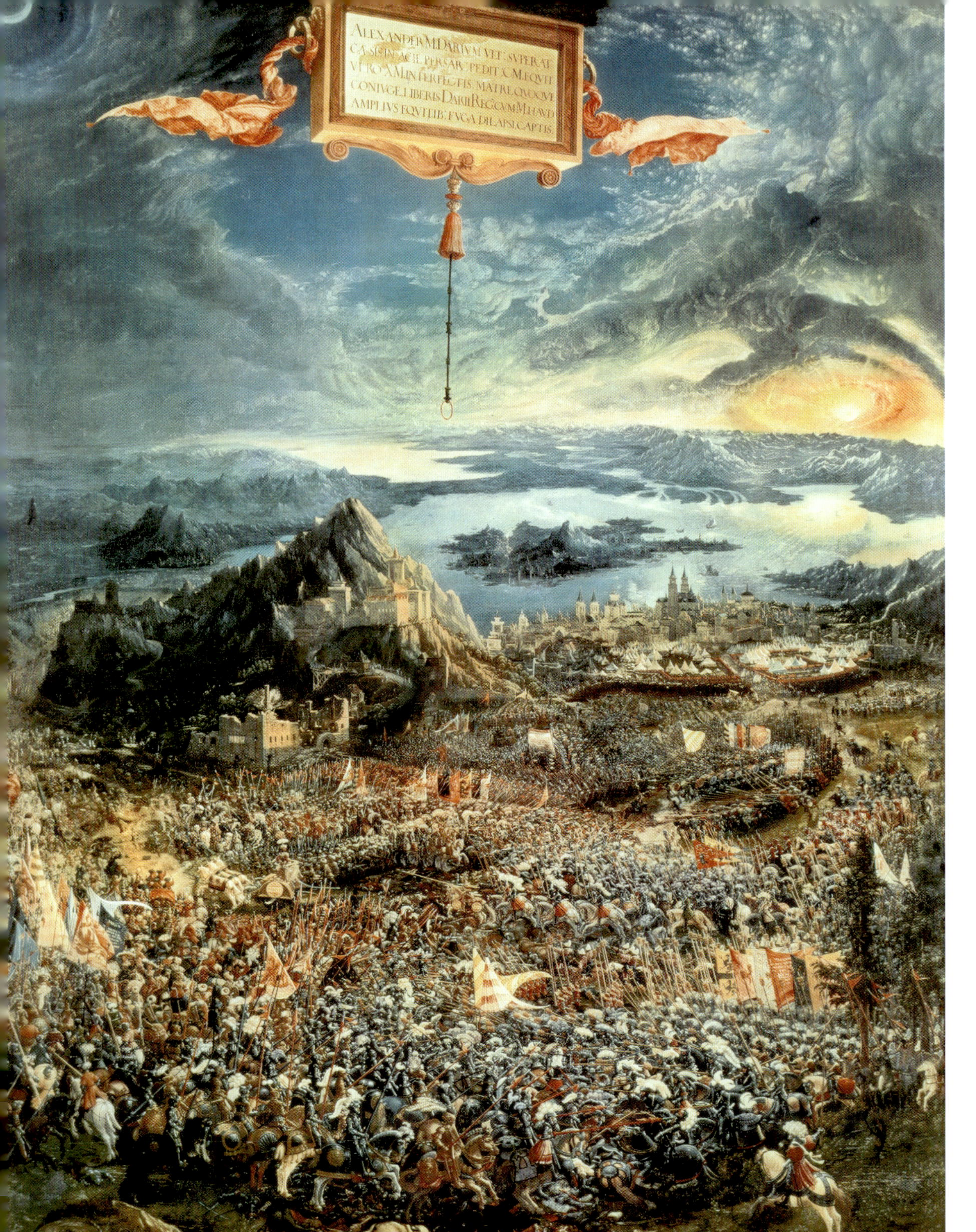

Albrecht Altdorfer
The Battle of Issus
1529
oil on panel, 158.4 x 120.3 cm
Alte Pinakothek, Munich

THE GOLD CONDOTTIERE

The painter Albrecht Altdorfer of Regensburg was one of the most brilliant artists of the German Renaissance. The best-known master of the Danube School, an intense interpreter of nature in forests and mountains, in 1513 he was called to Innsbruck by Emperor Maximilian of Habsburg to play a leading role in court commissions. In proximity to Maximilian ('the last knight' in the waning of the Middle Ages), Altdorfer gave his painting the tone of a fairytale, a chivalric romance, in which heroes assume legendary traits in fabulous settings. A characteristic example is Altdorfer's great masterpiece *The Battle of Issus*, painted in 1529 for Duke William of Bavaria, in which Alexander the Great is wearing gleaming armour of gold.

In the desire to confer a 'classical' aspect upon his residence, Duke William IV of Bavaria engaged a humanist man of letters to devise an iconographic programme, and then many painters to execute panels of historical episodes related to illustrious heroes and heroines of antiquity. Altdorfer was assigned the theme of the final battle between Alexander the Great and the Persian forces of King Darius, which occurred at Issus in 333 BC. The panel is in good condition. All areas are perfectly legible, and the refined superimpositions of light and colours can still be appreciated.

The commission came during a period of bloody battles on European soil, and the victory of the 'Greek' Alexander over the 'Oriental' Darius could be seen as a metaphor for the on-going war with the Ottoman Empire, advancing ever nearer to the heart of Europe. The crescent moon in the sky, soon to vanish with daybreak, can be interpreted in this context. It is also quite probable that Altdorfer wanted to create a striking illustration of recent famous battles – for example the Battle of Pavia in 1525, at which the French king Francis I was defeated – transferring the historical episode into a time and landscape familiar to him and his patron.

The painting offers an overhead view of one of the most attractive landscapes in all of art history, perhaps inspired by the Salzburg region. The relationship between the hillside fort, convent and city huddled around the cathedral corresponds to the actual Austrian city, but the water and mountain setting is imaginary. Thus, Altdorfer brought his investigation of landscape and natural atmosphere to a culmination. In a scene of exceptional grandeur, the sun rises behind endless mountain chains as clouds scurry across the sky. The landscape blends into the tumult of battle, underscoring in the tension of its atmosphere the importance of the outcome of the military event. The two formations, the movement of the troops and the camps are clearly distinguishable. Alexander, in golden armour, sets out in pursuit of the golden chariot in which Darius is attempting to flee.

THE GOLDEN CALF

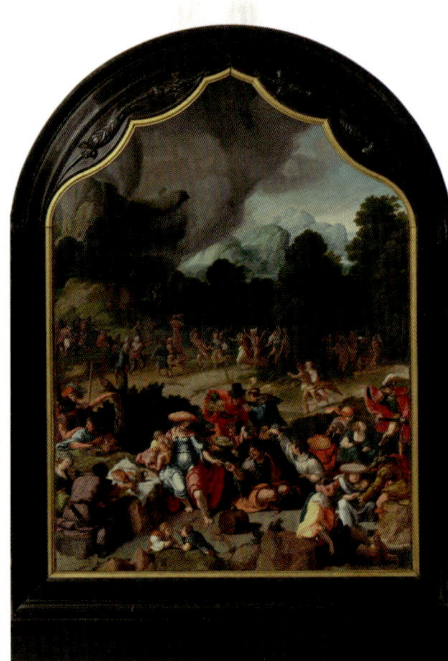

Lucas van Leyden
The Dance around the Golden Calf
(centre panel of the triptych)
c. 1530
oil on panel, 93.5 x 66.9 cm
Rijksmuseum, Amsterdam

The complex and controversial relationship between gold and religion comes to the fore in the Biblical episode described in Exodus, chapter 32. The Hebrew people, fleeing from Egypt to the Promised Land, feel abandoned and become disheartened while Moses is on Mount Sinai. The rumour spreads that Moses has died and, acting on the malicious suggestion of some Egyptian sorcerers, the Jews melt down their gold to create the effigy of a new god in the form of a calf (a reference to one of the main Egyptian gods, Hathor, who has the features of a cow). Even Moses' brother, Aaron, worships the idol. Returning from the mountain, Moses discovers his people's idolatry. Enraged, he shatters the Tablets of the Law (upon which were written the Ten Commandments), destroys the Golden Calf and has those responsible for the sacrilege punished. The gold from the statue is used to decorate the Ark of the Covenant.

The 'deviation' from faith in one God to the Golden Calf brought about a strict Jewish prohibition against building and depicting 'idols', or representing God in any way – not even through the depiction of human beings, who were created 'in his own image'. The contrast between the calf and the divine word (represented by the Tablets of the Law) symbolizes the age-old choice between naturalistic representation and the austere aniconism of the sacred art of Judaism, Islam and some Protestant Reformation sects. The fact that the calf was made of gold while the people of Israel were fleeing in the desert increases the sense of contrast and sinfulness.

In art history, the Adoration of the Golden Calf is represented in various ways. Drawing inspiration from the classical world, Poussin saw the Jews' dance around the statue as a sort of Old Testament bacchanal. A century earlier, in a remarkable triptych painted by Lucas van Leyden towards the end of his career, the irreverent dance is shunted to the background. The foreground seems to depict a peaceful country excursion on a beautiful day. Small and far distant, Moses appears twice in the background: above, prostrating himself before the cloud that conceals the manifestation of God; and a little lower, at the foot of the rocky ridge, as he angrily smashes the Tablets of the Law.

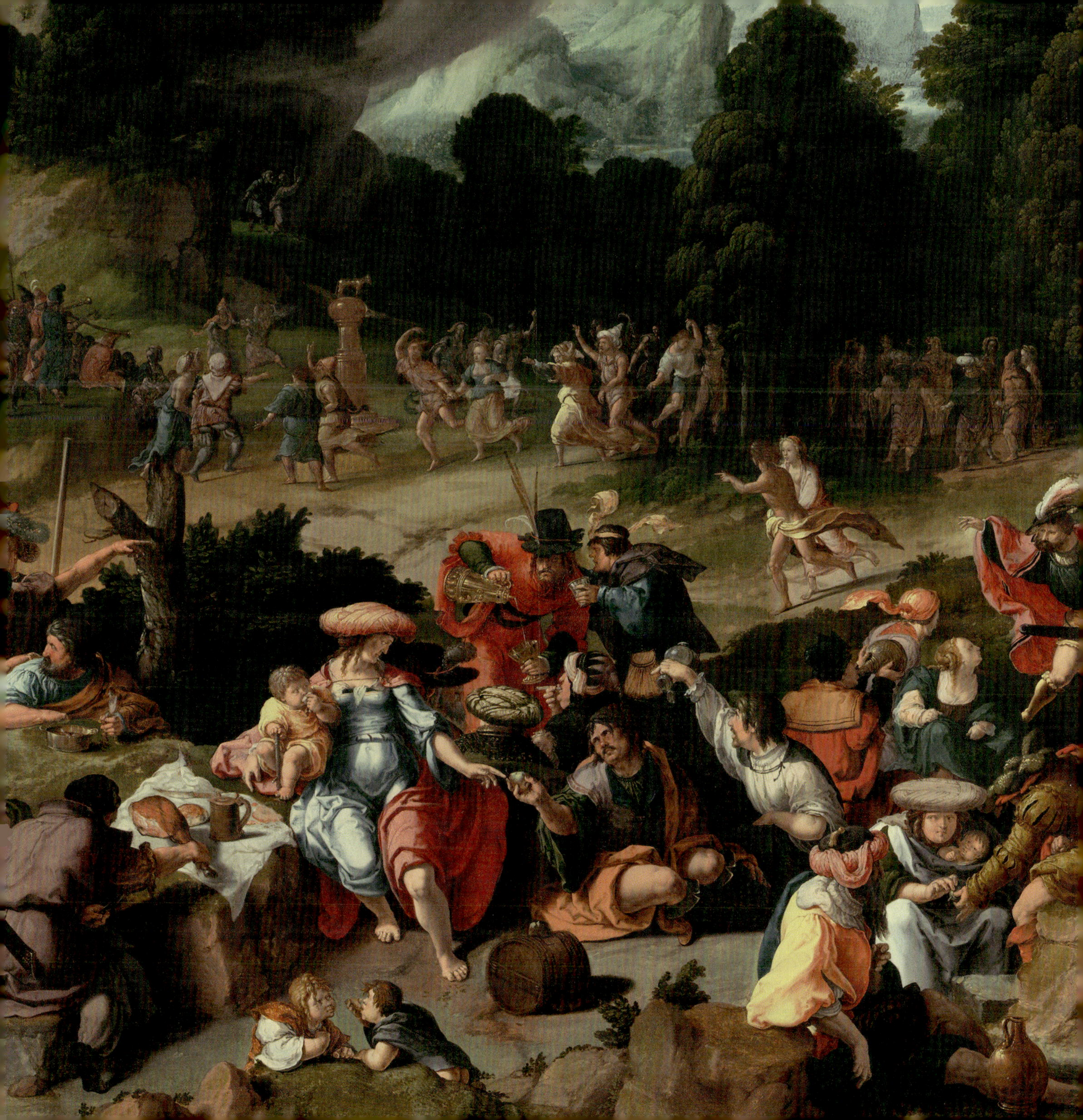

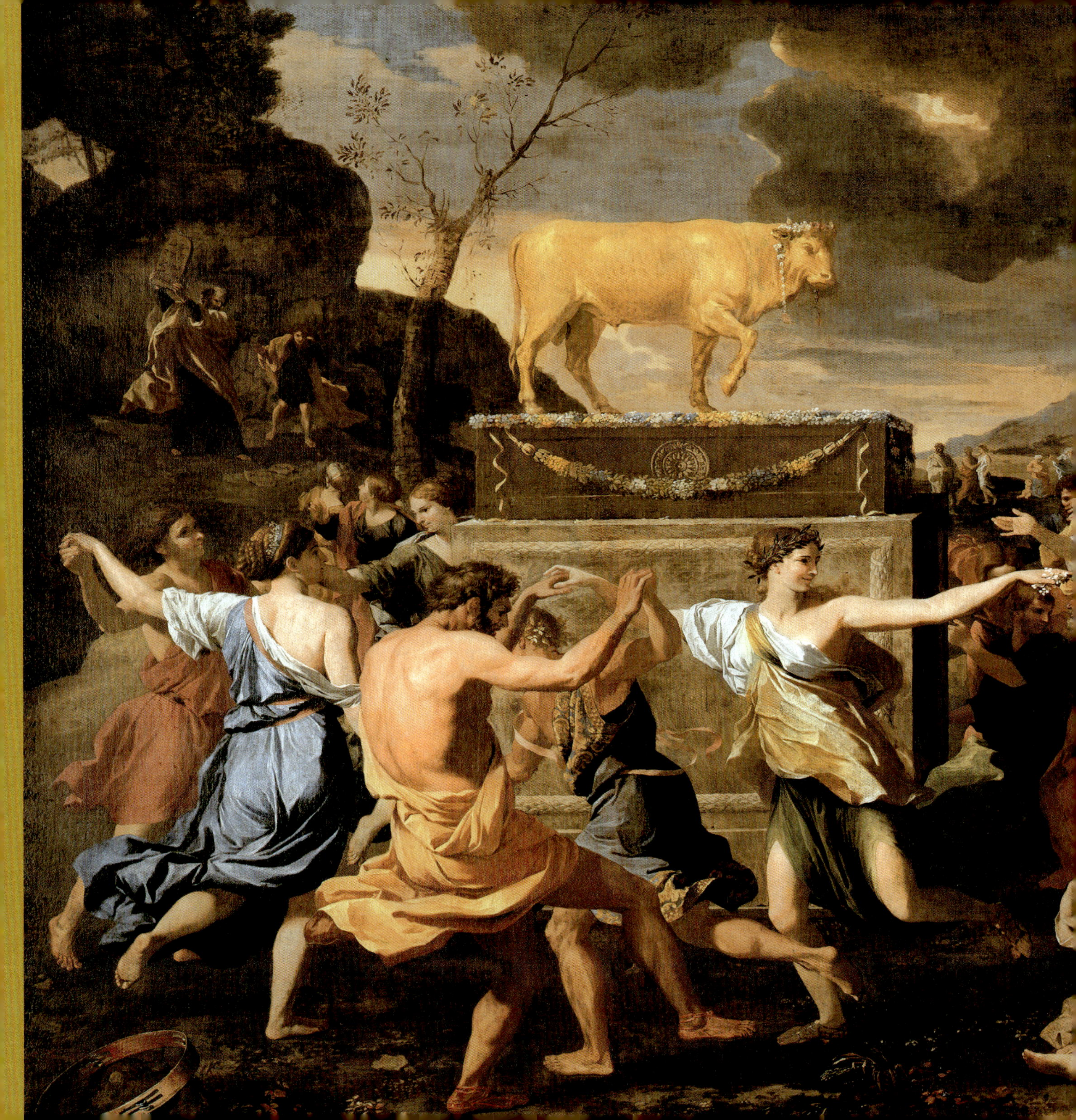

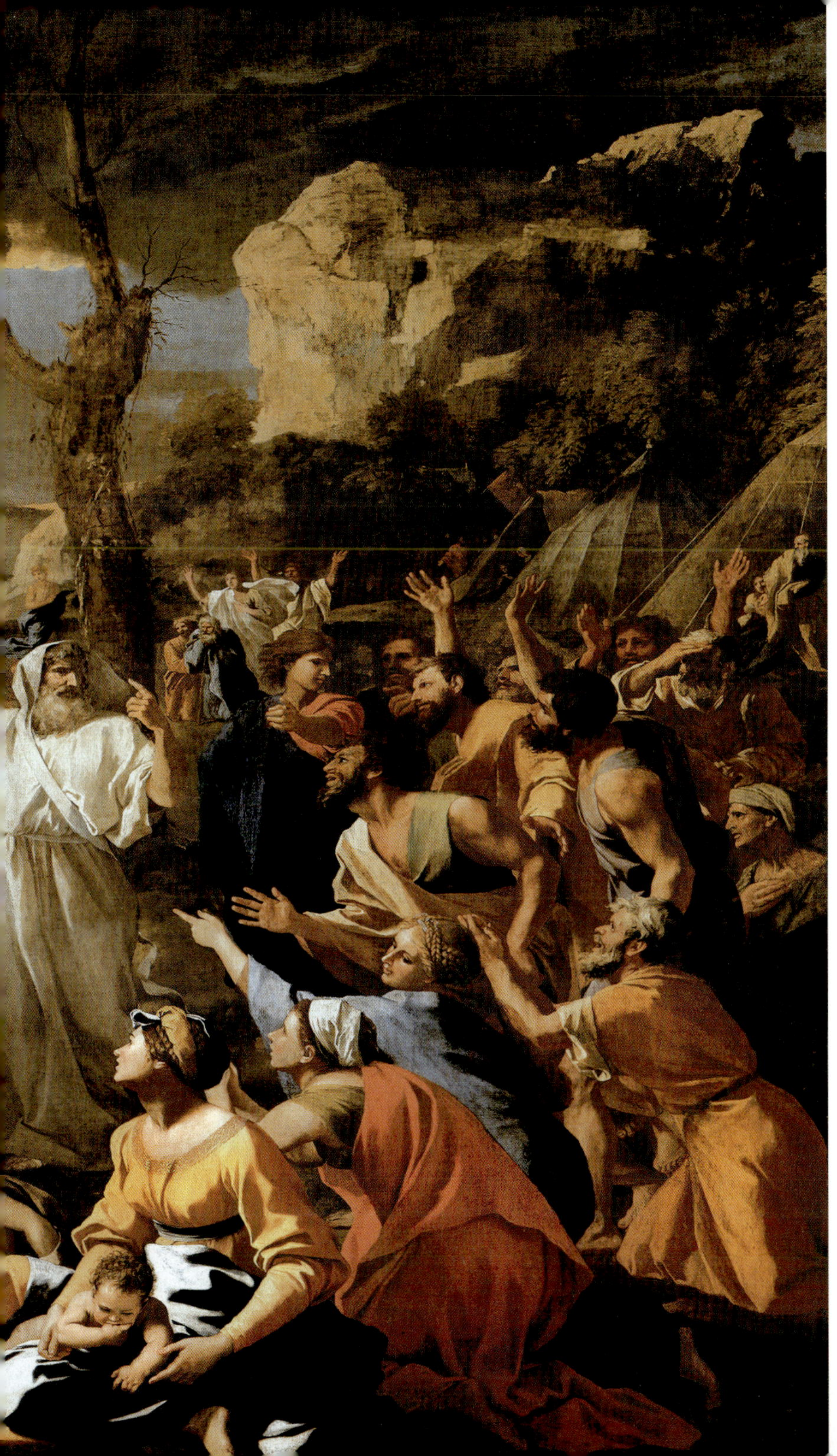

Nicolas Poussin
The Adoration of the Golden Calf
1633-1634
oil on canvas, 153.4 x 211.8 cm
National Gallery, London

GOLD AND LOVE

A common theme in art is the relationship between money and venal love. Titian – who had no qualms about dealing with money and oriented all his activity towards production and economics – repeatedly painted the classical subject of Danaë, the wife of the King of Argos, who was ravished by Jupiter in the form of a shower of golden rain. In Titian's earliest version, painted for Cardinal Alessandro Farnese (who was apparently not shocked by the provocative nude woman's explicit pose), the gold descends into Danaë's lap as a cloud. In the somewhat different version at the Prado, the gold appears as coins, which are eagerly gathered up by the housekeeper. In this prosaic yet effective way, Titian alludes to the gratuity offered to the woman who opens the door, if not exactly to payment for Danaë's 'services'.

The theme of love for hire (also treated in Central and Northern European art to illustrate the parable of the Prodigal Son) provided Lucas Cranach with various opportunities to display his narrative talent and mastery of grotesque facial expressions; however, his condemnation of moral decay is often diluted with a smile of complicity. In the contrast between the unpleasant old man and the available young woman, Cranach underlines that this is a business transaction (and indeed the girl does not hesitate to add to her compensation by stealing more coins).

Many paintings from the Renaissance to Impressionism refer to the relationship between money and love. It is a delicate subject, however, and one that can raise passions: even though money is not in view, Manet's masterpiece *Olympia* sparked a scandal when it was exhibited at the Salon of 1865. Explicitly inspired by Titian's *Venus of Urbino*, the painting had a defect that was intolerable to the morals of the time: it did not depict a nymph, goddess or mythological character but a wholly real woman. The organizers of the Salon relied on a permanent complement of guards to prevent enraged Parisians, offended by the provocative young woman, from striking the painting with their canes and umbrellas.

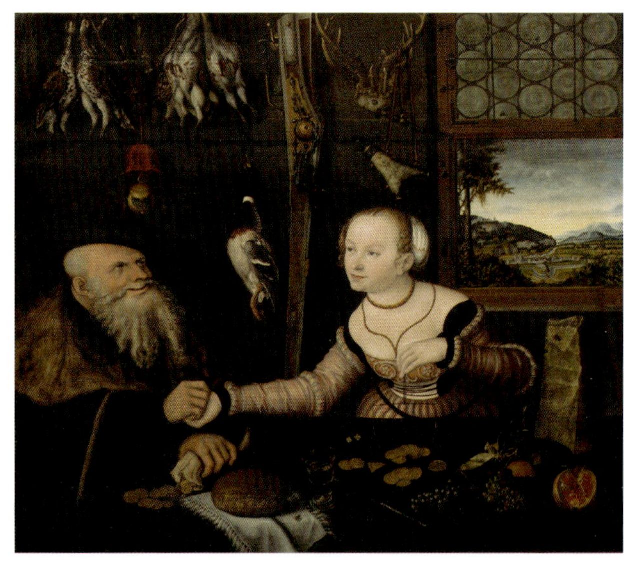

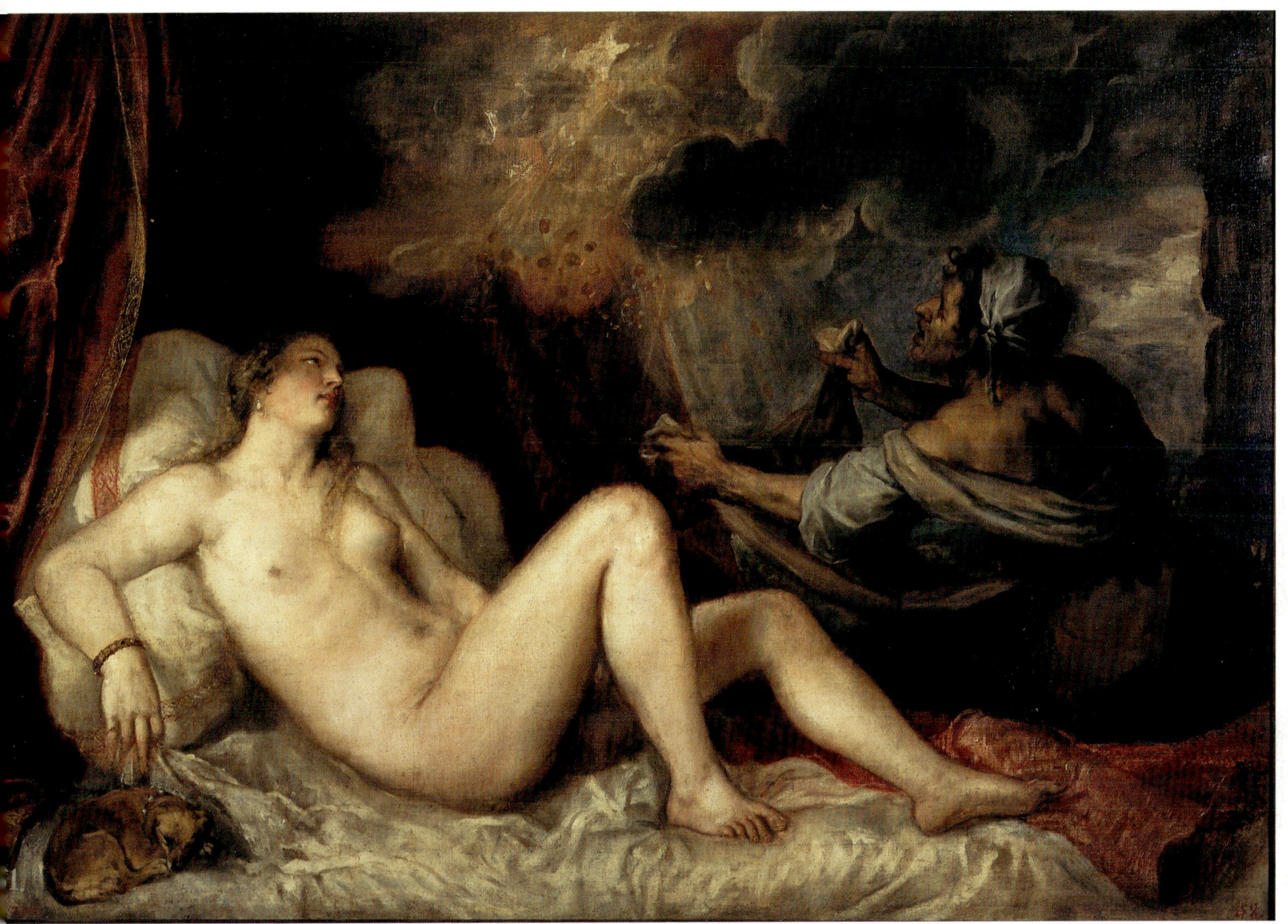

Lucas Cranach
The Ill-matched Couple
1532
oil on panel, 108 x 119 cm
Nationalmuseum, Stockholm

Titian
Danaë
c. 1551-1553
oil on canvas, 129 x 180 cm
Museo Nacional del Prado, Madrid

KLIMT

In the spring of 1903, Klimt made a journey to Venice and Ravenna where he was strongly impressed by the Byzantine mosaics – their formal simplicity, the reduction of space to two dimensions, the rarefied, unreal atmosphere, the stately nobility of the figures and the use of richly decorated gold backgrounds. This led to some of his best-known masterpieces, those of his 'golden period'. Previously, Klimt's art had looked modern, anti-academic, innovative, even provocative; now, his elegant, costly 'products', which amply showed off his technical ability and the quality of the materials, were aligned with the taste and purchasing power of high society patrons and collectors. Klimt's sparkling paintings reflect the gilded world of the Belle Époque.

Freely inspired by the subtle atmosphere and solemn spirituality of Byzantine mosaics, *The Kiss* is a perfect synthesis of Klimt's golden period. The faces of the two young figures are surrounded by an aura of gold that recalls the halos of saints in old paintings. This isolates them from the real world and places them in a dimension beyond this earth, a dimension of pure and perfect emotions. The man's head is bent towards his beloved. We see only his thick black hair, solid neck and a small portion of the face. His large, virile hands clasp the woman with extreme gentleness in a protective and affectionate attitude. The woman, her eyes closed, is completely rapt in the tender, yearning kiss. Her relaxed features reveal her inner feelings: she knows she is truly loved, understood, protected and defended by her man, to whom she gives herself with sincere and total abandon.

Even though the two figures' tight embrace almost forms a single being, Klimt succeeds in distinguishing the lovers through form and colour. The man's clothes are decorated with a rectangular geometric pattern in gold, white and black, while those of the woman display undulating lines and circles in ample zones of red, blue and other brighter hues. The theme of the kiss and eternal love between a man and a woman, to which the Austrian artist devoted his entire existence, appears in another painting expressing extreme longing: *Adam and Eve*, painted between 1917 and 1918. One of his last works, it remained incomplete at his death.

Gustav Klimt
The Kiss
1907-1908
oil on canvas, 180 x 180 cm
Österreichische Galerie Belvedere, Vienna

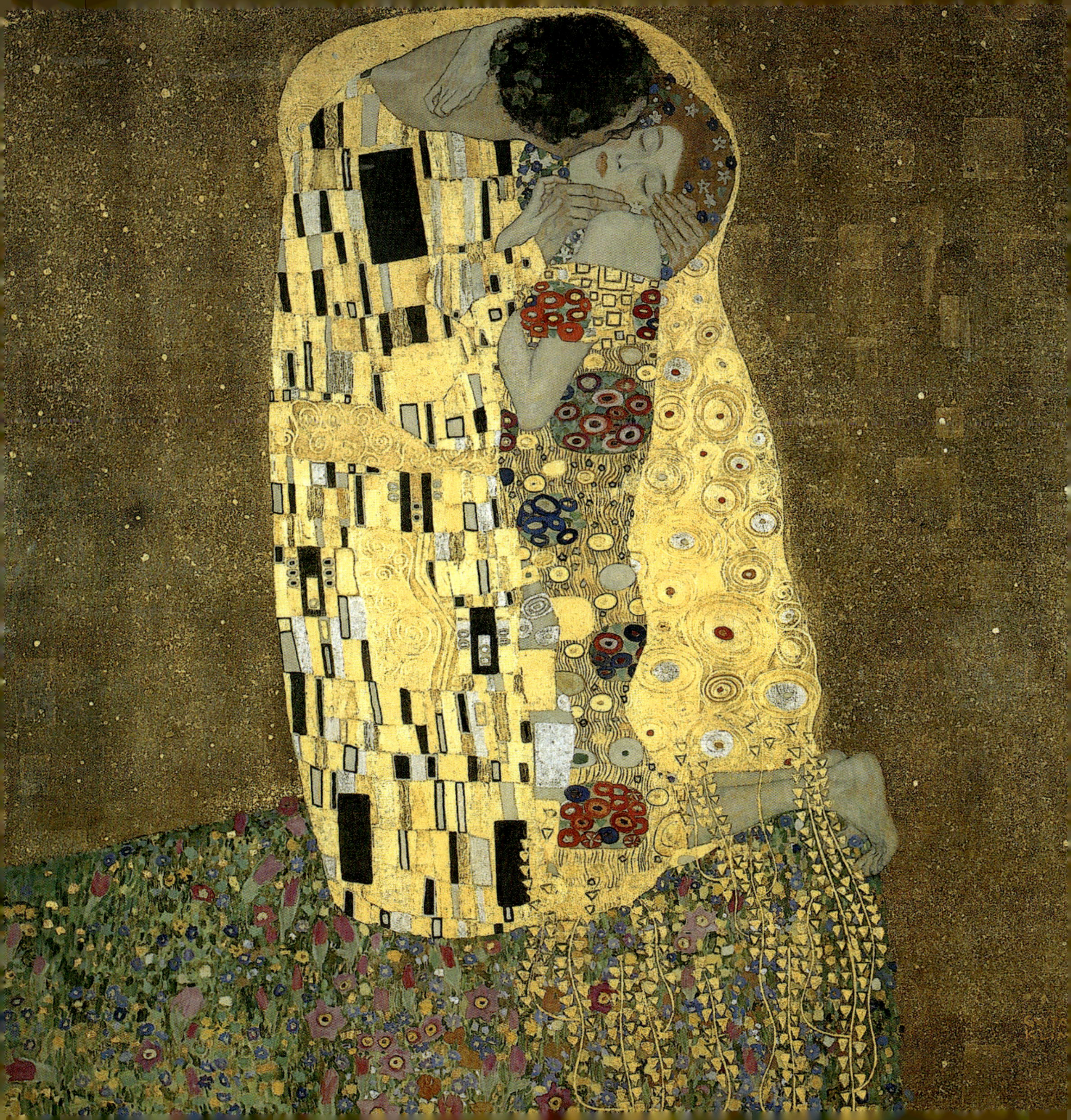

WHITE

INTRODUCTION

White is constantly praised in modern Western society as a symbol of cleanliness (if not exactly of purity, as in the past). Washing machines, detergents and stain removers will eliminate any blemish to make our shirts and table linens 'whiter than white' again. On TV, the white lab coats worn by medical doctors and health workers, as well as by specialized laboratory technicians and forensic police agents, denote extraordinary success.

The pairing of black and white has come to represent a schematic contrast between good and evil, between the shining angel and the dark demon, life and death, light and dark. Ingmar Bergman made masterful use of it with the chessboard in *The Seventh Seal* (a black-and-white movie, of course). In the Christian tradition, 'snow white' has symbolic implications of moral and spiritual immaculateness – it is the colour of bridal gowns at weddings and newborns' gowns at baptisms, as well as the colour worn by priests during Mass. The vestments of the Pope – the highest authority of the Roman Catholic Church – are white, as is the raiment of blessed souls in heaven. Thus, the colour white inspires a sense of the absolute, of divine perfection. Many of the examples illustrated in the following pages (the ermine, the Mystic Lamb, the lily, the Empyrean realm) draw on similar references. Still, we must not forget that in Asian cultures and for many peoples of Sub-Saharan Africa, white has the entirely opposite meaning: it is the colour of mourning and death, and also of evil. For that matter, in the West white does not refer solely to elevated and paradisiac thoughts but can underlie fear. Think of a cadaver's pallor, the winding-sheets of ghosts, the colossal symbol of evil that is the white whale Moby Dick. So once again, we encounter a somewhat unexpected ambivalence.

It is still a matter of debate whether white is to be considered a colour or an 'absence', a void. Beyond questions of physics, metaphors prevalent in every language (white noise, white space, white as a sheet, white-out, the 'white cube' and so on) attribute to white the meaning of a lack, a gap. The history of language presents some surprising vicissitudes. In Latin, there were two distinct ways of referring to white: *candidus* is gleaming white (the word was used to describe the togas of those who held public office, hence our word 'candidate', someone who aspires to public office), while *albus* is the opaque or translucid white of alabaster and albumen – the white of an egg. However, the term used for white in almost all of the Romance languages (*blanco, bianco, blanc,* etc.) does not derive from Latin but from the Old High German *blanc*, meaning 'brilliant, white', as opposed to *weiss*, opaque white, which has survived into German, Dutch and Modern English.

For many years, the walls of museums and hospitals were invariably whitewashed. For hospitals, the choice is easily understandable as a reference to hygiene and cleanliness, but for museums and other public spaces, white eventually – and perhaps a bit monotonously – became a sign of neutrality. In the arts themselves, however, white is clearly an active 'choice'. Since the time of palaeolithic cave art, ceruse and lime have been used in the execution of artworks, along with a great diversity of materials. The quest for absolutely white porcelain was achieved through a unique blend of chemistry and artistic creativity. White as a specific 'value' in art was prized by the Neoclassical aesthetic: Winckelmann thought (erroneously) that Greek statues were perfectly white, and the greatest sculptors of his era, such as Canova and Thorvaldsen, were repeatedly compared and judged on this assumption. With refined sensitivity, Canova understood that the absolute whiteness of marble statuary could be enhanced through subtle 'correction'. Thus, he not only skilfully varied the surface work and degree of polish, but also inserted gilded metal details, contrasts of black (the deep door in the centre of the tomb of Maria Christina of Austria, for example), and treated the idealized flesh of Paolina Bonaparte with a thin coating of pink wax.

THE MYSTIC LAMB

A guiltless victim of a pre-ordained fate, the white lamb is the sacrificial animal par excellence. White, on the other hand, has always been linked to the theme of the sacrifice of the just man to a supreme truth. In antiquity, while black animals were immolated for the gods of the underworld, the fleece of the victims destined for the celestial gods was bright white: a famous example from the *Odyssey* is the white heifers reserved for the sun god.

Since Early Christian art, the white lamb has been used to symbolize the sacrifice of Christ on behalf of humankind. The purest and whitest creature, the lamb was sacrificed by the Hebrews during Passover. John the Baptist points to Jesus as the Lamb of God who takes the sins of the world upon himself. A symbol of sacrifice, but also of redemption and triumph over death, the white animal makes its most splendid appearance in art in the *Ghent Altarpiece* by Jan van Eyck. The focus and heart of this complex altarpiece is the panel depicting the Adoration of the Mystic Lamb. The altar upon which the Lamb spills its blood into a chalice, surrounded by angels holding the symbols of the Passion, falls on the polyptych's vertical axis, between the Fountain of Grace and the Dove of the Holy Spirit. It occupies the centre of a large clearing, in a rolling landscape where the verdant foliage of the trees alternates with the Gothic spires of fabulous cities in the distance. The intense green of the lush Garden of Paradise further emphasizes the animal's white coat – symbol of the revealed truth that triumphs over death – for which the white garments of the angels, emblems of glory and the path to heaven, provide a backdrop.

While Van Eyck concentrates on the theme of Resurrection and Redemption, Francisco de Zurbarán draws upon the white lamb's sacrificial aspect. Zurbarán, a fascinating artist, painted images of penetrating spiritual force from a viewpoint that mainly dwelt on the idea of martyrdom. With half-closed eyes, the dying animal stretched out on a funereal black sill emanates a tremendous emotional charge. The light, coming from the left, does not describe the white fleece precisely but lingers on the cords binding tight the animal's legs, evoking the inescapability of the sacrifice.

▲

Jan van Eyck
The Adoration of the Mystic Lamb, centre panel of the Ghent Altarpiece
1425-1433
137.7 x 242.2 cm
Cathedral of St Bavo, Ghent

▶

Francisco de Zurbarán
Agnus Dei (The Lamb of God)
1635-1640
oil on canvas, 38 x 62 cm
Museo Nacional del Prado, Madrid

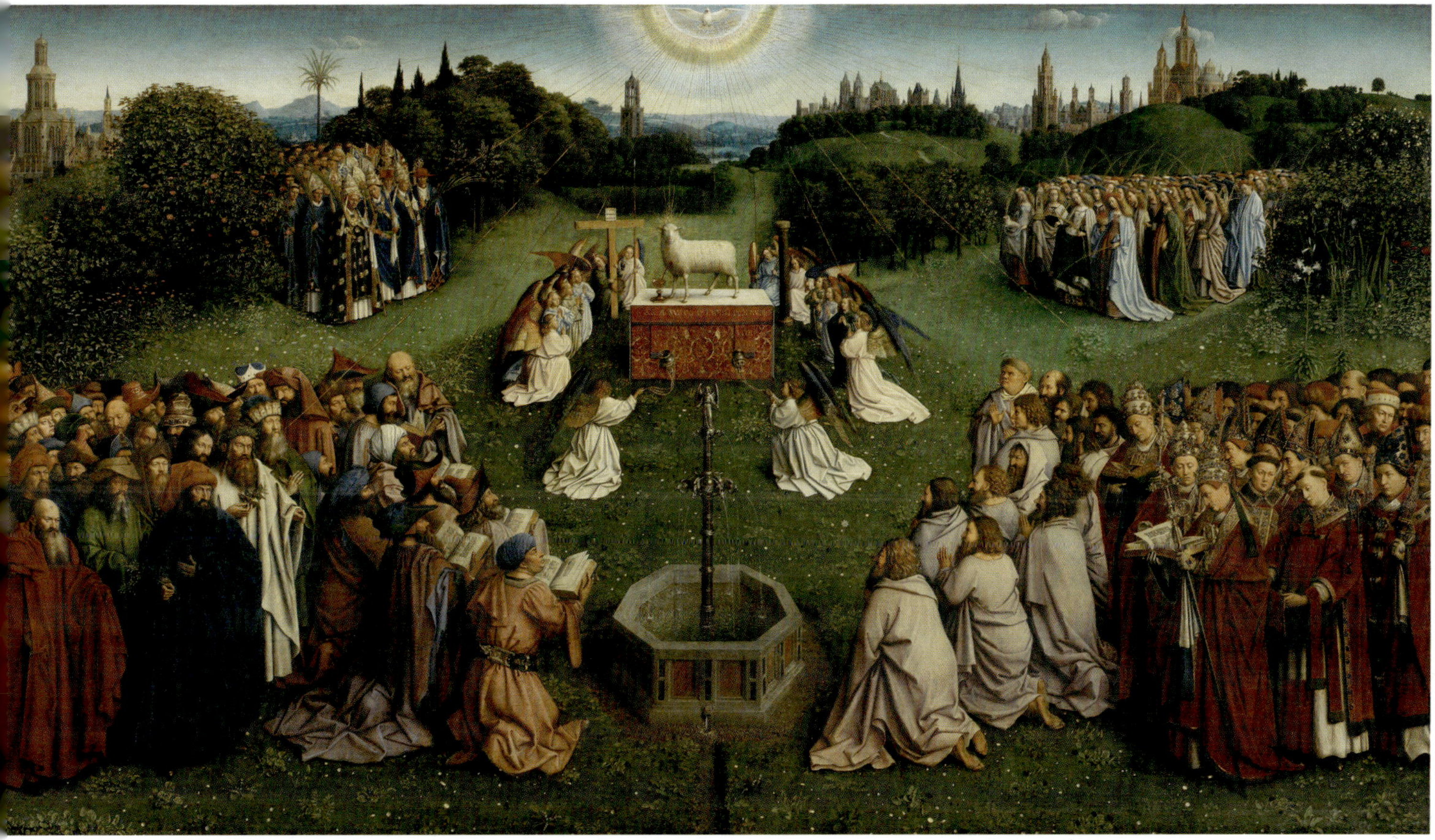

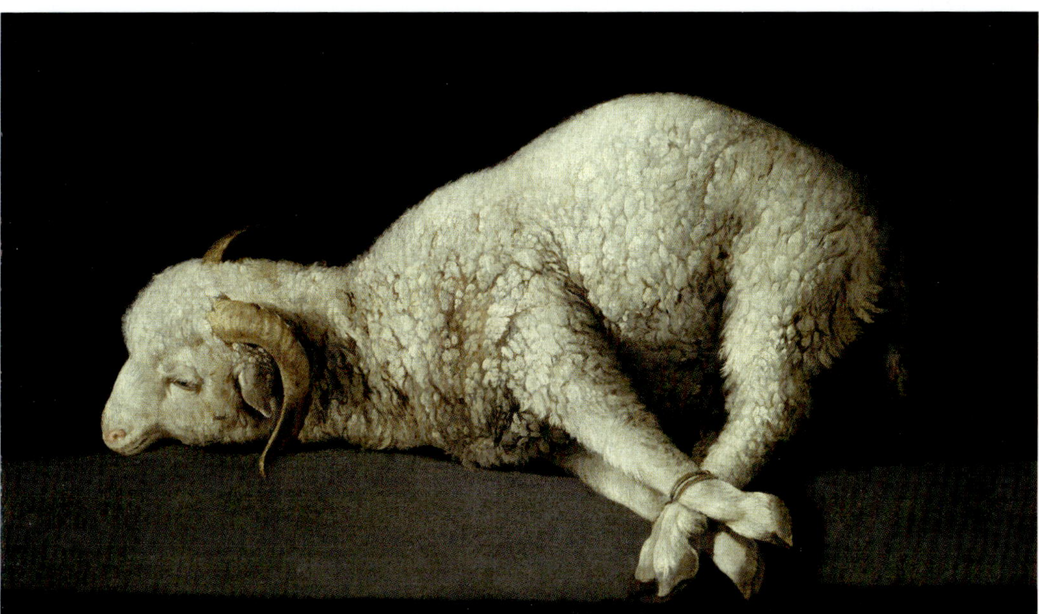

THE TRANSFIGURATION

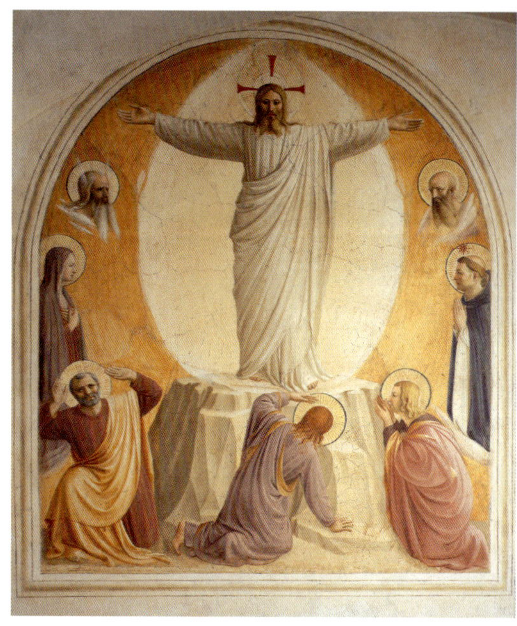

Fra Angelico
The Transfiguration
1439-1442
fresco, 193 x 164 cm
Convento di San Marco, Florence

Clothing, cloaks, cloths, bed sheets, bandages, swaddling and veils all appear repeatedly in the Gospels, from the Nativity to the sepulchre and the Resurrection. All four of the Evangelists mention the white bandages and *sudarium* (Holy Shroud) in which the dead Christ was wrapped, offering artists opportunities to depict these. For two thousand years, Christian art has sought to convey these scriptural passages through images.

The mystical episode of the Transfiguration is one of the most mysterious and solemn passages in the Gospel. Yet the account by Mark (probably a record of the memories of Peter, who was present at the Transfiguration) conjures up an image of homely simplicity, as Christ hovers in the air, flanked by Moses and Elijah: 'His raiment became shining, exceeding white as snow, so as no fuller on earth can white them.' This reference to the dazzling white of Christ's robes became a challenge to artists.

One of the most fascinating interpretations of the Transfiguration is from a cycle of Gospel scenes painted by Fra Angelico in the cells of the Dominican brothers at the Convent of St Mark in Florence. The series was designed to aid the monks' prayer and contemplation – these suspended scenes of rarified beauty without doubt rank among the most moving works of 15th-century art. The fresco panels are in predominantly light tones to match the large plaster walls, giving the scenes an even greater luminosity. However, the fresco technique, which uses lime as an ingredient, does not allow the transparency and lustre of oil paint.

In his *Transfiguration*, Fra Angelico has accentuated the whiteness of Christ's clothing through a double contrast of light tones: first, the diffuse gold background, and second the glow of an almond-shaped halo that envelops the figure of Christ like a medieval nimbus. In this unusual and highly effective virtuoso tone-on-tone effect, the luminous white of Christ's robes stands out against the white but nearly opaque halo.

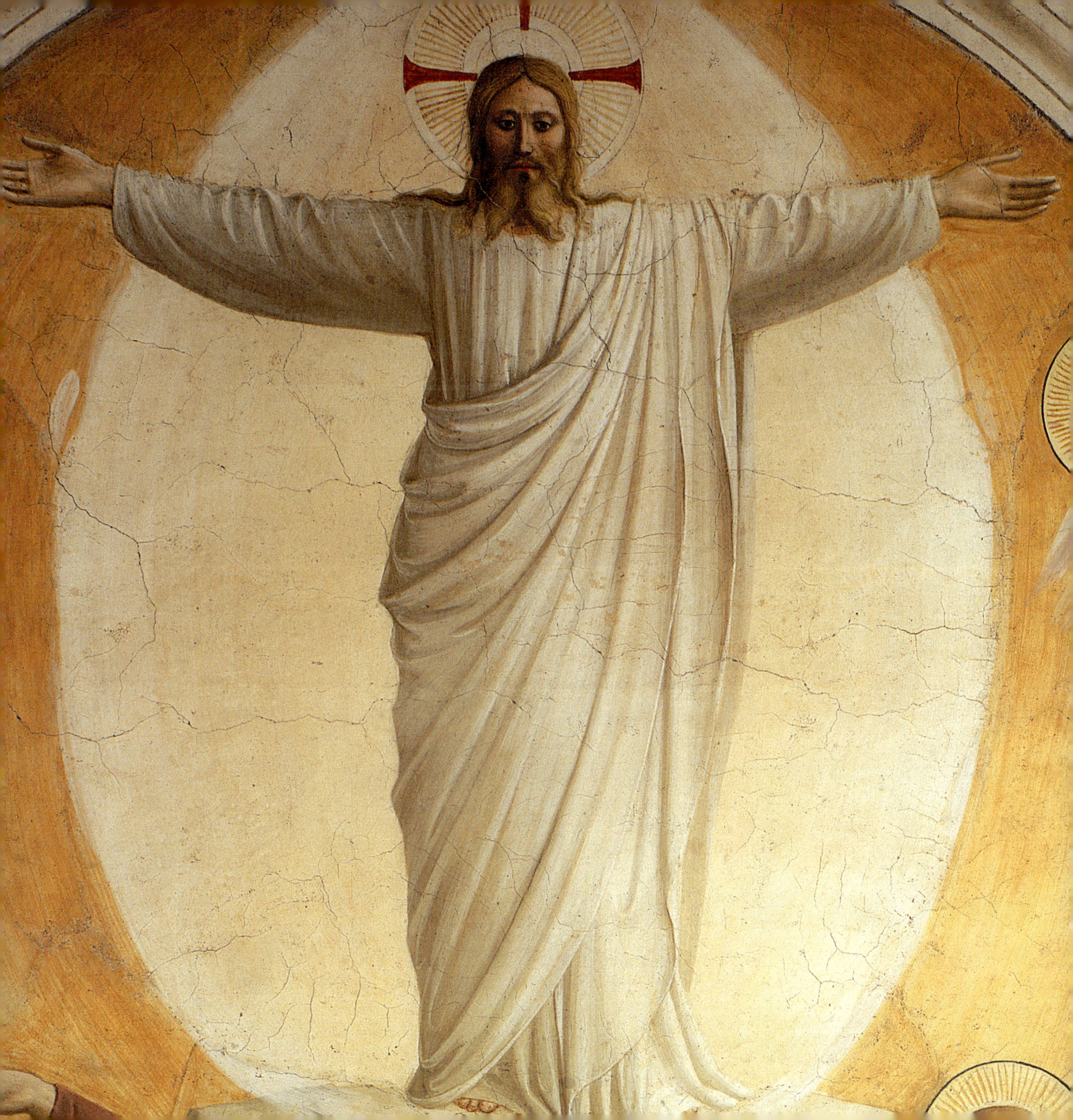

THE LILY

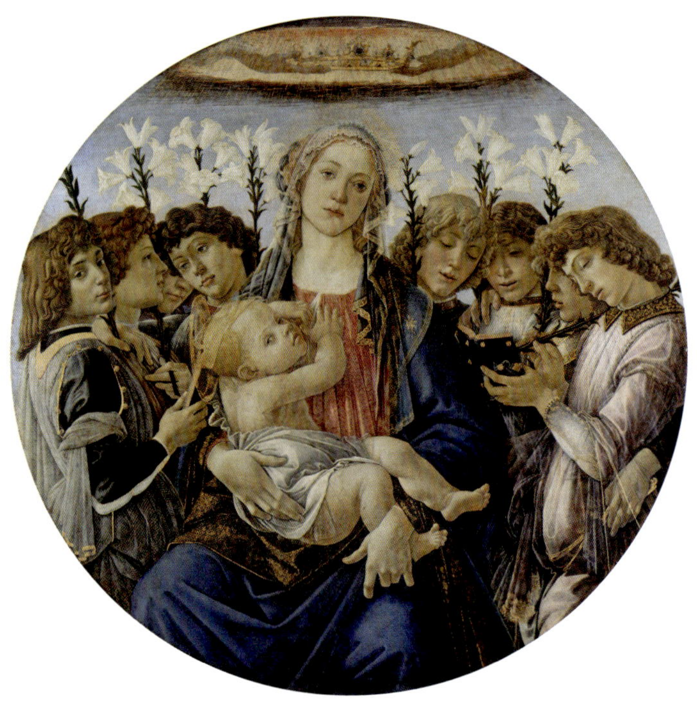

▲
Sandro Botticelli
Raczynski Tondo (Virgin and Child with Eight Angels)
c. 1477
oil on panel, diameter 135 cm
Gemäldegalerie, Berlin

▶
Gaetano Previati
The Madonna of the Lilies (Madonna dei Gigli)
1893
oil on canvas, 181 x 220 cm
Galleria d'Arte Moderna, Milan

The Gospel of St Matthew (6:28) asks us to consider the lilies of the field – not even Solomon at the height of his glory can compare with their splendour! The white lily is one of the most common flowers in Christian art and, more generally, is a symbol of chaste if gratuitous beauty. In a burst of aestheticism in *The Stones of Venice*, John Ruskin states, 'Remember that the most beautiful things in the world are the most useless; peacocks and lilies, for instance.'

In Christianity, the lily represents pure love, and its white petals allude to purity and innocence. In depictions of the Annunciation, the Archangel Gabriel often appears to Mary with a lily in his hand. Furthermore, the open calyx, capacious and ready to receive, is an evident reference to the womb of Mary, who herself had been conceived 'immaculately', as free of guilt as a lily.

The subject of the lily in combination with the Virgin is developed in a striking manner in Sandro Botticelli's *Raczynski Tondo*. Painted about 1477, it dates from the time when Botticelli was taking his place as a leading figure in the artistic scene in Florence, in the age of Lorenzo the Magnificent. Eight angels form a sort of living niche around the Virgin and Child. Standing out against an azure sky, the tall lilies thrust upwards towards where we see the hands of God the Father holding a crown.

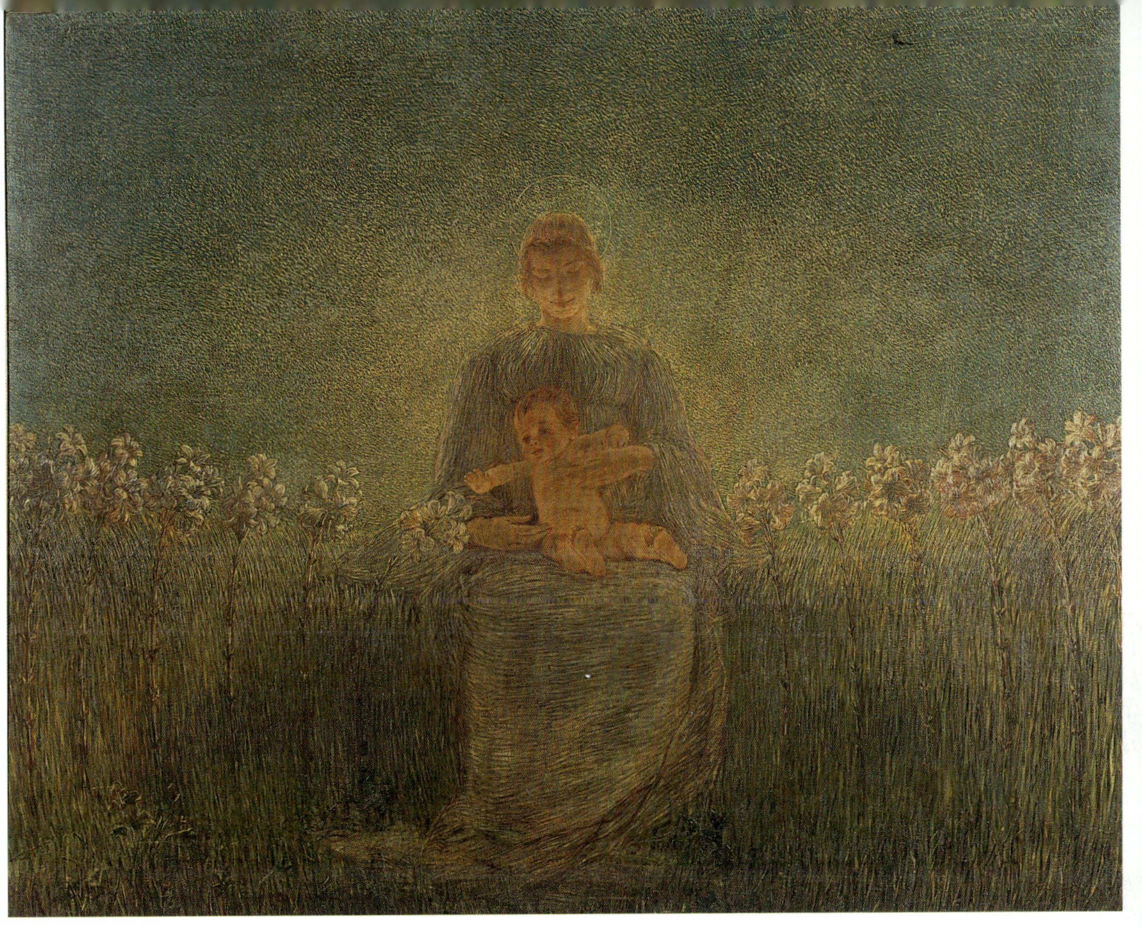

More than four centuries after Botticelli, another Italian artist returned to the same subject, in a painting of remarkable size. Previati's *Madonna of the Lilies* is an important but controversial contribution to the history of religious painting just before the dawn of the 20th century. Initially rejected by the jury for exhibition at the Accademia di Brera in Milan in 1894, the canvas was later cautiously accepted. Previati was invited to exhibit 'at his own risk', and became the object of controversy because of both his original painting technique and the work's symbolic content. The Madonna, at the centre of the canvas, is flanked on either side by six lilies growing in a regular row. Mary's light, simple clothing and the white reflection of the flowers, which create a golden, luminous halo around her in the blue sky, suggest the profound sense of devotion and religious fervour that Previati derived from Renaissance artists like Botticelli but reinvented through the technique of Divisionism.

PEARL

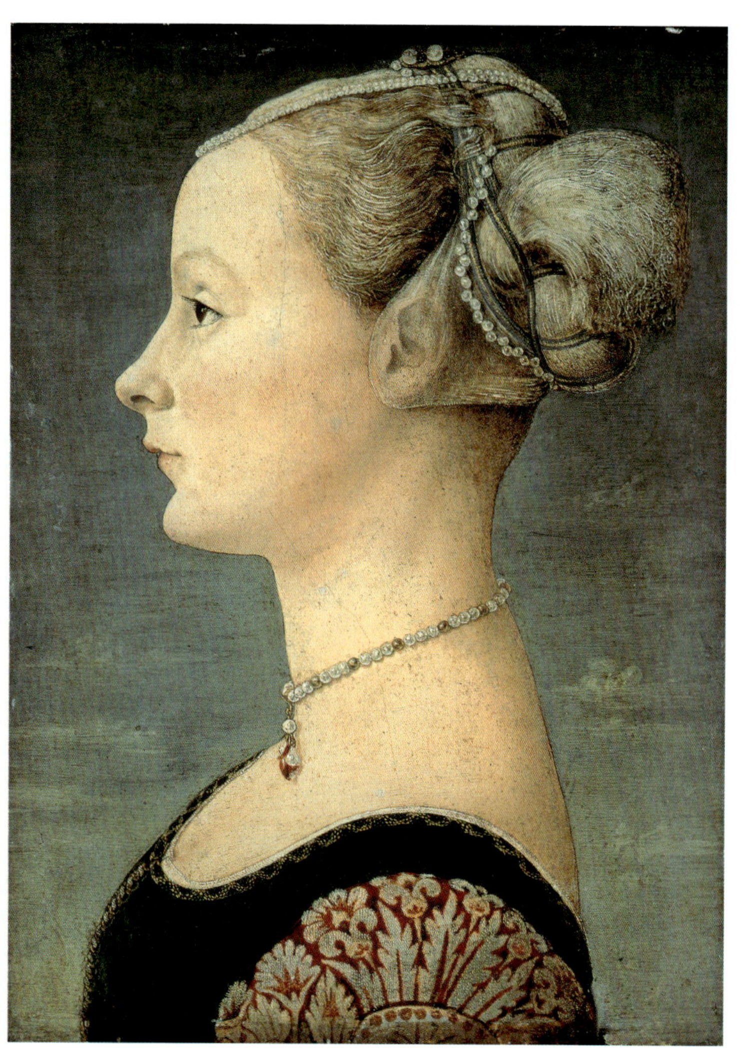

With its iridescence and transparency, its (normally) perfectly spherical shape, its origin in the animal and not the mineral world, and its symbolism, being treated in various passages of the Gospels, the pearl has always been highly treasured and has had an enormous presence in art. This has even extended as far as defining an entire cultural period: the word 'Baroque' derives from the old Portuguese word *barrueco*, which means 'pearl of imperfect appearance' (that is, incompletely formed, adhering to the shell or of an unusual, oblong form).

Pearls confer a fascinating and elegant luminescence upon whoever wears them, and they appear frequently in Renaissance portraits. The spheres' moonlike opalescence appears not only in necklaces, earrings, bracelets and brooches, but also as a decoration on garments and hair bands. A famous example is the portrait of a young woman by Antonio del Pollaiolo. The clearly delineated silhouette of the young noblewoman with an intricate hairstyle is heightened by details like the shaven brow (a fashion intended to make the forehead look higher) and the pearls in contact with her pale flesh. The comparison was already made by Dante in the *Paradise*, where he describes a pearl set against a pallid forehead.

A pearl earring features prominently in Vermeer's most famous portrait, a work of both great precision and immediate freshness in which the painter from Delft yet again offers the miracle of a light that seems to permeate the paint itself. The mysterious identity of the enchanting girl has inspired a novel and a film.

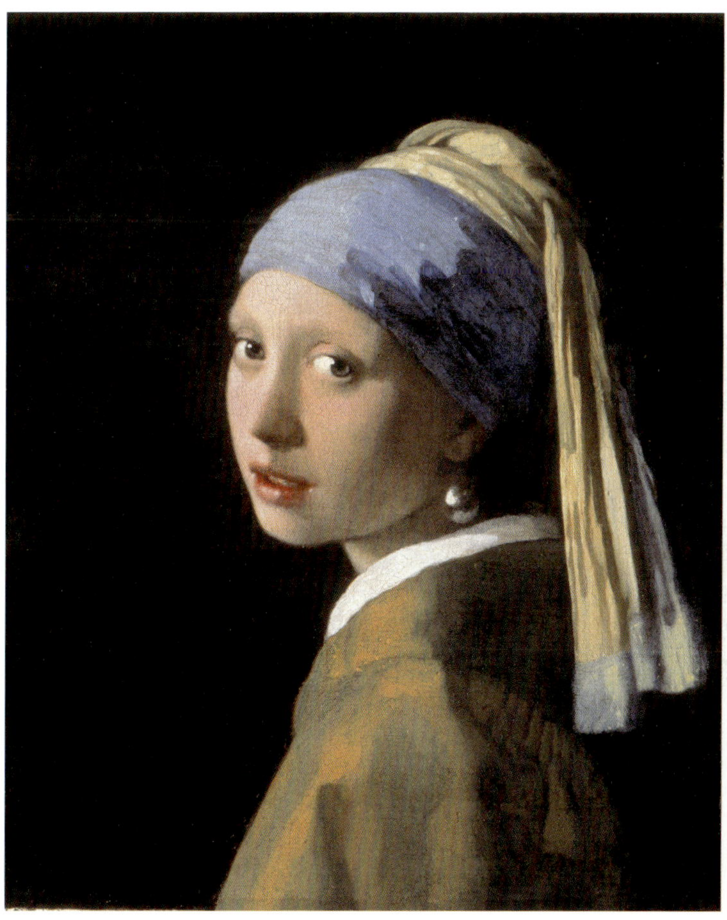

◂
Antonio del Pollaiolo
Portrait of a Woman
c. 1470
tempera on panel, 46 x 34 cm
Museo Poldi Pezzoli, Milan

▸
Johannes Vermeer
Girl with a Pearl Earring
c. 1665-1667
oil on canvas, 44.5 x 39 cm
Koninklijk Kabinet van Schilderijen Mauritshuis, The Hague

UNICORN

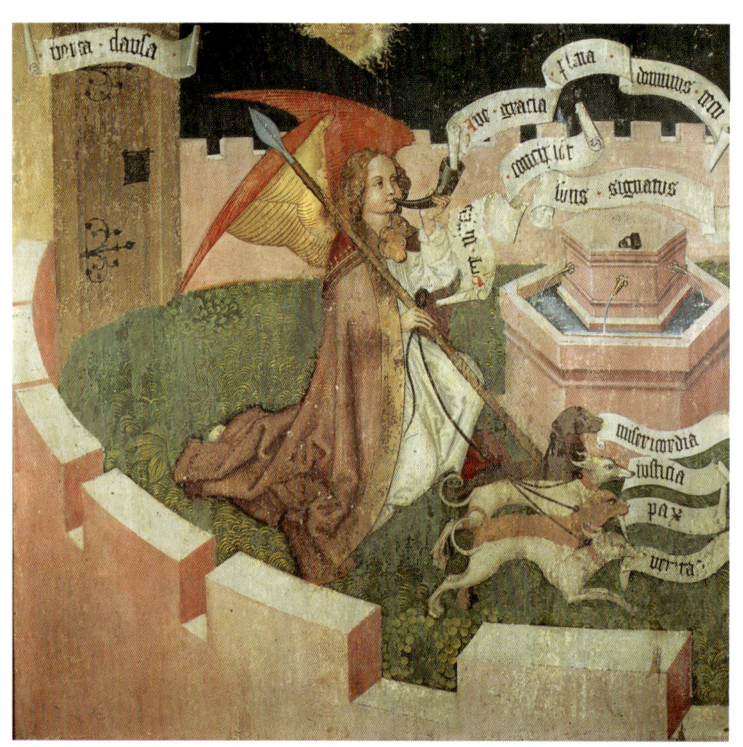

After the success of the *Madonna of the Rose Arbour* (1473), the Dominicans of Colmar commissioned an altarpiece from their city's celebrated citizen Martin Schongauer. The two panels that presented an allegory of the Annunciation in the form of a 'mystic hunt' decorated the interior, while the outside showed episodes of Christ's Passion. One of the main figures in this interior scene is the white unicorn, the mythological animal that, according to traditional medieval bestiaries, always escapes capture but meekly takes refuge in the arms of a virgin. Hence, in symbolic Christian iconography, a white unicorn in the Virgin Mary's lap is a metaphor for Christ. The theme of the mystic hunt was persistently spread by the Dominican order through the *Speculum humanae salvationis* (Mirror of Human Salvation), a handbook that was popular throughout Central Europe.

Martin Schongauer (who probably drew the scene and left its execution to the artists in his workshop, among them his three brothers) offers an interpretation rich in symbolism, where white prevails as a symbol of purity and chastity. This Annunciation takes place within an atypically pink enclosure. The classical attributes of Mary's virginity are present, from the fenced-in *hortus conclusus* (enclosed garden) to the fountain of pure water, the white unicorn and the white lily. The Archangel Gabriel blowing a hunting horn and holding greyhounds on a leash is unusual. Alternately white and brown, the dogs reflect the fact that the altar was a Dominican commission (*Domini canis* meaning 'Dogs of the Lord'), and represent the virtues.

The theme of the unicorn as an emblem of chastity and virginity was fairly prevalent in Renaissance painting (there are examples by Raphael and Domenichino). It also inspired two magnificent late 15th-century tapestry cycles: one with a red background in the Musée de Cluny in Paris, and another with a blue background in the Cloisters (the medieval section of the Metropolitan Museum of Art) in New York.

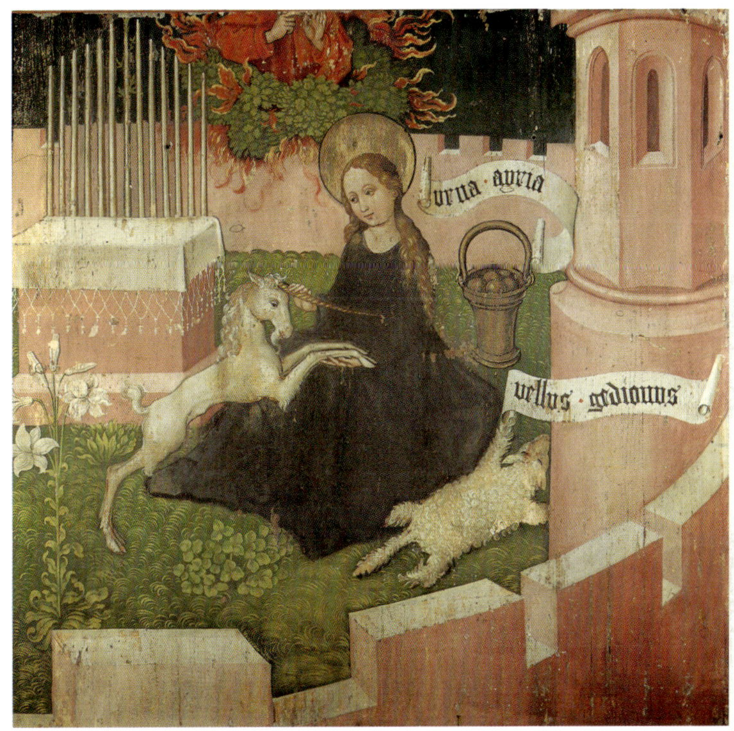

Martin Schongauer and workshop
The Mystic Hunt from the Altar of the Church of the Dominicans
c. 1480
oil on panel, 116 x 116 cm (each)
Musée d'Unterlinden, Colmar

THE ERMINE

The precious white fur of the ermine, being reserved for sovereigns, judges and university rectors, is associated with the highest aristocratic, juridical and intellectual dignity. In art history, the ermine is inseparably linked with the image of Cecilia Gallerani, the beautiful mistress of Ludovico il Moro, Duke of Milan. This highly innovative portrait by Leonardo offers an exceptional insight into feminine psychology. The presence of a live ermine brings in a series of symbolic references – including to purity and nobility – and gives the scene a vivid quality. With the hint of a smile, the attractive young woman slowly turns her eyes towards an unknown companion. Her hands graze the animal's soft fur, and her shoulders turn slightly, initiating a complex interplay of torsions and movements of the upper body, neck, head and eyes, which are directed towards a light source beyond the frame.

The painting became famous as soon as it was painted. A court poet wrote a sonnet about it, and Isabella d'Este – the sister of Ludovico il Moro's wife, Beatrice – asked the duke's permission to keep it in Mantua for a month so that local portrait painters could draw inspiration from it. Then, for almost three centuries, the masterpiece mysteriously disappeared from view. It resurfaced in the collection of a young Polish nobleman and underwent dramatic adventures. The damage caused by a soldier of Napoleon who trampled the priceless painting is still visible.

Some years after Leonardo, an ermine appeared in another important Italian Renaissance work, by Carpaccio (a portraitist of moderate fame). His painting symbolizes a bygone era of chivalry. The heraldic arms and other details have led to the highly plausible suggestion that the sitter is the twenty-year-old Francesco Maria della Rovere, future Duke of Urbino, whose portrait was also painted at different times by Raphael and Titian. The flowers, animals and details of the armour and architecture are reproduced with great care, and often with a symbolic reference. The white ermine is placed beside the motto 'I would rather die than incur dishonour'. According to legend, the ermine dies if its snow-white fur is sullied.

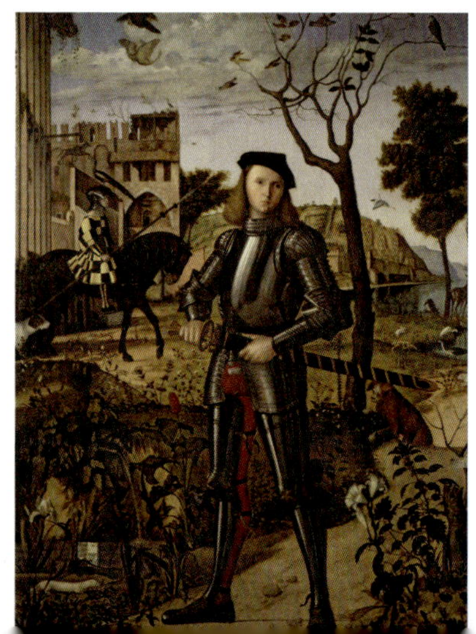

▸

Leonardo da Vinci
Lady with an Ermine
1485-1490
oil on panel, 54.8 x 40.3 cm
Museum Czartoryski, Cracow

◂

Vittore Carpaccio
Young Knight in a Landscape
1510
oil on canvas, 218.5 x 152.2 cm
Museo Thyssen-Bornemisza, Madrid

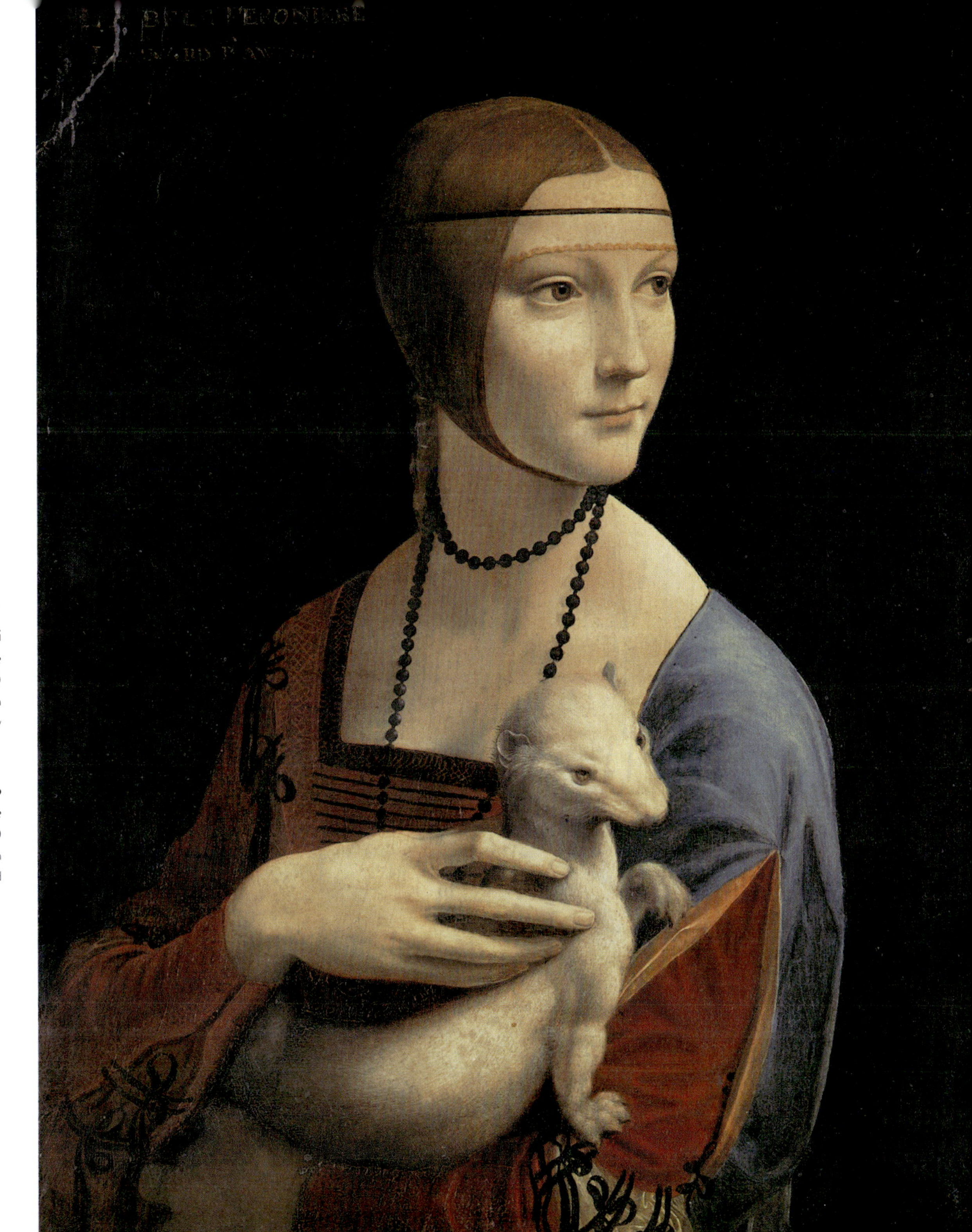

THE EMPYREAN REALM

José Saramago's novel *Blindness* describes the progressive spread of an illness that leads to an obliterating, blinding whiteness. The great Portuguese novelist thus reverses the usual association of blindness with black and the anxiety of impenetrable darkness. White, too, can be the colour of the total absence of image, an absolute void. On the other hand, Dante described the approach to Paradise as a flood of increasingly radiant light, a brightness too strong for human eyes.

In art history, Paradise has always proved more difficult to depict than Hell. For over a thousand years, the imagination of painters and sculptors has given form to the diabolical confusion of the place of eternal punishment. The many fewer images of Paradise show well-arranged (and inevitably monotonous) formations of smiling blessed souls, bathed in an often golden light. Fifteenth-century artists like Van Eyck and Fra Angelico found enchanting solutions for depicting Eden, the earthly paradise that was a prelude to the true Empyrean, but it is extremely difficult, if not impossible, to convey the concept of heavenly bliss in painting. A fascinating attempt is that of Hieronymus Bosch, who used white and the circle as metaphors of the absorption of individual humans into the divine light.

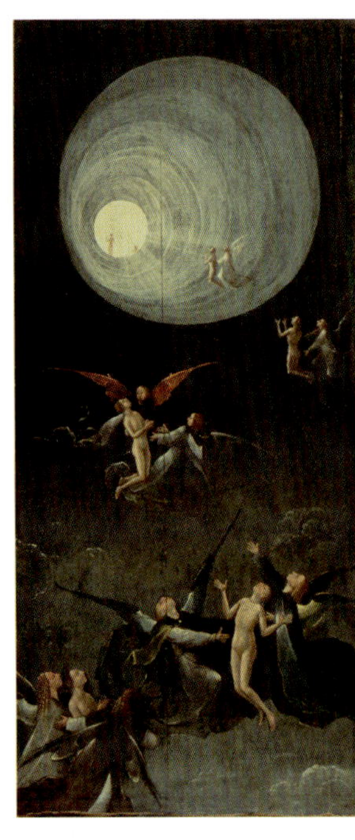

Hieronymus Bosch
The Ascent of the Blessed to the Heavenly Paradise
from the polyptych *Visions of the Hereafter*
c. 1490 or later
oil on panel, 87 x 40 cm
Palazzo Ducale, Venice

The striking image is from a cycle of four visions of the afterlife that were originally side panels of a polyptych that has since been dismantled. They provide evidence of Bosch's probable journey through northern Italy en route to Venice. In the painting, against a predominantly brown background, souls accompanied by guardian angels ascend to heaven along a rising path. Circular forms that look like entrances to a tunnel of light show the way. As the souls ascend, they seem to be liberated from their bodily essence, losing material consistency, until they dissolve into the blinding vortex of gleaming white light that leads towards the invisible, the Absolute.

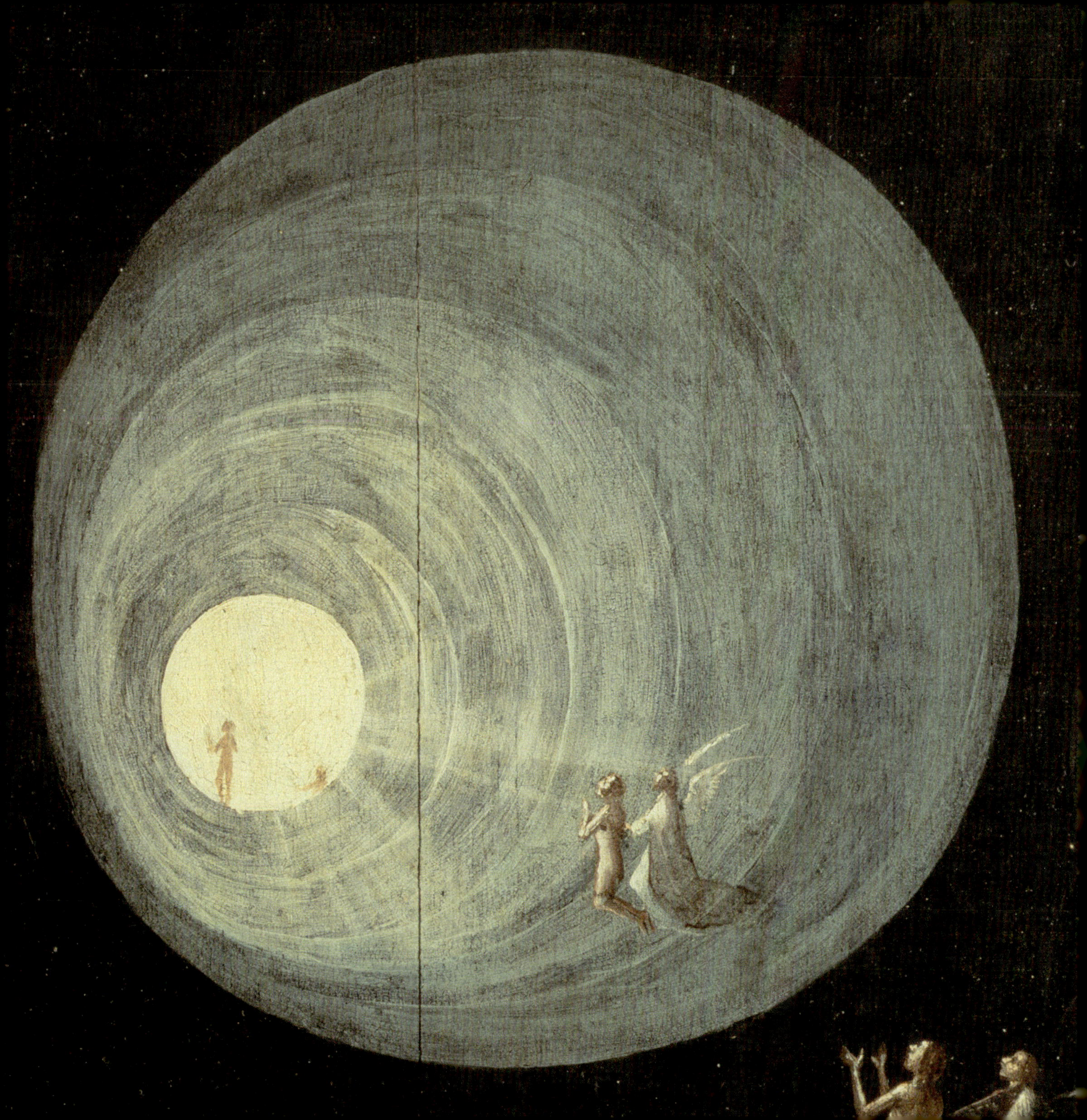

Pieter Bruegel
Hunters in the Snow
1565
oil on panel, 117 x 162 cm
Kunsthistorisches Museum, Vienna

SNOW

The so-called 'Months' cycle constitutes the most organic and important nucleus of the mature production of Pieter Bruegel the Elder. It entered the Prague collection of Emperor Rudolf II and corresponds to the tastes of that nonconformist collector from Augsburg. All the paintings in the cycle show exceptionally well-developed landscapes, with views of solemn breadth. In the past, the immediate and almost journalistic enjoyableness of Bruegel's narrative episodes has led to the artist being considered a 'naive' illustrator of peasant life, of the static, almost medieval world of traditions, proverbs and the 'perpetual calendar' of field labourers. The Months cycle, however, demonstrates the great originality and full stylistic awareness of the painter from Antwerp. Dispersed when Prague was sacked during the Thirty Years War, the cycle has been preserved only partly. Five paintings remain today: *The Harvesters*, in New York; *Haymaking*, which recently entered a private collection in the Czech Republic; and three at the Kunsthistorisches Museum in Vienna (*The Gloomy Day*, *The Return of the Herd*, and the winter scene *Hunters in the Snow*).

This famous image is inspired by a human, social, climatic and natural state that goes beyond the time and logic of a painting cycle to become the very image of winter's intense cold and silence. Bruegel constructs the composition from a viewpoint higher than the foreground, concentrating on the fundamental contrast between the white snow and the black figures, tree trunks and buildings – a pattern of absolute simplicity and immediate effect that heightens the exceptional luminescence achieved by the master, above all in the background landscape. Born and raised in Flanders' flat countryside, Bruegel had been strongly impressed when crossing the Alps during his journey to Italy. His memory of the snow-capped peaks and rocky mountaintops took form in an image where reality and fantasy combine in an extremely striking way.

Bruegel's use of white is masterful, and before the advent of Impressionism, it is difficult to name a winter scene that so effectively conveys a sense of brisk cold air and the immensity of a snowfall on the highest jagged peaks. The skeletal branches of the bare trees form a black screen against the compact background of the sky. On the valley floor below, at the foot of the huge mountain, huddles a tiny village. The games the children are playing on the frozen pond add a delightful note of life to the scene.

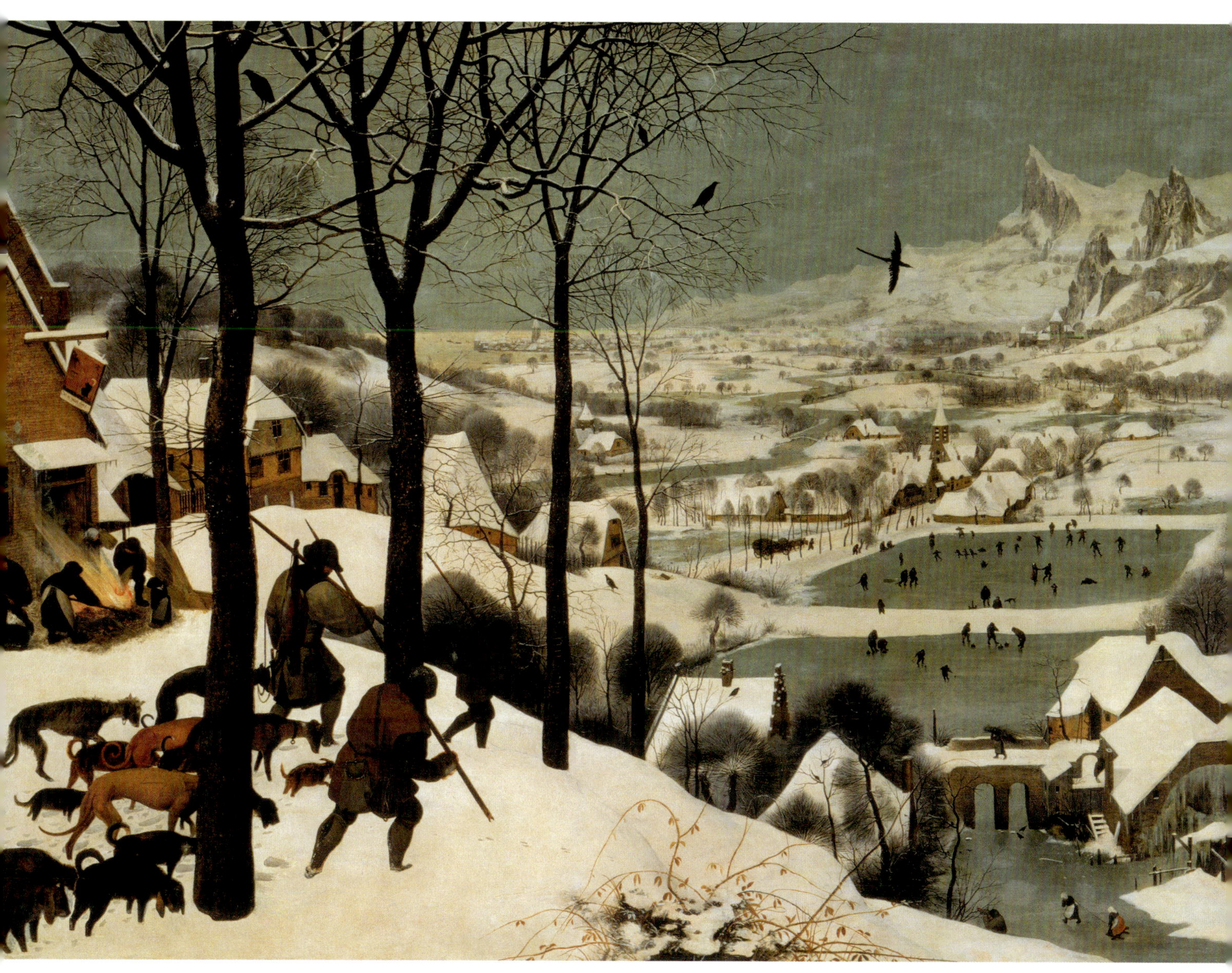

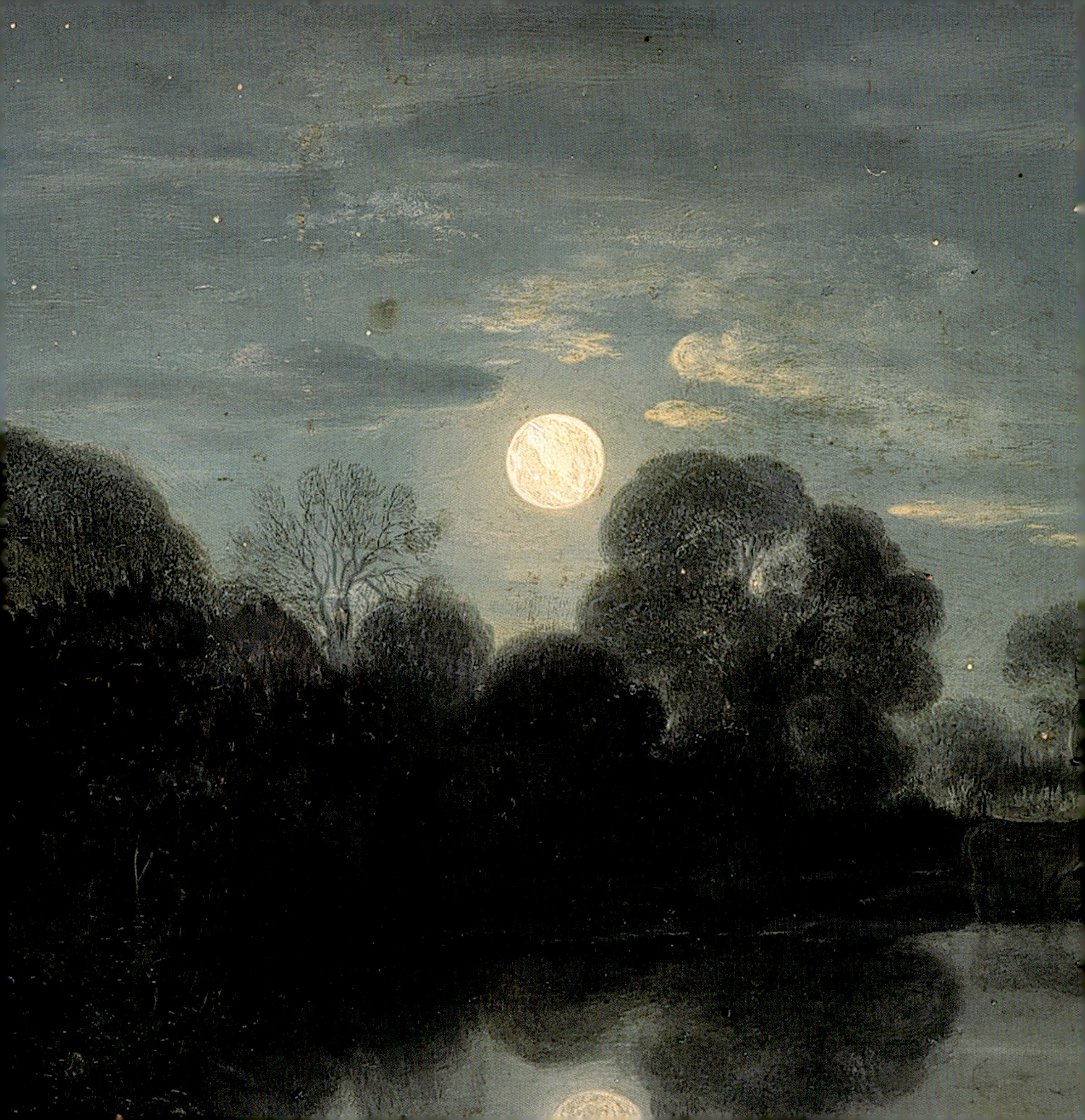

MOONLIGHT

Adam Elsheimer
The Flight into Egypt
1609
oil on copper, 31 x 41 cm
Alte Pinakothek, Munich

Immanuel Kant celebrated the magic of night in an unforgettable manner: 'Two things fill the mind with ever new and increasing admiration and awe the oftener and more steadily we reflect on them: the starry heavens above and the moral law within. I have not to search for them ... I see them before me and connect them directly with the consciousness of my existence.' (*Critic of Practical Reason*, 1786, trans. Thomas Kingsmill Abbott). Moonlight is an often-repeated motif in poetry, art and music, reaching its culmination in the Romantic period: we need only think of Beethoven's 'Moonlight' Sonata, Chopin's Nocturnes and Vincenzo Bellini's 'Casta diva' aria.

The moon is seen by painters variously as white, yellow, red or golden. Nevertheless, in the dark of night its light remains the silent and elusive inspiring Muse – at least until the early 20th century, when the Futurist poet Filippo Tommaso Marinetti proclaimed: 'Let's kill the moonlight!'

The enchanting nocturnal elegy *The Flight into Egypt*, even though of small dimensions, is without doubt the best-known work by Elsheimer, a refined painter of the same generation as Caravaggio and Rubens. Born in Frankfurt and active mainly in Italy, Elsheimer died at quite an early age, breaking short a career that began with extreme subtlety and fascinating results in the realm of landscape, at once classical and Romantic, idealized and scientific. The perfect description of the celestial vault, with the Milky Way and the constellations sparkling in a sky illuminated by the full moon, is a remarkable demonstration of Elsheimer's attention to science, in particular the studies of Galileo. The year of this painting, the Italian scientist had officially presented his invention, the telescope, at the University of Padua. The limpid full moon is doubled by its reflection in the water of a pond.

THE HOLY SHROUD

The Holy Shroud or *Sudarium* at the cathedral in Turin is one of the most important and mysterious relics of Christianity. It is an ancient linen sheet, certainly of Middle Eastern production, that bears an image of a man who has been beaten and crucified. According to pious tradition, it is the impression left by Christ's body at the moment of the Deposition. The white funeral shroud of Christ appears repeatedly in painting and is the focus of *The Deposition* painted by Rubens as part of a spectacular altarpiece for the cathedral in Antwerp. Taken down from the cross and supported with difficulty by the many figures, Christ's body collapses heavily as the last rays of light glow in the background.

Having recently returned to Antwerp after eight years in Italy, and still under the profound influence of the masterpieces of Caravaggio, Rubens conceived a work that is directly comparable to Italian models in its spectacular compositional force and intense expressiveness of the gestures. At the same time, it pays tribute to Flemish tradition in the accurate rendering of surfaces, fabric and details, as well as in the intensity of the colours. Composed in a single block of powerful physical and chromatic masses, the nine figures stand out against a dark background. They are almost completely immersed in the darkness of night, illuminated only by a last glimmer of daylight on the horizon. The shroud down which the body of Christ descends stands out all the more brilliantly. This is the central motif of the painting and distinguishes Rubens from his Italian models. Indeed, according to Sir Joshua Reynolds, the contrast between the white sheet and the ashen coloration of the dead Christ is too violent for any Italian painter. The powerful liveliness of St John's bright red clothes seems a clear tribute to 15th-century Flemish painting.

Along with the innovative force of the colours and light, in *The Deposition* Rubens shows a special interest in a compositional structure based on a diagonal – in this case determined by the bleeding Christ. The figures are distributed on three different horizontal planes: at the top, two men bend over precariously on the ladders, hanging on to the sheet as best they can – one of them holds it tight in his hand – which forms a kind of slide along which to guide the lifeless body of Christ into the hands of Nicodemus and Joseph of Arimathea. The lower portion at the left is entirely occupied by the weeping Virgin Mary and the anguished yet sensual figures of the kneeling pious women – they are a reference to the Venetian tradition. For the body of Jesus, Rubens draws inspiration from classical statuary, with a direct reference to the torso of the *Laocoön*.

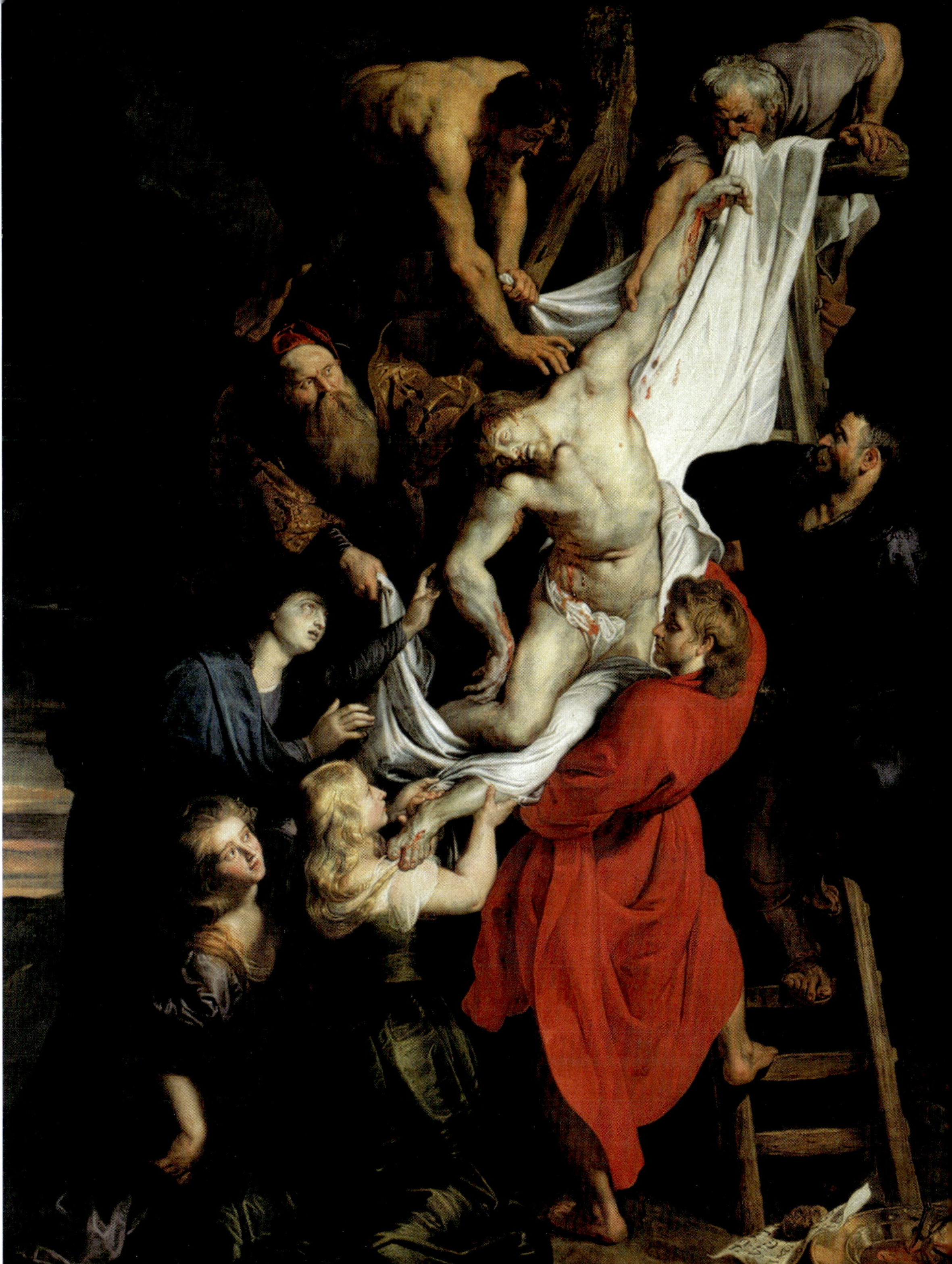

Peter Paul Rubens
The Deposition
1611-1614
oil on panel, 420 x 310 cm
Cathedral, Antwerp

SPIRITUAL WHITE, OR WHITEWASH?

In his famous treatise *On the Art of Building* (c. 1452), Leon Battista Alberti, drawing on the writings of Cicero, maintains the necessity of plastering church walls, since lime white is the only appropriate colour for reflection and meditation. And in fact the churches built in the 15th century by Brunelleschi and by Alberti himself adhere to this principle. In addition, over the centuries, coinciding with plagues and epidemics, various churches were whitewashed with lime for hygienic reasons. The use of white plaster in the interiors of religious buildings found particular application in the centre of Europe, and especially in the Low Countries, following the spread of Calvinist doctrine.

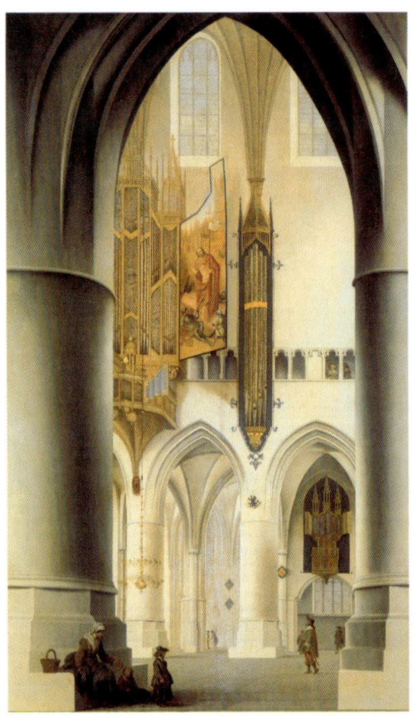

Pieter Jansz. Saenredam
Interior of the Church of St Bavo in Haarlem
1636
oil on panel, 95.5 x 57 cm
Rijksmuseum, Amsterdam

Firmly rejecting the cult of images and the opulent furnishings that had previously adorned places of worship, in the second half of the 16th century the Calvinist movement stripped many churches and destroyed artworks across a geo-cultural path that ran from Zurich to Antwerp. And while retaining a reasonable degree of religious tolerance, the United Provinces embraced Calvinism as their official faith. Dutch churches are sober and austere, whitewashed, devoid of pictorial and sculptural decorations. One interpreter of Calvinist and Dutch asceticism was Pieter Jansz. Saenredam, who specialized in bare, almost metaphysical views of the main Dutch churches that were being reformed.

A little older than Rembrandt, Saenredam left about fifty nearly monochrome canvases of interiors of religious buildings, distinguishing himself as the most gifted and poetic specialist in a genre that had other worthy exponents in the Low Countries. In silent, majestic naves peopled with small isolated figures, a cold light falls from above, emphasizing the white architectural framework and analysing with almost scientific expertise every least detail of construction. The plastered walls convey a sense of alienation and solitude, an emptiness that sharpens the building's brightness, underscoring human beings' relationship to spirituality.

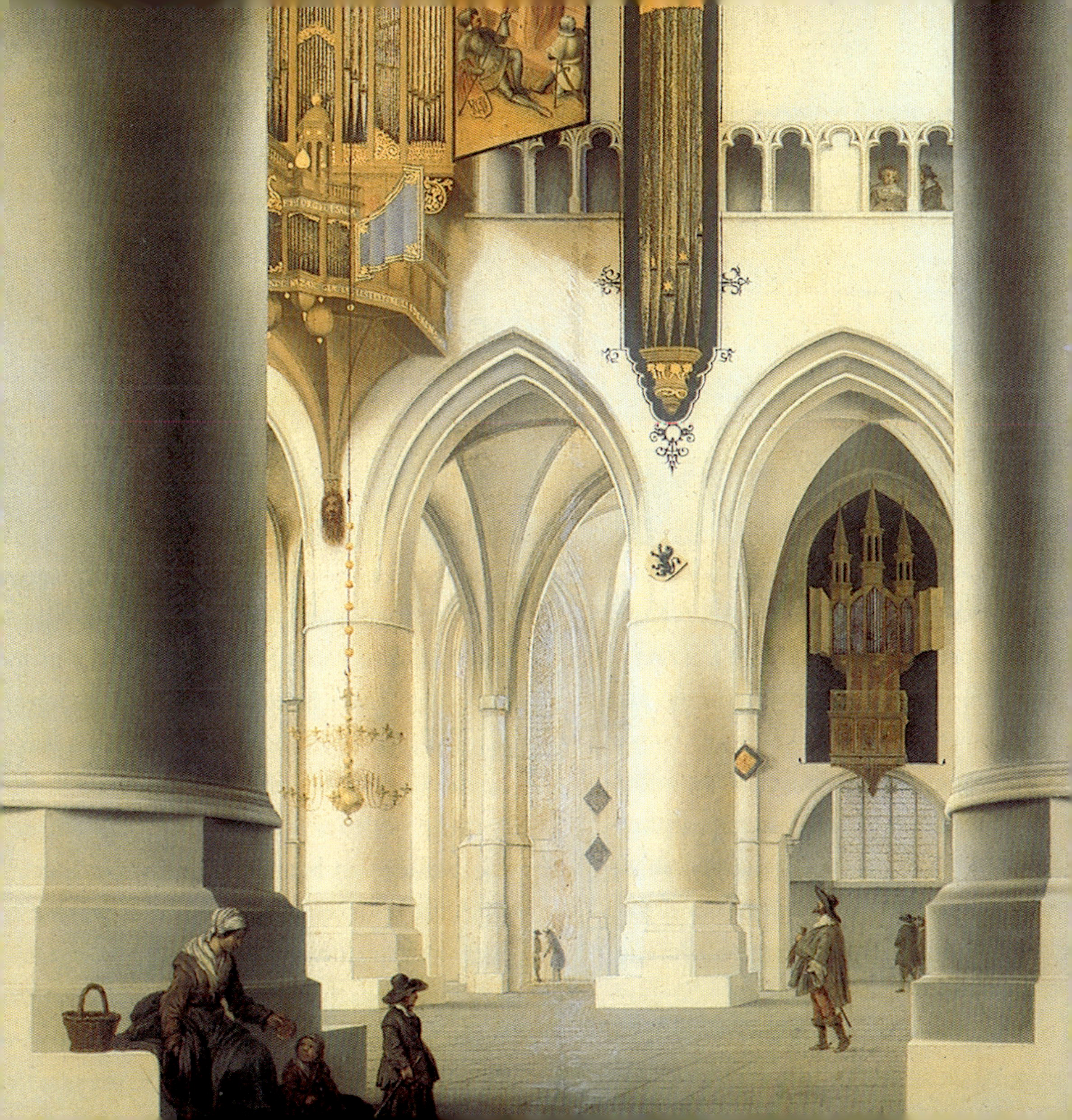

MILK

Johannes Vermeer
The Milkmaid
c. 1657-1658
oil on canvas, 45.5 x 41 cm
Rijksmuseum, Amsterdam

White expresses a sense of primordial purity, of spiritual and material nourishment: we might think of milk, the soft inside of a loaf of bread, the host of the Eucharist. Milk's whiteness and its symbolic value are celebrated in *The Milkmaid* by Vermeer. The stream of milk trickling from the jug is the luminous highpoint and focus of the action. With full awareness, Vermeer gives the buxom woman a solemn pose that refers to the traditional iconography of the Christian virtue of temperance. According to the social and religious ethic of the Low Countries, a housewife is responsible for maintaining exemplary moral 'cleanliness' in the domestic environment and for the moral management of the family.

The point of view is slightly above eye level. In this case, Vermeer forgoes the usual setting of a comfortable middle-class room to depict a plain kitchen where the floor does not shine and the wall, hung with functional objects, is spotted and peeling in places. The only decorative element consists of a skirting board of blue-and-white glazed ceramic tiles, a typical product of Vermeer's city, Delft.

The perfectly balanced canvas offers an extraordinary visual rendering of many different types of surface – from the braided breadbasket to the rudimentary foot warmer on the floor, from the wicker hamper to the polished metals, from the ceramic vessels of various thicknesses to the loaves – attuned to the dual yellow-blue tonality so often used by Vermeer. However, the exceptionally tactile re-creation of the objects does not distract from the robust figure of the woman, in her almost devotional gesture of pouring the milk without spilling so much as a drop. *The Milkmaid* has also been considered an allegorical personification of the 17th-century Low Countries, and not only in its ethical values: Holland was, and still is, famous for raising cattle, dairy products and a rich, varied diet.

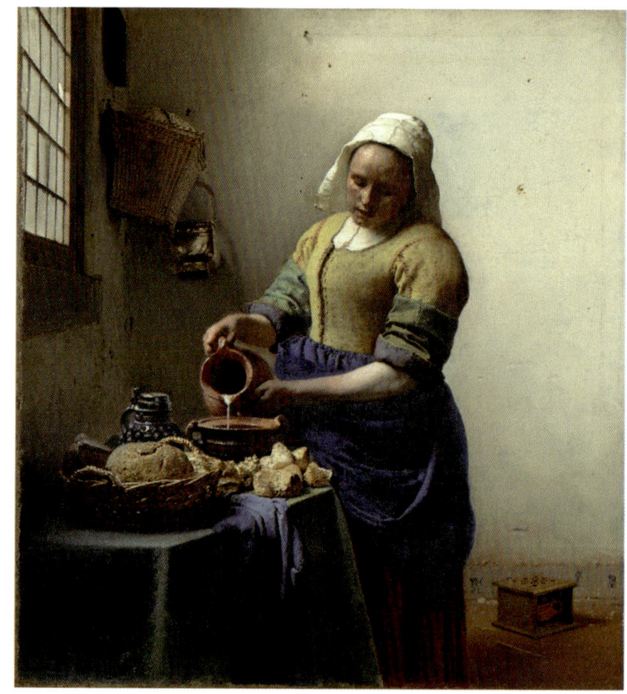

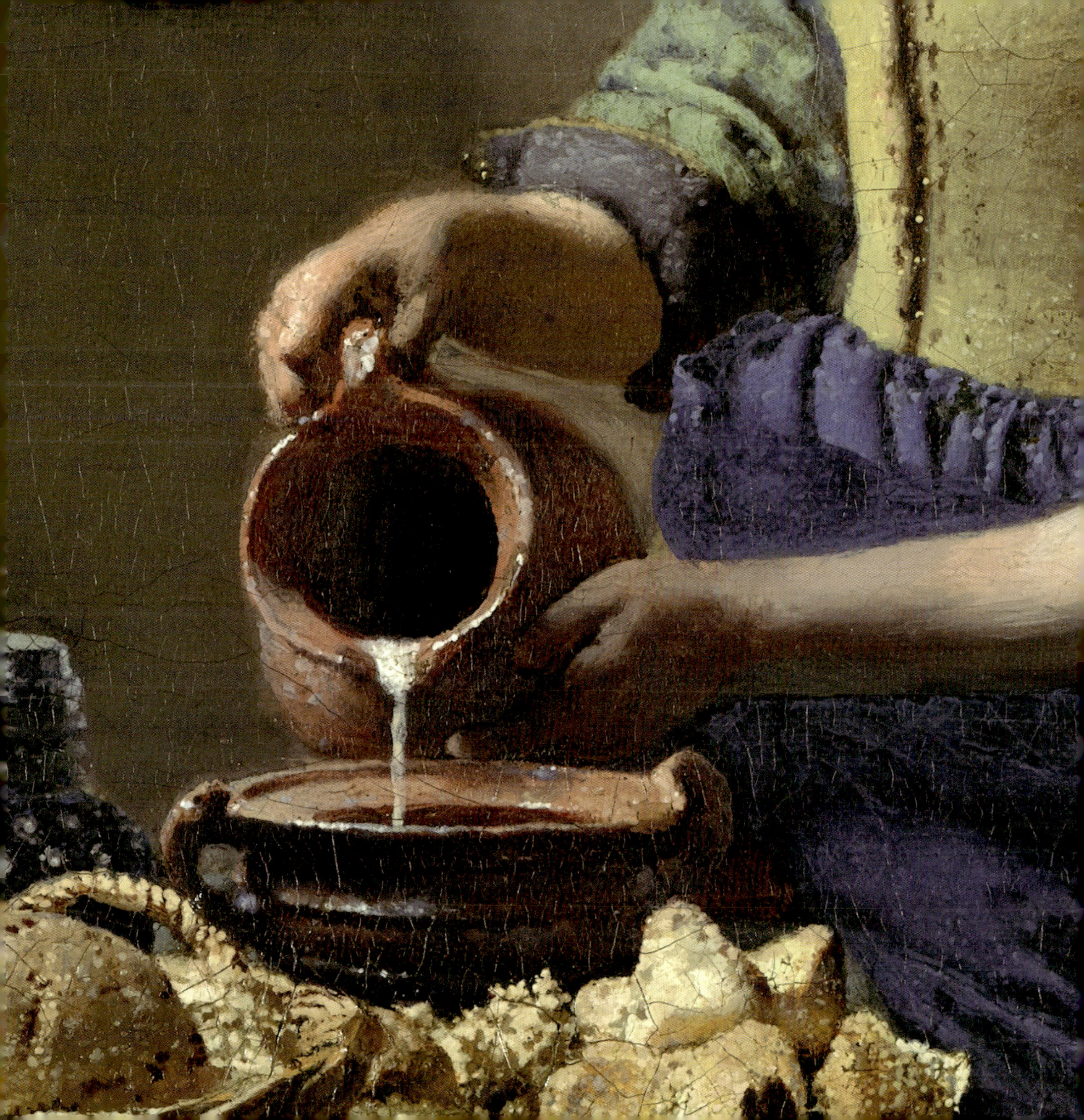

PORCELAIN

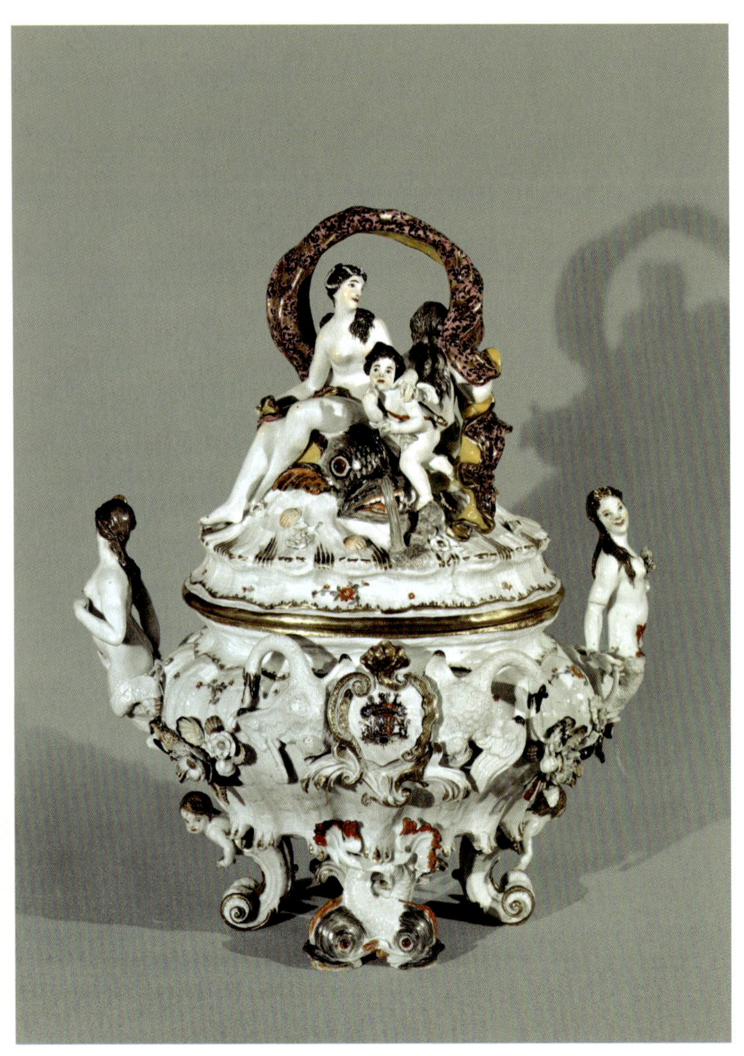

The expressive pinnacle of the Rococo style, both from the technical standpoint and in terms of sheer artistry, came with the advent of European porcelain production. Until the early 18th century, porcelain was exclusively an Oriental import and hence very costly. The history of the introduction into Europe of the technique of white hard-paste porcelain was tinged with intrigue. The discovery of the formula for the paste and firing was made in 1708 by Johann Friedrich Böttger, an alchemist who was held secretly in the castle of Meissen by Prince Augustus II of Saxony. After various unsuccessful attempts that resulted in brown porcelain, Böttger at last succeeded in finding the correct formula to produce a compact ceramic body that was white inside, and not just on the glazed surface. For some years, thanks to the exploitation of veins of kaolin and the jealous safekeeping of the secret of production, Meissen maintained a European monopoly over porcelain. After the clandestine theft of the formula in Vienna, however, the rest of the 18th century saw the foundation throughout Europe of other factories, often owned by monarchs or the nobility. In Germany, factories at Frankenthal (founded by the Prince-Elector Charles Theodore, Count Palatinate), Hoechst and later Berlin were set up at the behest of Frederick the Great of Prussia; in France Madame de Pompadour inspired the factory of Sèvres; in Italy the Marchese Ginori inaugurated the factory at Doccia, near Florence.

The basic production of these factories was table service that was truly exceptional at times. The 'Swan' service, created at Meissen for the powerful Prime Minister Count Brühl, contained more than two thousand pieces, executed from models designed by Jacob Joachim Kändler. A substantial part of this set of dishes is now at the Porzellansammlung in Dresden, but many pieces have been dispersed and are now the pride of decorative arts museums and collections. Porcelain, the 'Swan' service and Kändler's incomparable skill inspired the brief but delightful novel *Utz*, the last work of Bruce Chatwin.

Kändler was without doubt the most imaginative and delicate modeller of statuettes and sculptural groups. His inspiration was quite varied, though often characterized by a touch of irony. His work ranged from Oriental-style figures to charming ladies-in-waiting, burlesque figures and animals represented with great refinement. For the garden of the Prince-Elector of Saxony, Kändler executed almost life-size animal figures. The unusual dimensions made firing extremely difficult, and many pieces had to be redone several times. The cost of the operation was considerable.

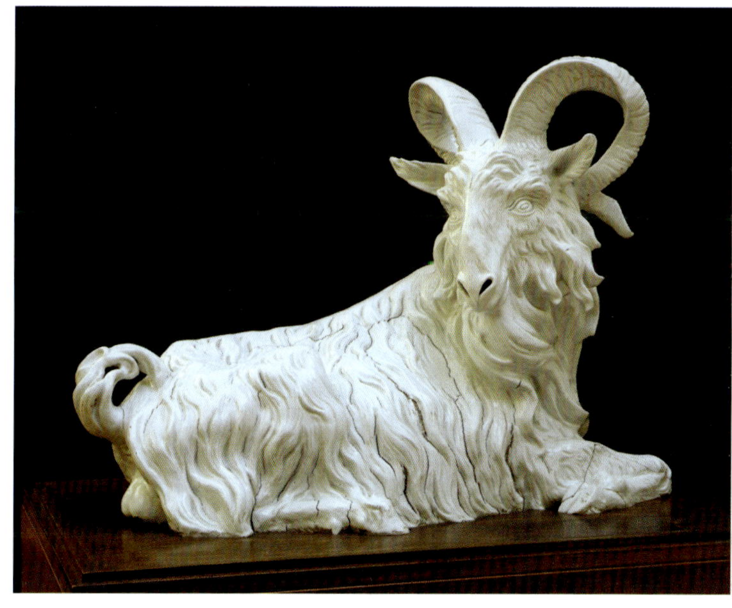

◂

Jacob Joachim Kändler
A piece from the 'Swan' service
1738-1739

▴

Jacob Joachim Kändler
Goat
c. 1732
hard-paste porcelain
Victoria & Albert Museum, London

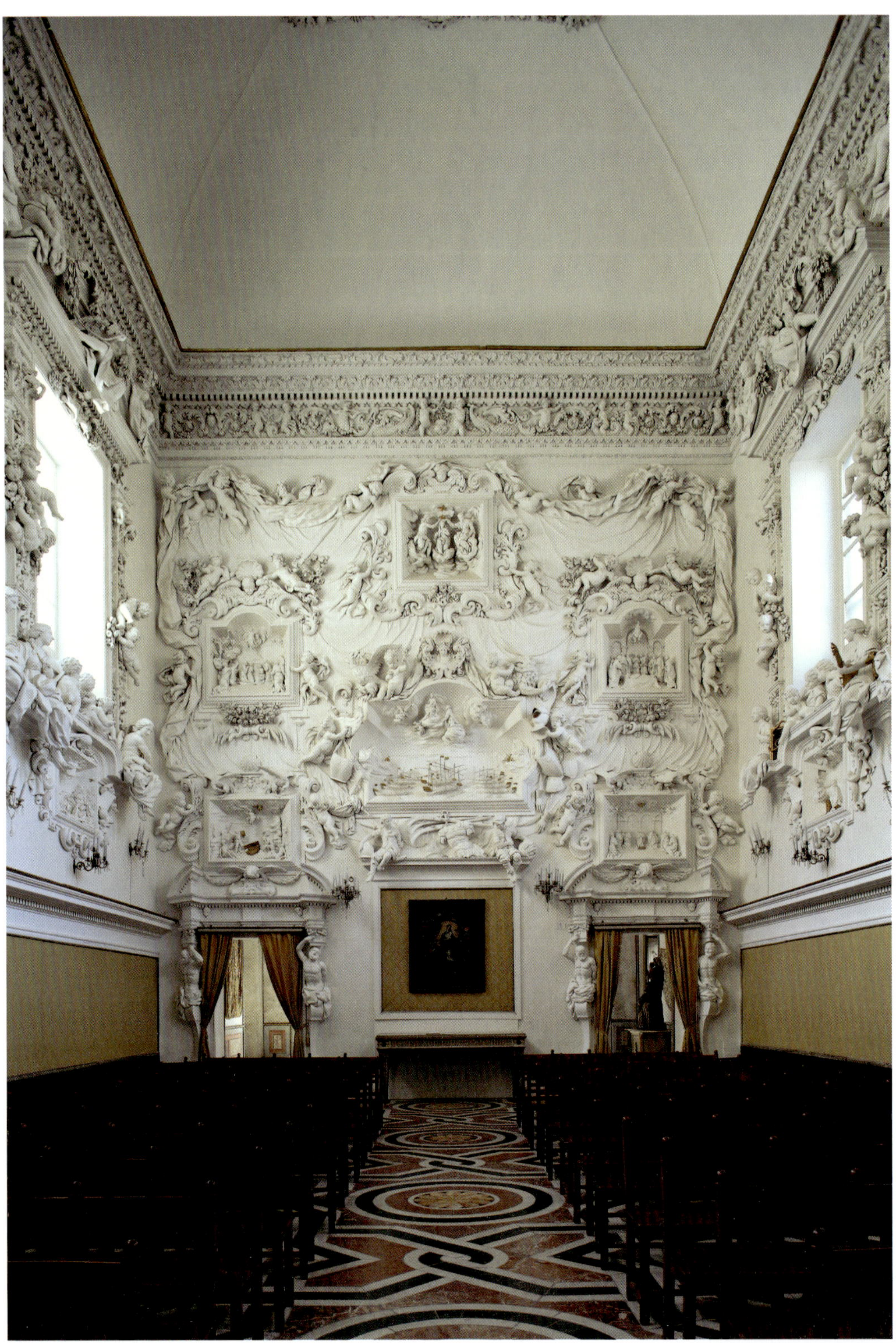

STUCCO

Giacomo Serpotta was born in Palermo in 1656. He was the most illustrious member of a prolific family of sculptors that crossed four generations. Although they were afflicted by serious economic crises, Giacomo amassed his own fortune through his great creative ability and innovative technique for transforming a humble material like stucco into sumptuous scenes. He studied Baroque Roman models, in particular those of Bernini, but mainly experimented with a different mixture of ingredients for his sculptures: limestone, sifted and washed sand, casein glue and marble dust. Thanks to a process that was kept strictly secret, Serpotta succeeded in avoiding the usual opaque and somewhat floury tone of stucco, instead making his surfaces shine like marble. By using a complex armature of metal wire, he created statues of increasing size and movement, while his interior spaces show a pleasing theatrical tendency.

For the oratorios of Palermo, Serpotta created altars with spiral columns, flights of angels, sculptural cycles, stucco 'paintings' and novel architectural settings. Allegorical figures of the Virtues became fashion parades of female figures dressed and coiffed in the latest style with flurries of plumes, ribbons, accessories, scarves and cloaks. His first masterpiece was the Oratory of St Zita (1686–1718), with its military trophies, allegorical statues, Mysteries of the Rosary and enchanting figures of street urchins – the latter as beautiful as angels though dressed in rags, and of compelling veracity and sincerity. In 1699, he began a seven-year project at the Oratory of St Lawrence and St Francis, embellishing the white stucco surfaces with gold borders and details. Then came the Oratory of the Rosary, near San Domenico, which also boasts an altarpiece by Antony van Dyck.

Serpotta's style is a hymn to freedom, inventiveness and creative inspiration, but even in the overwhelming richness and unpredictability of many details, his best works demonstrate a perfect organization. The Sicilian light then plays an important role in kindling the lucid white surfaces with reflections. Because of the different settings, it is fascinating to compare these works with similar contemporary creations in Austria and Bavaria, where the masters of the school of Wessobrunn and the Asam Brothers covered renovated 18th-century Benedictine abbeys and Rococo residences with stucco decorations, often polychromed and lavishly gilded.

Giacomo Serpotta
Stuccos from the Oratory of the Rosary
Palermo

CANDOUR

An ingenuous, sincere person without a strong personality is often described as 'candid'. The term was confirmed in literature by Voltaire's novella *Candide* (1759), in which the title character is in fact an excessively optimistic, easy-going and easily manipulated young man. Forty years earlier, in the disenchanted period of the Regency, Jean-Antoine Watteau, the most sensitive pre-Enlightenment 18th-century artist north of the Alps, produced a celebrated image of the 'candour' of a defenceless, fragile character. An assiduous theatre-goer, Watteau knew the rules of dissimulation, play-acting, the play of gestures, expressions and interconnections. The Commedia dell'Arte's world of masks became the stage of uneasiness, ambiguity and a sense of the transitory and the precarious.

Gilles is one of Watteau's two largest paintings (a little under two metres tall and a metre-and-a-half wide) and one of very few with almost life-size figures. The subject is probably drawn from *The Education of Gilles, or How to Wash a Donkey's Head*, a farce staged at the Opéra Comique, which Watteau attended regularly. Besides the main character – the equivalent of Pierrot – four other characters are identifiable: Cassandro, on the donkey at the left; the pair of lovers Leandro and Isabella; and at the far right, the dandy who vexes poor Gilles in various ways.

The scene is set in an outdoor space that resembles an Italian-style park with a maritime Umbrella pine and, on the right, a herm with a fawn's head. The white figure of Gilles, the pathetic buffoon of burlesque shows, is seen from slightly below against a background of sky. This unusual viewpoint further accentuates the emptiness of Gilles' expression and the awkwardness of his gestures. Watteau did not place the main figure at the exact centre of the canvas and so has made a series of corrections and re-balancings. At the right, the thriving trees are taller and the three figures toward the bottom are dressed in bright colours (white, yellow, red, orange). On the more constricted left side, riding the donkey, is Cassandro, dressed in a black suit and mostly brown tones. The gestures and glances between the figures completely exclude Gilles, who is all the more isolated. The parting of the trees behind him opens a spatial void, with a pale, washed-out sky, like the character's elusive personality. The curved lines of the hat, ruffled collar, arm and hand placement, and even the folds of the trousers compose a sort of secular halo, like a nimbus of uncommunicativeness.

Jean-Antoine Watteau
Gilles
c. 1718–1719
oil on canvas, 184.5 x 149.5 cm
Musée du Louvre, Paris

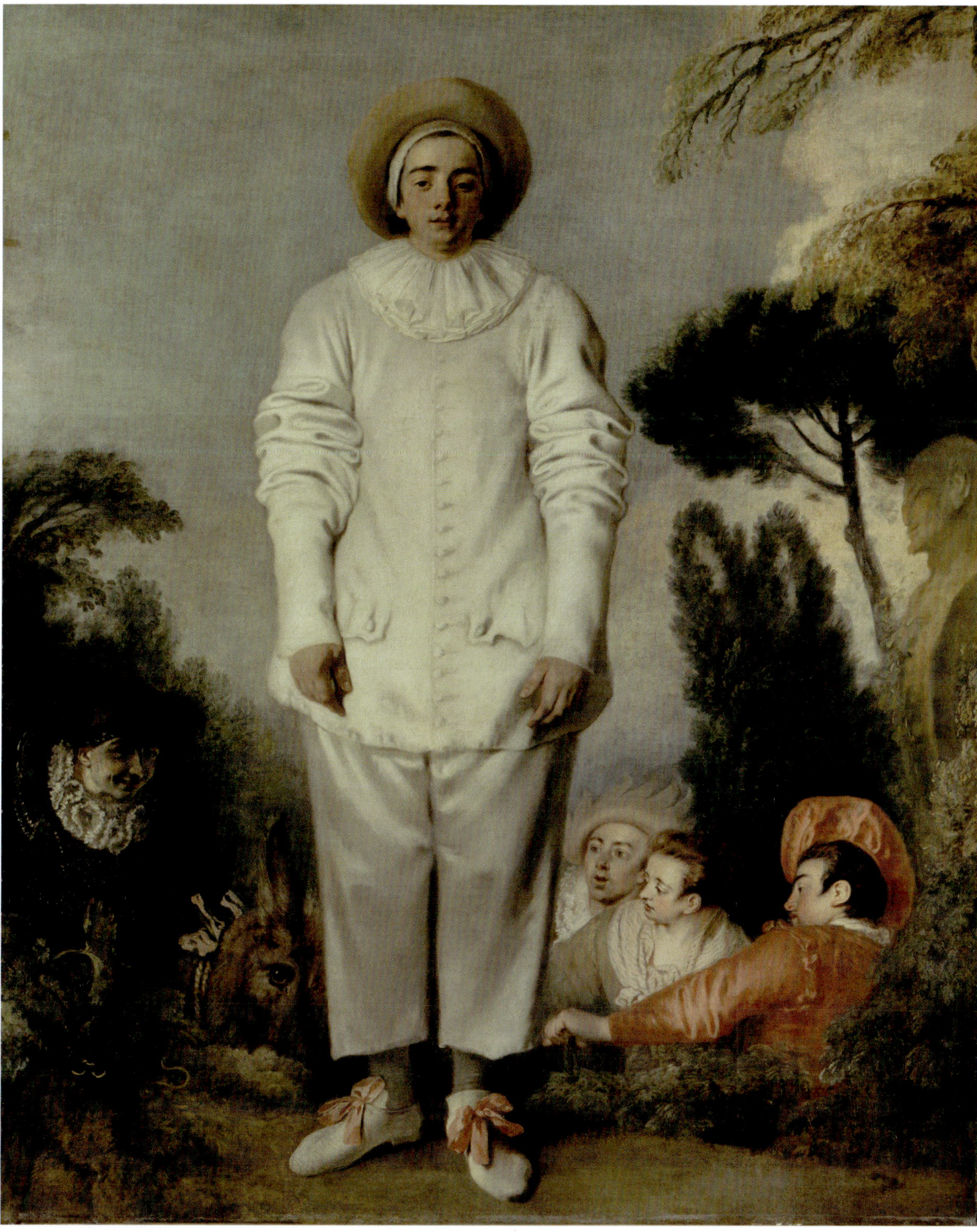

GHOST WHITE

In some countries – Japan, for example – white is the colour of mourning. In Western culture, too, it can be associated with the pallor of death. Ghosts, witches, phantasms, creatures from beyond the grave and zombies are often a cadaverous white or dressed in pure white. At the dawn of Romanticism, especially in England, this terrible and frightening aspect of the colour pervaded the works of a generation of writers and painters intent on examining the fantastic, occult forces of the dream and the beyond, and transforming fear of the unknown into aesthetic pleasure. This is the context in which the frightful, irrational visions of Henry Fuseli were painted. The Swiss-born painter was one of the first to explore the realm of the subconscious, using his paintbrush to capture the worst nightmares: nocturnal spirits and apparitions are displayed on the canvas with all the macabre impact of their lifeless pallor.

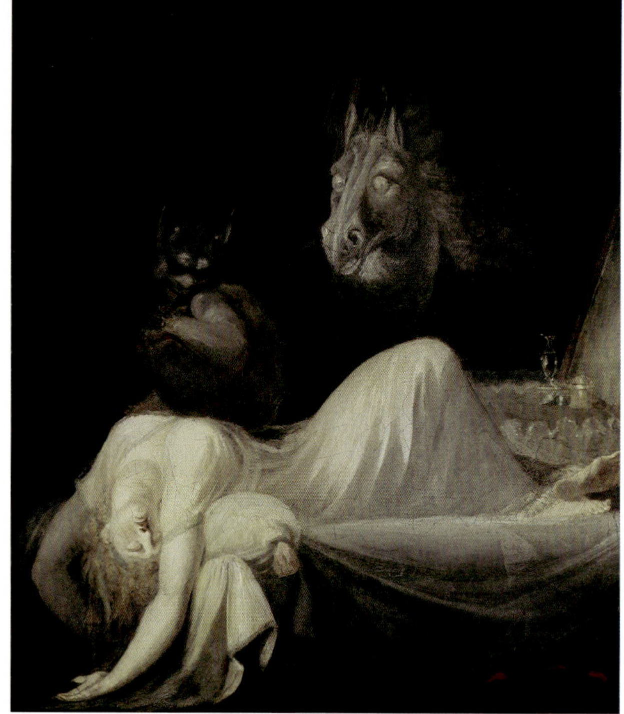

Henry Fuseli
The Nightmare
1790-1791
oil on canvas, 76.5 x 63.5 cm
Goethe Museum, Frankfurt

Known in various versions, *The Nightmare* is one of Fuseli's most famous works. The setting is a middle-class interior: a young woman lies sleeping in the silk sheets of her bed. The extreme transparency of the flesh tones, heightened by the white nightgown, the distorted pose and her obvious inner turmoil express the nocturnal dimension of an anguished nightmare. A grotesque little monster sits on the woman's upper body, and a ghostly horse with phosphorescent white eyes and quivering nostrils emerges from the parted curtains hanging behind. The nightmare takes shape before the eyes of the viewer, forcing us to participate in the sleeper's inner torment.

The presence of a white horse in dreams is often connected with a presentiment of death, to which the pallor of the woman's body may also allude. On the other hand, the white clothes symbolically underscore her virginal purity. Nightmare and innocence meet in the restricted range of colour, which stands out the more intensely against the dark background.

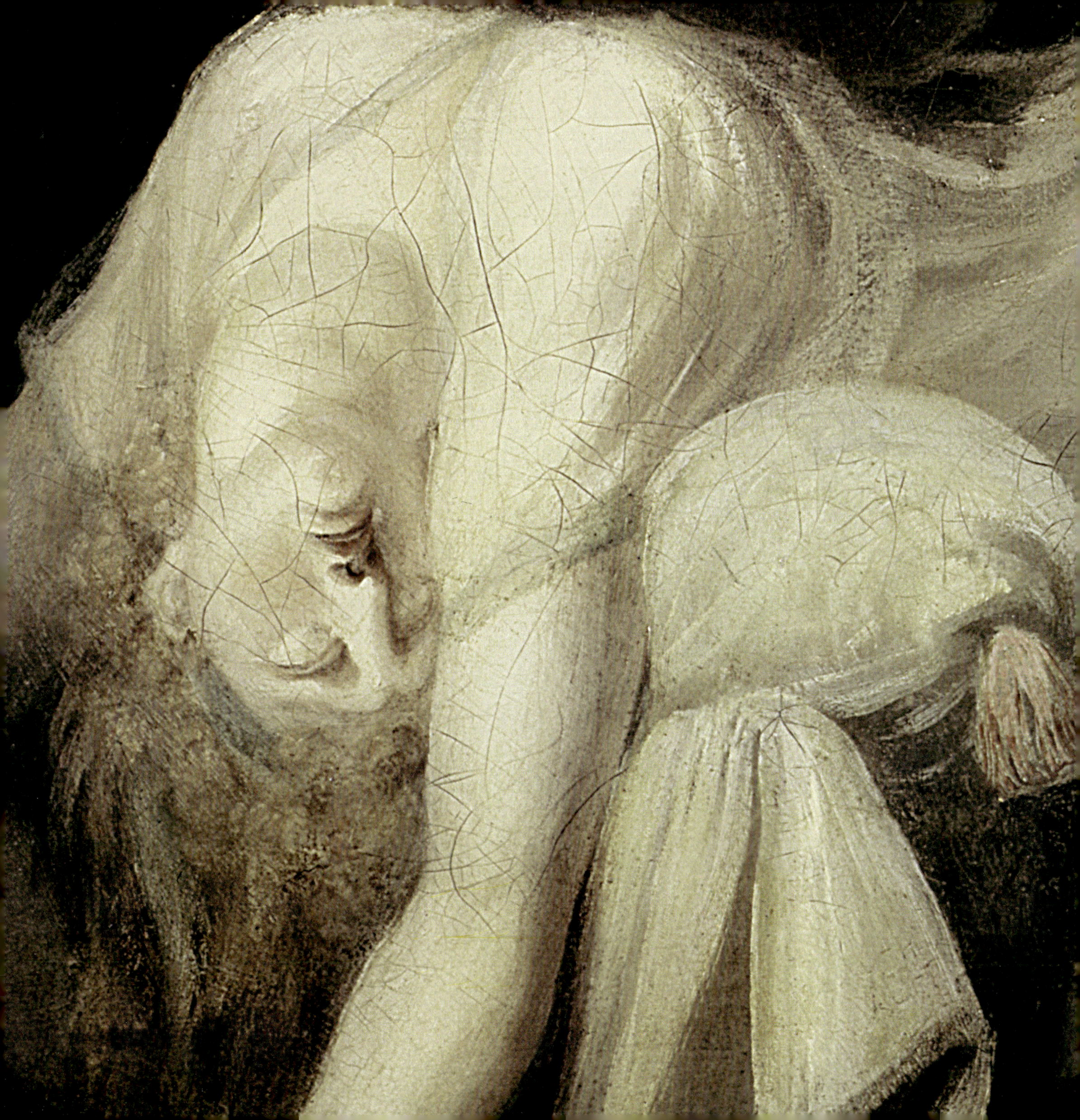

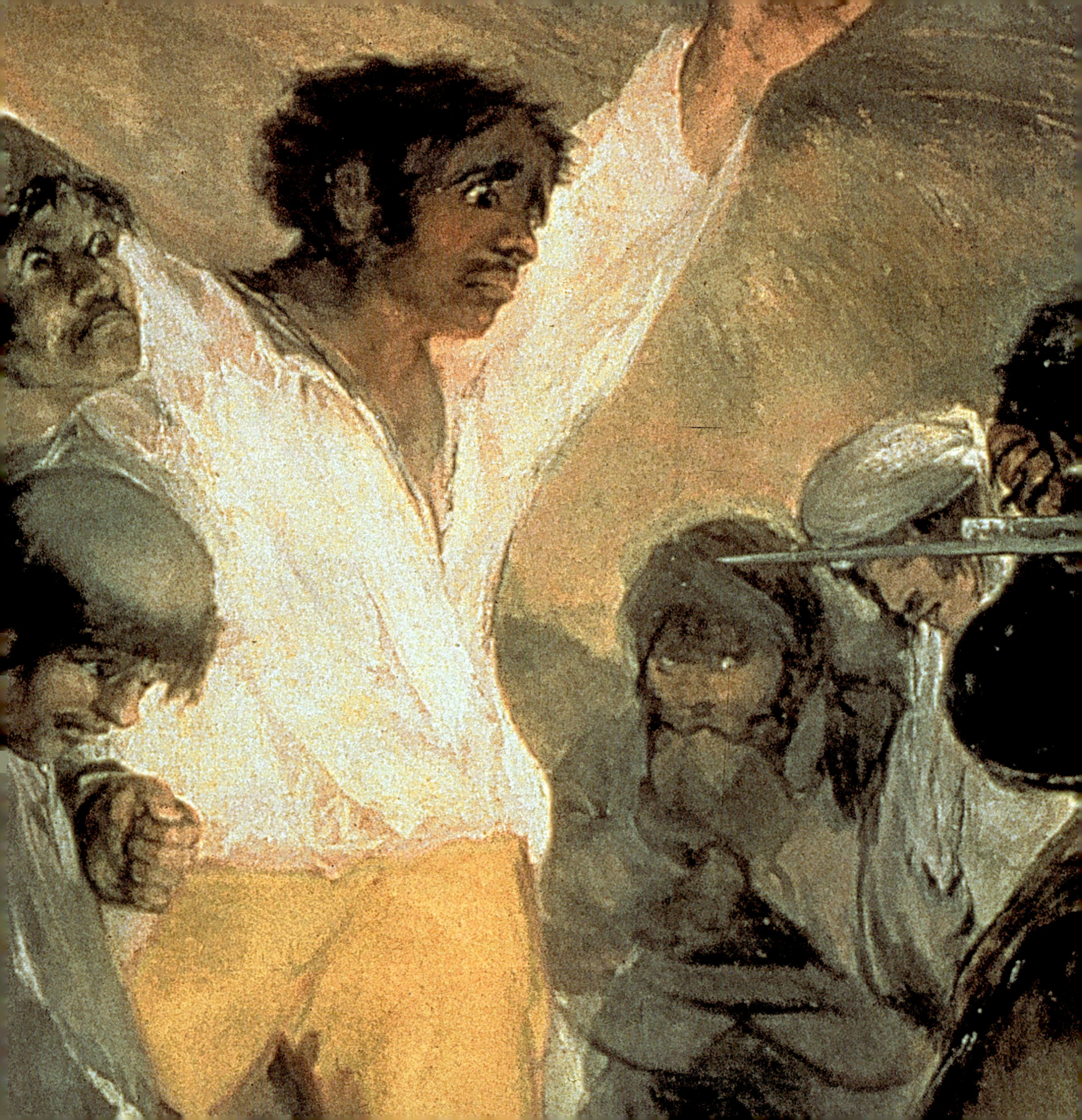

Francisco de Goya
The Third of May 1808 in Madrid:
The Executions on Príncipe Pío Hill
1814
oil on canvas, 266 x 345 cm
Museo Nacional del Prado, Madrid

THE WHITE FLAG

The historical origin of waving a white flag as a sign of surrender is uncertain. It is thought to have developed in the early 15th century, during the Hundred Years War between France and England, coinciding with the spread of firearms and increased use of multicoloured flags, banners and showy uniforms. Before then, in order to declare defeat at the hands of the enemy it was customary for shields to be raised above the head or for weapons to be dropped to the ground. At any rate, a white cloth (handkerchief, article of clothing, sheet or some rag) was always easier to find than any other colour. A widespread practice during five centuries of warfare, the use of a white flag to request the cease of hostilities was officially sanctioned by the Geneva Convention of 1949.

A few years after the people of Madrid rebelled against the occupying Napoleonic troops, Madrid's city council asked Goya to celebrate two eventful days in May 1808: the assault against the occupying Mamelukes, and the firing squads that executed the insurgents. It is a dramatic page from what Goya himself called 'the disasters of war'. Shunning rhetoric, the painter placed the scene of the execution in the deep of night, partly illuminated by a large lantern in the foreground. The perfectly aligned soldiers of the firing squad are seen from the back. They perform their task mechanically, betraying no human emotion.

Seen from the front, the disarray of the group of the condemned is in total contrast. As corpses lie on the ground, the faces and gestures of those who are about to be shot express a wide variety of emotions. There is no hint of a heroic Romantic disdain for death. On the contrary, Goya shows the anxiety of the common people, who appear to appeal for mercy to the last.

Standing out from the prevailing dark tones of the group of the condemned is the spotless shirt of a man who raises his arms with an impotent gesture of surrender – his 'white flag', however, will not deter the shooting. Rather, he will soon be riddled with bullets and spattered with blood. In fixing the instant that precedes the volley, Goya launches an indictment against war, violence and terror. The commemoration of a precise historical fact takes second place: Goya's painting has a universal value and meaning.

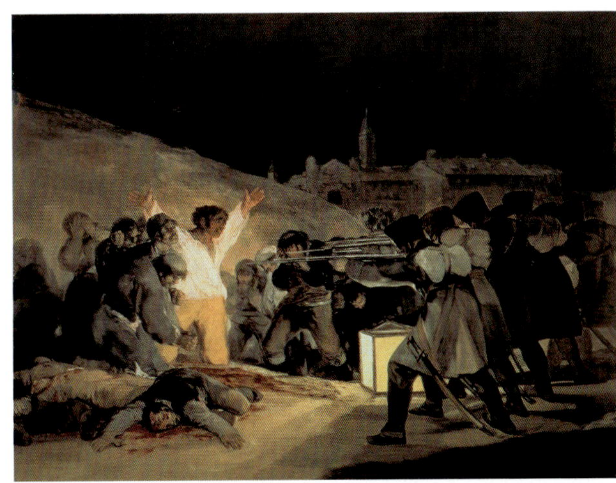

NORTHERN LIGHT

Light colours, comfortable but pared-down decoration, simple, white-painted furniture, and wooden window frames and floors seen through a soft grey-white light: this is the atmosphere of the silent domestic interiors painted by the Danish artist Vilhelm Hammershøi.

Hammershøi, who also painted landscapes and portraits, may be considered late 19th-century Scandinavian painting's human and artistic antithesis to Munch. While the Norwegian screams his own anguish through colour, Hammershøi immerses his paintings in absolute silence, in the solitary interior event, spreading out light colours with patient skill. Recently, his intensely poetical atmospheres have been reassessed thanks to important exhibitions of his work in Paris, London and New York.

The Danish painter is clearly inspired by the example of Vermeer and 17th-century Dutch interior scenes, revisited in the spirit and style of Scandinavian intimism, with light colours but also a slightly blurry quality that comes from the milky northern light. A master of subtle psychological atmospheres, Hammershøi is a sensitive interpreter of the feminine world, capturing the secret vibrations and emotions that are repressed in the everyday flow of ordinary life. Very often in Hammershøi's paintings we do not see the faces of the young women, who are instead viewed from the back or in profile, always dressed in severe clothes, with long skirts. The painter does not seek a direct relationship with the gaze but prefers to allow feelings to seep through only slowly.

Hammershøi spent his entire life in Copenhagen, but extensive study trips to Paris and London brought him into close contact with international art movements. By conscious choice, he did not adhere to the avant-gardes but pursued his own path with consistent reserve. The palette, reduced to the essential in a range of light colours, and the neat geometric regularity of the furniture convey an almost Puritanical rigour and minimalism.

Vilhelm Hammershøi
A Woman Sewing in an Interior
1901
oil on canvas

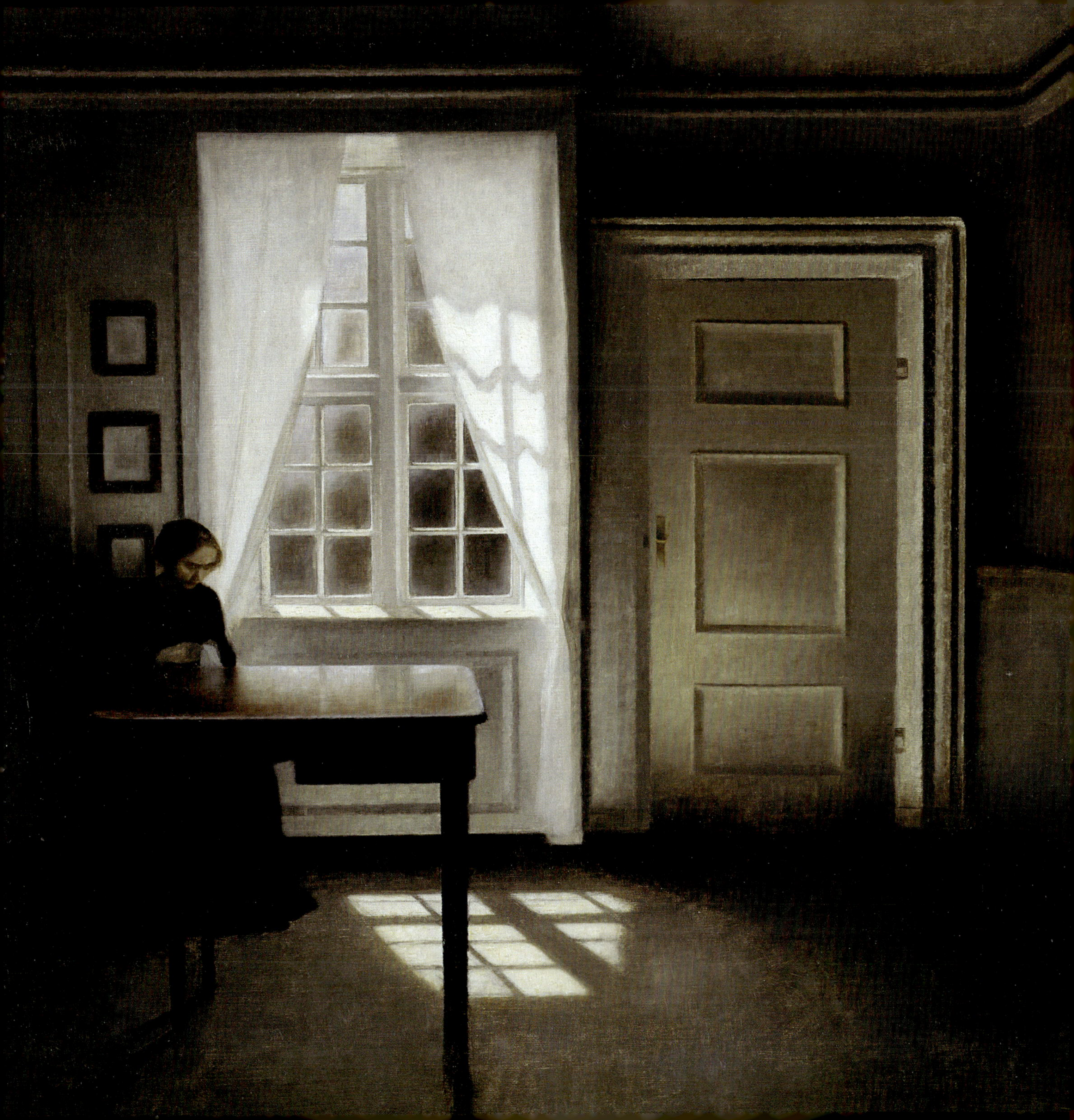

SILK

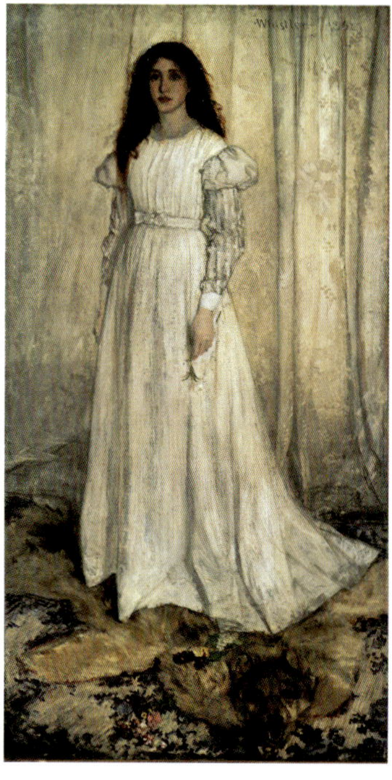

James Abbott McNeill Whistler
Symphony in White, No. 1: The White Girl
1862
oil on canvas, 213 x 107.9 cm
National Gallery of Art, Washington

James Abbott McNeill Whistler was born in Massachusetts in 1834 and died in London, England, in 1903. He was a leading figure in late 19th-century international art, particularly for European (especially English) painting, rather than the American school, from which he kept his distance. After early training in the United States, where he worked as a cartographer for the Coast Guard, Whistler moved to France in 1855, coming immediately in contact with the exponents of realism and then later the nascent Impressionism. In 1859, he went to London, where he soon became the most sensitive portrayer of Victorian high society. Whistler's extraordinary technical skill supported an artistic conception that saw painting as a pure aesthetic experience wherein chromatics acquire a tactile value. His portraits are the image of a world of convention, of sought-after shared formality beneath which seethed quivers of emotion that, though held in check, were nonetheless perceptible.

Whistler was aware of the subtle divide between the portrait that gives a true likeness and the literary, aestheticizing image more typical of Symbolism. The titles of many of his paintings do not name the figure portrayed but include the word 'harmony' or 'symphony', along with an indication of the dominant colour or tone. In *Symphony in White, No. 1: The White Girl*, Whistler interprets as a musical vibration the abstract harmony that plays on a two-dimensional chromatic recalling Japanese prints. The delicacy of the white clothing is made apparent by a rapid, light brushstroke. The young woman's bewildered gaze loses itself beyond the painting's frame.

Exhibited at the Salon des Refusés in Paris in 1863, this portrait is one of the earliest and most emblematic of the painter's masterpieces. Whistler gauges the tones of white with elegant refinement, highlighting the silky reflections of the virginal purity of the young woman's clothing. The artist's mistress, Joanna Hiffernan, posed for this painting. The ivory brocade curtain and bearskin rug form a sumptuous aristocratic setting that provides the opportunity for a new display of virtuosity in variations on white.

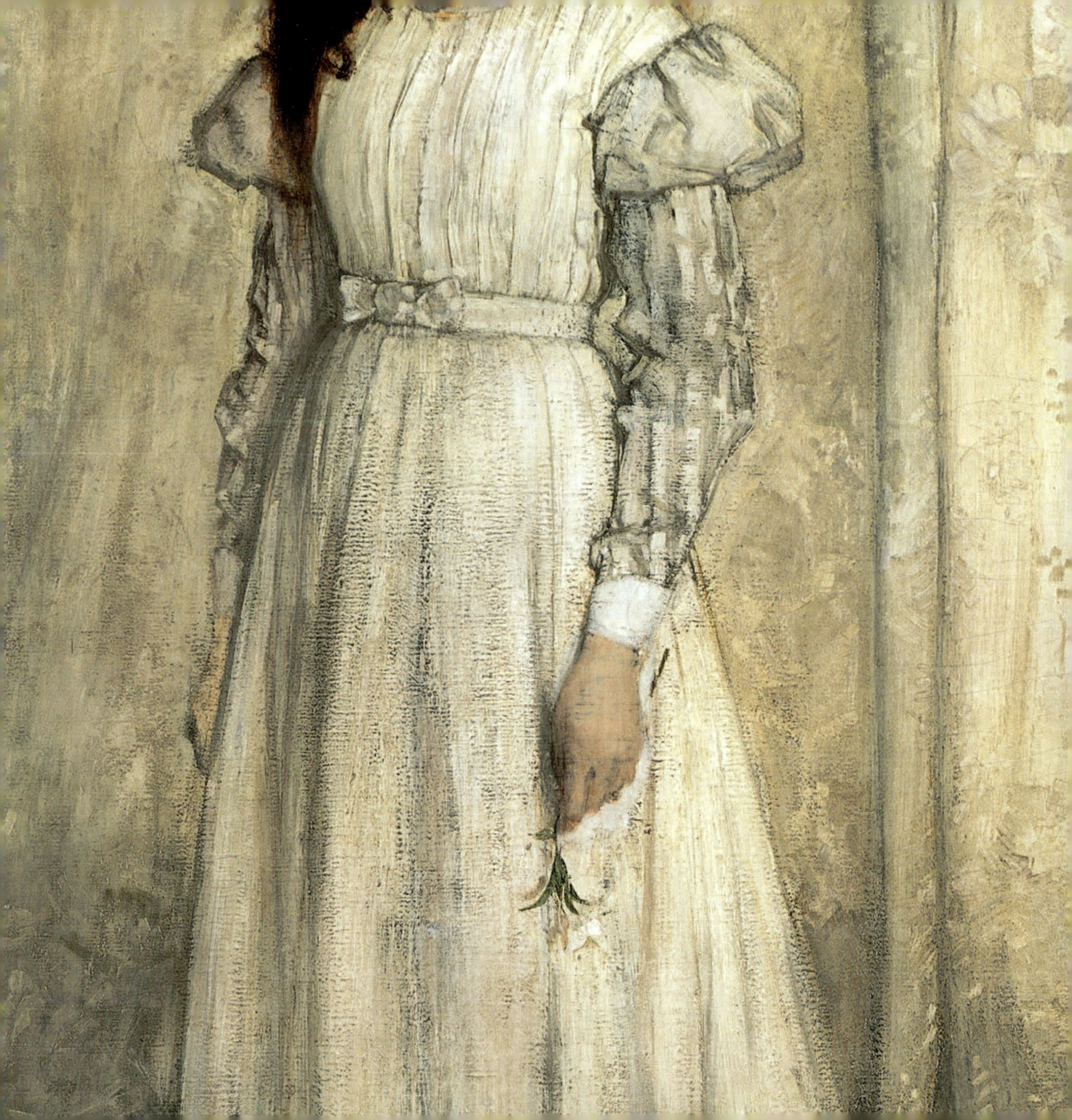

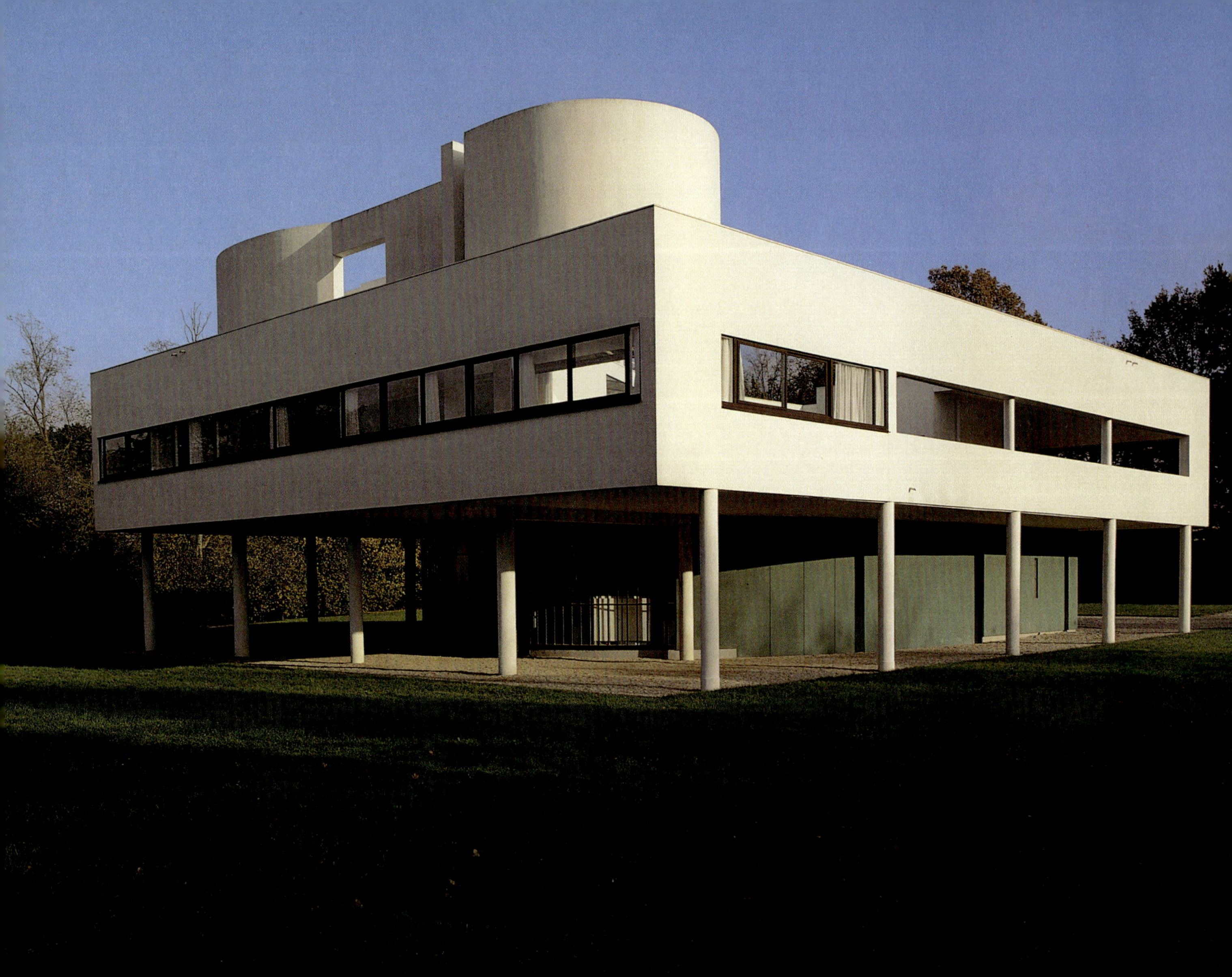

Le Corbusier
Villa Savoye
1928–1931
Poissy

PURE WHITE

'A great epoch has begun, moved by a new spirit: a spirit of building and of synthesis, guided by a clear conception.' In 1920, Le Corbusier began the first issue of the magazine *L'Esprit nouveau* with these words proclaiming his own architectural theories based on the choice of clean, functional volumes that are in close contact with the surroundings. His architectural theories are related to his experiments in painting, which were allied with Purism's clear and simple geometry, in which space and light enhance one another. Outstanding among his residential projects is the Villa Savoye, constructed between 1928 and 1931 in Poissy, a small town near Paris.

The villa seems to rise spontaneously from a large grassy clearing in a sort of symbiosis with its surroundings. The white of the building opens to the four cardinal points, further underscoring the free interplay of spaces typical of Le Corbusier's architecture. The use of pilotis, small pillars of reinforced concrete, frees up the plan and also frees the architect from the need to create a main façade. From the ground floor, under the pilotis, a ramp gradually rises in a sort of centripetal movement towards the roof garden and solarium, which is surrounded by curved light walls that block the view from the outside while their circularity opens onto the greenery of the horizon.

The volumes of the villa are dominated by the white of its walls, which sharpens the functionality and rationality of the various spaces without giving them a sense of closed orderliness. The spatial openness that the choice of the light colours gives to the structure plays on the light, establishing the idea of a finite construction that extends into the natural surroundings.

Marc Chagall
The Bride and Groom of the Eiffel Tower
1938-1939
oil on canvas, 150 x 136.5 cm
Centre Pompidou, Paris

NUPTIAL WHITE

Although the traditional white bridal gown popular in the West is rapidly changing, it persists in the shared imagination. Born in 1887 in Liozna, near Vitebsk, Marc Chagall was from a poor Jewish family. His art always remained firmly rooted in his impoverished childhood environment, the Jewish religion and popular Russian traditions, despite his many travels to Paris, Europe and the United States. A kind of childlike, fairytale ingenuousness imbues his paintings, in which figures levitate in a gravity-free poetical space, populated by fanciful images and good-natured magic.

In *The Bride and Groom of the Eiffel Tower*, a pair of newlyweds – their marriage having been celebrated under a simple canopy on a rocky spur barely sketched in the background – float in the air as they are fêted by little dancing angels. A goat plays the violin, and a large rooster accompanies them in what appears to be a dance of love. The rooster's presence reflects the popular belief that this animal was a good omen for male offspring. A symbol of virility, it may refer to the groom's gesture of delicately placing one hand on the belly of his beloved.

The bride's white gown, an emblem of virginity still intact, stands out in a swirl of movement and colour. Beyond proscriptions forbidding a woman who has already had children to be married in white, the choice of this colour for the wedding gown is rooted in the desire of any young woman who (like the one depicted here) dreams of being abducted by the groom in a sort of celestial feast – an expression of the universal dimension of her love.

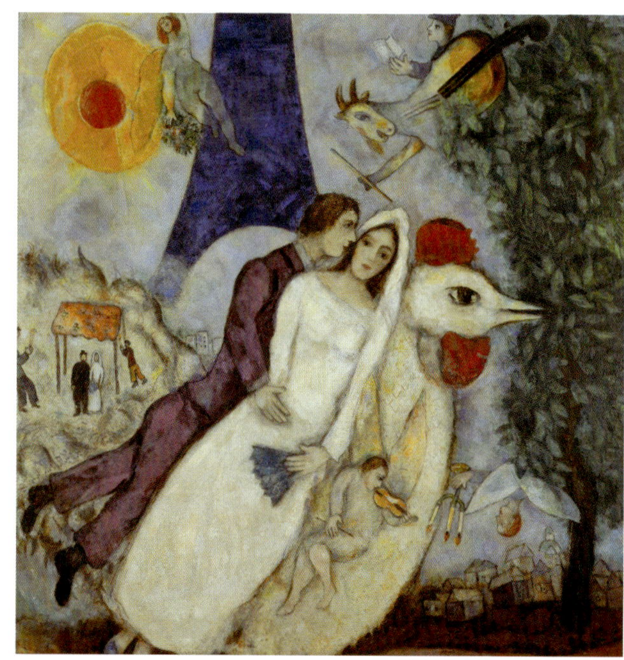

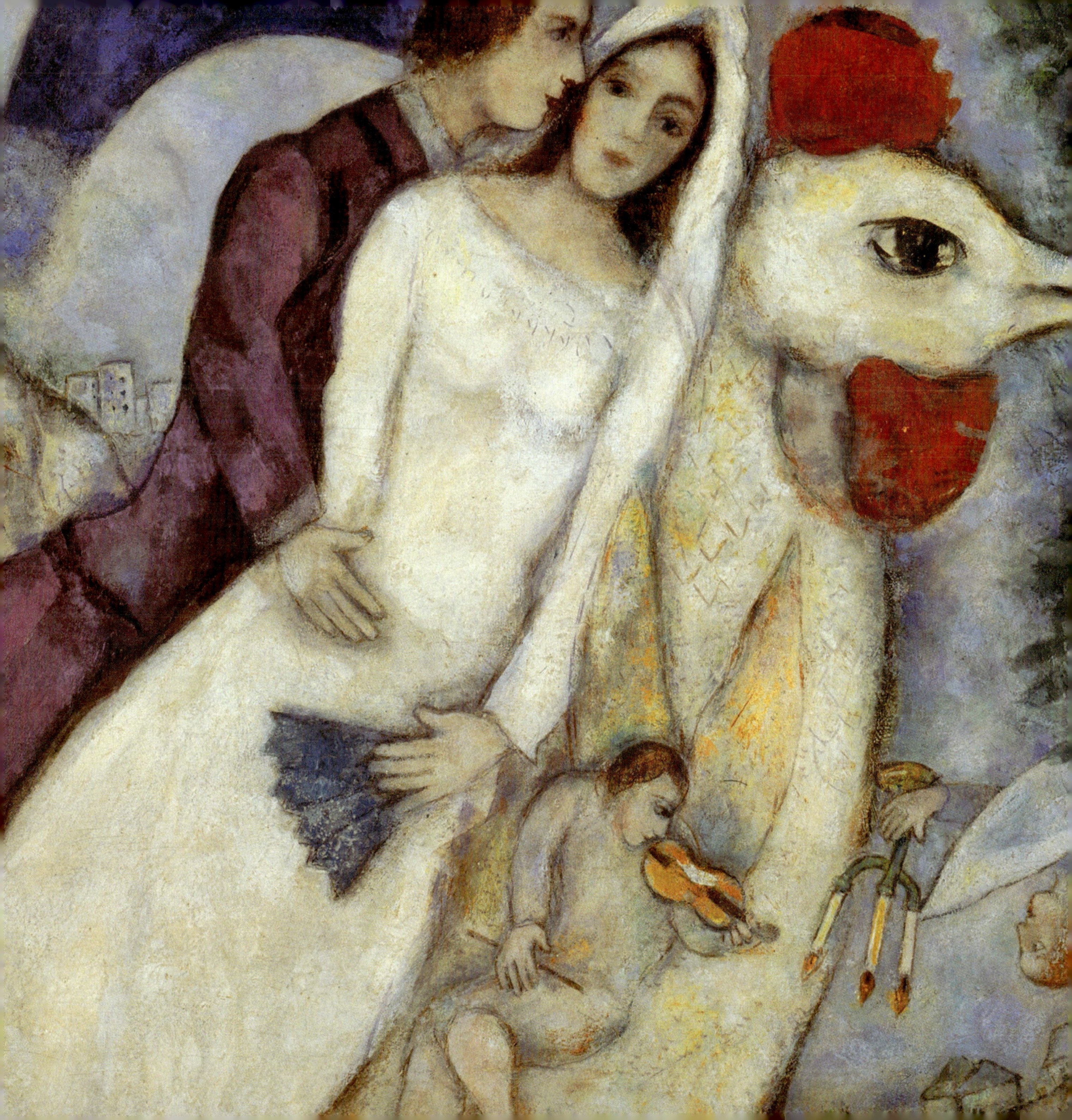

BLACK

INTRODUCTION

'Any colour, so long as it's black.'

Henry Ford

Black is the colour of night, of the underworld gods, of the moon's mysterious far side – or more precisely the 'non-colour', the ultimate negation and cancelling out of all colour. It is associated with darkness, and if darkness was the origin of all mysteries, fears and insecurities, it may also be considered a starting-point, the preparatory moment necessary for birth, growth, entry into the daylight. This is the meaning of *nigredo*, the initial black phase in the process of alchemy, as Dürer so masterfully shows in his celebrated engraving *Melencolia I*.

The metaphor of black as a 'primal state' is widespread in cosmogonies throughout the world. There is no religious culture – from Judeo-Christianity to the Greeks, from Norse saga to Egyptian myth, from the India of the terrifying Kali to Shinto Japan, from Mesoamerica to Oceania – in which the world does not begin in the darkness of a night that envelops the universe. Black is not infrequently associated with the profound, mysterious darkness of a primordial ocean engulfing the world. Then, a God intervenes to initiate creation.

Though seemingly unequivocal in its lugubrious symbolism, black may in fact be seen in a different key. In ancient Egypt, for example, the gods and rites connected with the afterlife were associated with black, while the precious dark silt of the Nile stood for moist black earth, fertile and alive. In Africa, the arrival of rain-filled black clouds is still awaited anxiously.

White and black form a basic dialectic, and though on a chequerboard the two colours bear no moral significance, white is traditionally associated with good and black with bad. With few exceptions (Zorro and Batman, both of whom prefer to act at night), bright, shining superheroes combat dark enemies. However, the one facet is indispensable to the other, as shown by the Balinese fabric with black and white squares that drapes statues of the guardian spirits of temples, bridges and doorways.

For over five centuries, black – or at least dark grey – has been considered the quintessence of male elegance. From El Greco to Van Dyck, from Velázquez to Rembrandt, late 16th- and 17th-century art offers a gallery of figures dressed uniformly in black, with the only possible exception variously ruffled or pleated lace collars. Even cursory analysis allows us to perceive the quality, weft and softness of these refined and prized fabrics, quite different from ordinary cloth.

Through various transitions in the 19th century (frock-coat, tailcoat, dinner jacket), black remained the basic colour of elegant, high-ranking men. It extended from clothes to accessories and then to objects with a specifically masculine connotation, such as cars. In fact, this is the context of the quotation from Henry Ford when advising on which colour of Model T to choose.

In art history, black has an obvious fundamental importance. It is the basic colour of drawing, the stroke that defines the shape. Broad sectors of figurative art (drawing and, for a long time, intaglio prints, film and photography) are essentially black and white. Moreover, it must be said that the history of painting has had a controversial relationship with black, which was eventually rejected by the Impressionists. There is a famous anecdote about the funeral of Claude Monet in Giverny on 5 December 1926. Having arrived slightly late to the ceremony at the village church and seeing the artist's coffin covered with a traditional black drape, President Georges Clemenceau exclaimed, 'No black for Monet. Black is not a colour!' And so, coloured curtains, hastily removed from a nearby window, were used at the painter's funeral.

EXEKIAS:
THE PINNACLE OF BLACK FIGURE CERAMICS

Archaic Greek ceramics can be divided into two main trends according to technique (see also p. 30).

Attic black figure ceramics reached their peak between 560 and 530 BC through the activity of artists of very different temperaments.

Active between 550 and 525 BC, Exekias was without peer as both painter and potter. His absolute mastery of incision and the effects of line on a neutral background brought a sophisticated, intellectual stylization to black figure painting. His austere, solemn language focuses strongly on the main action, involving few figures. He imprints the heroism of epic poetry on these dramatic, synthetic scenes, which are sometimes motionless and charged with inner tension, and at other times characterized by the explosion of inevitable tragic violence. The search for larger surfaces better to convey the breadth of his painted scenes led him to introduce the kylix krater. With small handles toward the bottom and a slightly flared mouth, it offered the necessary space for painters of succeeding generations to unfurl more complex compositions, so transferring the progress made in monumental painting to a smaller format.

This amphora with Achilles and Ajax, two heroes from Homer's *Iliad*, concentrating in absolute seriousness on what would seem to be a simple pastime is one of Exekias's greatest masterpieces. The absence of other figures and the reduced number of descriptive details make the two figures appear completely absorbed in the game table (used for dice, though it may be a chequerboard), toward which turn their gazes; their arms, spears and feet all converge at the same point. An impressive charge of potential energy animates the composition, superbly regulated by the outline of the two shields, the heroes and the parallelepiped that serves as a table. The black contrasts with the bright yellow-orange background. The scene is viewed as if from within, and its harmony is the result of lucid intellectual discipline.

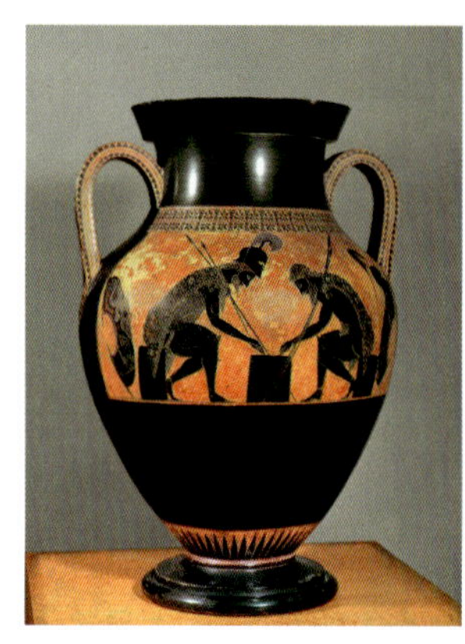

Exekias
Attic black figure amphora depicting Ajax and Achilles Gaming
c. 540-530 BC
painted terracotta, 61.1 cm (h)
Vatican Museums, Vatican City

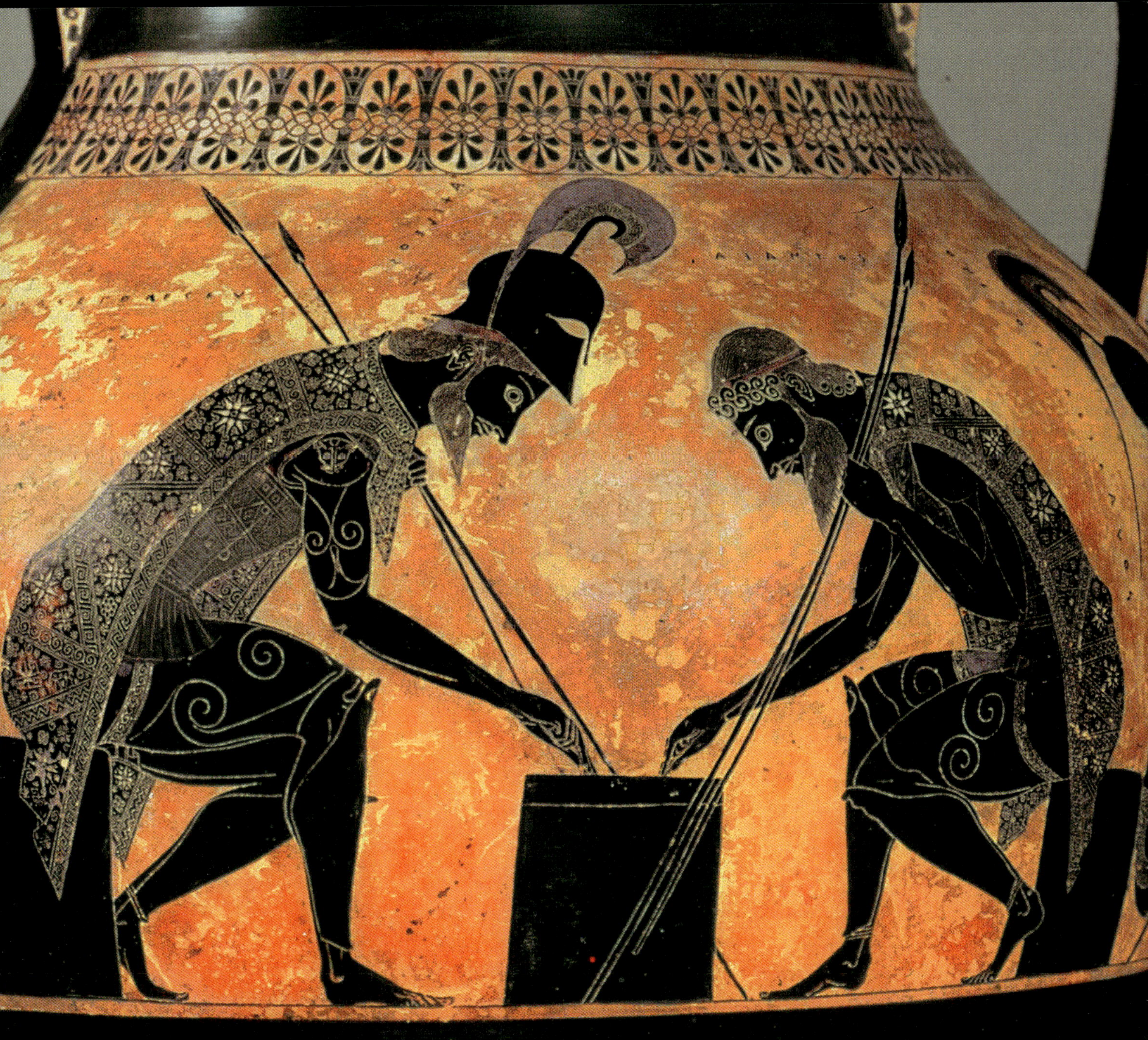

BLACK DEVIL

The Holy Scriptures offer no clue as to what the Devil looks like. He exists as an antagonist and sometimes direct interlocutor of God, but the Bible does not linger over his appearance, leaving ample leeway for the imagination of artists and the faithful. The Devil in Christian iconography evolved from the satyrs of Greek mythology, taking on their physical features, like shaggy hooves and goat horns. For centuries, the Lord of Darkness was represented as a little black monster. The animals of his court – cats, goats, pigs and frogs – were also black. Later on in Western sacred art and literature (the character of Mephistopheles, for example), the Devil assumed human shape and proportions; in the Byzantine tradition, however, he remained of a reduced size.

The Sienese artist Duccio di Buoninsegna worked within the figurative norms and schemata of the Byzantine tradition, albeit renewing them with a new sensitivity to colour and line that influenced the early careers of Simone Martini and Lorenzetti. Duccio's first works already show the attention to drawing and the use of the limpid colours that characterize his greatest masterpiece, the magnificent *Maestà*, executed between 1308 and 1311 for the high altar of Siena Cathedral. Most of the altarpiece is now kept at the Museo dell'Opera del Duomo, but some panels from the predella are in museums in Berlin, London and New York.

The panels of the *Maestà* mark a transition between Byzantine symbolic elegance and the narrative concreteness of the new Italian art. In the scene in which Christ dispatches Satan, Duccio develops a contrast between the moral and physical nobility of Jesus and the rough appearance of the Devil – robust but clumsy, and covered entirely in bristly black hair.

Duccio di Buoninsegna
The Temptation of Christ on the Mountain
1308-1311
tempera on panel, 43.2 x 46 cm
The Frick Collection, New York

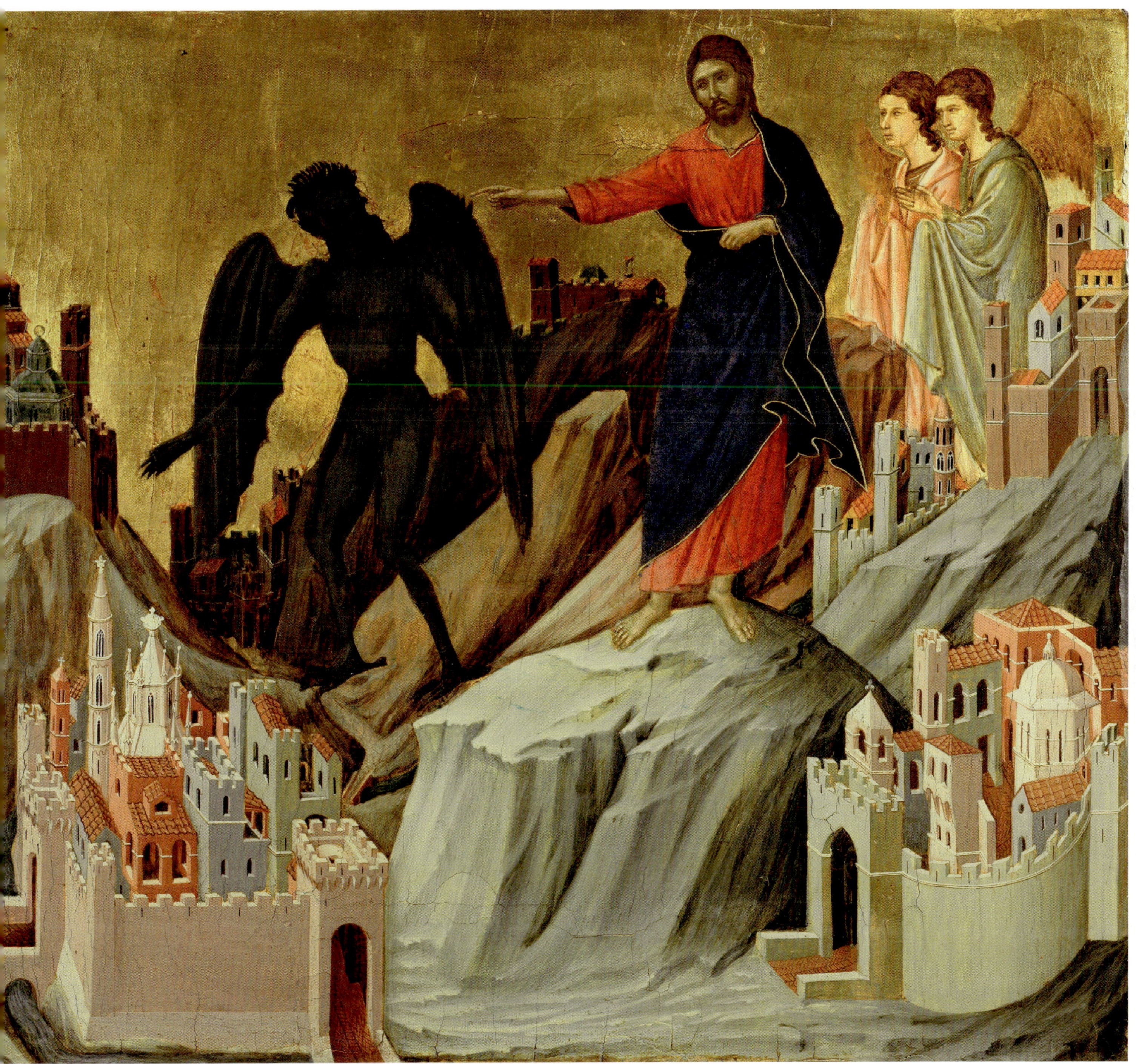

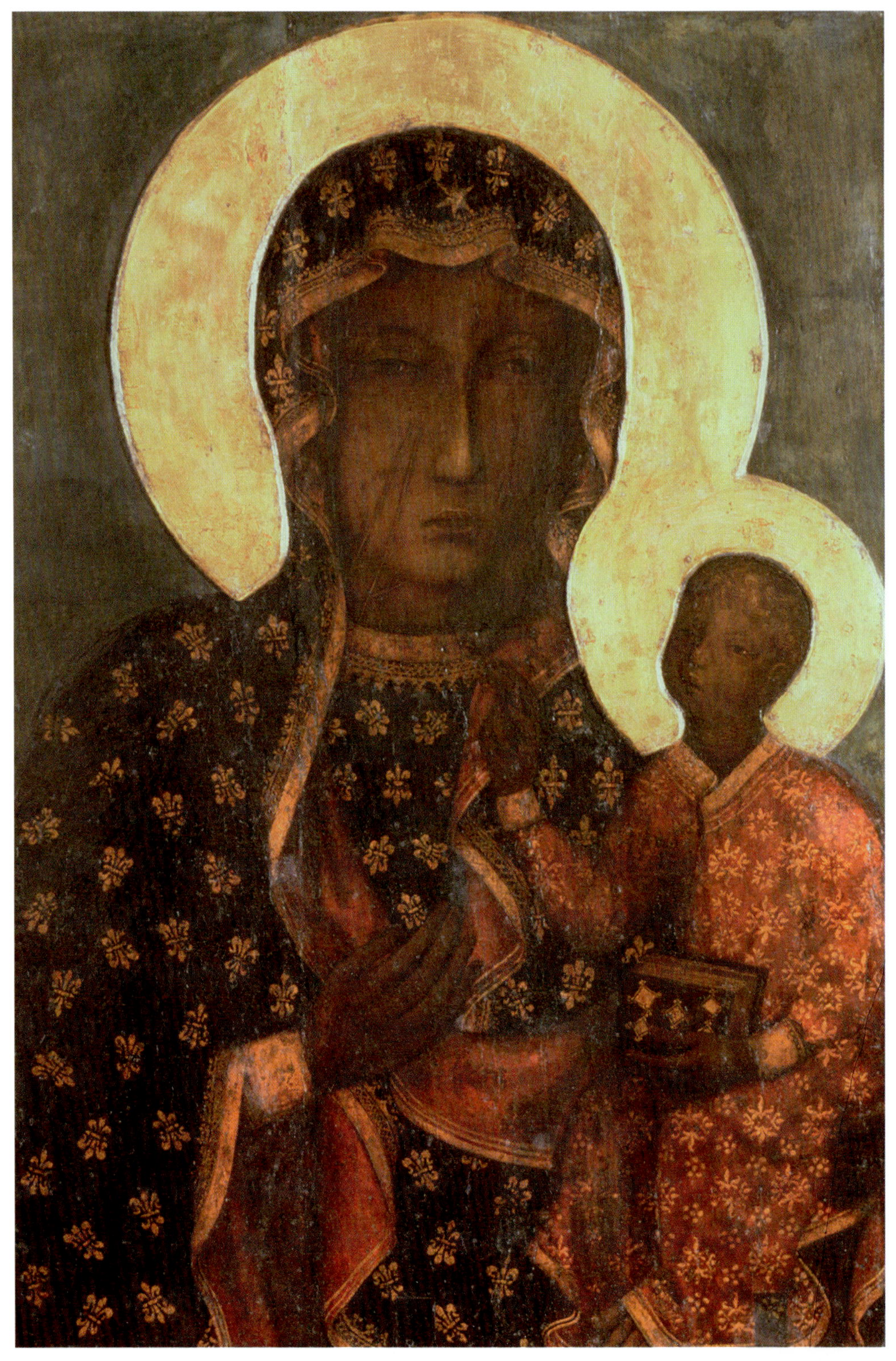

BLACK MADONNAS

The colour of the depths of caves, of mysterious chasms and the darkness of the earth, black is obviously associated with the underworld. The chthonic 'Great Mothers' of various mythologies are often black – for example, the Egyptian Nekhbet, represented as a black vulture, and the terrible dark-skinned Indian goddess Kali, adorned with necklaces and belts of severed heads and hands. The Indo-European roots of the names of the fearful enchantresses Circe and Calypso evoke the memory of caves and shadowy ravines. The profound darkness of the earth can also become the cradle in which nature's seasonal rebirth is prepared, as in the well-known episodes of Proserpine, Demeter and especially Isis, whose maternal image in the act of nursing the little Horus is probably the origin of the many 'black Madonnas' found in early medieval art and Christian devotion.

'Black Madonnas' can be either statues, carved out of dark wood, or paintings – especially icons whose painted surface darkens from smoke and flames or, more often, through the deterioration of the lead oxide-based pigments. In any case, the cult of the 'black' Virgin, attested from the 4th century, had a revival in the powerful Marian preaching of St Bernard of Clairvaux (who associated the Madonnas' dark colour with the description in the Song of Songs) and was further spread in colonial times: in Mexico, Our Lady of Guadalupe gained tremendous popularity because the colour of her skin is close to that of the Native American Indians.

The Black Madonna at the Polish sanctuary of Częstochowa – according to tradition it is a portrait of Mary painted by St Luke – became famous in the Catholic world during the pontificate of John Paul II. It is a large medieval icon of the Virgin Odigitria ('the guide') who shows worshippers the Christ Child she holds in her arms. Taken to the sanctuary of Jasna Góra ('white mountain') by Prince Władysław of Opole in 1382, the icon was damaged in 1430 during the Hussite Wars. Scarlike hatchet marks may be seen on the Madonna's face.

The Black Madonna of Jasna Góra
14th century
tempera on panel
Jasna Góra Monastery, Częstochowa, Poland

WOMAN IN BLACK

The technical innovation of oil painting enabled the Flemish masters to achieve an extraordinary luminosity and chromatic freshness. Moreover, flax oil brings out the transparency of colours, allowing exceptional results even when superimposing various shades of the same hue. In portraits by Petrus Christus, the range of colours is often very limited. An example is this masterpiece, a highly refined exercise in a very limited range of tones. The young woman is lightly touched by a radiant light that reveals an astonishing range of fragile features and sensations.

Like the other great Flemish masters of the first half of the 15th century, Petrus Christus clearly distinguished two genres. Sacred paintings include many descriptive details, examined and enumerated by limpid, diffuse light. Portraits on the other hand are almost always presented against a neutral background. Descriptive details of the setting are kept to a minimum, and the sitters are motionless, striking absorbed, thoughtful poses.

Petrus Christus belongs to the second generation of 15th-century Flemish artists, who came after the 'founding fathers' Van Eyck, Campin and Van der Weyden. In 1444, Christus moved to Bruges, where he remained the rest of his life. He and his wife joined two confraternities devoted to Mary, whose followers included high-ranking nobility, among them the Duke and Duchess of Burgundy, and powerful members of the emerging middle class. The artist's highly personal pictorial language stems from Van Eyck's realism but concentrates on the rendering of the space, making him the first Northern painter to adopt a rational spatial construction based on a single vanishing point. After the middle of the century, his paintings took on a monumental air, following the example of Van der Weyden.

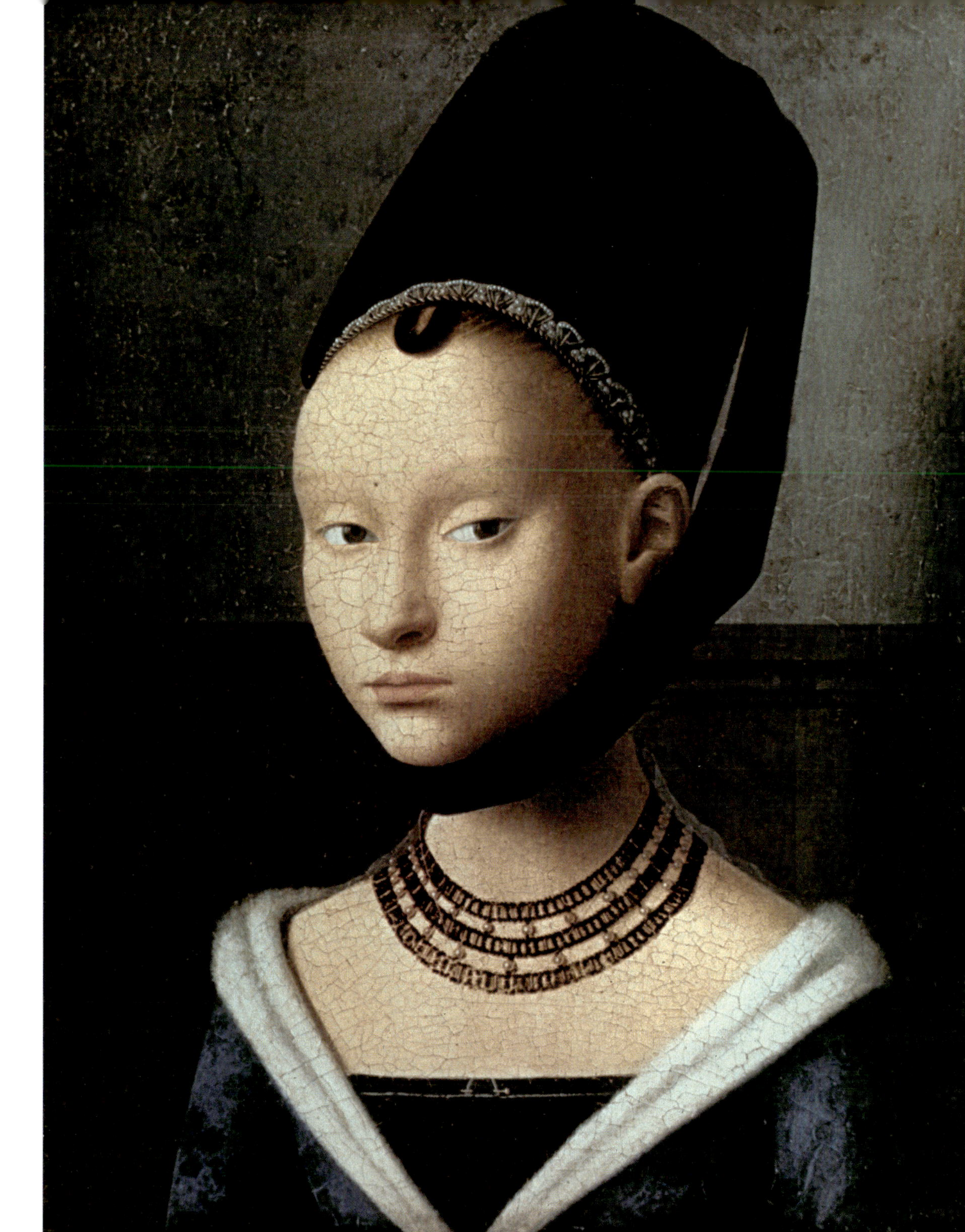

Petrus Christus
Portrait of a Young Girl
c. 1470
oil on panel, 28 x 21 cm
Gemäldegalerie, Berlin

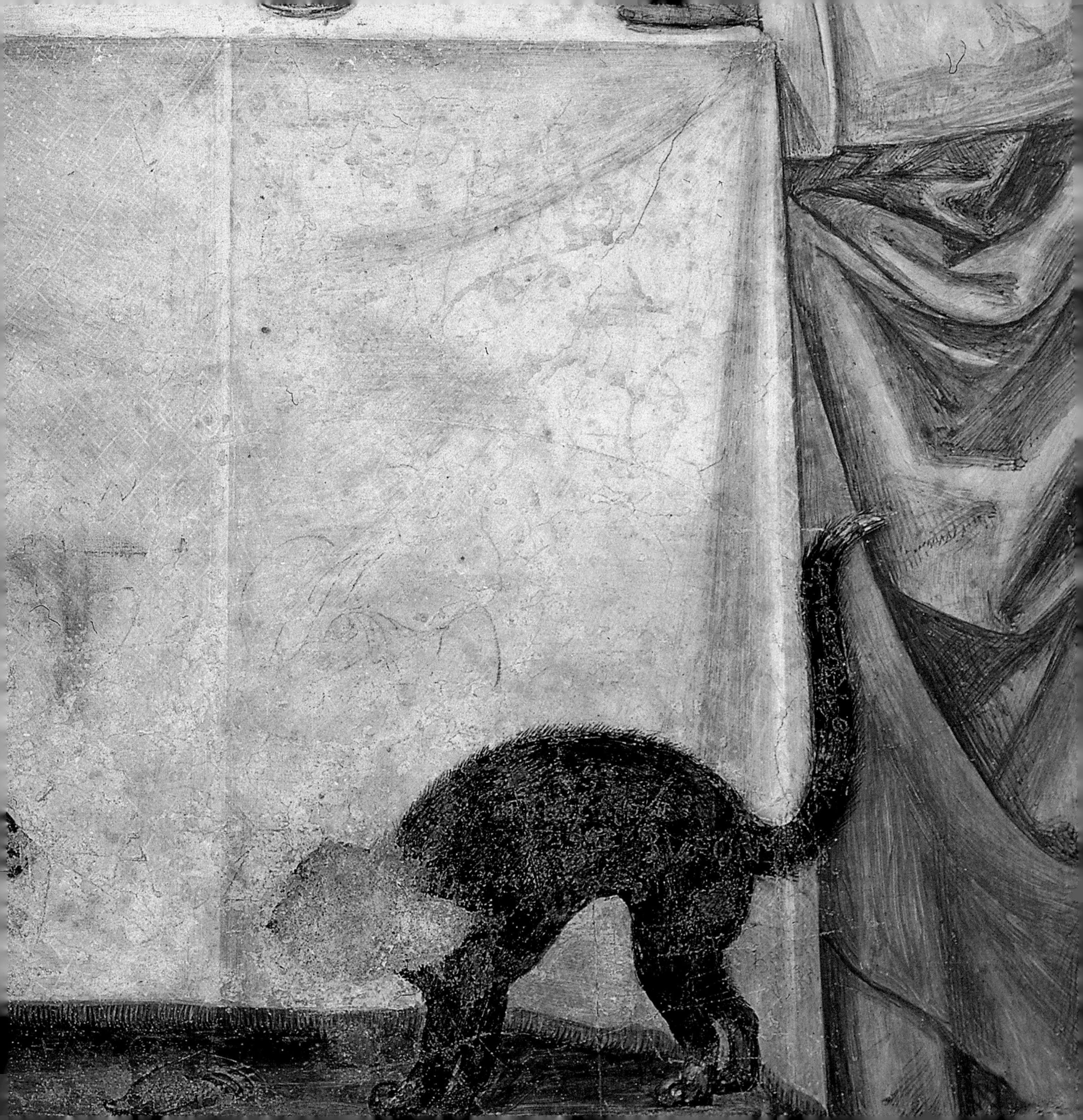

BLACK CAT

Il Sodoma (Giovanni Antonio Bazzi)
The Story of St Benedict,
The Saint and his Monks Eating in the Refectory
1505
fresco
Abbey of Monte Oliveto Maggiore

According to an aphorism of Honoré de Balzac, the cat has heaven in its eye and hell in its heart. Their iridescent, flashing eyes, mysterious nocturnal habits (including the ability to hunt in the dark), the sparks produced by the static-electrical charge of their fur, their sudden changes of humour, extreme agility and skill in torturing their prey are all characteristics that cast heavy suspicion on them. The proverbial bad luck caused by a black cat crossing one's path is an extremely widespread survival of medieval superstition.

In the Celtic religion of the Germanic people, the cat was associated with the goddess Freya and was commonly offered in sacrifice. The traditional Kattenstoet, in which cats were thrown from the belfry of the Lakenhallen (Cloth Hall) in Ypres, began as a ritual to ward off witchcraft. The cat suggests a number of female characteristics – wile, domesticity, and a nocturnal and lunar existence – that appeared incomprehensible to a tenaciously male-dominated society incapable of fathoming the subtleties of the female (or feline) spirit. By the Early Middle Ages, the cat had become the witch's loyal companion, the demonic animal par excellence.

Begun by Luca Signorelli and continued by Il Sodoma in 1505, the frescoes of the cloister of the Abbey of Monte Oliveto Maggiore make up one of the most fascinating cycles from the Italian Renaissance. Judging by the frequency with which images of cats appear in various parts of the abbey, the monks at the mother house of the Olivetan order must have been very fond of their feline companions. Here, a black cat arches its back, its fur standing on end, its ears lowered, and spits threateningly at a dog twice its size. The cat's black fur contrasts with the white of the tablecloth, walls and monks' habits that dominate the scene. The demoniacal appearance of the animal is related to the fresco's subject of a sin being committed by a monk under the Devil's influence: during a period of abstinence, the brother in the foreground is stealing his neighbour's bread.

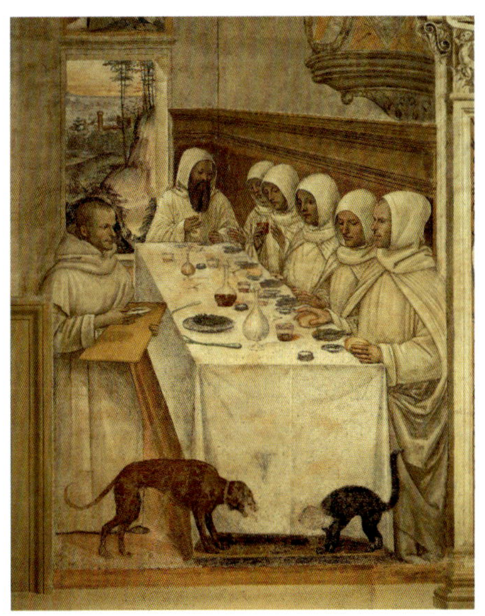

Fra Bartolomeo
Portrait of Girolamo Savonarola
1517
Museo di San Marco, Florence

THE FRIAR'S CLOAK

Strictly speaking, the term 'Black Friars' refers to the Benedictines, an old monastic order that wore an entirely black habit. However, Benedictine abbeys were isolated in the country, far from inhabited centres. On the other hand, Dominican convents (like those of the Franciscans) were often located in the heart of the city. The Dominicans wore a white habit, often covered in a black hooded cloak. In symbolic iconography, the brothers are represented by little black-and-white dogs (the *Domini canes* or hounds of the Lord) with flaming torches in their mouths.

Among the most eminent figures of the Dominican order was the controversial Girolamo Savonarola. Born in Ferrara, he wielded great influence over Florence's cultural, political and religious scene in the last decade of the 15th century. The posthumous rehabilitation of this great preacher is reflected in this impressive portrait, a strictly ascetic image of the firmest determination: the strong-willed profile, severe and concentrated, emerges from a black monastic robe.

In 1492 – the year Columbus reached the New World and Piero della Francesca died – Lorenzo Medici, the Magnificent, de facto ruler of Florence, died at the age of forty-three. Alas, his celebrated lines 'Whoever wants to be happy, let him be so: / Of tomorrow there's no knowing' turned out to be prophetic.

The spiritual and political climate of the city soon changed radically. The preaching of Fra Girolamo Savonarola, prior of the convent of San Marco, stirred people's consciences. For the next six years, the city was pervaded by a feeling of penitence and meditation. Immodest clothing and unbecoming works (like the profane paintings of Botticelli) were burned by Savonarola's followers in huge bonfires in the squares. The aristocratic secular government of the Medicis was succeeded by a kind of theocratic republic. In the context of a general religious ferment on the eve of the Protestant Reformation, the austerity and mysticism urged by Savonarola were ill-tolerated in the Curia in the Vatican. Pope Alexander VI (Rodrigo Borgia) finally decided to excommunicate Savonarola and have him executed. And so, on 23 May 1498, Savonarola and some of his followers were burned at the stake as heretics in the Piazza della Signoria. His ashes were scattered in the Arno so that his tomb would not become a cult site for his followers.

The most famous portrait of Savonarola is by the Dominican Fra Bartolomeo (Bartolomeo di Paolo del Fattorino). He began his career at a young age working alongside Mariotto Albertinelli, but a deep mystical crisis aroused by Savonarola's preaching led him to abandon painting for some years and take Dominican vows. Having returned to art in 1504, the painter-monk followed in the footsteps of his predecessor Fra Angelico, establishing a workshop within the convent of San Marco.

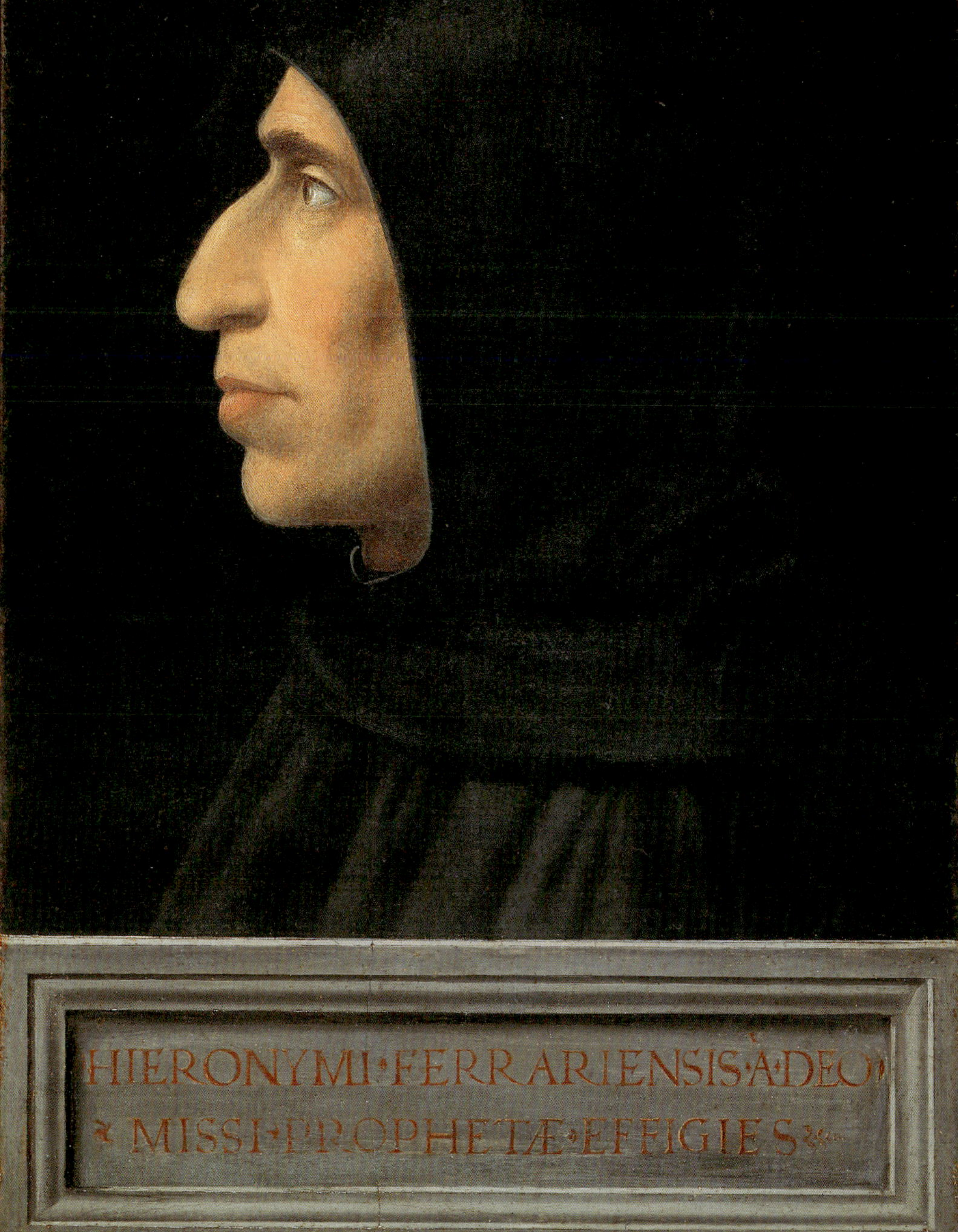
HIERONYMI·FERRARIENSIS·A·DEO
MISSI·PROPHETÆ·EFFIGIES

BLACK BILE

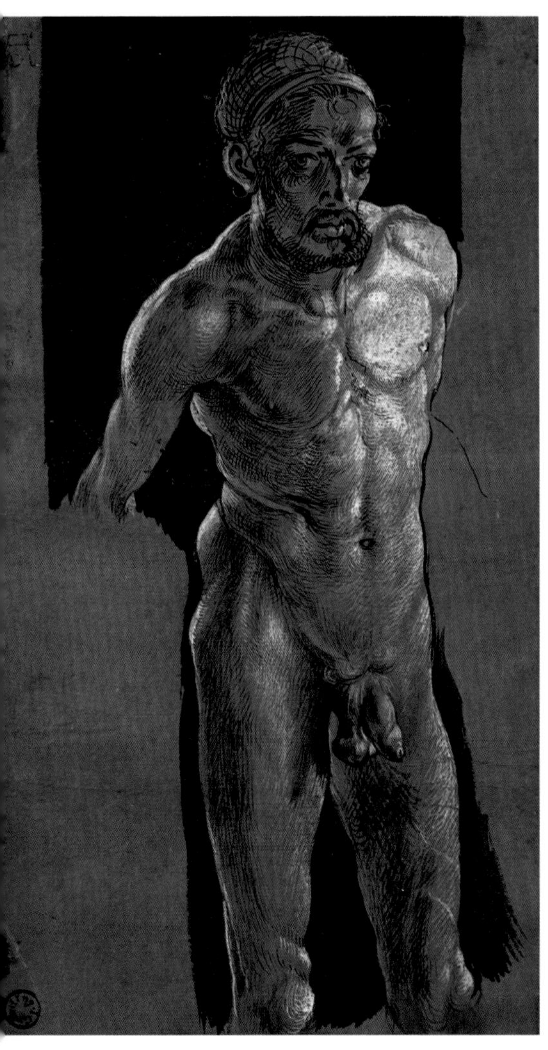

Between 1513 and 1514, Dürer executed three masterpieces of printmaking that he called 'Meisterstiche': *The Knight, Death and the Devil*, the most complete version of *St Jerome in His Study*, and the famous *Melencolia I.* Although conceived separately, the three engravings are considered as a unit, an ideal trilogy, not least because of their similar dimensions (about 24 x 19 cm). To reduce their complex and profound philosophical and symbolic meaning to its simplest expression, the print of the knight represents the active life, the *St Jerome* represents the contemplative life, and the allegory of Melancholy stands for a radical existential alternative, projected onto an interior horizon dense with references.

A bat with wings spread holds a scroll inscribed with the work's title, related to the 'first state' of melancholia, closely linked with alchemy. The engraving illustrates the initial phase of the creative moment – meditation, preparation of the raw material and its transformation.

The main figure is the winged allegorical figure symbolizing the melancholy 'humour'. According to the theory of humours, four liquids flow through the human body: blood, phlegm, yellow bile and black bile (*melan cholè* in Greek), influenced respectively by four planets. Dürer considered himself to be of a melancholic temperament, dominated by the planet Saturn. According to his conception, the indispositions and illnesses he suffered were due to uncontrolled excesses of black bile in his system. Another example is the disturbing self-portrait 'in black' in Weimar (c. 1505), in which the artist depicts himself completely nude with an almost diabolical expression.

▸

Albrecht Dürer
Melencolia I
1514
engraving, 23.9 x 16.8 cm
Musée d'Unterlinden, Colmar

◂

Albrecht Dürer
Self-portrait
c. 1505
brush and ink on paper, 29 x 15 cm
Kunstsammlung, Weimar

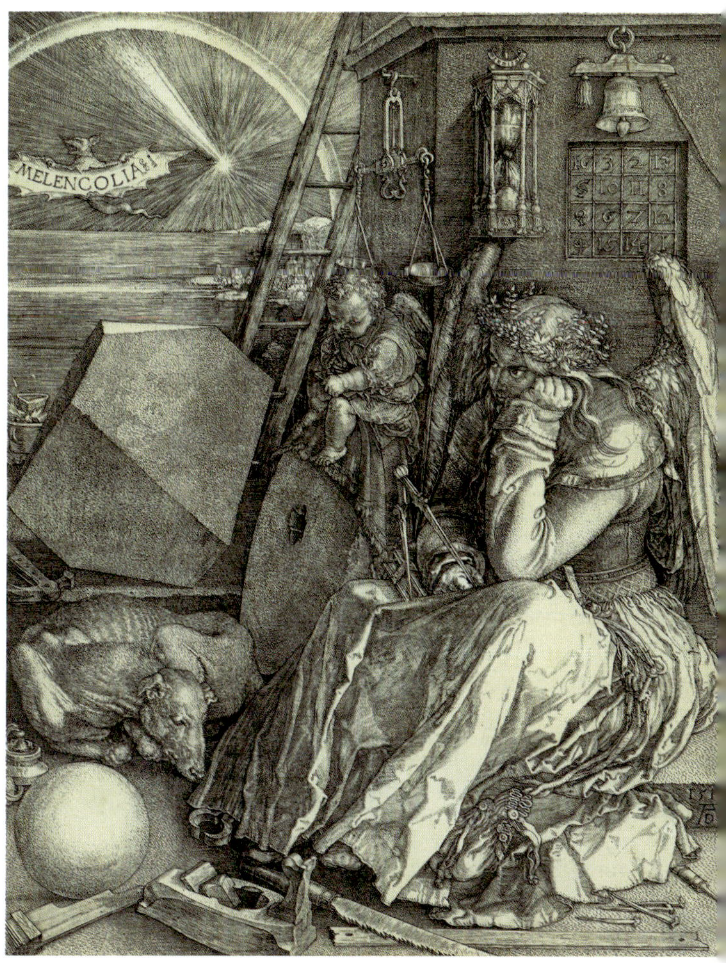

'AND DARKNESS COVERED ALL THE EARTH'

All three of the synoptic Gospels (Matthew, Mark and Luke) tell of a frightening cosmic phenomenon during Christ's agony on the Cross: darkness at midday. The Evangelists unanimously agree that this darkness fell over 'all the earth'. It lasted three hours, from noon until three o'clock. Luke (23:44) adds an astronomical detail: 'And the sun was darkened.' Various scientific interpretations and explanations have been advanced for this phenomenon, but none is convincing.

For this reason, scenes of the Crucifixion are often set against a dark background. The most spectacular of these is the series of paintings by Mathias Grünewald for the Anthonite monastery in Isenheim, Alsace – the resulting altarpiece is a landmark in figurative culture and religious feeling in the heart of Europe on the eve of the Protestant Reformation. The scenes were painted on the doors of the large case that housed the altar proper and were hinged into a structure with movable wings. The panels, with scenes of very different themes and atmospheres, were opened or closed according to the liturgical calendar of Advent, Lent and Eastertide.

The scene of the *Crucifixion* originally constituted the 'first view' of the closed polyptych. It is therefore the least well preserved, since the polyptych was kept closed for most of the church year, and the *Crucifixion* was consequently subjected to longer exposure to candle smoke and other microclimatic agents than the remaining panels. Perfectly unified in composition, the scene is physically made up of two separate panels, a structural necessity for opening the panels so the carved case could be viewed. Therefore, Grünewald had to place the figure of Christ slightly to the right in order to avoid the joint. He acted with great expressive freedom in regard to the proportions of the figures: the difference in scale between the small Magdalene and the monumental John the Baptist is striking.

Treating the Gospel theme of the darkness that envelops all the earth, Grünewald's *Crucifixion* unfolds in a gloomy, uninhabited landscape. The gigantic figure of Christ stands out forcefully against a sky that becomes completely black at the top. He is nailed to a cross of rough-hewn tree trunks, riddled with wounds, livid, in agony, and has turned an appalling ashen colour; his head is tortured by a hideous crown of thorns, while his hands and feet are pierced by nails in one of the harshest images in all of art history. In fact, it provided a point of reference for 20th-century art, in particular the German Expressionist movement.

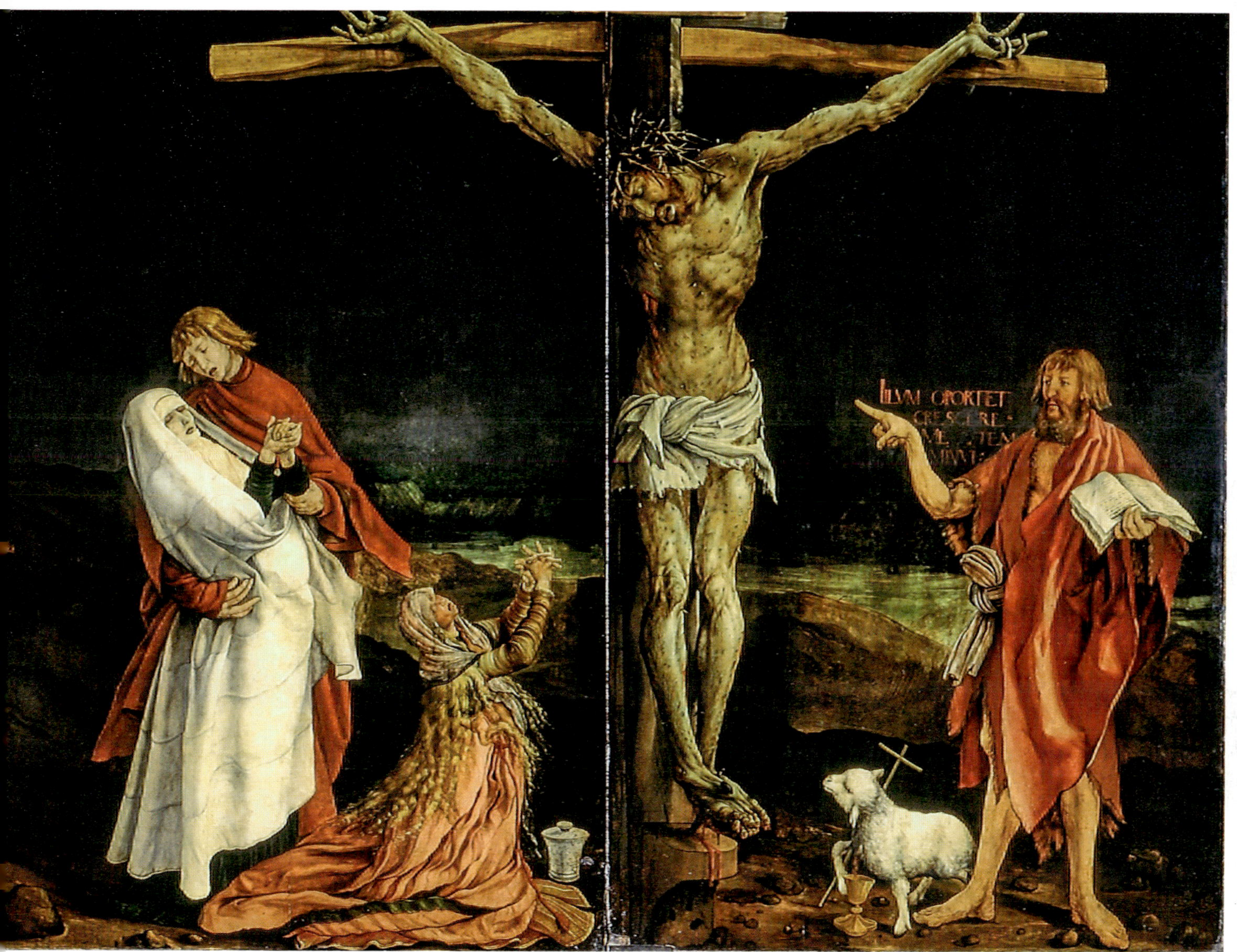

Mathias Grünewald
The Crucifixion from the *Isenheim Altarpiece*
1512-1516
oil on panel, 300 x 328 cm
Musée d'Unterlinden, Colmar

WIDOW

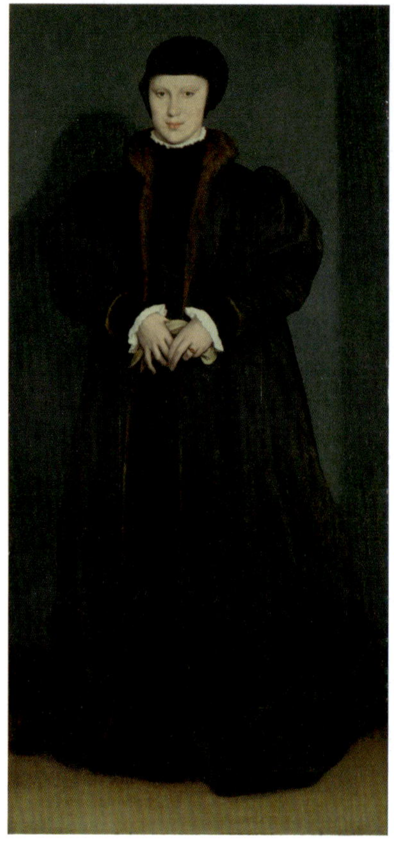

Hans Holbein the Younger
Christina of Denmark, Duchess of Milan
1538
oil on panel, 179.1 x 82.6 cm
National Gallery, London

Black is still largely the universal colour of mourning and widowhood. Certainly it appears in several 16th-century paintings in which the costumes and the sitter's bearing are intended to suggest the recent loss of a loved one, usually a spouse.

Widowed at the age of thirteen upon the death of Francesco II Sforza, Duke of Milan, the younger daughter of the King of Denmark was celebrated in Europe for her kindness and beautiful hands. Two years later, Henry VIII, king of England, lost his third wife, Jane Seymour, who died in childbirth in October 1537. Wishing to remarry, in March 1538 he sent Holbein to Brussels, where the princess was staying. Accompanied by a diplomat, the famous German painter, who had become the official portrait painter of the English court, had to execute a full-length portrait of the potential spouse, sixteen years old at the time and still in mourning. The sittings lasted only three hours – an extremely short time, but long enough for Holbein to capture the young woman's features and then transfer them in a manner deemed 'most perfect' into a portrait of penetrating simplicity and energy. Despite the effectiveness of Holbein's painting, Henry VIII decided not to marry the charming princess, choosing instead Anne of Cleves, the sister of a Protestant duke. Anne, too, was portrayed by Holbein, and the wedding was celebrated on 6 January 1540. It was not, however, a happy marriage, and after a few months it was annulled, with Anne declaring that the union had not been consummated.

Holbein portraits clearly indicate the symbols of the sitter's social rank but do not stop at simple appearances. The artist's extraordinary awareness of volumes, psychological involvement and unfailing realism, make him without doubt one of the most balanced and important portrait painters of the European Renaissance.

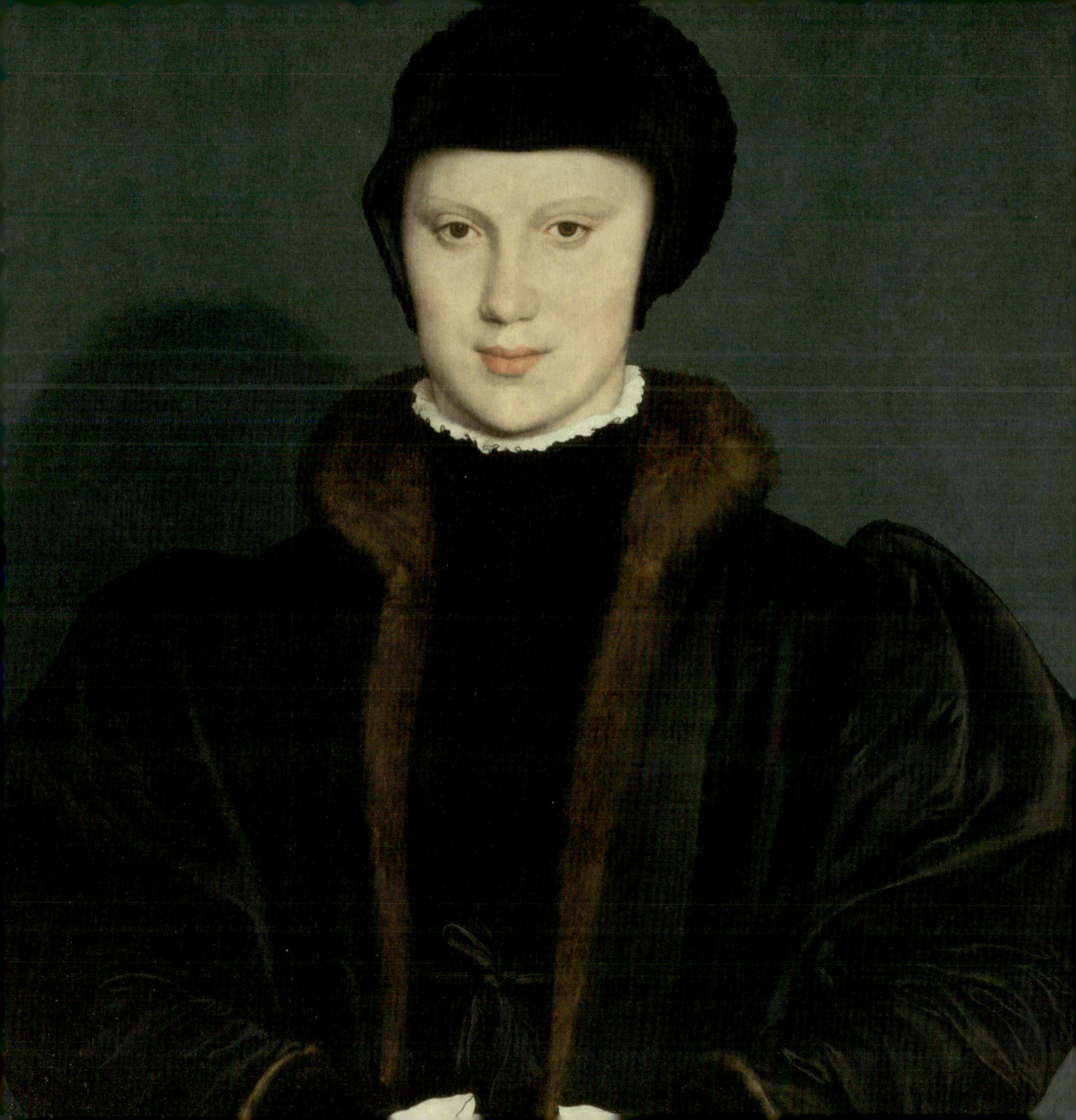

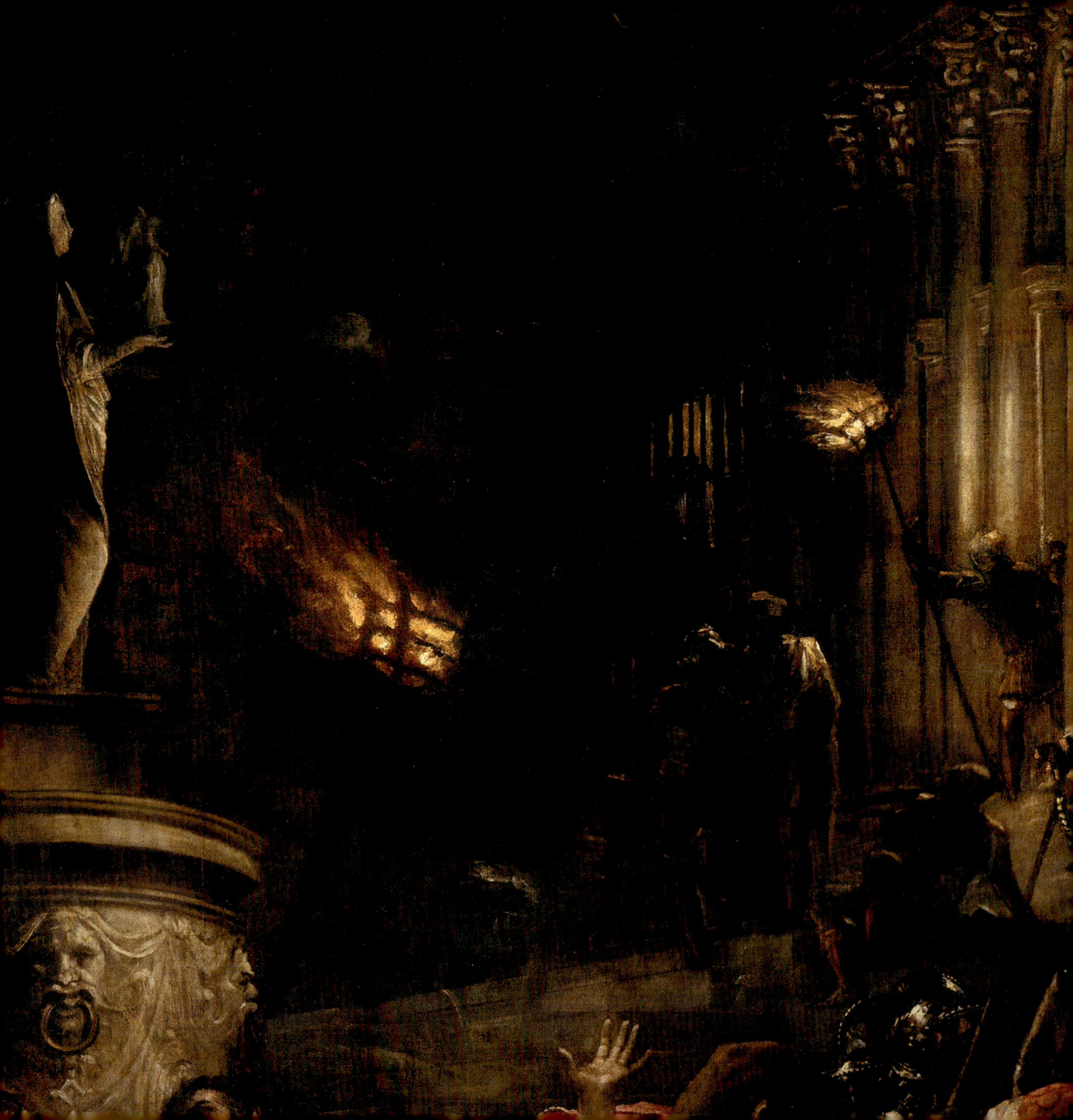

FIRES BY NIGHT

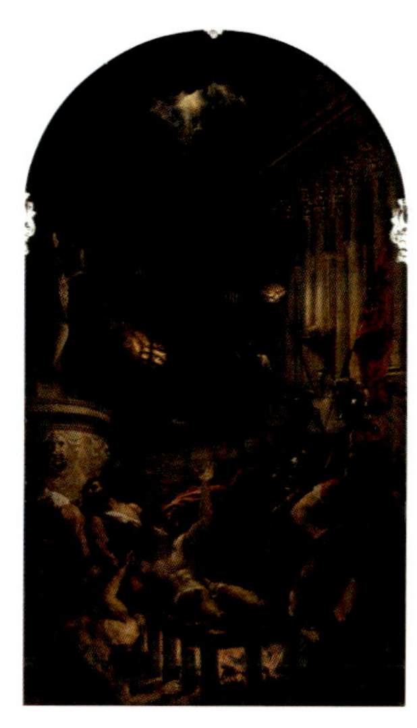

Titian
The Martyrdom of St Lawrence
c. 1548-1557
oil on canvas transferred from panel
493 x 277 cm
Jesuit Church, Venice

From the spectacularly colourful palette of his early years, Titian gradually reduced the number of colours to a range of predominantly whites, blacks and reds. The decision to set some works against a homogeneous dark background, or even at night, showed off his skilfully modulated use of black.

In *The Martyrdom of St Lawrence*, Titian abandons the Renaissance heritage for a composition of exaggerated expressionism, built upon a dramatic quest for light. The deep night is illuminated by a violent source of light within the scene, creating a remarkable effect.

The altarpiece remains in its original site. But the church was completely remodelled and redecorated in exuberant Baroque forms, creating a strident contrast between the gay colours of the interior and the painting's almost 'charred' appearance. With an intuition that even surpasses the bold experiments of theatrical lighting techniques initiated by Tintoretto, Titian shrouds in shadow the place of martyrdom, which is surrounded by dim but towering buildings. One of the main figures in the scene is the fire – earthly, heavenly and divine – that smoulders, flares up or is quenched at various points in the large painting.

Giorgio Vasari, who certainly did not approve of the convoluted iconography in some of Titian's works, tried to follow these flames, but his initially detached analysis becomes increasingly overtaken by emotion. The surprising play of light and shadow was effectively described by Vasari in the biography of Titian in the second edition of the *Lives* (1568): 'the painting, which is on the altar of the Church of St Lawrence, within which is the martyrdom of that Saint, with a large tenement full of figures, and a foreshortened St Lawrence lying half on the grate, below him a great fire, and around some that are lighting it. And because he has painted a night scene, two servants hold two torches that cast light where the glare of the fire under the grate, which is often very lively, does not reach; and in addition he has painted a lightning flash coming from the sky and piercing the clouds that overpowers the light of the fire and the torches, being above the Saint and the other main figures; and besides the said three lights, the people he has painted in the distance at the windows of the tenement have the light of the oil lamps and candles that are near them, and overall, the whole is accomplished with fine art, talent and judgement.'

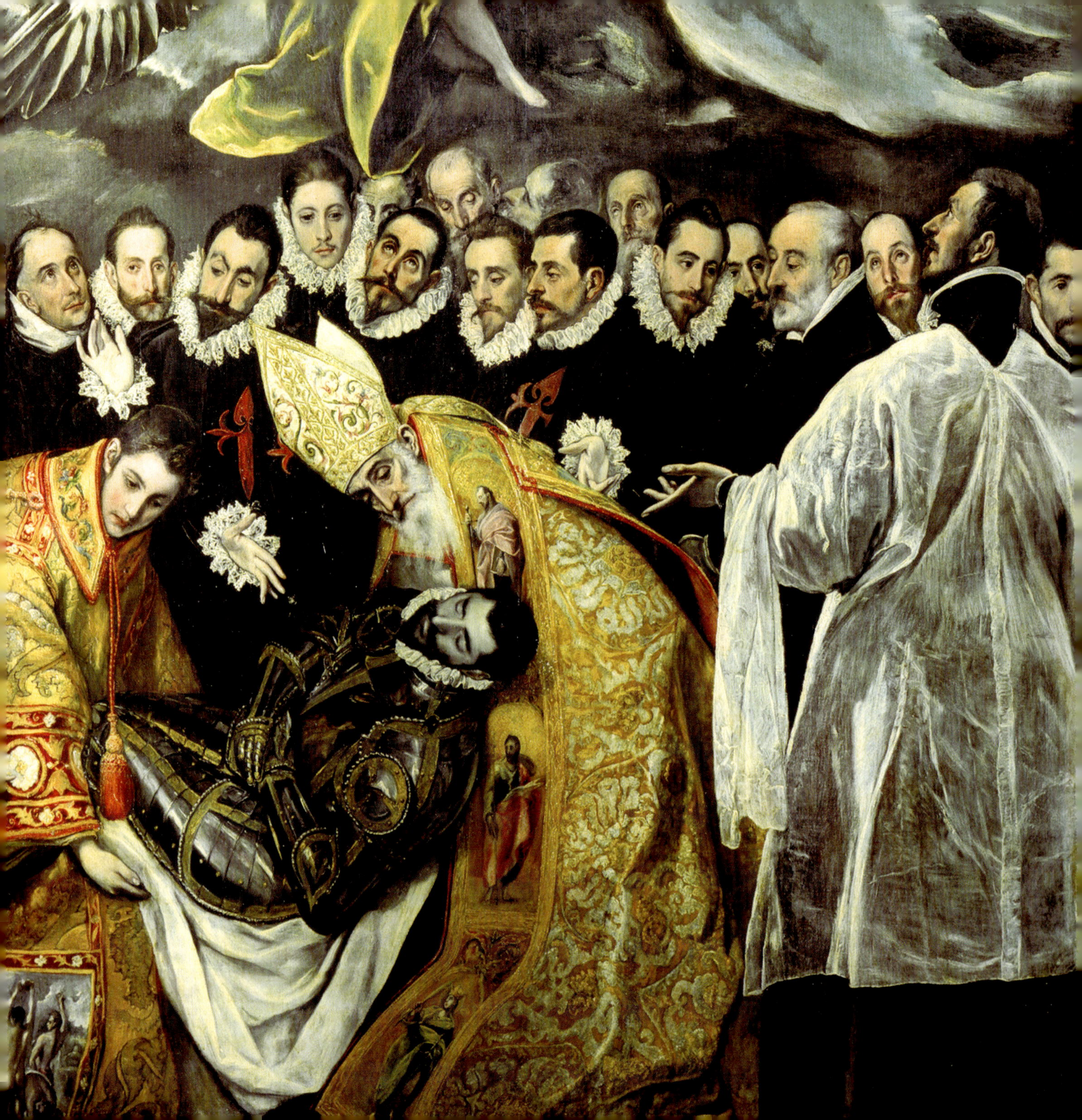

SPANISH FASHION

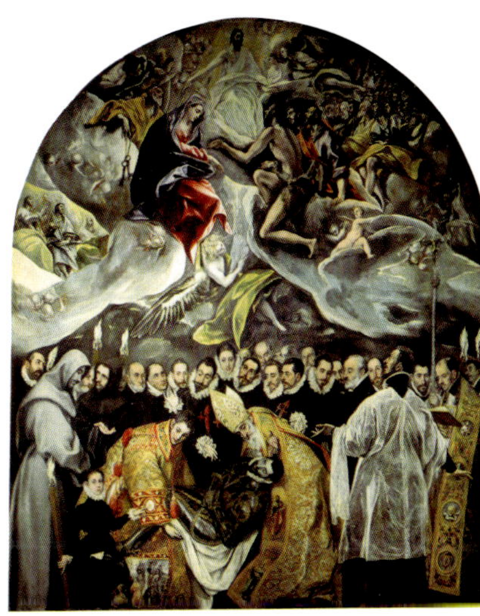

El Greco
The Burial of the Count of Orgaz
1586
oil on canvas, 460 x 360 cm
Santo Tomé, Toledo

For five hundred years, black has been synonymous with masculine elegance, and is often required at official receptions. This in large part came from the 16th-century Spanish fashion initiated by Charles V, who brusquely abolished the previous gaudily coloured clothing and replaced it with strictly sober black and white. The emperor had adopted black in mourning for the untimely death of his beloved wife, Queen Isabella of Portugal. In the space of a few years, it became the symbol of the renewed vigour of the Counter-Reformation. One might add, somewhat unkindly, that Charles V was not very good looking, with his typically Habsburg protruding chin, meagre stature and skinny, unsteady legs. He must certainly have been ill at ease in front of colossi brimming with health and energy like Francis I of France and Henry VIII of England, who both liked to wear colourful, fanciful clothes. However, the fact remains that black was absolutely indispensable for men's clothing among Europe's upper echelons, whether Catholic, Lutheran or Calvinist.

One of the first painters to perceive the elegant rigour of this severe clothing was El Greco, who had settled in Toledo, Spain, after a youthful itinerary that had taken him from his native island of Crete to Italy, where he pursued his training eclectically in Venice and Rome. His style shows the influence of Byzantine icons, the colours of Titian, the classicism of Raphael and Michelangelo, the magical effects of light of Tintoretto and Jacopo Bassano, the torsions of Mannerism and perhaps even the series of figures by Dürer. Yet El Greco's style was radically new. The contrast in his works between pallid, almost feverish faces and dark cloth is highly effective.

One of the painter's greatest and most famous canvases illustrates a miraculous event that occurred in the 14th century. St Stephen and St Augustine are said to have appeared at the funeral of the pious gentleman Don Gonzalo Ruiz, count of the town of Orgaz, and placed the deceased in his tomb. To all present there appeared a vision of Christ in glory, surrounded by saints and angels, into whose presence the count's soul was delivered. El Greco clearly divides this grandiose scene between the earthly and celestial planes. There is a palpable, throbbing uneasiness that makes the facial expressions febrile, the hands agitated, the eyes moist, especially in the exceptional gallery of gentlemen severely dressed in black.

CARAVAGGIO'S DARK SIDE

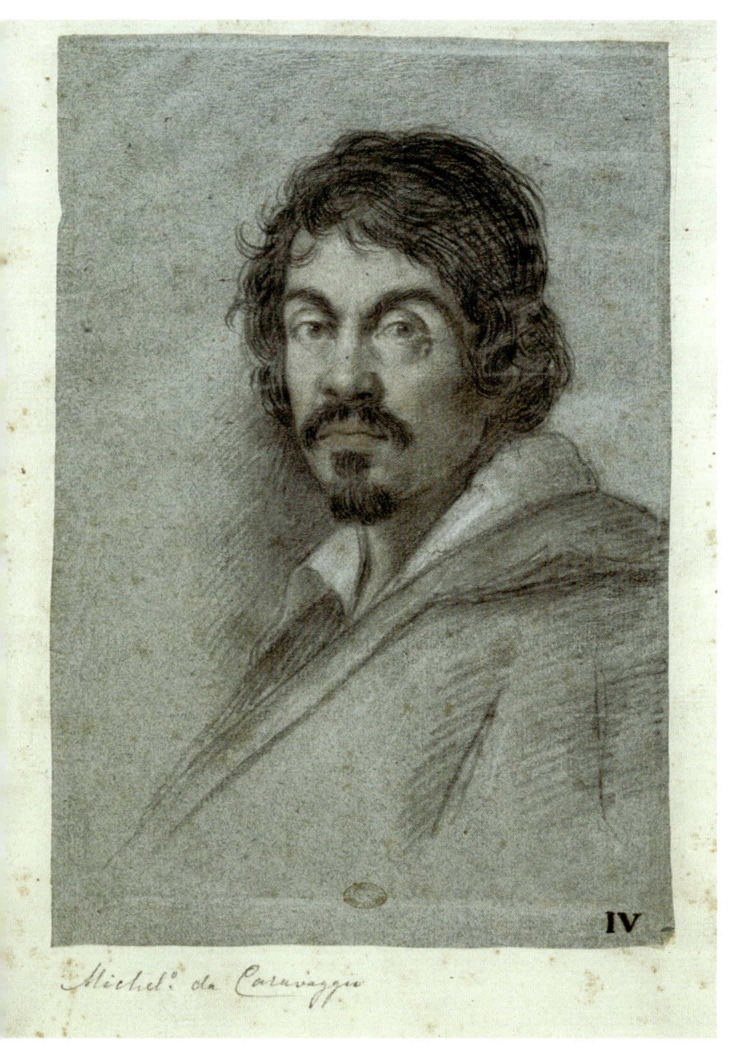

Unlike all the other painters of his period, Caravaggio did not leave a dedicated self-portrait. However, on several occasions he included himself among the figures in his paintings. We can recognize his face a number of times through the years, always in dramatic situations: as a boy, pale and emaciated, eaten away by malaria, the illness that eventually brought about his death (*The Young Sick Bacchus*); at the age of thirty, assisting in a murder (*The Martyrdom of St Matthew*); not long after, amid a group of persecutors, holding a lantern during a tempestuous night-time arrest; then attending the funeral of a girl, overcome by the impending void of death (*The Burial of St Lucy*); and twice in the last months of his brief life, first as a dumbfounded, impotent witness to a girl's murder by a crazed thug (*The Martyrdom of St Ursula*) and finally as the defeated giant, slashed and decapitated (*David with the Head of Goliath*).

Caravaggio's 'official' portrait is provided in two charcoal and chalk drawings, presumably quite faithful, by Ottavio Leoni, a minor painter and companion-in-adventure of the master. Some interesting details are also provided by Caravaggio's biographers, who on the whole were quite ungenerous towards the painter from Lombardy. His physical description evokes the gloomy image of an almost diabolical man, and black takes on a clearly negative connotation. Giovanni Pietro

Bellori, a fierce critic of Caravaggesque naturalism, recalls, ‘He had a dark complexion and dark eyes, black hair and eyebrows.’ In another even shorter and blunter passage, Caravaggio is described as ‘small of stature and ugly of face’.

The theme of the severed head recurs in this work painted by Caravaggio during his second stay in Naples. The body of David emerges dramatically from the dark background as, with a sad and melancholy expression, he looks at the head of the giant Goliath, still streaming with blood. This tragic image conceals an anguished self-portrait, perhaps a sign of Caravaggio repenting the murder that had forced him to flee Rome, or simply his reckless life in general. The rapid, simplified brushstroke, particularly in the rendering of the youth’s shirt and sword, is typical of Caravaggio’s late period.

◂
Ottavio Leoni
Portrait of Caravaggio
c. 1614
drawing, 24.2 x 17 cm
Biblioteca Marucelliana, Florence

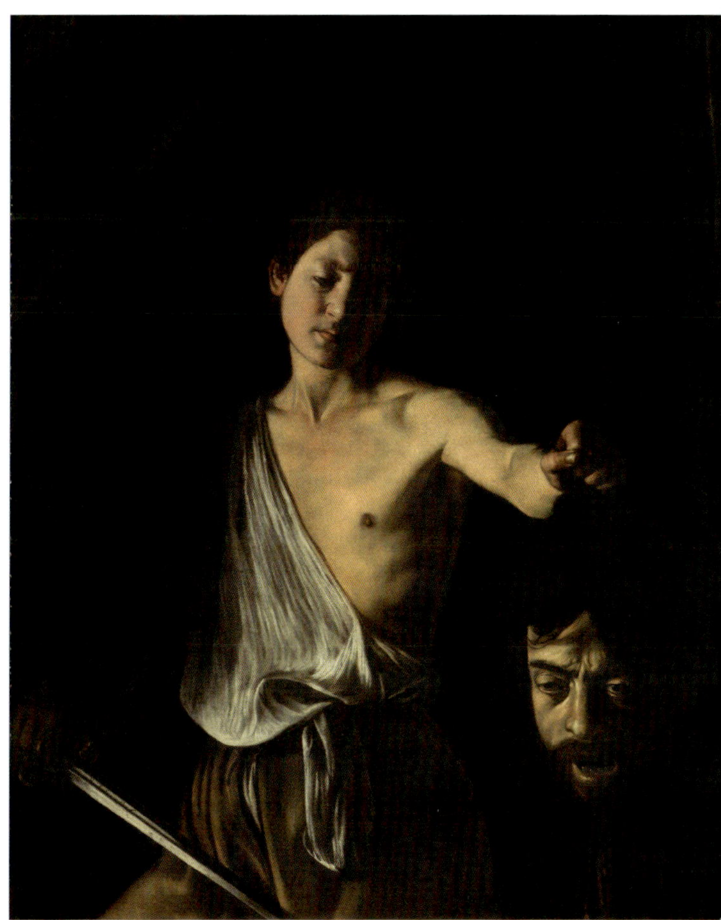

▸
Caravaggio
David with the Head of Goliath
1609-1610
oil on canvas, 125 x 101 cm
Galleria Borghese, Rome

REMBRANDT AND DE RIGUEUR 'BASIC' BLACK

A sublime draughtsman and engraver, Rembrandt knew perfectly well the value of black. The painting technique of the mature and late works – often very dense, granular and almost three-dimensional – makes them particularly difficult to illuminate, exhibit, restore and reproduce. It is easy to become submerged in the shadowy density of the dark tones. The painter's extreme sensitivity to the smallest variations of shade and thickness means that the black in his paintings contains an almost infinite range of expressive potential. According to the surfaces or section of the painting (for example, the background or the fabrics of the figures' clothing), black can appear opaque or lucid, dull or vibrant.

The testimony of the French critic André Félibien des Avaux is interesting. In the years he spent in Rome as secretary to the French ambassador, he became a devoted admirer of Poussin and classicism. Nonetheless, he was struck by Rembrandt's power, his vital, primitive force. He describes the Dutch painter in his *Entretiens sur les vies et sur les ouvrages des plus excellents peintres anciens et modernes* (volume 4, 1685): 'All his paintings are painted in a personal manner, so different from the overly polished manner into which Flemish painters usually fall. In fact, he often limits himself to tracing with broad strokes, applying colours alongside one another, without concerning himself about combining or blending them.'

This large painting depicts the councillors of the Drapers' Guild in Amsterdam. The centre of the scene is the set of samples (which we may naturally assume are black); around them, intense conversation rages. The series of seated figures is interrupted by the second one from the left, rising with a gesture that disrupts the gathering. The secret of the enthralling strength of Rembrandt's portraits, the unmistakable and inimitable vital flux that springs from them, derives from this new communication established between the work and the viewer. Rembrandt understood the importance of drawing the viewer into an 'action' unfurling here and now before their eyes. The low vanishing point and the convergence of the councillors' attention on the viewer are ingenious strokes. The busy gentlemen raise their eyes from the ledger they are discussing, their words and gestures hanging in the air as they gaze at us.

Rembrandt
The Syndics of the Drapers' Guild, or The Sampling Officials
1662
oil on canvas, 191.5 x 279 cm
Rijksmuseum, Amsterdam

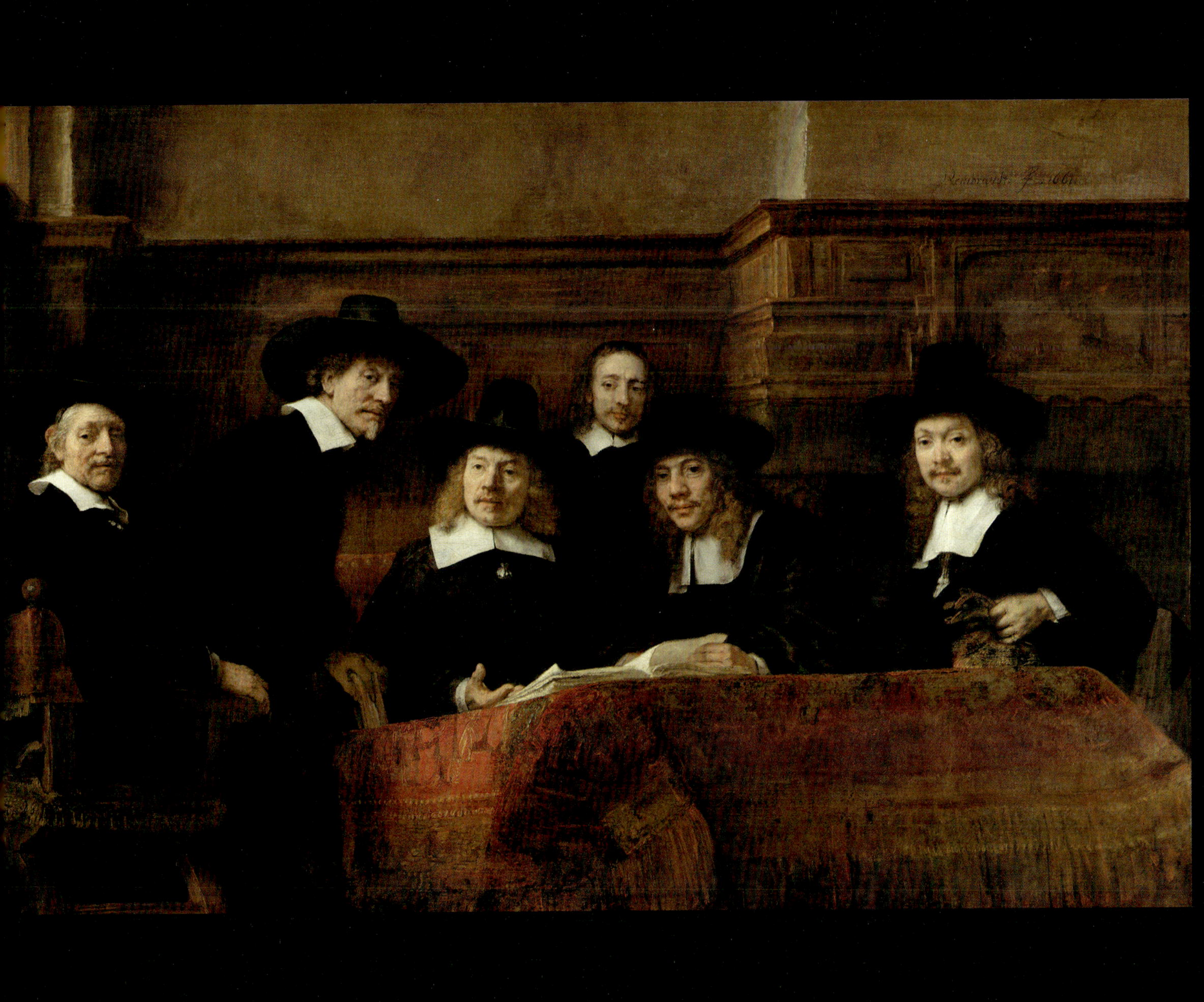

'BLACK' SKIN

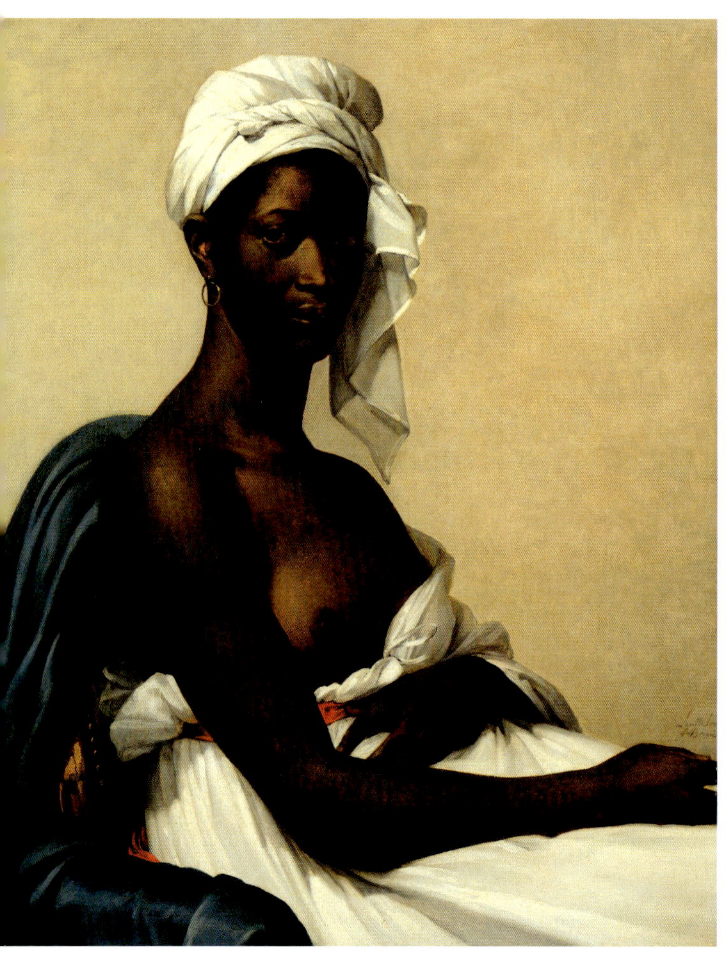

Marie-Guillemine Benoist
Portrait of a Black Woman
1800
oil on canvas, 81 x 65 cm
Musée du Louvre, Paris

In European culture and art before the 19th century, Africans were obviously well known in the Mediterranean region but were hardly unheard-of in Central Europe either. With the development of trade during the 15th century, followed by new geographical discoveries and the great sea voyages, inhabitants of sub-Saharan Africa also began to appear frequently in images. 'Black' skin still had an exotic appearance but soon became almost obligatory in, for example, scenes of the Three Wise Men.

The cult of the Magi takes as its starting-point the Gospel of Matthew, but art and devotion mostly draw on the apocryphal Gospels and popular tradition. Matthew describes the last stages of the journey of the Magi – their meeting with Herod and then the Christ Child, the gifts, and the dream of an angel who suggests taking a different route home, to avoid Herod. But the Evangelist does not actually state the number, identity, royal rank and names, exact place of origin, age or race of the Wise Men. He tells of 'wise men from the east' – probably Persian astronomers connected with Zoroastrian culture.

Early Christian iconographic tradition set the number of the Magi at three, coinciding with the gifts of gold, frankincense and myrrh named in the

Hieronymus Bosch
The Adoration of the Magi (detail)
1485-1500
triptych, oil on panel, 138 x 72/144 cm
Museo Nacional del Prado, Madrid

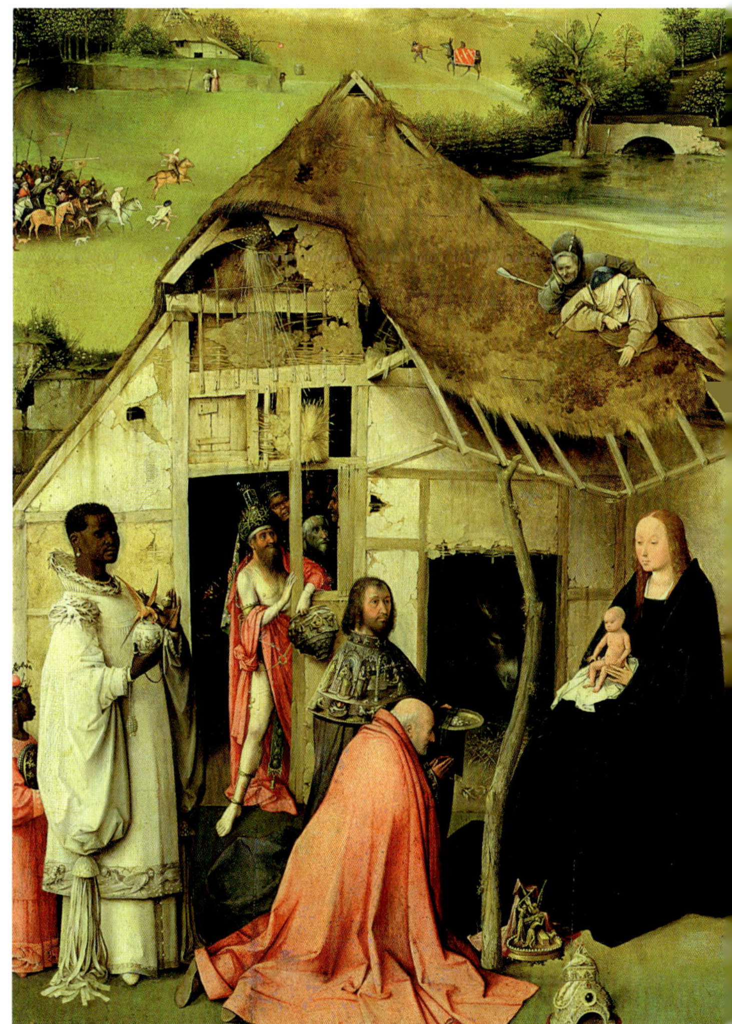

Gospel. Until the Gothic period, the Eastern sages (who became kings only in the Middle Ages) all have a similar appearance derived from illustrations of chivalric romances and differ only in age if at all. The procession that accompanies them to Bethlehem becomes increasingly opulent until it achieves a tone of absolutely fabulous magnificence. Then, in 15th-century Flemish art, the Magi assume distinct physical characteristics and take the names Caspar, Melchior and Balthazar. The latter is identified by his dark skin and is often the most exotic and fascinating figure of the entire scene.

However, images of dark-skinned men and women remained relatively rare and, on the threshold of the modern era, became entangled with the debate over slavery. The portrait of an African woman exhibited at the Salon in Paris in 1800, the work of Marie-Guillemine Benoist, is interesting in this regard. As a woman artist, Benoist, a pupil of Élisabeth Vigée-Le Brun, had to deal with prejudice and discrimination. It is easy to understand the emotional involvement and intensity with which she depicts a woman whose inward nobility triumphs over a difference of skin colour and social rank.

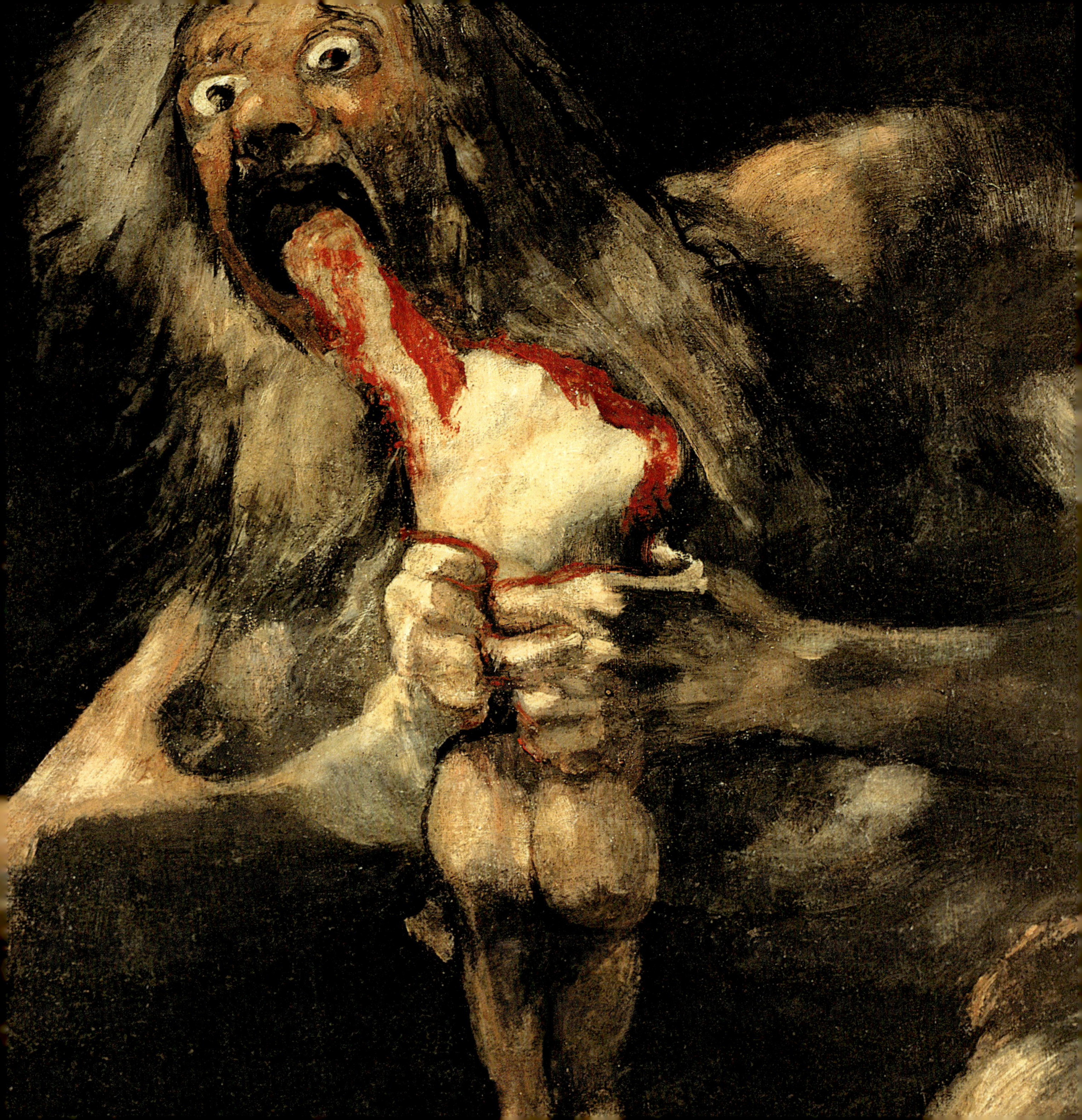

GOYA'S 'BLACK PAINTINGS'

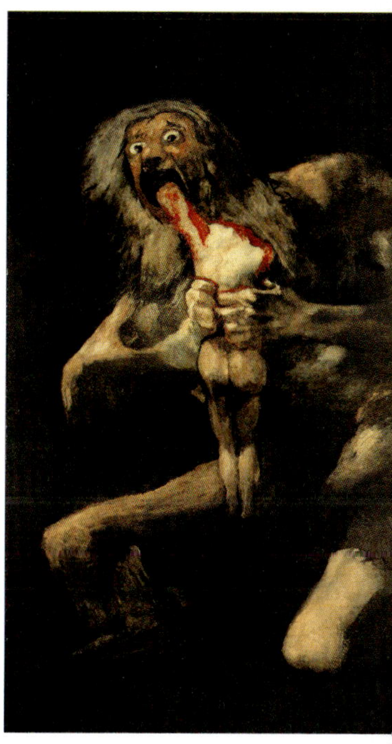

Francisco de Goya
Saturn Devouring One of His Sons
from the cycle of
Black Paintings
at the Quinta del Sordo
1821-1823
canvas (originally on plaster),
143.5 cm x 81.4 cm
Museo Nacional del Prado, Madrid

Although Goya was not an intellectual or a philosopher, he had a depth of thought and an expressive force based on the political and historical contrasts of his time that had resonances in later periods. A quarrelsome and immoderate youth, twice expelled from the Royal Academy of Fine Arts in Madrid, as well as a voracious lover and a hunting and bullfight enthusiast, Goya underwent an artistic evolution that took him from refined aristocratic Rococo scenes to the bitterest and most disenchanted reflections on humankind. One of his main themes, developed in paintings and above all in prints and drawings, is the infinite variation of physical violence, a true obsession that culminated in the *Caprichos* and the 'Black Paintings'.

Deeply disturbed by the war of 1808 and the repression of the popular insurrection against Napoleon's invading troops, Goya indiscriminately condemned bloodshed, violence and savage behaviour. His figures gradually lose the chromatic richness and assured appearance of his early years and are set in hallucinatory empty spaces. His sense of solitude and isolation was intensified by the illness that made him almost totally deaf. Anguished and horrified by the violence he considered a widespread, ineradicable evil, Goya gradually moved away from reality and ventured into the mysterious, shadowy images of an unsettling, macabre fantasy. The peak of this spectral vision came with the 'Black Paintings', the wall paintings he executed in about 1821–1823 at his country house known as the Quinta del Sordo.

Goya called these wall paintings (today at the Prado) 'black' not only because of the predominant colour but also because of their frightful subject-matter. Representative of the cycle is the torn body in *Saturn Devouring One of His Sons*, the expressionistic vein of which anticipates Ensor and Bacon. With works like these, Goya offered himself as a universal 'moral witness', a critical consciousness pointing to the eternal abyss of evil, the recurring fear of violence and the desperate vacillation between reason and unreason.

Gustave Courbet
Self-portrait with a Black Dog
1842
oil on canvas, 46.5 x 55.5 cm
Petit-Palais, Musée des Beaux-Arts de la ville de Paris

THE BLACK DOG

One of the most energetic personalities of the 19th century, Gustave Courbet was a provocateur and a revolutionary in both life and art, and a confirmed supporter of art's social function as candidly expressed through Realism. The two large canvases he exhibited at the Salon of 1850 (*A Burial at Ornans* and *The Stone Breakers*) attracted the attention of the critics for their creator's unquestionable technical ability but also sparked debate between supporters of his realistic style and its detractors, who were still bound to classicism. In both paintings, black plays a dominant role: in the *Burial*, it is the colour of the priest's robes and the clothing of many of those in attendance; in *The Stone Breakers*, it crudely defines the workers' figures, as if sculpting their outline.

In 1855, Courbet conceived and executed his most ambitious painting, *The Artist's Studio* (Musée d'Orsay, Paris), a synthesis of his art up to that point, and the starting-point for what he was to embark upon next. Submitted to the 1855 Paris World's Fair, this masterpiece was rejected by the jury. Disappointed and bitter, but not defeated, Courbet assembled forty rejected works and, at his own expense, set up an alternative exhibition in a tent, which he called the Pavilion of Realism. His friendship with the thinker Proud'hon led to the strengthening of his socialist and republican political convictions, which caused him not a few problems under Napoleon III's reign. At the close of the Second Empire, Courbet was among the leading figures in the formation of the Paris Commune, by which he was appointed delegate for the Fine Arts. With the repression of the government of the Third Republic, Courbet was considered a ringleader of the revolt. Accused of ordering the destruction of the Vendôme Column, he was imprisoned and brought to trial. He managed to take refuge in Switzerland but was sentenced to pay for the column. The state obtained the money it was owed by requisitioning many of his paintings and selling them at auction. Courbet died in exile in La-Tour-de-Peilz, near Vevey, Switzerland, in 1877.

In this early painting, executed a few years after Courbet settled in Paris, the young painter's proud gaze seems to defy the viewer, an effect accentuated by the low viewpoint. Among the composition's significant details are the wide-brimmed hat, pipe, walking-stick, sketchbook (an indication of the artist's intention to work *en plein air*) and wonderful, gleaming black dog, which lends the work its title. Though symbolically the painter's loyal companion, from a compositional standpoint the animal represents a skilful chromatic device in the foreground, drawing the eye towards the background landscape.

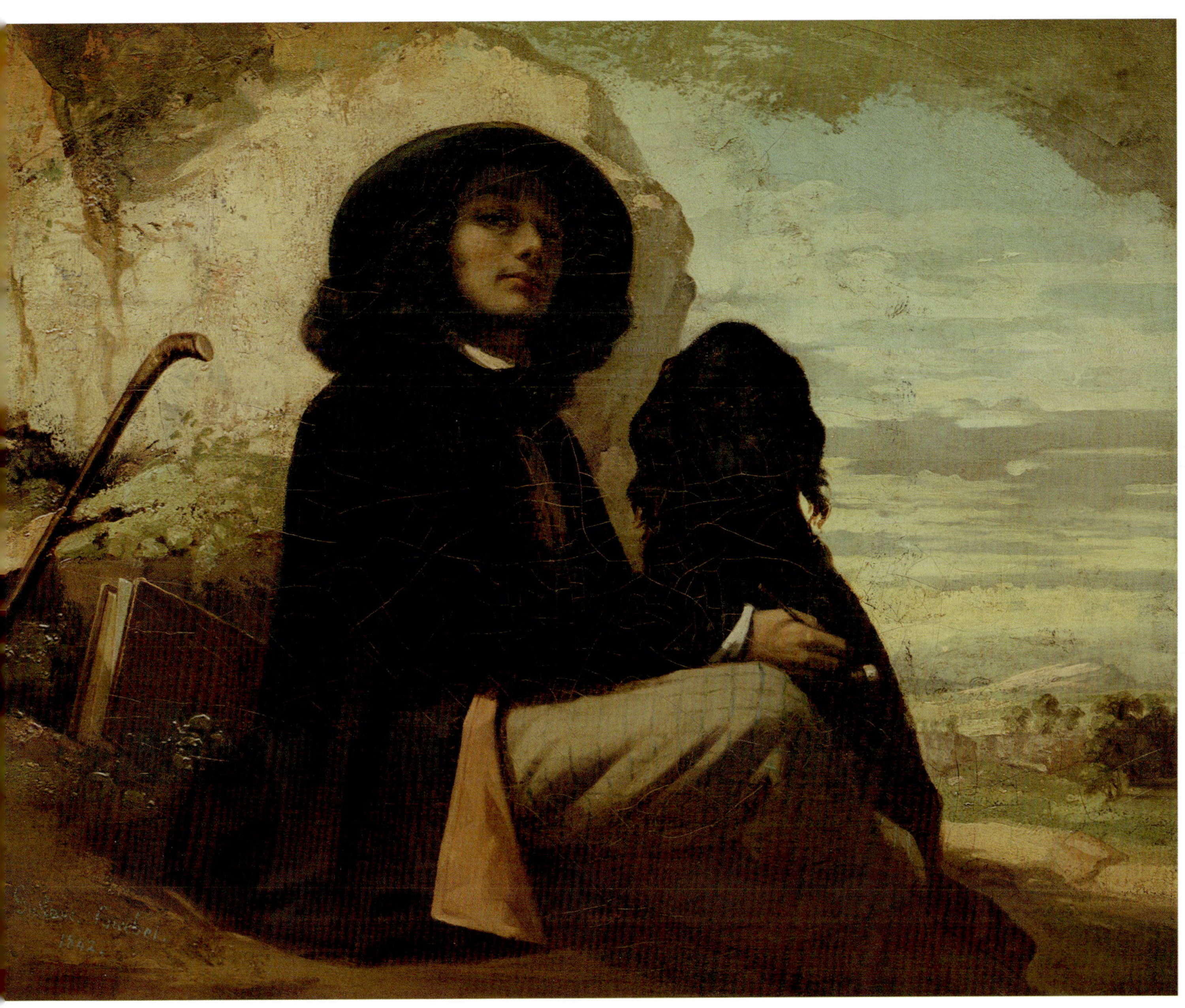
1842.

MANET AND BERTHE MORISOT

Berthe Morisot was an important painter in the Impressionist panorama. She showed a particular sensitivity in treating moments of tenderness, quiet and intimacy. Many of her paintings represent interior family scenes, in which she often portrays her sister and other relatives. Particularly charming – people described her as a 'Spanish' beauty – Morisot was repeatedly portrayed by various fellow painters, especially by Manet, whose brother Eugène she married in 1874.

The series of portraits of Berthe Morisot signals Manet's return to painting after serving in the National Guard during the Franco-Prussian War in 1870–1871. When discussing *Le Triomphe de Manet*, a large retrospective exhibition at the Orangerie in 1932, Paul Valéry (who married Morisot's niece and lived in the Paris house previously inhabited by Morisot) regarded the 'absolute' black Manet used for these portraits with emotion. To the poet's mind, the portrait of Morisot with a bunch of violets was the painter's masterpiece: 'I do not place anything in Manet's oeuvre above a certain portrait of Berthe Morisot dated 1872.'

It depicts the sitter close to the picture plane, with a strong contrast of shadow and light between the figure and the neutral background. Although in reality Morisot had green eyes, in the portrait her eyes are black, like her clothes and hat. Manet innovatively develops the use of black, giving it an extraordinary power and immediacy. This aspect furthermore signals Manet's independence from the Impressionists – including Morisot herself, who tended to reject black, considering it a non-colour.

Edouard Manet
Berthe Morisot with a Bouquet of Violets
1872
oil on canvas, 55.5 x 40.5 cm
Musée d'Orsay, Paris

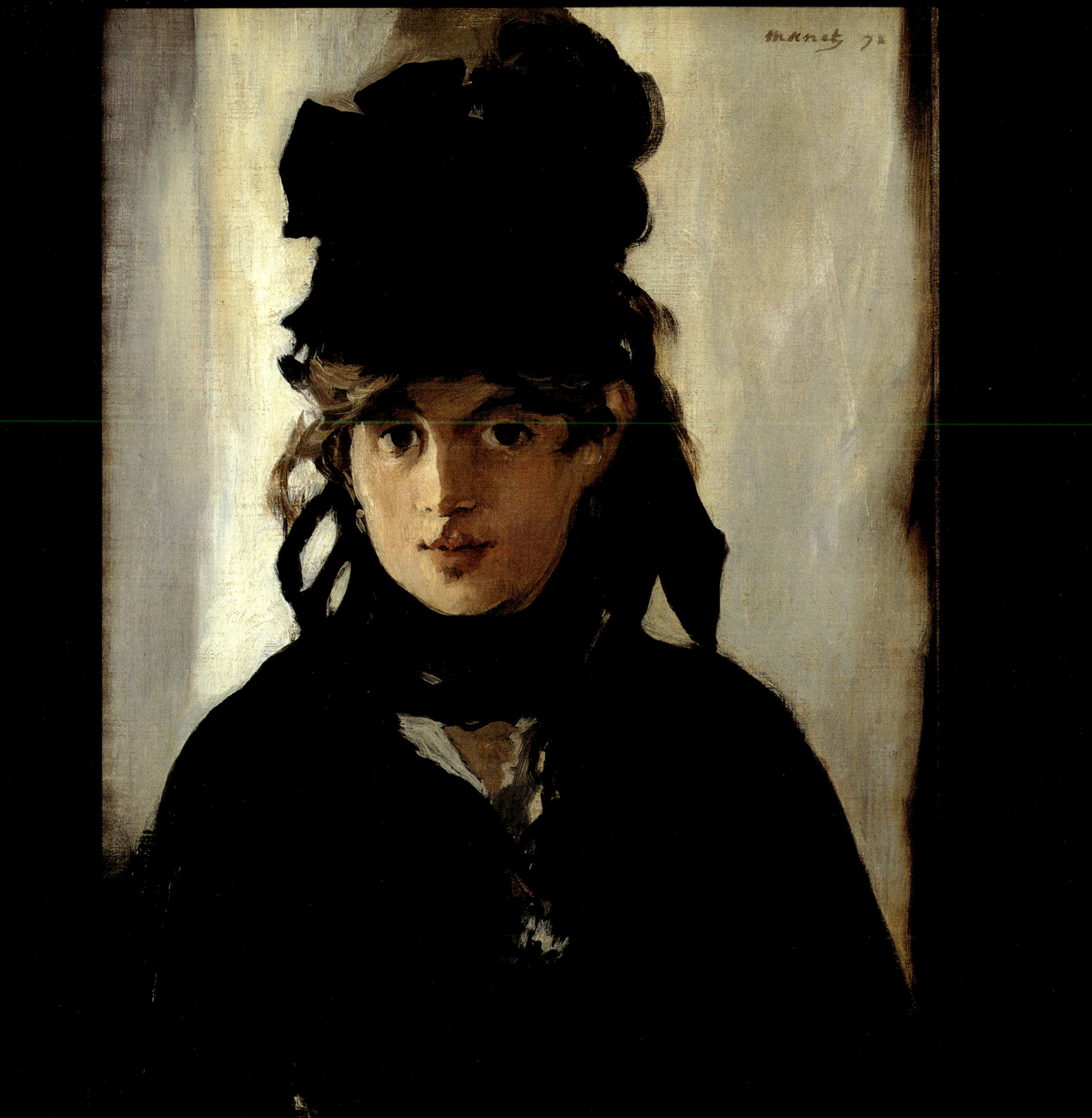
manet 72

BLACK, WHITE AND MATHS

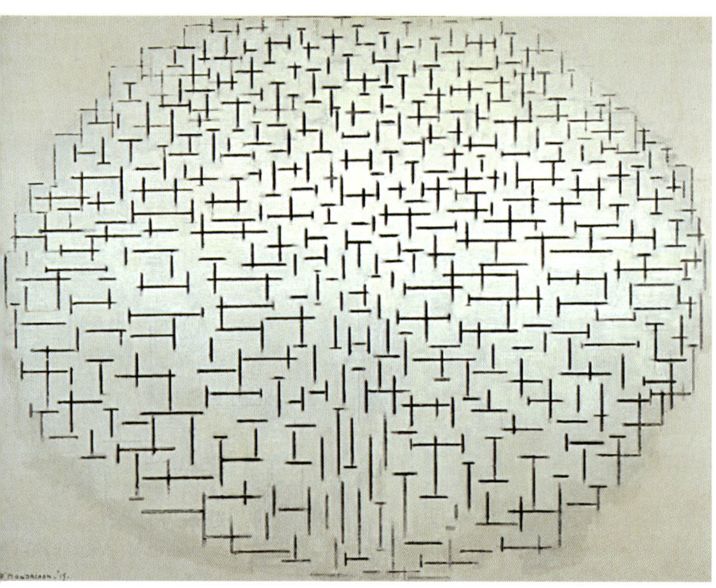

Piet Mondrian
Composition 10 in Black and White
1915
oil on canvas, 85 x 108 cm
Kröller-Müller Museum, Otterlo

Black and white offer a clear-cut opposition. They correspond to the mathematical 'plus' and 'minus' signs, and the works of some 20th-century artists who adhered to the logic of algebra may be interpreted in this light.

Piet Mondrian began his career painting figurative works in Post-Impressionist styles. Forced to remain in Holland during the First World War, he declared that it was during these years that he began to see the landscape, and especially the horizon of the North Sea, as a succession of mathematical plus and minus signs. In *Pier and Ocean* (or *Composition 10 in Black and White*) the thick graphic mark of intersecting black lines forms an irregular series of right angles. It is one of the last paintings to contain a reference to reality, at least in its title. From then until his death, Mondrian would be strictly faithful to abstraction, and with just a few exceptions his paintings were entitled *Composition* and identified by a sequential number. Mondrian's world became reduced to a purely mathematical and geometric essence. The 'grid' of straight lines over a solid white background is completed by squares in the three primary colours – yellow, red and blue.

The love of mathematics and calculations, as well as a taste for mental games, characterizes the vast

M.C. Escher
Sky and Water I
1938
woodcut

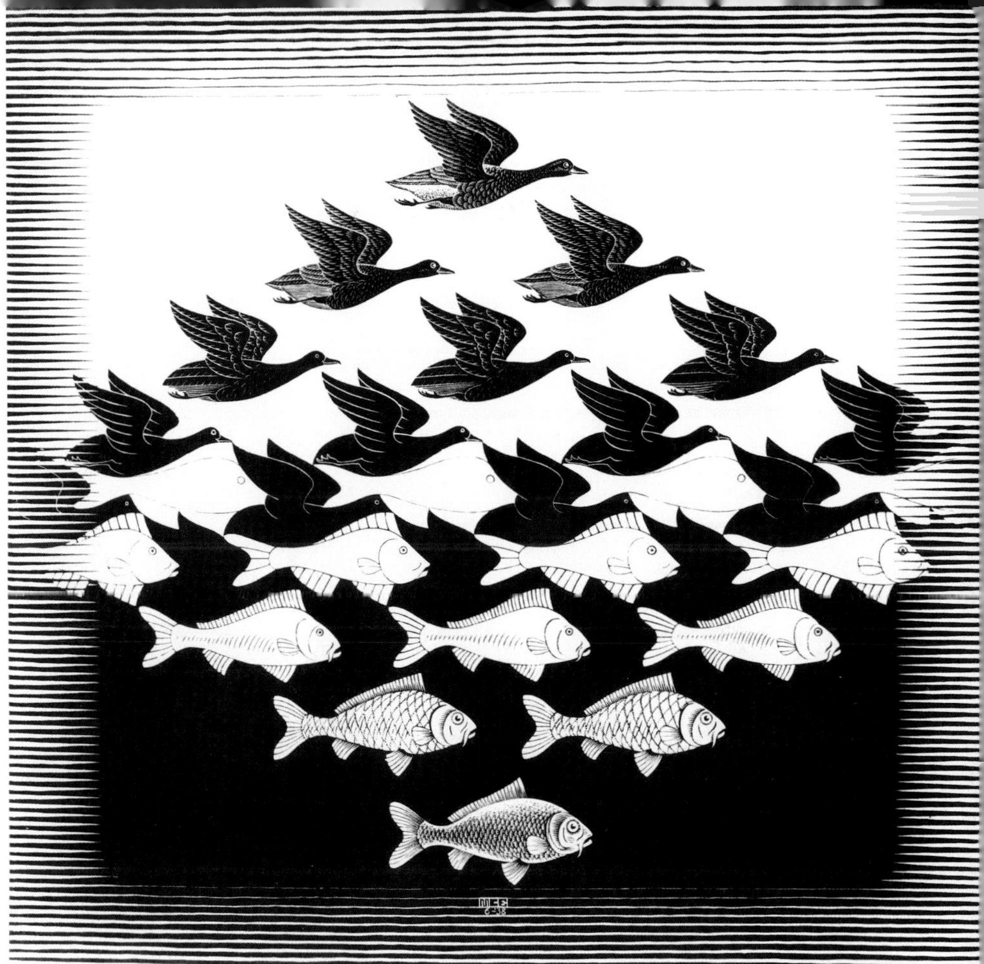

production of Maurits Cornelis Escher. His art revolves around a single basic concept – that of space – reproduced not according to the scientific laws of perspective but by means of geometric devices that push our perception to the limit, showing us an ambiguous world of 'impossible' objects. Escher applies the theme of the double to spatiality, so that two contrary versions of an object may coexist in the same image: what is in front ends up looking like it is at the back, the concave looks convex, and the overhead view merges with the view from below. This doubleness is reinforced by the black-and-white contrast typical of engravings, the artist's preferred medium.

THE SUPREMACY OF BLACK

During the second decade of the 20th century, a period of war and revolution, the Russian avant-garde artist Kazimir Serverinovich Malevich created images based on the radical simplification of form and colour using essential relationships of pure geometry. What was important was a perfect balance of parts. *Black Square on White* marks the beginning of the current known as Suprematism. For Malevich, art was a means of profound transformation and research, not ornament and decoration. Malevich was in search of a new image of the world, and Suprematism became the most suitable tool for 'the renewal of life'.

Malevich's interest in Byzantine art (with its aesthetic and intellectual symbolism verging on abstraction), Eastern philosophies, yoga and esoteric doctrines ripened into the conception of an almost magical role for the artist – a being who could stand apart from earthly reality and rise to a cosmic dimension. Open to the latest European trends, having gradually progressed through the experience of Symbolism, primitivism and Cubo-Futurism to a surpassing of the objective view of the world, Malevich arrived at a very personal interpretation that went beyond phenomenological reality to embrace infinity. The birth of Suprematism around 1915 was his turning-point towards abstraction – 'the new pictorial realism', or 'non-figurative creation', as the artist defined it. The dominant idea was that of the void, an absence that culminates in the rigour of black and white – with a meaning quite opposed to that of the Blue Horseman and the bright colours of Kandinsky.

In his many writings, Malevich emphasized the philosophical nature of his conception of art. Art was not only 'art', but also a 'thought'; in fact, he wrote, 'The brush rebels and cannot penetrate the convolutions of the brain. The pen is sharper. The painted work is no longer simply the imitation of reality but is this very reality, like any other object in the phenomenological world. It is not a demonstration of ability, but the materialization of an idea.'

Kazimir Malevich
Black Square on White
1915
oil on canvas, 80 x 80 cm
State Tretyakov Gallery, Moscow

ELEGANT EVENING ATTIRE

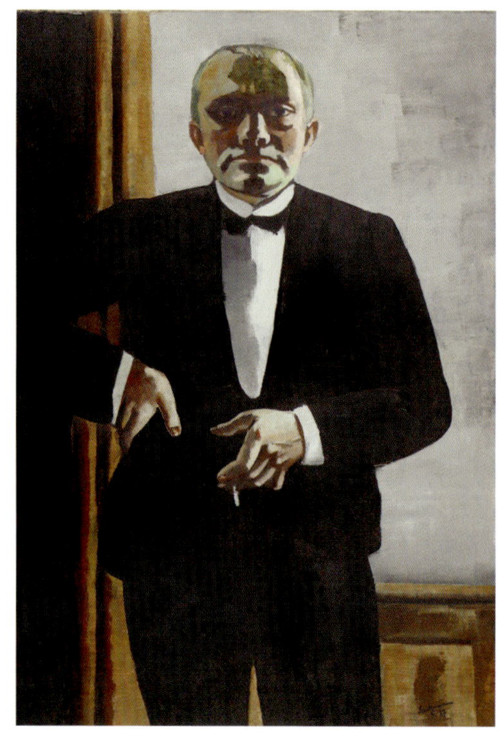

The typically masculine 19th-century custom of spending part of the evening smoking cigars or cigarettes, often in special smoking parlours, led to one's formalwear smelling of tobacco. And so, as tradition holds, in 1865 the London tailor Henry Poole & Co. created an alternative to the tailcoat for the Prince of Wales (the future King Edward VII): the 'smoking jacket'. Originally a black dressing gown, it soon became the 'dinner jacket'. The first to wear the smoking jacket on the other side of the Atlantic was Griswold Lorillard, a member of the Tuxedo Club in Tuxedo, Orange County, New York State. For this reason, in the United States, the smoking-dinner jacket is called a tuxedo.

An intense and independent personality, Beckmann followed an artistic and human trajectory that exemplifies the status of the artist during the troubled period between the two World Wars. Alternating activity as director of the School of Fine Arts in Frankfurt with trips to Paris, Beckmann had a predilection for scenes and figures with simplified monumental volumes in which the Expressionist graphic style is accompanied by a strong taste for dominant colours that define a painting's tone.

In this self-portrait from 1927, the hard facial features, the volumes clearly articulated by black and white, the outline and graphic character place Beckmann clearly within the pattern of German Expressionism. Yet in his choice of costume Beckmann reveals himself to be a refined, ironic interpreter, integrated into Berlin society. In 1937, his activity was suddenly interrupted when he was forced to leave Germany during the Nazi persecution. He spent the war years in Amsterdam and then moved to the United States in 1947.

Max Beckmann
Self-portrait in Tuxedo
1927
oil on canvas, 139.5 x 95.5 cm
Harvard Art Museums, Busch-Reisinger Museum, Cambridge, Massachusetts

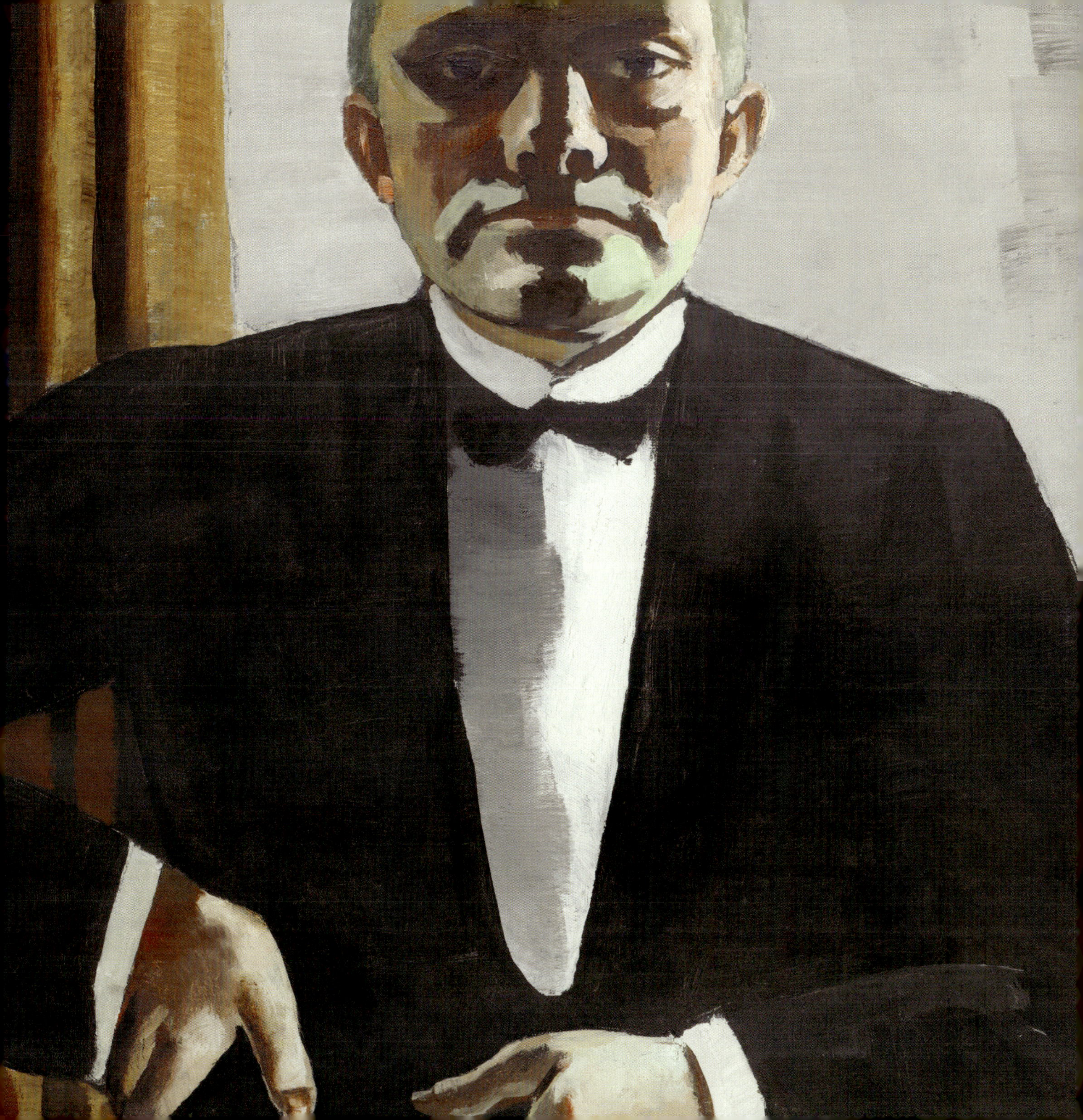

Pablo Picasso
Guernica
1937
oil on canvas, 350.5 x 782.3 cm
Museo Nacional Centro
de Arte Reina Sofía, Madrid

PICASSO OPTS FOR BLACK AND WHITE

Unlike many of his fellow artists and intellectuals, Picasso took no interest in politics or international matters for decades, showing a thorough disregard for the upheavals of the First World War and the totalitarian age that followed it. Not until the outbreak of the Spanish Civil War did he take a close interest in the social and political reality, as demonstrated by the large canvas *Guernica* – one of the greatest masterpieces of painting in black and white. The 'making' of *Guernica* was documented in a series of photographs taken by Dora Maar, Picasso's companion during the 1930s. These images provide a direct and emotional account of the artist's intuitions and variations as the work advanced.

In January 1937, the Spanish Republican government, in exile after the Civil War, commissioned Picasso to paint a mural for the Spanish Pavilion at the Paris World's Fair. On 26 April, while the artist was still working on the initial preparatory drawings, German and Italian planes bombed Gernika (Guernica in Spanish), an ancient Basque town. Moved by the dramatic news reports, Picasso radically changed the layout of his painting and completed it in a few frenzied weeks. It is not a realistic illustration – Picasso had only a few blurry newspaper photos available to consult – but an anti-war allegory.

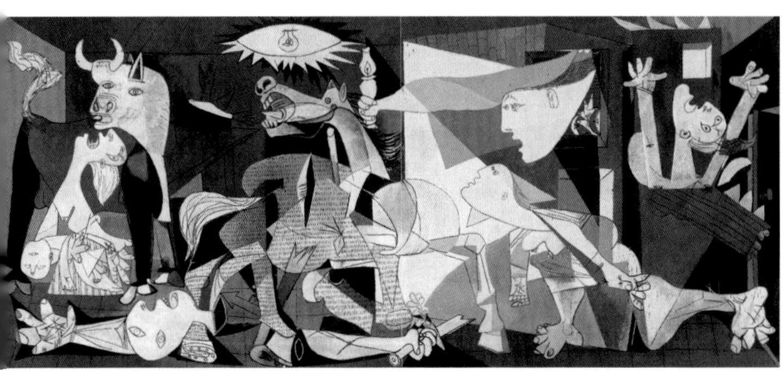

The varied interpretations critics have given of the many symbolic figures in the composition demonstrate the richness of Picasso's creative inspiration.

Guernica is a funeral lament that recalls medieval Depositions. It is the artist's grief for a nation and, at the same time, a symbol of universal pain in the face of death and violence. The figure of the bull emerges at the left, a symbol of instinctive brutality but also of indestructible resistance. Near it, a woman holding her dead child in her arms expresses desperate grief. At the right is a terrified woman, her arms raised in a gesture of anguish and a vain plea for help. In the centre, Picasso has placed the head of a horse that has been pierced by a spear. Above it is a stylized light, towards which the two women at the right seem to turn in an attitude of prayerful supplication.

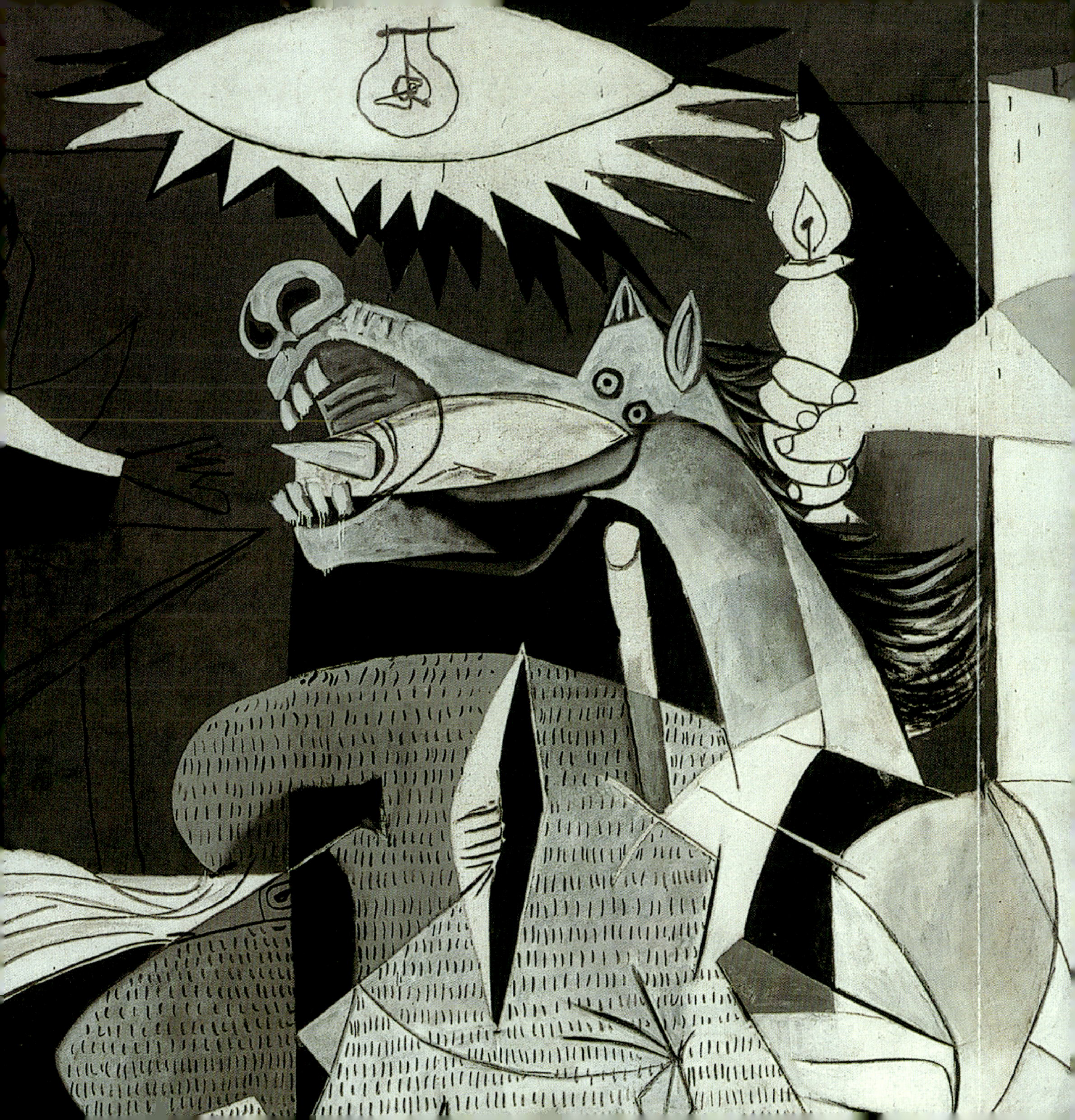

BIBLIOGRAPHY

Josef Albers, *Wechselwirkung der Farbe*, Ulm, 1963 (new complete edition, Interaction of color, New Haven, 2009)

Jane Alison (ed.), *Colour after Klein: re-thinking colour in modern and contemporary art*, London, 2005

Selim Augusti, *I colori pompeiani*, Roma, 1967

Jenny Balfour-Paul, *Indigo*, London, 1998

Philip Ball, *Bright earth : the invention of color*, London, 2001

Christophe Ballare, *Traité de miniature pour apprendre aisément à peindre sans maître et le secret de faire des plus belles couleurs*, Paris, 1676

Manlio Brusatin, *Colore senza nome*, Venice, 2006

Manlio Brusatin, *Storia dei colori*, Turin, 1999

Manlio Brusatin, *Lezioni sui colori*, Venice, 1995

Cennino Cennini, *Il libro dell'Arte*, Fabio Frezzato (ed.), 2. ed., Vicenza, 2004

Michel-Eugène Chevreul, *De la loi du contraste simultané des couleurs*, Paris, 1839

Henry-Claude Cousseau (ed.), *Colour since Matisse: French painting in the 20th century*, London, 1985

Jo Crook and Tom Learner, *The impact of modern paints*, London, 2000

François Delamare and Bernard Guineau, *Les matériaux de la couleur*, Paris, 1999

Maria Fernanda Ferrini, Pseudo Aristotele, *I colori*, Pisa, 1999

John Gage, 'Goethe as a historian of color' in Michel Hochmann and Danielle Jacquart (eds.), *Lumière et vision dans les sciences et dans les arts: de l'antiquité au XVIIe siècle*, Genève, 2010, pp. 341–354

John Gage, 'When warm was cool: on the history of colour temperature' in Werner Busch unter Mitarb and Elisabeth Müller-Luckner (eds.), *Verfeinertes Sehen: Optik und Farbe im 18. und frühen 19. Jahrhundert*, Munich, 2008, pp. 91–99

John Gage, *Colour in art*, London, 2006

John Gage, *Colour and meaning: art, science and symbolism*, London, 1999

John Gage, 'Rothko: Color as Subject' in Jeffrey Weiss (ed.), *Mark Rothko*, New Haven, 1998

John Gage, *Colour and culture: practice and meaning from antiquity to abstraction*, London, 1993

John Gage, 'Color in Western art, an issue?' in *The Art Bulletin*, 72, 1990, pp. 518–541

John Gage, 'A Locus Classicus of colour theory : the fortunes of Apelles' in *Journal of the Warburg and Courtauld Institutes*, 44, 1981, pp. 1–26

John Gage, 'Colour in history, relative and absolute' in *Art History*, 1, 1978, pp. 104–130

Johann Wolfgang von Goethe, *Zur Farbenlehre*, Tubinga, 1810 (English translation, Theory of Colours, trans. Charles Lock Eastlake, Cambridge, MA, 1982)

Marcia B. Hall, *Color and meaning : practice and theory in Renaissance painting*, Cambridge, 1992

R. D. Harley, *Artists' pigments, c. 1600–1835: a study in English documentary sources*, 2. ed., London, 1982

Johannes Itten, *The Art of Color: the subjective experience and objective rationale of color*, New York, 1961

Johannes Itten and Faber Birren, *The Elements of Color: A Treatise on the Color System of Johannes Itten Based on His Book The Art of Color*, New York, 1970

Toby Kamps (ed.), *Ellsworth Kelly: red, green, blue; paintings and studies*, 1958–1965, San Diego, 2003

Martin Kemp, *The science of art: optical themes in Western art from Brunelleschi to Seurat*, New Haven, 1990

Trevor Lamb and Janine Bourriau (eds.), *Colour: art & science*, Cambridge, 1995

Kazimir S. Malevich, 'An attempt to determine the relation between colour and form in painting' in Troels Andersen (ed.), *K. S. Malevich, Essays on art, II*, 1928–1933, Copenhagen, 1968

Isaac Newton, *Opticks*, London 1704

Michel Pastoureau, *Couleurs: toutes les couleurs du monde en 350 photos*, Paris, 2010

Michel Pastoureau, *Noir: histoire d'une couleur*, Paris, 2008

Michel Pastoureau and Dominique Simonnet, *Le petit livre des couleurs*, Paris, 2007

Michel Pastoureau (ed.), *Couleur, travail et société du Moyen Age à nos jours*, Paris, 2004

Michel Pastoureau, *Les couleurs de notre temps*, Paris, 2003

Michel Pastoureau, *Bleu: histoire d'une couleur*, Paris, 2000

Michel Pastoureau, *Jésus chez le teinturier: couleurs et teintures dans l'Occident médiéval*, Paris, 1997

Charles A. Riley, *Color codes: modern theories of color in philosophy, painting and architecture, literature, music, and psychology*, Hannover, 1995

Georges Roque, *Art et science de la couleur: Chevreul et les peintres de Delacroix à l'abstraction*, Nîmes, 1997

Patricia Sloane (ed.), *Primary sources: selected writings on color from Aristotle to Albers*, New York, 1991

Bruce R. Smith, *The Key of Green: Passion and Perception in Renaissance Culture*, Chicago, 2009

Heinrich Zollinger, *Color: A Multidisciplinary Approach*, New York, 1999

INDEX OF PROPER NAMES

Pages numbers in *italics* refer to illustrations

Aaron 212
Achilles 270, *270*
Acrisius of Argos 216
Adam 48, 78, 218
Adonis 64
Ahmet I, Sultan 115
Ajax 270, *270*
Albers, Josef 21-22
Alberti, Leon Battista 244
Albertinelli, Mariotto 280
Albizi, Giovanna degli 40, *40*
Alexander I, Czar 162
Alexander the Great 211
Alexander VI, Pope 280
Allah 114
Altdorfer, Albrecht *210*, 211
Amerling, Friedrich von *105*
Anne of Cleves 286
Anubis 185
Apollinaire, Guillaume 21, 138
Apollo 82, 82
Arcimboldo, Giuseppe 85, *85*
Aretino, Spinello 149
Artemis 82
Asam Brothers 251
Athena 126, 182
Augustus II of Saxony 248
Augustus, Emperor 190
Aztecs 112

Bacon, Francis 299
Baldassare, Castiglione 11
Baldung Grien, Hans 154, *154*
Balzac, Honoré de 279
Bassano, Jacopo 291
Bataille, Nicolas 119
Batman 268
Baudelaire, Charles 137
Beatles 70
Beatrice d'Este 234
Beckmann, Max 308, *308*
Beethoven, Ludwig von 21, 241
Bellini, Giovanni 127, *127*
Bellini, Vincenzo 241
Bellori, Giovanni Pietro 293
Benoist, Marie-Guillemine *296*, 297
Bergman, Ingmar 222
Bergotte 86
Bernini, Gian Lorenzo 34, *34*, 251
Bingen, Hildegard von 40, 204
Birren, Faber 22
Bonaparte, Paolina 223
Bosch, Hieronymus 48, *48*, 76, *76*, 128, 206, *206*, 236, *236*, 297
Böttger, Johann Friedrich 248
Botticelli, Sandro *125*, 228-229, *228*, 280
Boudin, Eugène 137
Boudolf, Jan (Hennequin de Bruges) 119, *119*
Bourbons 33, 66
Brown, Lancelot 146
Bruegel, Pieter the Elder *84*, 85, *128*, 128, 238, *238*
Brühl, Heinrich von 249
Brunelleschi, Filippo 201, 244
Burgundy, Dukes of 276

Cadmus 152
Calypso 275
Campin, Robert 43, 276
Canaletto 133
Canova, Antonio 223
Caravaggio 55, *55*, 88, 209, 241, 242, 292-293, *293*
Cardon, Émile 13
Carpaccio, Vittore 152, *152*, 234, *239*
Carter, Howard 184
Casa, Giovanni della 11
Cassandro 252
Cennini, Cennino 196
Cézanne, Paul *132*, 133
Chagall, Marc 264, *264*
Charlemagne 58, 190
Charles I of England 94
Charles V, Emperor 58, 291
Charles VII of France 120
Charles the Bold 199
Chatwin, Bruce 249
Chevalier, Etienne 120
Chirico, Giorgio De 178
Chopin, Frédéric 241
Christie, Agatha 104
Christus, Petrus 276, *277*
Churchill, Winston 7
Cimon 56, *56*
Circe 275
Clemenceau, Georges 269
Codde, Pieter 78, *78*
Coladarci, Luca 7
Colombus, Christopher 280
Comnenus, dynasty 75
Constable, John *158*, 159
Constantine, Emperor 75, 75
Corot, Jean-Baptiste-Camille 160, *160*
Correggio 156, *156*
Courbet, Gustave 137, 161, 300, *300*
Cranach, Lucas 216, *217*
Cromwell, Oliver 94

Daedalus 92
Dalí, Salvador 64, *65*
Danaë 216, *217*
Dante 72, 76, 230, 236
Daphne 82
Darius the Great 211
Daubigny, Charles-François 160
David 292, 293, *293*
Decamps, Alexandre Gabriel 160
Degas, Edgar 172, *172*
Delaunay, Sonia 21
Demeter 275
Denis, Maurice 17
Descartes, René 88
Diesbach, Johann Jacob 132
Dionysus 33

Dolce, Ludovico 11
Domenichino 233
Duccio di Buoninsegna 34, *34*, 272, *272*
Dunant, Henry 56
Dürer, Albrecht 48, *48*, 78, *78*, 154, 199, *199*, 268, 282, *282*, 291
Dyck, Anthony van 94, *94*, 134, 251, 268

Edward VII of England 308
El Greco 52, *52*, 268, 291, *291*
Elsheimer, Adam 241, *241*
Ensor, James 299
Equicola, Mario 11
Erasmus, Desiderius 128
Escher, Cornelis Maurits 305, *305*
Espine, Malies de l' *33*
Eve 48, 218
Exekias 270, *270*
Eyck, Jan van 36, *37*, 43, 224, *224*, 236, 276

Farnese, Alessandro 50-51, *51*, 216
Farnese, Ottavio 50-51, *51*
Félibien des Avaux, André 294
Fénéon, Félix *15*, 16, 170
Ford, Henry 268-269
Fouquet, Jean 118, *118*
Fra Angelico 107, 226, *226*, 236, 280
Fra Bartolomeo 280, *280*
Francesco II Sforza 286
Francis I of France 211, 291
Frederick the Great 248
Freya 279
Fuseli, Henry 254, *254*

Gabriel, Archangel 228, 233
Gainsborough, Thomas 133, 134, *135*
Galileo 241
Gallerani, Cecilia 234
Ganelon 71
Garibaldi, Giuseppe 46, 66
Gauguin, Paul 16, 17, 94, 96, *96*, 137, 174
Ghirlandaio, Domenico 40, *40*
Ghislieri, Michele 52
Gilles 252, *252*
Ginori, Carlo 249
Giotto 72, *72*, 196, *197*, 206
Giulio Romano *83*
Goethe, Wolfgang 6, 12, 146
Gogh, Theo van 168
Gogh, Vincent van 19, 70, 94, *94*, 96, *97*, 168, *168*
Gogh, Willemien van 96
Goliath 55, 292, 293
Goncourt, Edmond de 160
Goncourt, Jules de 160
Gonzaga, Francesco 44
Goltz, Hans 140
Goya, Francisco de 257, *257*, 299, *299*
Grimm Brothers 150
Gropius, Walter 21-22
Grünewald, Mathias 23, 154, 284, *285*
Guevara, Fernando Niño de 52
Guttuso, Renato 66, *66*

Hammershøi, Vilhelm 258, *258*
the Habsburgs 75, 130, 291
Harvey, William 55
Hathor 212
Hawks, Howard 108
Hawkwood, John 149
Hennequin de Bruges see Jan Boudolf
Henry VIII of England 286, 291
Hephaestus 182
Hercules 186
Hermes 82
Herod 296
Herodotus 186
Hey, Jean see Master of Moulins
Hiffernan, Joanna 260
Hitler, Adolf 112
Hokusai, Katsushika 60, *60*, 133, *133*
Holbein, Hans the Younger 286, *286*
Hölderlin, Friedrich 112
Holofernes 55, *55*
Homer 126, 270, 275
Horace 76
Horus 185, 275

Icarus 92, *92*
Ingres, Jean-Auguste-Dominique 58, *58*
Isabella d'Este 234
Isabella of Portugal 291
Isis 275
Itten, Johannes 21-23

Jacob, Max 138
James, Henry 161
Jawlensky, Alexei von 140
Jesus (Christ) 34, 43, 44, 52, 72, 76, 116, 120, *125*, 132, 146, 182, 183, 185, 192, *193*, 198, 199, 204, 206, 208, 224, 226, 232, 242, 272, 284, 291, 296
John II (the Good) of France 119
John Paul II, Pope 275
Jongkind, Johan Barthold 137
Joseph of Arimathea 242
Judas 71-72, 204, 206
Judith 55, *55*
Jupiter see Zeus

Kalf, Willem *91*
Kandinsky, Wassily 19, 102, *103*, 140, *140*
Kändler, Jacob Joachim 249, *249*
Kant, Immanuel 241
Kapoor, Anish 55
Kasparov, Garry 113
Klee, Paul 22, 140
Klein, Yves 142, *143*
Klimt, Gustav 21, 218, *219*
Klinger, Max 21

La Tour, Georges de 88,
Lancret, Nicolas 133
Latona 82
Le Corbusier *262*, 263
Leenhoff, Ferdinand 164

Leenhoff, Suzanne 164
Leighton, Frederic *98*, 99
Lenin, Vladimir Ilyich 66
Leningrad Painter 31, *31*
Leo X, Pope 51, *51*
Leonardo da Vinci 156-157, *156*, 205, 234, *235*
Leoni, Ottavio 292, *293*
Leviathan 113
Leyden, Lucas van 212, *212*
Loredan, Leonardo 127, *127*
Lorillard, Grisworld 308
Lothair II of Lotharingia *192*
Louis I d'Anjou 119
Louis XIV of France 82, 168
Lucifer 72, 177
Lucretia *46*
Ludovico il Moro, Duke of Milan 156, 234
Lüscher, Max 7
Luther, Martin 154

Maar, Dora 310
Macke, August 140
Magritte, René 178, *178*
Mahler, Alma 22
Malevich, Kazimir Serverinovich 306, *306*
Mañach, Pere 138
Manet, Édouard 14, 164, *165*, 216, 302, *302*
Manet, Gustave 164
Mantegna, Andrea 44, *44*
Mao Tse-tung 66
Marc, Franz 8, 140
Maria Christina of Austria 223
Marinetti, Filippo Tommaso 241
Mars 46, *47*, 201
Marsyas 55
Martini, Simone 272
Mary Magdalene 34, *88*, 284
Mary, The Virgin, Madonna, Our Lady 43, *43*, 44, *44*, 58, 113, 116, 120, *120*, *121*, 122, 125, *125*, 134, 154, 190, 192, 194, 196, 204, 205, *205*, 208, 228-229, *228*, 232, 242, 275-276, *275*
Massys, Jan 46, *46*
Massys, Quentin 208-209, *208*
Master of Moulins 205, *205*
Matisse, Henri 16, 63, *63*, 174
Maupassant, Guy de 137
Maxentius 75, *75*
Maximilian of Habsburg 211
Mayas 112
Medici 201, 280
Medici, Cosimo the Elder de' 202
Medici, Lorenzo de' (the Magnificent) 280
Medusa 44, 55
Melandroni, Fillide 55
Meléndez, Luis Egidio *90*
Memling, Hans 9, *10*
Mephistopheles 272
Meurent, Victorine 164
Michelangelo Buonarotti 28, 81, *82*, 291
Millais, John Everest 167, *167*
Millet, Jean-François 160
Mohammed, Prophet 114
Mona Lisa 108
Mondrian, Piet 306, *306*
Monet, Claude 13, 60, *60*, *137*, 137, 160, 161, 182, 269
Monet, Léon Pascal 60
Montefeltro, Federico da 36, *37*
Monna Vanna 108
Monroe, Marilyn 108, *108*
Montale, Eugenio 91
Montferrand, August Ricard de 162
Morato, Fulvio Pellegrino 11
Morisot, Berthe 302, *302*
Moses 212, 226
Motherwell, Robert 22
Mucha, Alphonse 177, *177*
Munch, Edvard 70, *98*, 99, 258
Münter, Gabriele 140
Mussorgsky, Modest 21
Myron of Eleutherae 50
Nadar, Félix 13, 60
Napoleon 58, *58*, 82, 92, 234, 257, 299
Napoleon III, Emperor 164, 300
Ness, Beatrice Whitney Van 2, 104, *105*
Newton, Isaac 6, 11
Nicodemus 242
Nicolas of Verdun 194-195, *194*, 199
Noah 149, *149*
Noland, Kenneth 22
Notke, Bernt 152

Odysseus 152
Olbrich, Joseph Maria 21
Ophelia 167, *167*
Osiris 148
Otto I, Emperor 190
Otto II, Emperor 75
Otto III, Emperor 190

Pacher, Michael 150, *150*
Palladio, Andrea 147
Pastoreau, Michel 6
Pater, Jean-Baptiste 133
Paul III, Pope 50-51, *51*
Pellizza da Volpedo, Giuseppe 16, 101, *101*
Pero 56, *56*
Perseus 44, 152
Perugino 125
Pesello, Il 201, *202*
Phaeton 92
Philip IV of Spain 130, *130*
Piacenza, Giovanna 156
Picabia, Francis 21
Picasso, Pablo 21, 101, 138, *139*, 174, 310, *310*
Piero della Francesca 36, *37*, 75, *75*, 120, 204, *204*, 280
Pietro, Sano di *38*
Piper, Reinhard 140
Pisanello *33*
Pissarro, Camille 14, 160
Pius V, Pope 52

Poinçon, Robert *119*
Pollaiolo, Antonio del 230, *230*
Pompadour, Jeanne-Antoinette Poisson, marquise de 248
Poussin, Nicolas 88, 212, *215*, 294
Previati, Gaetano 16, 101, *101*, *228*, 229
Prévost, Jean see Master of Moulins
Proserpine 275
Proust, Marcel 86

Raimondi, Marcantonio 164
Raphael 51, *51*, 58, 156, 164, 204, 233, 234, 291
Rauschenberg, Robert 22
Rembrandt (Harmenszoon van Rijn) *208*, 209, 244, 268, 294, *294*
René of Anjou 202
Renoir, Pierre-Auguste 160
Reymerswaele, Marinus van 208
Reynolds, Joshua 134, 242
Rimbaud, Arthur 7, 19-20
Robbia, Luca della 122, *122*
Rolin, Nicolas 43
Romanovs 75
Rossetti, Dante Gabriel *108*, 167
Rothko, Mark 107, *107*
Rousseau, Henri (Le Douanier) 174, *174*
Rousseau, Jean-Jacques 146
Rousseau, René-Lucien 6
Rousseau, Théodore 160
Rovere, Francesco Maria della 234
Rubens, Peter Paul 56, *56*, 92, *92*, 108, 241, 242, *243*
Ruiz, Gonzalo 291
Runge, Philipp Otto 12
Ruskin, John 228
Rysselberghe, Théo van 16

Saenredam, Pieter Jansz. 244, *244*
Saint Augustine 150, 291
Saint Bernard of Clairvaux 275
Saint George 152
Saint Jerome 282
Saint John the Baptist 55, 226, 284
Saint Lawrence 289
Saint Luke 198, 275, 284
Saint Marc 226, 284
Saint Matthew 228, 284, 292, 296
Saint Paul 56
Saint Peter 52, 72, 226
Saint Stephen 120, 291
Saramago, José 236
Saturn 78, 201, 283, *299*
Savonarola, Girolamo 280, *280*
Schoenberg, Arnold 19, 102, *103*, 140
Schongauer, Martin 43, *43*, 232, *233*
Schopenhauer, Arthur 12, 92
Segantini, Giovanni 16
Seljuk dynasty 115
Serpotta, Giacomo 251, *251*
Sérusier, Paul 16, *17*
Seurat, Georges 14, 16, 170, *170*
Seymour, Jane 286
Shakespeare, William 167
Siddal, Elizabeth 167
Signac, Paul 14, *15*, 16
Signorelli, Luca 279
Simon of Cyrene 34
Sisley, Alfred 160
Sodoma, il 279
Solomon 228
Sorel, Agnès 120
Suger 183

Tarquin 46, *46*
Theophilus 26, 116
Thorvaldsen, Bertel 223
Tiepolo, Giambattista 82, *82*
Tintoretto 289, 291
Titian 50, 51, *51*, 126, *127*, 216, *217*, 234, 289, *289*, 291
Tornabuoni, Lorenzo 40
Toscanelli, Paolo Dal Pozzo 201
Toulouse-Lautrec, Henri de 172
Trakl, Georg 7
Troyon, Constant 160
Turner, Joseph Mallord William 12-13, *13*, 81, 92, *92*
Tutankhamun 184, 185
Twombly, Cy 22

Uccello, Paolo 149, *149*

Valentino 64, *65*
Valéry, Paul 302
Vasari, Giorgio 125, 149, 289
Velázquez, Diego *130*, 268
Venus 64, 108, 201
Vermeer, Johannes 86, *86*, 231, *231*, 246, *246*, 258
Verne, Jules 174
Veronese, Paolo 8
Vigée-Le Brun, Élisabeth 297
Virgil 206
Vollard, Ambroise 138
Voltaire 146, 252

Warhol, Andy 108, *108*
Watteau, Jean-Antoine 133, 146, 252, *252*
Wells, H.G. 174
Werff, Pieter van der 132
West, Mae 64, *65*
Weyden, Roger van der 198, *198*, 199, 276
Whistler, James Abbott McNeill 19, *19*, 260, *260*
William II of Altavilla 192
William IV of Bavaria 211
Winckelmann, Johann 223
Władysław of Opole 275

Zeus (Jupiter) 82, 201, 216
Zorro 268
Zurbarán, Francisco de 224, *224*

PHOTOGRAPHIC CREDITS

Every effort has been made to trace copyright holders. If, however, you feel that you have inadvertently been overlooked, please contact the publisher.

ADAGP, Paris / Scala, Florence – 264, 265

AISA / The Bridgeman Art Library – 114

AKG Images – 109, 150, 151, 154, 155, 162, 163, 191, 248, 277

AKG Images / Werner Forman – 184, 185

Alamy Images – 162, 163

Biblioteca Estense, Modena, Su concessione del Ministero per i Beni e le Attività Culturali – 47

Bridgeman – 76, 77, 78, 80, 82, 85, 88, 89, 90, 94, 96, 98, 195

C.H./ADAGP, Paris – 179

Christie's Images / The Bridgeman Art Library – 106, 107, 258, 259

Collezione d'Arte Banca Intesa – 30, 31

Corbis – 64

Courtesy of the Huntington Art Collections – 135

DACS / The Bridgeman Art Library – 141

De Agostini Picture Library / A. Dagli Orti / The Bridgeman Art Library – 278, 279

FineArtImages/Leemage – 133

Giraudon / The Bridgeman Art Library – 28, 46, 58, 59, 60, 161, 175, 205

J.P. Zenobel / The Bridgeman Art Library – 132, 234

Jean Bernard / Leemage – 117

Kunsthalle Bremen – Der Kunstverein in Bremen, photo Lars Lohrisch – 79

Musée d'Unterlinden, Colmar – 42, 43, 232, 233, 283, 285

Musées royaux des Beaux-Arts de Belgique, Brussels – 92

Museo Nacional del Prado, Madrid – 48, 49

Museo Thyssen–Bornemisza, Madrid – 40, 41, 42, 91

National Gallery, London – 286, 287

National Museum of Women in the Arts, Washington – 105

Palazzo Chigi, collezione Fagiolo dell'Arco, Ariccia – 34

Peter Willi / The Bridgeman Art Library – 254, 255

Photo Erik Cornelis / Nationalmuseum, Stockholm – 216

PhotoScala, Florence – 38, 52, 53, 193, 197, 209, 228, 249, 260, 261, 293

Photoservice Electa – 33, 54, 55, 61, 66, 67, 74, 75, 83, 100, 101, 115, 123, 148, 149, 152, 153, 156, 157, 204, 226, 227, 229, 236, 237, 250, 262, 263, 281, 292, 303

RMN (Musée d'Orsay) / Martine Beck-Coppola – 172, 173

RMN (Musée du Louvre) / Jean-Gilles Berizzi – 44, 45, 253

Sotheby's / AKG-Images – 176, 177

Tate, London – 93, 108

The Bridgeman Art Library – 29, 72, 73, 104, 124, 125, 127, 136, 158, 187, 188, 200, 202, 214, 215, 270, 271, 274, 282, 296, 297, 298, 299, 300, 301, 310, 311

The M.C. Escher Company – 305

The Maas Gallery, London / The Bridgeman Art Library – 99

Translation
Donald Pistolesi

Editing
Christopher Dell

Design and typesetting
quod. voor de vorm.

Colour separations and printing
ebs Editoriale Bortolazzi ste s.r.l., Verona

Cataloging-in-Publication Data has been applied for
and may be obtained from the Library of Congress.
ISBN 978-1-4197-0111-5

COVER:
Salvador Dalí
Athens Is Burning! The School of Athens and the Fire in the Borgo (Stereoscopic work, left component) (detail), 1979-1980, Fundación Gala-Salvador Dalí, Figueras

Printed and bound in Italy
10 9 8 7 6 5 4 3 2 1

ABRAMS
THE ART OF BOOKS SINCE 1949

115 West 18th Street
New York, NY 10011
www.abramsbooks.com